DATE DUE

DEMCO 38-296

Transition Banking

Transition Banking

*Financial Development of
Central and Eastern Europe*

RONALD W. ANDERSON
AND CHANTAL KEGELS

CLARENDON PRESS · OXFORD
1998

Clarendon Street, Oxford OX2 6DP

New York

Bogota Bombay Buenos Aires
Delhi Florence Hong Kong Istanbul
Madrid Melbourne Mexico City
Paris Singapore Taipei Tokyo Toronto Warsaw
and associated companies in
Berlin Ibadan

Oxford is a trade mark of Oxford University Press

Published in the United States
by Oxford University Press Inc., New York

© Ronald W. Anderson and Chantal Kegels 1998

The moral rights of the author have been asserted

British Library Cataloguing in Publication Data
Data available

Library of Congress Cataloging-in-Publication Data
Anderson, Ronald W., 1946–
Transition banking : financial development of Central and Eastern
Europe / Ronald W. Anderson and Chantal Kegels.
p. cm.
Includes bibliographical references (p.) and index.
ISBN 0–19–829013–6
1. Banks and banking—Europe, Eastern. 2. Banks and banking—
Europe, Central. I. Kegels, Chantal. II. Title.
HG2980.7.A6A53 1997
332.1'0943—dc21 97-31979
CIP

1 3 5 7 9 10 8 6 4 2

Typeset by Best-set Typesetter Ltd., Hong Kong
Printed in Great Britain
by Biddles Ltd, Guildford and King's Lynn

To my parents, Nels and Bernice Anderson,
in deepest appreciation of their love and support.

To Pol,
for his supporting love.

Preface

This book is our account of the efforts since 1989 to develop financial sectors within the formerly socialist economies of Central and Eastern Europe. While almost all aspects of economic organization in this region have been affected by the changes taking place since the collapse of the Soviet bloc, the developments in banking and finance are sufficiently important as to merit a detailed treatment of their own. Probably in no other domain are the organizing principles of the Soviet-style central planning and of the capitalist market economy so radically opposed as in matters of finance. Under centrally planned socialist systems, finance is restricted to implementing the monetary payments and accounting system which helps facilitate production decisions taken elsewhere in the planning system. Under capitalism, the pursuit of financial return is directly linked to the allocation of capital. To move from one to the other requires the creation of a series of totally new institutions as well as the education of not only of the workforce for the new financial sector but also the whole business community which will be required to compete for capital under a whole new set of rules. This is a major undertaking whose success will be of crucial importance in determining whether these countries succeed in growing at the rates they hope for and ultimately join the mature capitalist countries of the West as equals.

We have tried to give a comprehensive treatment of the financial sectors in the transition economies of Central and Eastern Europe. Thus our coverage ranges from monetary policy and central banking to the development of stock and bond markets to the establishment of stable, solvent commercial banks, to banking competition to the development of corporate control through the banks or the stock market. Furthermore, we have attempted to survey the range of experiences in Central and Eastern Europe outside the former Soviet Union. We know of no other attempt to carry out an in-depth comparison of the alternative directions taken in financial development by the countries of the region. Given the time and effort involved in collecting and organizing the relevant data, we have not been able to investigate all the countries in the region to the same degree. Indeed, our most detailed analysis has been restricted to three countries: Hungary, Poland, and the Czech Republic. This choice was dictated first by the fact that these countries are widely considered as relatively advanced in the transition to the market. Knowledge of developments in these countries will be of particular importance to efforts to develop business relationships and to otherwise integrate these economies in the mainstream of the West. Furthermore, the analysis of these transition leaders may produce lessons that can be used by other countries who are not so far advanced along the transition path. Finally, we have worked with these countries because we have been able to assemble roughly comparable data sets for each.

This book has been written with several distinct audiences in mind. The first are the readers with a general knowledge of economics who wish to learn about recent developments in Central and Eastern Europe either out of general curiosity or because they have dealings in the region. The second are the professionals in finance or government who may have a detailed knowledge of some aspect of finance or banking somewhere in the region who wish to have an account that places their area of competence in a more general context. The third is the community of academic economists interested in the field that is now known as 'the economics of transition' who wish to review all the data relevant to the financial sector which have been collected in one place and distilled into a convenient form.

The events in Eastern and Central Europe since 1989 have been widely recognized as being of major historical importance and they have inspired many of our fellow economists to study one or another aspect of these developments. However, we know of no other study that approaches the subject as we do. As we have already emphasized we attempt to range very wide since we feel this is needed in order to study a system-wide change of regime. Furthermore, we have attempted to keep our study down-to-earth by making it thoroughly empirically-based. In the pages that follow the reader will find a great number of tables which report the main facts relevant to the financial sectors in our target economies. While most of these data have been published in some form elsewhere we generally have found it necessary to manipulate them further in order to make them most revealing. Around these facts we have attempted to weave the story of emerging financial practices in countries on their way to the market. The result is our own particular vision which undoubtedly will not be shared by all. However, we have given the readers the basic information necessary to form their own alternative accounts of the same subject.

A word about economic data in transition economies is in order. It is sometimes stated that data in these economies are so poor as to make empirical analysis very difficult. This is not exactly true. Central planning bureaucracies generated large amounts of data much of which was collected in a very professional manner. However, often these data are of relatively little interest as these economies move to the market. And the data series needed in a market economy were unavailable at least initially. For example, in Poland one can have monthly observations on prices of a variety of specific categories of grain purchased by official granaries in some forty-seven separate provinces of the country. However, until January 1992 there was no consolidated balance sheet for the banking sector for the economy. In Hungary, Poland, and the Czech Republic there have been major efforts to develop statistical information useful for a market economy where private enterprises are taking on ever increasing importance. We have found that the data do present problems, notably in changes in series where coverage has been expanded as more organizations are included in the statistical universe. However, we have found that with effort we were usually able to find the data that interest us and to learn something of how they were constructed. Furthermore, in many cases good data are available on a consistent basis for a period to three or more years. As a result we are strongly committed to the idea that the systematic review of the data is preferable to relying on hearsay or anecdotes.

We have supplemented our information from publicly available sources by repeated fact-finding visits to Hungary, Poland, and the Czech Republic. During these, we have interviewed central bankers, commercial bankers, participants of securities markets, and officials in finance and privatization ministries. Furthermore, we have met with a number of bankers and investors from the West who have had experiences in Eastern and Central Europe. Finally, we have had the pleasure of discussing our subject with a large number of academic researchers in the region as well as specialists in transition economics from the West. There is now a large literature on transition economics from which we have drawn very liberally and cite in the appropriate places. However, we make no pretence of making a comprehensive survey of this secondary literature. Undoubtedly, there are many interesting contributions touching on finance that we have overlooked and for which we are correspondingly the poorer.

Our book is organized in a way that will allow readers to read selectively if they see fit. The field of transition economics has developed its own conceptual framework, its own models, and a vocabulary that is all its own. We do not attempt to survey transition models, and we have tried to keep the jargon down to the minimum. However, we have felt that the non-academic reader in particular would like to have available a brief account of the ideas emerging in this new academic literature. Therefore, in Chapter 1 we provide a brief survey of the main concept arising in the analysis of finance in transition economies. The empiri analysis begins in Chapter 2 with a review of the macroeconomic context of Hungary, Poland, and the Czech Republic. Chapter 3 is devoted to the main relations between these economies and the economies of the West including international trade, the foreign debt, and relations with multinational organizations. We provide these two surveys because financial development does not occur in a vacuum but rather is formed by the constraints and the expectations arising from the rest of the economy. Having thus set the stage, we turn to the detailed, empirical analysis of financial developments of Hungary, Poland, and the Czech Republic in Chapters 4, 5, and 6 respectively. These chapters contain the results of our efforts to compile and organize all the available, important data on the financial sectors in these countries. We regard them as the heart of the book. Our attempt to understand the many important developments in these three countries inevitably leads us to deal with a large number of details. In order to make sure that the big picture emerges clearly we provide in Chapter 7 a comparison of the main aspects of financial development in the three countries we have covered in detail. Then in Chapter 8 we broaden our perspective further and consider the main issues of public policy that emerge in the financial sectors of a transition economy. Here we draw on the experiences of transition countries other than the three we have studied in detail. In effect, this chapter distills whatever wisdom that our empirical analysis has given us into a series of policy lessons. Our final reflections on the subject of finance and banking in a formerly socialist economy are collected in Chapter 9.

In carrying out our research we have accumulated many debts. First, we have received financial support first from the 'Fonds de Développement Scientifique' of the Catholic University of Louvain-la-Neuve and subsequently from 'Actions de Recherches Concertées' No. 93/98–162 of the Ministry of Scientific Research of the Belgian French Speaking Community. Beyond this great many people have been very generous in helping us to amass the information that we have reported in this book. The following have been particularly helpful in preparing our analyses of the three countries we have studied in detail:

The Czech Republic: Randall Filer, Miroslav Hrnčir, Vratisláv Izák, Kamil Janáček, Martin Kalovec, Jan Klacek Jiří Koliha, Miroslav Kučera, Radek Laštovička, Michal Mejstřík, Jan Mládek, Ivo Řihola, Jiří Šebánek, Pavel Štěpánek, Miroslav Šinger, and Jan Švejnar.

Hungary: Lóránd Ambrus-Lakatos, Gábor Obláth, Balazs Hámori, Jávori Jenö, Kálmán Mizsei, Judi Neményi, Ágota Rozsályi, György Sándor, István Székely, Magdona Szöke, János Száz, and Janos Vincze.

Poland: Piotr Bednarski, Marek Belka, Jarosłav Biernacki, John Bonin, Władysław Jaworski, Tomasz Karecki, Janusz Lewandowski, Ewa Mikaszewska, Witold Orłowski, Brian Pinto, Zbiginiew Polanski, Sławomir Sikora, Jan Solarz, Adam Szulc, Mariusz Tamborski, Paweł Wyczański, and Teresa Zemplinska.

In addition, our thinking has been influenced by discussions with a great many others. In particular, we would like to thank: Erik Berglöf, Wendy Carlin, David Begg, Marek Dąbrowski, Mathias Dewatripont, Peter Dittus, Rumen Dobrinsky, Lado Gurgenidze, Janet Mitchell, Joan Pearce, Enrico Perotti, Richard Portes, Gérard Roland, Mark Schaffer, Bernard Snoy, and Paul Wachtel. We would also like to express our appreciation to Rachel Brivio and Thérèse Davio for their excellent assistance in the preparation of the manuscript. Finally, we thank Cheng and Pol for their support and understanding.

Contents

1

Financial Development of Post-Socialist Economies: The Main Issues

1.1. The Scope of Financial Transition

In the chapters that follow we tell the story of the development of finance in the former socialist countries of Central and Eastern Europe in the aftermath of the fall of communism. In pursuing this very down-to-earth purpose we shall marshal a huge number of facts concerning banking, privatization, securities markets, and monetary policy in the region. Thus our approach is decidedly empirical in nature. However, in order to let the data speak they need to be organized according to some conceptual framework. The study of the ex-socialist economies attempting to develop into full-fledged market systems has given rise to a set of concepts generally known as 'transition economics', and our analysis will draw freely on this literature. Since the preoccupations of this field as well as the language employed may be unfamiliar to the general reader, we start our study with a discussion of the main ideas encountered in this new field.

The term 'transition' itself implies a passage from one point to another, and in the context of Eastern and Central Europe this is broadly accepted to mean moving from a socialist organization of the economy to a capitalist system centred around private property with a high degree of decentralization in decision-making. Furthermore, it is widely recognized that this transformation involves a wide range of changes to the economic and social system that can be roughly grouped as falling into *stabilization*, *liberalization*, and *deep institutional restructuring*. We will discuss all three as they relate to the financial sector.

What can we say about the starting points and end points of financial transition? Within the planned socialist system, it is difficult to identify a financial sector as such.[1] There are banks which create money and

---

[1] We are referring to what Kornai (1992) calls the 'classical socialist system'. For a description of money and banking in this system see Kornai (1992: ch. 8) and also Nuti (1992c).

implement the monetary payments of the economy in something like the way this occurs within capitalist economies. This is where the resemblance of socialist banking and capitalist finance ends. Socialist banking is the monetary adjunct of the planning process. It allows for an accounting of real activities in monetary terms. However, because of restrictions on the uses of various categories of monetary balances, even these monetary aggregates do not have the same interpretation as they do in the West. That is, money is not a universal means of payment. Instead, some money balances are designated for equipment purchases, others are used for paying personnel, and so on. In particular, the monetary relations of the household sector are intentionally segmented from those of the enterprise sector. As a result the flow of savings to investments is inevitably intermediated by the State. Beyond facilitating payments and accounting, the banking system has little scope for making independent decisions which have an impact on the real economy. The banking system collects the savings of the population since funds not spent on consumption can be held only as currency or as bank balances. However, the interest rate paid on savings deposits is set administratively. The banking system also extends credits to state enterprises and cooperatives. However, these advances are those required to carry out the quantitative production targets set in the planning process. The banking system undertakes no independent credit evaluation of a recipient, and if the borrower has failed to repay advances in the past this does not affect the necessity of granting future credits. Borrowers are meant to repay their loans with interest. However, if they fail to do so, the bank cannot force payment by threatening bankruptcy and liquidation. Furthermore, the interest charges are often omitted in the calculation of socially necessary costs which are the basis for establishing prices for firms. And the interest rates on bank credits are again set administratively.

Since the banking sector has so little scope for independent decision-making, there is little apparent need for banking competition. There may be separate banking organizations servicing different segments of the economy; however, these are administrative artefacts of the organization of the state bureaucracy. All important decisions affecting the interest rates and the granting of credits are taken centrally. Thus it is common to think of all socialist banking as taking place within a single monobank. The particular form this takes matters relatively little since the banking sector as a whole exercises very little impact on the allocation of capital or other resources.

In contrast, the financial sector of a capitalist economy plays a crucial role in determining the allocation of resources. The form it takes can have an impact on the equilibrium of savings and investment that is reached within the economy. Specifically, agents who save seek to make their funds available to the agents with real investment projects which will pay the greatest *returns* in the future. They may do this directly by acquiring securities (e.g. stocks and bonds) issued by the real investors. More likely, they do this by placing their funds with a financial intermediary who then lends the funds to borrowers or acquires securities. In either case, the future welfare of the saver is linked to the return generated by real investments. When those returns are uncertain, the form of financial contracting will determine the kinds of *risk* borne by the saver. In some cases such as company shares the link between fluctuations in the returns in the investment project and the saver's earnings are direct. Other contracts, such as bonds or bank deposits promise a known, fixed interest rate. However, such contracts may carry a risk that the borrower will default, a consideration that the saver must bear in mind. Other contracts, such as government bonds or insured bank deposits may avoid such credit risks and their return may be lower as a consequence.

Within a capitalist system the choices of how to allocate savings to alternative investment uses are made in a *decentralized* manner. In such a context, *financial competition* can have a clear impact on the outcome: if at the margin savers choose between borrowers with similar risks, the one who promises the lower return will be denied credit. Competition allows savers to choose from a larger universe of borrowers, so that unattractive projects are weeded out leaving only relatively high-return or low-risk projects. Furthermore, since savers will feel the consequences of the choices they make, they will have an interest in making them in an informed manner. Some savers will be more active in acquiring *information* than others. Many will choose financial intermediaries on the basis of their perception of the intermediaries' expertise in collecting and processing information. Information gathering does not stop at the time the saver contracts with the borrower. The saver will have a continuing incentive to *monitor* the borrower to assure that funds are used for the investment purpose declared in the financial contract. When it is discovered that the borrower has defaulted on terms of the contract, the saver can seek corrective actions under the law governing financial contracts. This may ultimately result in *bankruptcy* of the borrower which is a means by which inefficient projects are terminated.

These stylized descriptions of the starting points and end points of the transition process do not do justice to the historical and social diversity of the countries of Central and Eastern Europe nor to the great variety of capitalist institutions found in practice. These factors are important, and much of our attention in this book will be devoted to understanding how they weave together to define the distinct transition approaches of different countries. However, there is much that is common across these countries and it is fair to say that in order to develop a financial sector based on market principles each country must implement a number of clearly identifiable reforms.

Imposing financial discipline. A country wishing to adopt capitalist finance must recognize that economic investment projects should be accepted on the basis of their return and risk. While this may seem obvious, the experience of socialism has not prepared these countries to implement this principle. In particular, the techniques of project appraisal and valuation were underdeveloped under the socialist regime. As a consequence, developing the necessary skills and the adaptation of decision-making to make use of them are high priorities within the transition process. In particular, in a market economy, the riskiness of a project plays a central role in the decision to invest or not, whereas risk evaluation enters little if at all in a traditional planning process.

Decentralization. In the practice of socialism, routine planning and decision-making were never totally centralized; however, the decentralization that prevailed was the result of pragmatic arrangements which grew up because the central authority was generally less well-informed than the enterprise it was meant to direct. This gave the enterprise some effective bargaining power *vis-à-vis* the planning bureaucracy, but it had few legal guarantees to establish its right to make decisions. Furthermore, there were few bureaucratic barriers to prevent the centre from intervening in enterprise decisions when it deemed appropriate. One of the tasks then in a transition economy is to establish clear boundaries between the State and economic decision-making. In finance, generally the first step has been to establish a *two-tiered banking system* whereby central banking and commercial banking are separated. More generally the process of decentralization involves the withdrawal of the State from most financial decisions. The void left by the departure of the State is to be filled with a large number of private organizations created either by *privatizing* state enterprises or by starting entirely new ones.

Introducing competition. The socialist system had little reason to create competition since in theory the activities of an organization were adapted to the objectives established by the State. As a consequence, the bureaucracy was organized on the principle that any given administrative task should become the exclusive responsibility of a single organization. This practice was reinforced by the tendency to believe that the potential for economies of scale were very great in virtually every area of economic activity. Thus a state savings-bank bureaucracy had the responsibility of banking for individuals, an export-import bank handled affairs of firms involved in international trade, and so on. An implication of this is that if existing socialist institutions were merely reconstituted on a commercial basis the result would very likely be the creation of powerful monopolies. This implies that another important aspect of transition is the *demonopolization* of the economic organizations carved out of the state bureaucracy.

Information for investment decisions. Since under socialism the banking sector had few rights to make credit decisions, there was little need to assure that accurate information on borrowers was given to the banks. Getting the necessary information to the savers or their chosen financial intermediaries is an important new activity for the transition economy. The experience of capitalist economies suggests that this will not take place spontaneously. In particular, the establishment of *accounting and reporting standards* is often the responsibility of the public sector or of a quasi-public self-regulatory body (e.g. a stock exchange).

Establishing investors' control rights. In a socialist system enterprise managers are intended to carry out the objectives established by a higher authority. In the capitalistic firm, the management is appointed by the firm's owners. Even if the owners can hire and fire managers, the fact that top managers may be few in number whereas the firm's owners may be many and that the managers may have superior information about the enterprise creates one of the thorniest problems for the functioning of a capitalist economy. These so-called agency problems of the firm give rise to a variety of methods for exercising *corporate control*. Developing these within a transition economy is in part a matter of the company and securities law. However, it is also a matter of ensuring that at least some ownership groups have a clear incentive to carry out monitoring activities. In general the greater the concentration of ownership the greater are the incentives to monitor. It is clear then that the need to create effective monitors may conflict with the desires for demonopolization.

Reconciling conflicting interests. Decentralization of financial decisions in capitalist economies must come to grips with conflicts of interests other than those of managers and owners. Firms finance investment through a variety of financial contracts, thus creating separate creditor classes whose interest may not coincide. In particular, debtholders' interest may differ from those of shareholders. The debt contract may establish the responsibilities of the firm and the rights of the creditor. When the firm fails to respect the terms of the loan contract it becomes *financially distressed.* Capitalist economies have adopted a variety of bankruptcy laws and administrative procedures which govern the operations of distressed firms. Experience has shown that the managers and shareholders of distressed firms may have perverse incentives in the sense that may work against the interests of the creditors and may lower the value of the firm as a whole. These problems can be even more acute for transition economies since bankruptcy laws must be written and the bankruptcy courts need to start functioning. At the same time, the many shocks to the enterprises of transition economies may mean that the scale of financial distress may far exceed that experienced in mature capitalist economies even in severe recessions.

In the remainder of this chapter we develop conceptual problems that must be addressed in formulating reforms in each of these dimensions. We take up first those related to stabilization and liberalization measures and then move on to those that require deep institutional restructuring.

1.2. Financial Aspects of Stabilization in Transition

The suddenness of the political changes which swept the socialist countries of Central and Eastern Europe from 1989 to 1991 exposed their economies to a number of very important, system-wide shocks. There was a risk that the economies would veer off towards high inflation, severe recession, or both before the natural stabilizers that exist in a market economy could be put into place. Thus one of the first priorities of policy-making in transition was to stabilize the economy. The fact that these economies were exposed to more than one shock made the task of stabilization complex. Liberalization was the source of many shocks. *Price liberalization* was aimed at allowing consumer and producer prices to adjust to market-clearing levels.[2] Given very large discrepancies in relative prices between the socialist economies and capitalist economies these adjustments were often very severe.[3] An economy in transition is in many instances subjected to *major* changes in the *state budget*. Prior to 1989 many socialist economies had made efforts to remove direct subsidies to loss-making enterprises. However, few such enterprises had been shut down and many of the structural

---

[2] Nuti (1992*b*) describes the liberalization measures taken by the post-socialist countries of Central and Eastern Europe.

[3] e.g. in 1989 the price of bread (expressed in terms of units of wheat) was about 3.5 times higher in West than in East Germany. At the same time the price of washing machines in West Germany was one-half of that in the East. See Kornai (1992, table 8.4).

losses were covered from the state budget or the banking system. Many of the reforming governments which came to power in 1989 or after placed high priority on *removing direct subsidies*. When implemented this exposed their economies to a contractionary shock which threatened major job losses and loss of sales to suppliers. In order for competitive forces needed for a market to function, many of the reforms sought to promote the growth of the private sector by *removing barriers to entry*. The hope of course was that the growth of the private sector would help to offset contractionary forces. In particular, labour shed from inefficient manufacturing industries could be absorbed by the service sector which had been neglected under socialism and where large untapped demand would be found. However, increased competition would force existing firms to speed their adjustments and thereby could serve to reinforce contractionary tendencies.

Transition countries are also exposed to major changes in their foreign economic relations. The economic by-product of the fall of the Yalta order was the *break-up of the system of foreign trade* that had applied to these countries. Under the Council for Mutual Economic Assistance (CMEA) foreign trade flows among socialist countries were determined through an administrative bargaining process at terms which were divorced from those prevailing in the world's hard currency trade. This broke up starting in 1991 so that from that time on, foreign trade of the former socialist countries both among themselves and with the West was conducted on a hard currency basis. This was profoundly disruptive to trade. In particular, no payments union among the former CMEA countries was established, and, in its absence, trading relations among these countries collapsed. Instead they had no choice but to orient their trade activities towards the West (Rosati 1992). Despite being ill-prepared to do so, trade patterns shifted dramatically towards the West in the early stages of transition. As a consequence these countries were exposed to major changes in their terms of trade. These shocks could have both negative and positive effects for the economy. On the negative side, energy prices increased, exporters may have found their traditional foreign markets disappear, and domestic producers may have been exposed to low-cost imports. On the positive side, firms might find new export opportunities or lower-cost input sources and consumers could benefit from new and lower-cost goods. All of the transition economies were open prior to 1991. Consequently, there was no way that the governments of these economies could have avoided this shock. And there were only limited policy tools, mainly border measures (such as tariffs or quotas) and exchange rate policy, available to help moderate or modulate the shock.

Given our focus on the financial development of transition economies, we are particularly concerned with the monetary aspects of macro-
stabilization. Here it was widely recognized that the socialist economies
generally faced a problem of *monetary overhang*. Specifically, in the face
of widespread rationing of consumer goods households had positive
savings and had little choice but to keep their wealth in the form of
currency or savings deposits. As a result holdings of monetary assets far
exceeded the amounts required for transactions purposes. For example,
in East Germany in 1989 individuals' monetary holdings including
savings accounts were 237 billion Eastmarks; whereas, assuming the
same velocity of circulation as in West Germany, the appropriate figure
would have been 150 billion marks. Thus there was a monetary overhang of 87 billion marks (Sinn 1991: 19). Upon liberalization this was a
component of personal wealth that would be deployed in one way or
another. Either it could be used to acquire less liquid financial assets
such as government bonds or company shares; alternatively, it could
be used to acquire consumer goods, in particular durables, which were
rationed prior to liberalization.

The fear was that either by overstimulating investment or by directly
inducing price increases, this monetary overhang when unleashed could
initiate an inflationary spiral (Calvo and Kumar 1994). These considerations guided fiscal and monetary authorities in transition economies,
and they were at the centre of the early debate between the advocates
of a radical approach to transition and those who espoused gradualism.
The radical approach to stabilization was exemplified by Poland.[4] There
inflationary tendencies of monetary overhang were exacerbated by
nominal wage increases far in excess of real productivity growth which
the last communist government had granted in a vain effort to quell
labour unrest. The first post-communist government chose to free
virtually all prices as of 1 January 1990. Immediately, prices rose at
hyperinflationary rates and in so doing virtually wiped out the monetary
overhang. The risk in this was that this inflation would perpetuate itself.
In order to combat inflationary expectations, a very restrictive monetary
policy was adopted aimed at imposing high real interest rates on the
economy.

Other countries have elected to allow the repressed inflation of the
communist regime to continue into the transition period. Consequently,
they have liberalized prices and foreign trade in a more gradual manner.[5] In principle, one approach to resolving the monetary overhang is

[4] See the discussion of these issues in Balcerowicz (1993).
[5] Countries slow to pursue price liberalization include Ukraine, Turkmenistan, Kazak-
shstan, Georgia, Belarus, and Romania. See EBRD (1994*b*: 10).

through the sale of government bonds to the population.[6] Finally, in the case of East Germany, reunification with West Germany involved the conversion of all Eastern monetary contracts into Deutchsmarks. The rate of exchange rate rule that was adopted meant that Eastern monetary assets were converted at an average rate of 1.8 Eastmarks per DM; whereas, estimates of the purchasing power parity exchange rate ranged from 0.98 to 1.28 Eastmarks per DM (Sinn 1991: 13–15). As a consequence, the monetary conversion wiped out between 29 and 44 per cent of financial wealth in purchasing power parity terms. This compares to the monetary overhang which was estimated to be about 36 per cent of total financial wealth.

1.3.   Financial Liberalization

In the traditional socialist economy the State is present in almost all segments of the economy. Given this origin, it is clear that for the post-socialist countries a central element of the transition to a market economy involves the liberalization of a large range of economic activities. The liberal principle is that of freedom in contracting with whom one wishes at terms, including price, that are determined by the contracting parties. In the financial sphere, this means that the terms of loan contracts and of securities can be set freely and their price or interest rate are determined in the market place without state intervention.

The naïve liberal prescription for transition is very simple: take the State our of the contracting between private parties. However, the reality of post-socialist economies makes this prescription difficult to follow in an immediate way. In the first place, socialist habits in contracting are not those known in a mature capitalist economy. In part, this may be because of difficulties in the prevailing contract law. At least as important is that there may be a lack of an enforcement mechanism. When enforcement is difficult, it is natural that contract terms are routinely the subject of renegotiation. This means that terms of an economic transaction become contingent on changeable circumstances that may be difficult for either or both parties to verify. A reasonable policy in such circumstances is to restrict contracting to simple contracts that are consummated immediately or to contracts with agents with whom one has long-standing relations. An example of this in the area of finance is that in the socialist economies of Eastern Europe, borrowers

---

[6] Bulgaria has not been rapid in liberalization but started issuing government securities in 1990.

were sometimes subjected to changes in the interest rate after their loans were negotiated.

A further difficulty in liberalizing exchange is that in a post-socialist economy there may be a lack of clarity of ownership. When ownership rights are not clear, contracting between agents cannot be expected to produce efficient results.[7] To see how this can affect financial contracting in a transition economy consider the case of a new firm which seeks a bank loan to acquire and operate equipment. If it is difficult to establish that the seller of the equipment is its owner under the law, the sale may not be valid. If so, the equipment would not be a security for the loan. Uncertainty of this sort may be sufficient for lenders to decide not to grant the loan.

Given the structure of the socialist system, liberalizing existing financial institutions essentially means bank reform. The object of liberalization in this areas is to remove the State from setting interest rates on deposits and on bank loans. This is accomplished by introducing two-tiered banking. One part of the ex-monobank becomes the central bank. Commercial banking activities are diverted to independent institutions either carved out of the ex-monobank or newly created. Individuals are given the freedom to hold deposits in the bank of their choosing, and banks are free to set rates on deposits as they wish. At the same time, borrowers are allowed to select their bank and to negotiate the rate and other terms of their loan agreement.

Liberalizing the banking sector is unlike liberalizing other economic activities because banks are the conduits of monetary control. At times central banks of the capitalist economies have exercised monetary control through restrictions on the quantity of credits that banks are authorized to grant. Another quantitative credit tool is the provision of refinance credit. Such tools tend to give the central authorities control not only of overall monetary conditions but also of the allocation of funds among potential borrowers. Clearly, this works against the principle that credit decisions should reflect free negotiation between private borrowers and lenders, and for this reason in most mature capitalist countries central banks have increasingly relied on less indirect policy tools such as reserve requirements and open market operations. Refinance credit is restricted to short-term liquidity provision such as Lombard credit or discount credit.

Given that the central bank in a transition economy may be struggling to establish its mastery in monetary control, it may oppose rapid liber-

---

[7] In such a case, the basic conditions of the Coase theorem are not fulfilled. See Coase (1960).

alization throughout the banking sector. In particular, the market for government securities may be very underdeveloped so that open market operations are infeasible. Furthermore, policies aimed at influencing market interest rates may be ineffective if financial discipline is not in force. A distinct but similar concern is that rapid liberalization may disrupt operations of state-owned enterprises with long-standing debts and continuing needs for credit. This may provoke liquidity crises for such firms even if they are solvent. Thus in banking reform as elsewhere the objectives of liberalization and stabilization tend to come into opposition.

The monetary authorities in a transition economy possess very considerable powers over the economy and the course of transition. However, the heritage of banking under socialism does little to prepare the newly constituted central bank for implementing monetary policy in a very assured way. It is a commonplace opinion that an effective anti-inflationary policy requires the central bank be independent of the government budget. However, this raises the questions of the accountability of the central bank authorities and of how the objectives of monetary policy are to be determined.[8] Furthermore, even if the central bank is given nominally independent status, it might be effectively controlled by the government either because of informal links that exist between the two or because the bank is reluctant to pursue a policy that diverges too greatly from the thrust of the government's policies.

Even if the monetary and governmental authorities are committed to financial liberalization, at the microeconomic level there tend to be some structural features which produce hold-overs which perpetuate socialist banking practices.[9] We have already mentioned that in socialist banking financial relations tended to be highly segmented. Certain monetary accounts were not directly convertible into others. Furthermore, agents had little or no choice in restricting its financial dealings with a single banking institution. Changing this requires a series of administrative changes which may take time to put into effect. Furthermore, as in other sectors there are monopolistic tendencies in the banking sector even though the sector is formally thrown open to competition. For example, there may be entry of new banks, but if these banks simply open a home office without establishing a network of branches, individuals may have few practical alternatives to keeping their deposits in

---

[8] During the period 1991–4 the Russian central bank was independent of both parliament and the president. Under its chairman Viktor Geranshchenko, it used its freedom to pursue a very highly inflationary policy aimed at counteracting the effects of the liberalization measures promoted by the government. The result was a dramatic collapse of the rouble.

[9] For a more detailed discussion of these points see Nuti (1992*a*).

the same place they always did, even though this institution may change its name. The same applies to enterprises which may find that credit is difficult to obtain from new banks with which they have had no previous dealings and which may be unfamiliar with their industry or region. Achieving effective competition in a liberalized banking environment may be a matter of simply allowing the time for entry to result in a new industry equilibrium. However, it may require active intervention as a matter of anti-monopoly policy.

Perhaps the most pervasive socialist banking practice and the most difficult to change is the passive behaviour of creditors. This is one of the main factors contributing to what has come to be known as the 'soft budget constraints' faced by socialist enterprises (Kornai 1992: ch. 8). An enterprise with revenues insufficient to allow it to service its outstanding debt was not likely to receive any severe sanction for this shortcoming. Certainly the bank could not force the liquidation of the firm in order to recover the amounts owed. Instead, it was more likely that additional credits would be accorded to allow it to meet its production and other objectives. As a result, the banking sector at the start of transition has no experience in disciplining its borrowers; rather, banks' experience was that tolerating non-performing loans was sanctioned by the State. Furthermore, giving the banks the means of enforcing contracts requires the implementation of effective bankruptcy laws. Even if these laws exist, they may be administered, either intentionally or not, in a way that makes bankruptcy very costly. In such a circumstance, the rational course may be to allow the enterprise to continue operations in the hopes that something will be recovered in the future. Enterprises tend to recognize this, thereby reducing their incentives to service their debts.[10]

We have described some of the possible difficulties in pursuing liberal banking reforms in transition economies. All that we have discussed can be described either as structural impediments or constraints deriving from the needs of stabilization policy. We should mention that there is a line of argument that even in the absence of these it may be inappropriate to leave real interest rate determination to market forces alone. In this line of reasoning, imperfections in the economy mean that some degree of subsidization of industry on a continuing basis is appropriate. However, rather than have the State choose in detail which firms should receive subsidies, this should be done with fewer distortions by providing credit subsidies that would be available for a wide range of borrow-

---

[10] In the parlance of game theory, the banks have no 'credible commitment' to enforce the terms of the loan agreement. For a theoretical analysis of this see Dewatripont and Maskin (1990) and Maskin (1994).

ers. Often this line of argument comes in the form of recommending subsidized long-term credit. The idea is that the market may apply an inappropriately high discount rate to projects because of risk aversion.[11] The Japan Development Bank is sometimes suggested as an example of the successful public intervention in the provision of long-term finance.[12] Others may argue that interest rates should be determined by the market but that the State should provide loan guarantees to borrowers who would otherwise be cut off from credit. Again, the rationale for this policy may be that the market is applying an inappropriate risk-premium to some borrowers.

Whatever the merits of these arguments in favour of credit subsidies, other considerations may suggest that, if anything, they can be even more distortionary and difficult to eliminate than direct subsidies from the state budget. Since they operate by distorting prices, credit subsidies do not appear on any government budget. Therefore, it is difficult to identify who receives the subsidies and who is paying the bill. Since they are difficult to account for and their incidence is unclear, there may be little effective resistance to granting such subsidies. Other forms of intervention in banking relations may produce subsidies that are similarly difficult to detect and to quantify. For example, in granting loan guarantees, the State gives borrowers access to credit at lower rates than they would have otherwise. The costs of this emerge only in the future and only in those cases where the borrowers experience difficulty. In the same vein, if the State indirectly pursues a policy that encourages extending credits to state-owned enterprises which do not service their debts, there is an implicit guarantee.

Some of the same remarks apply to deposit guarantees; however, in this case the public policy purpose which serves to justify such guarantees is more apparent, namely they are the most effective means of preventing bank runs which may otherwise exist in the private banking sector and which could threaten the effectiveness of monetary policy. Despite this, the experience in capitalist countries which have relied on deposit insurance systems, especially that of the USA, suggests that implicit guarantees may far outstrip the explicit ones which are needed to secure stable monetary policy. Furthermore, such schemes may have the unintended side effect of inviting improper risk-taking by the banking sector.[13]

In discussing financial liberalization we have concentrated on banking reform since this has the closest links to finance of the system in place at

---

[11] For a theoretical statement of this position see Arrow and Lind (1970).
[12] For a description of the Japan Development Bank see Harada (1994).
[13] For an analysis of the problems of deposit insurance in the USA, see Kane (1989).

the start of transition. The application of liberalization measures in the area of stock and other securities markets is in some ways less problematic. Even if securities issue and portfolio investment are totally free, they are likely to be relatively small, at least in the early stages of the transition. Some involvement of public authorities may be necessary to stimulate securities market development. Certainly in most mature capitalist economies some degree of regulation is used in securities market. In particular, basic company law must define the rights of securities owners. For example, the methods of registering and transferring ownership of share need to be clarified. The right of shareholders to participate in firm governance must be established as does the ability of debt-holders to enforce restrictions on asset sales or other actions which could be harmful to their interests.[14] Given the lack of previous investment experience of most individuals in transition economies, it may be felt that there are clear needs for strong investor protection. The problem with this is that many forms of investor protection, e.g. the regulation of insider trading or the policing of fraudulent trading practices, have proved to be among the most subtle of market regulations and the most difficult to implement in a low-cost manner.

1.4. Deep Institution Building: Establishing Property Rights

In virtually every former communist country of Eastern and Central Europe there was widespread recognition that the transition to the market economy must involve the privatization of state-owned enterprises. Economic efficiency is clearly the principal benefit sought through privatization. Socialism was inefficient because resources were controlled by agents and organizations who did not have a clear interest in using them well. In part, this was because the bureaucracies running the economy had diffuse authority to make decisions. It was also because managers with effective control may have been pursuing personal objectives. However, sometimes firms were clearly directed to pursue social or other state objectives that sacrificed or ignored efficiency.[15]

---

[14] Many difficulties in the areas of investor rights emerged in the early stages of the Russian stock markets, e.g., in order to register shares sales investors may be obliged to travel to the remote place of business of the company where they may find that the official authorized to make the transfer is absent for an unspecified period. An even more egregious abuse arose when managers of a company which had sold a controlling interest to outside investors succeeded in doubling the outstanding shares and sold these to a subsidiary over which they had control.

[15] This point has been emphasized by Boycko *et al.* (1994).

Some of these problems of resource allocation also exist in mature capitalist economies. Much production is directed by large firms which must employ heavy bureaucracies. Managers often pursue their own objectives rather than the owners'. And the State pursues social objectives by regulating and taxing firms. Despite this supporters of privatization believe that the inefficiencies are considerably greater in socialist state enterprises. However, the desire to privatize is not only aimed at increasing the degree of efficiency. It is also aimed at bringing about a fundamental, qualitative change in the organization of the economy. In the classical socialist economy, land and capital are owned collectively. Furthermore, in Marxist ideology economic output originates fundamentally from labour. Thus as we have noted, capital's return in the form of interest was often omitted from the calculation of socially necessary costs. Even when it was included in the calculation of price, assuring the return on capital is not a priority objective for the enterprise. Furthermore, the halfway reforms of market socialism did little to correct this. In essence under socialism there is no 'advocate' for capital.[16] In principle, privatization changes this because then the firm's capital and land belong to agents who can legally use them in a self-interested way. Thus it is in their interests to see that the return on capital is maximized.

One of the most fundamental justifications for the market system is set out in the Coase theorem which shows that efficiency will be served by clearly defining property rights.[17] It does not matter who has the property rights so long as it is clear that somebody does. With this idea in mind at the outset of transition many argued that it was important to privatize state-owned enterprises rapidly, whereas the precise form of privatization was of secondary importance. However, this view ignores the distributional implications of privatization. In part, because of these,

[16] In an influential article in the early days after the fall of communism in Eastern Europe, E. Hinds (1991) argued, 'In effect, having socialized enterprises owning themselves means that nobody owns them. Thus there is no direct advocate for capital in these enterprises. Workers are supposed to be the surrogate advocates, but they have little interest in preserving and increasing their enterprises' capital'.

[17] See Coase (1960). Other conditions are required as well to assure that efficient bargains are struck. A technical condition is that the courts are able to verify without great cost the information pertinent to the contract. More generally, this line of argument abstracts from monopoly power since in the presence of such power non-cooperative solutions are not generally Pareto optimal. Weitzman (1993) has argued that the emphasis on defining property rights in Eastern Europe may be misguided precisely because when competition is imperfect the uncoordinated maximization of individual rights may be very inefficient. He suggests that organizational forms which promote coordination may do better. He supports this argument which reference to the Chinese township-village enterprise which has ill-defined property rights but which nevertheless seems to be the origin of much of the rapid Chinese growth in recent years.

the choice of privatization method has become a hotly debated and highly politicized question. As a result in some transition countries privatization has been anything but rapid.

There have been a very large number of proposed methods to privatize state-owned assets of the former socialist economies.[18] These can be grouped into three broad categories:

(*a*) *The sale of state assets to the public for money*. This may or may not be open to foreigners. It may be carried out by auction, negotiated sale, or other means. It may involve leverage or not. A prime example of a privatization programme in this category is the sale of East German assets by the *Treuhand*. It has also been heavily used in Hungary. It has been part of the process employed in Poland and the Czech Republic.

(*b*) *Turn over firms to employees*. This may involve all employees or only subgroups (e.g. managers). It may require employees to pay for their stakes. They may be permitted to borrow to finance their purchase (i.e. leveraged buyout). Plant and equipment may be transferred to the employees or they may be retained by the State and leased to the employees. It may involve a mixture of sales to the public and to employees with the latter paying lower prices. Sales to employees have been a prominent feature in Polish privatization.

(*c*) *Free-of-charge transfers to the public*. This is intended to give the citizens specific claims on the assets which they previously owned collectively. They may be given specific assets (e.g. restitution of properties expropriated by the State). They may receive vouchers which are claims on assets. They may use vouchers to bid for specific assets. Vouchers may be tradeble or not. Assets may be bunched together to spread risks. This may involve intermediaries (mutual funds). The population may be required to pay a small amount of money for the claims. The voucher method has been a prominent feature of privatization in the Czech Republic and in Russia.

All three of these general approaches can be applied to one firm at a time on a case-by-case basis. However, there has been an emphasis on carrying out the privatization process rapidly on a massive scale, and to this end a number of former socialist countries have simplified procedures as part of a process of large-scale privatization. The Czech Republic and Russia stand out in this regard.

Depending upon the precise details of the privatization method employed these approaches can have very different consequences for the

---

[18] General references concerning privatization in Eastern and Central Europe are Frydman *et al.* (1993*a*, *b*) and Bolton and Roland (1992).

distribution of ownership and control both within the citizenry and between foreigners and the domestic population. Similarly, they can lead to different relations between owners and managers. In particular, an important issue is whether in post-privatization there are significant ownership groups with a clear incentive to monitor management who might otherwise pursue their own private objectives. If privatization results in the shares of the firm being held by a very large number of individual owners, it may be that no one owner will have the incentive to undertake the effort to follow the affairs of the firm very closely. On the other hand, a privatization process which bestowed a controlling interest in an enterprise to a single individual or a very small group of investors would probably be extremely inegalitarian. The alternative which attempts to reconcile a wide distribution of financial wealth with the concentration of control rights involves financial intermediaries.[19] However, this leaves open the issues of what form such intermediaries should take and whether the intermediaries themselves will be subjected to effective monitoring.[20] Perhaps equally important is the question of whether privatization is merely a matter of form with little substantial change in the control of the real assets. For example, before privatization many socialist enterprises' productive assets were owned by the State but control rights were vested in workers' councils. If privatization takes the form of an employee buyout with plant and equipment owned by the State to be leased backed to the employees, then there is very little effective change on the way the firm is operated.

In a market economy, the ownership and control of capital and land are directly linked to the markets for financial assets. With the exception of sole proprietorships where the owners and the managers generally coincide, firm managers obtain capital on the basis of their promises set out in their contracts with creditors and shareholders. In this sense, the purpose of privatization is to create financial wealth with clear links to productive capital. Sometimes this has been expressed by saying that the monetary overhang problem of socialist economies implied a comparable asset underhang problem (Sinn 1991). That is, assets owned collectively by the population did not give rise to financial assets which carry control rights. Instead, the population held its wealth in the form

[19] See Diamond (1984) for an analysis of the advantage that a financial intermediary has in monitoring firms.
[20] e.g. the Polish approach to mass privatization has featured having state assets allocated to mutual funds and in turn citizens receiving vouchers which they can invest in the competing mutual funds (see Frydman and Rapaczyski 1991*a*). This approach has been criticized on the grounds that this does not create strong incentives for the mutual funds to compete with one another and therefore results in passive ownership.

of money. Depending upon the approach taken in privatization, the financial wealth of the population can take a variety of forms. If state enterprises are sold to the population, the population holding the shares then has control rights and has claims returns on which depend directly on firm performance. When the population buys shares in mutual funds which in turn buy the shares, the link of individual return to firm performance is weakened but is still present. If banks or other depository institutions own the firms and the population holds deposits, the link is weaker still since the performance of firms is perceived by depositors only to the extent that it affects the probability of default. Finally, if state enterprises are sold to foreigners for money, the citizens lose their control rights over these assets. The wealth of the population is increased only indirectly in the form of lower future tax liabilities and/ or greater future public services.

This discussion makes it clear that a country's approach to privatization has direct implications for the development of the country's financial sector. Privatization that endows the population with shares or bonds necessarily tends to create a securities market. Privatization through mutual funds may also do this if both the funds and the population trade on a secondary market. On the other hand, privatization that has the banking sector as the main creditor of industry reinforces the intermediation process but does little to develop securities markets. Finally, selling state assets to large foreign enterprises does little to develop the domestic financial sector.

1.5. *Deep Institution Building: Discipline in Financial Contracting*

Privatizing enterprises is viewed as an important step in applying discipline in the use of economic resources. However, the fact that an enterprise is private does not always mean that it will use resources well. Even if it maximizes its profits, it may squander resources if relationships with the providers of the resources induce it to do so. Thus if the newly privatized firms in a transition economy perceive that their budget constraints are as soft as those of the preceding state-owned enterprises, they may change the direction of the firm little or those changes that are implemented may be inefficient.

If the State stands ready to provide subsidies in order to prevent firms from failing or in order to support employment, a privatized enterprise will probably persist in producing unwanted goods in an inefficient manner much as a state-owned enterprise would. The same remark applies to the cases when the State continues to subsidize the price of certain products (e.g. fertilizers or energy). Thus the removal of direct state subsidies is the first and most obvious step towards increasing the economic discipline of enterprises.

Privatization may serve indirectly to reduce the state subsidies to firms. When firms are the property of the State, the decision to close down an uneconomic firm leaves labour with an easily idcntified target for applying political pressure. The response may be for the State to allow the firm to continue operations and to provide it with subsidies to cover its operating losses. In contrast, when jobs are lost because of the failure of a private firm, the responsibilities of the State are less clear.

The State may provide an indirect subsidy to enterprises in the form of reduced taxes. Even if the State does not intend to grant a firm a tax break, in some cases the firm may try to take one anyway by simply refusing to pay taxes either on time or at all. Faced with mounting tax arrears, the State may have the choice of either letting the firm off or forcing it into bankruptcy. Given this stark choice, even a reforming government may decide that avoiding job loss is more important than strict enforcement of tax laws.

Similarly, an enterprise, either private or state-owned, may find that it can avoid or delay paying for some inputs. For example, its supplier may be a loosely run state enterprise. Alternatively, even a privatized enterprise may feel that it has little choice but to ship to a customer that is unable to pay immediately. Thus, using trade credit by letting payments arrears mount is one way for a firm to keep its budget constraints soft.

In the financial sphere, whether or not enterprises face hard budget constraints depends on whether they will be held to the terms of their loan agreements. In general, a profit-maximizing borrower will respect his financial commitments when the alternative of defaulting is made unattractive because of threat of sanction. Default will make sense if the contract enforcement is expensive, as it will be if bankruptcy courts are slow or are generally soft on borrowers. Alternatively, firms will default if lenders are passive. The most important source of external funds is likely to be the banking system. If the banks remain in the hands of the State, we might expect the credit discipline to stay somewhat lax. However, even if the banks are privatized, they may not necessarily become aggressive creditors if competition among banks is weak or if bank management does not maximize profits.

Thus privatization is not a sufficient condition for the imposition of economic discipline. It might not be a necessary condition either. In particular, there is a distinction between the privatization of enterprise and the *commercialization* of enterprise. Usually the transformation of a public sector firm into a joint-stock company with shares held by the state treasury is viewed as a preliminary step towards privatization. However, this can be an important step in itself. In part, it can create a clearer operating environment for management who now is responsible to the State only to the extent that it is the main shareholder. The State may choose to allow the manager considerable operating freedom. Furthermore, in the commercialized enterprise profits can be made the central focus by making them the criterion for rewarding and firing management.[21]

1.6.   Deep Institution Building: Cleaning up Bad Loans

In the socialist system enterprises were directed according to the priorities of the State. In decision-making profitability was only one consideration and often not the most important one. Furthermore, the profitability of an enterprise reflected the prevailing price structure which was set administratively. In light of this, it was expected that with the onset of economic liberalization many state enterprises would be very unprofitable. This would mean that much of the plant and equipment of these enterprises was worth less than it cost to produce them. From an accounting viewpoint, the changes in a transition economy would force the partial write-off of enterprise assets. This shrinkage of the asset base implied the loss of financial capital in the enterprise. However, enterprises were also financed by credits from the banks and from other enterprises. For many firms the declines in asset values were likely to be large enough to make it impossible to pay back all these loans.

If defaults on loans were an isolated problem, they do not pose a great difficulty for the economy. In a transition economy, however, there is a risk that they could occur throughout the system. An enterprise might be able to sell its products profitably after liberalization; nevertheless, if it had extended credits to other unprofitable firms, their default would handicap and possibly cripple the otherwise healthy firm. Thus there was a threat of a domino effect provoking a massive wave of bankruptcies. This could easily spread to the banks and thereby undermine their capacity to provide the liquidity that would allow a firm to survive a

---

[21] See Carlin *et al.* (1994) on the performance of enterprise restructuring with and without privatization in a variety of transition economies.

difficult period. These massive defaults could be very harmful for the future growth of the economy. If firms were mired down in drawn-out bankruptcy proceedings, they would not be able to undertake the changes necessary to adapt the enterprise to new circumstances. Beyond this, after a firm emerged from bankruptcy, it may have difficulty obtaining the credits it needs to grow.

Since this bad-loan problem threatens to make the creation of a more efficient, market-based economy slower and more difficult, treating it is one of the most important tasks for policy-markers in a transition economy. Fortunately, it is one area where the authorities of the State can exercise significant power. One view of the bad debt problem is that it is the heritage of state central planning. This suggests that its solution might be centrally administered as well.[22] In particular, both the enterprises which are unable to service their loans and the banks and other enterprises which hold them are owned by the State. If the State consolidated the balance sheets of all of these state-owned institutions, it would find that the debts would cancel. In the end it would be left with real assets, i.e. the plant and equipment of the enterprises, which constitute the net worth of the State. As owner of both the banks and the enterprises involved, the State should be able to bring about a clean-up of the accounts of these enterprises. In effect this would involve a general moratorium on old debts. This would allow the state enterprises to undertake the adjustment to the new economic environment unhindered by its old obligations. Furthermore, these enterprises could then be privatized more readily since purchasers would be acquiring in essence the assets of the old enterprise but not the liabilities.

In reality the bad-loan problem is not as neat and self-contained as this description suggests. Furthermore, the solution involving general debt forgiveness may also have adverse consequences for the future performance of the economy. In none of the socialist countries was the economy entirely centralized in state-owned enterprises. The cooperative sector was very significant in all socialist economies. Also, to varying degrees limited amounts of private ownership were tolerated. For example, in Poland much of agricultural output came from privately owned farms. Beyond this the various attempts to introduce market socialism meant that some effort had been made to establish legally binding and enforceable contract relations among the various institutions making up the state bureaucracy. Were these past efforts to be totally ignored?

[22] See Begg and Portes (1993) for a statement of the problem and a proposed centralized solution involving debt foregiveness.

Furthermore, bad loans were not entirely confined to the internal economic relations of a country. A number of socialist countries had very sizeable foreign debts. If the State declared debts of its enterprises null and void, it still would be left with the liabilities *vis-à-vis* the rest of the world. How was the State to pay these? Also, the state-owned enterprises and banks, especially those involved in foreign trade, may have directly established credit relations with foreign institutions. The liabilities of such enterprises could not be forgiven so readily.

Even when debt cancellation is feasible administratively, authorities may be reluctant to pursue it for fear that it would create very bad precedents for the future. One of the objectives of transition is to introduce the discipline of the contract and to harden budget constraints generally. To bring this about, it is important that the State be viewed as helpful in contract enforcement. From this perspective, nothing could be worse than for the State to start the transition process with a policy of general debt forgiveness. The outcome that the policy-markers would like is to clean up the old debts while still encouraging financial discipline in the future.[23] Therefore, it may declare that any debt forgiveness is a one time only affair. However, such declarations may not be entirely convincing. Somehow the State would like to tie its hands so that such declarations would be credible. Unfortunately, there are no obvious institutional means of making such commitments credible.[24]

The bad loan problem takes on special meaning within the banking sector. At the outset of transition the most important assets of the banks are the credits granted to state institutions. General debt forgiveness would wipe out most of the banks' balance sheet. Even without a debt moratorium, a large fraction of the banks' credits outstanding may be non-performing. This could be of a magnitude which means the banks are unable to pay back depositors. Thus there is a real chance that there could be bank runs and large bank failures at the outset of transition. This could shake the confidence of the population in reforms. Robbed of the political support, the efforts towards liberalization and privatization could be aborted as a consequence.[25]

---

[23] This is expressed by Begg and Portes (1993) by saying that the *stock* of old loans should be written down so that the *flow* of new credits will be managed in a disciplined way.

[24] Berglöf and Roland (1995) explore a model in which a bank gambles on the possibility of a future bailout in making its loan decisions. This is a new source of creditor passivity not present in other models of soft budget constraints.

[25] This is not inevitably the outcome. In 1992 Estonia restructured two banks on the verge of collapse and closed a third which had failed, leaving depositors with losses. However, this did not give rise to a generalized bank run. Nor did it seem to lead to a collapse in credit expansion as Estonia in 1993 had positive GNP growth for the first time sine the break-up of the former Soviet Union. See Baer and Gray (1994: 41).

This would be an extreme outcome. The bad loan problem of banks might be less severe than this, or it might be possible to prevent it from destabilizing the banking sector through other policy measures such as deposit insurance. Nevertheless, the heritage of bad loans could adversely effect the performance of banks in a liberalized financial environment. The reason for this is that loan losses hit directly the capital of the bank. With a given deposit base, this mean the banks become more highly levered. This can give the bank the incentive for risky lending practices.[26] For example, it may agree to finance risky borrowers who promise to pay a relatively high return. When these projects succeed most of the benefits accrue to the bank owners. When they fail, the losses accrue mainly to depositors or to the deposit insurance fund. As a result, starting the transition process with undercapitalized banks could be a major obstacle to efficient investment practices.

Basically two sorts of policy interventions could improve the health of the banks. Effort could be made to improve the quality of the assets, for example, government securities could be swapped for loans which threaten default. Alternatively, the State could intervene in order to assure the performance of the existing loan portfolio. The second class of measure would work on the liability side of the ledger. The State might give the banks capital infusions. Or it can give the banks access to cheap funds either by subsidizing deposit rates or through low-rate credits from the central bank. None of these policy interventions is entirely innocuous. In bond–loan swaps, who ends up holding the old, bad loan? Guaranteeing service of enterprise loans involves a subsidy which could distort firm behaviour. Similarly, subsidized deposit rates drive a wedge between lending and borrowing rates. And if banks benefit from capital infusions now, will they not come to expect the same in the future?

1.7. Deep Institution Building: Banks or Securities Markets?

In 1990, at a time when it was just becoming clear that Eastern Europe as a whole was rejecting communism, trading of commodity futures contracts began on the Budapest Grain Exchange. Commodity futures trading with its aggressive speculation and seeming lack of planning is for many people the extreme form of the free market system. The fact

---

[26] This 'asset substitution problem' is one of the main agency costs of debt. For an analysis within the context of banking see Dewatripont and Tirole (1994).

that it was introduced in the early, highly uncertain stages of transition was a powerful symbol—if Budapest had a commodities exchange, surely Hungary had given up all pretence of adherence to a planned, socialist economy. The commodity market was prominent in Budapest the Second World War so that the reopening of the exchange was viewed by some as the return to normalcy. Indeed, one of the traders in 1990 had been a broker as a young man. However, Budapest was not an isolated example. Throughout Eastern Europe and in Russia itself, early on in the transition process, there has been considerable early interest in stock markets and commodity markets.

It is a matter of debate whether the creation of securities markets is more than just a symbol of the change in regime. Not all are convinced that securities markets should be a very high priority in transition economies.[27] Finance takes on a variety of distinct forms in mature capitalist systems. It has become common to describe the main alternatives as being either 'bank-based' or 'market-based'.[28] The clearest example of the bank-based system is Germany where a small number of universal banks are permitted to pursue a wide range of commercial and investment banking activities and have representation in the supervision of many firms.[29] The clearest example of a market-based system is the USA where there are highly developed markets for stocks and bonds and where even short-term finance for many firms is obtained through the commercial paper market. Thus the transition economies of Eastern Europe have fairly distinct competing models around which the reforms of the financial sector could be organized.

Giving priority to the development of markets implies one set of reforms should be advanced first. Stock exchanges are needed. Specialized institutions such as stockbrokers and clearing companies must develop. Institutional investors such as mutual funds, pension funds, and insurance companies are needed to make the markets accessible to a broader investing public. Beyond the symbolism already mentioned there are distinct advantages of this type of development. In particular, this form of finance emphasizes a more direct relation between the saving population and the investing firms. This is removed from the monetary creation process and for this reason involves the government only in a relatively distant way. More generally, the development of the financial markets implies the creation of new institutions so that the break with the institutions of the previous regime will be more pro-

---

[27] See Corbett and Mayer (1991) and Grosfeld (1994) for sharply contrasting views on the issue.

[28] See Mayer (1990) for international comparisons of forms of financing that make this distinction.

[29] See Franks and Mayer (1994) for an analysis of German financial structures.

found. Furthermore, the creation of competitive conditions in securities markets should aid economic efficiency. Certain disadvantages are involved in market-based financial developments. For example, direct finance requires a more active portfolio choice which is relatively costly for small savers. Also, firms financed through widespread sales of securities may have passive shareholders which can lead to serious agency problems where managers pursue their own goals and do not maximize firm value. Furthermore, securities-based financing relies on well-developed companies law and securities regulation which are difficult to develop quickly in the context of Eastern Europe.[30] In particular, the experience of the USA and the UK has shown that maintaining public confidence in the markets requires elaborate investor protection which certainly does not exist in the former communist countries.

Creating a banking sector which can operate efficiently in a capitalist economy requires another set of reforms in a transition country. Existing depository institutions will inevitably have competitive advantages over new banks if only because they already provide the population banking services. Thus reforms must address the issue of how these hold-overs from the socialist banking bureaucracy can be transformed into modern, efficient organizations. For this reason, bank privatization is an important step even if the best timing of this may be unclear. Furthermore, some solution for the bad loan problem needs to be found before existing banks will have the right incentives when making credit decisions. Bankruptcy reform is an important complement to banking sector development since this will permit banks to become active in enforcing the terms of their loan contracts thus hardening budget constraints for enterprises. Finally, bank regulations are needed to assure the stability and solvency of the banking sector.

One of the advantages of a strategy for financial sector development emphasizing banks is that it builds on existing institutions. Thus there can be greater continuity in the introduction of reforms with less disruption to the economy as a result. At a deeper level, advocates of bank-based finance emphasize the usefulness of banks in collecting information on investors and monitoring the execution of projects once initiated. Indeed in the highly uncertain conditions of a transition economy one of the biggest challenges is to generate information useful for guiding investment decisions. The fact that in developed capitalist economies many

---

[30] There are numerous cases of Russian securities and company laws failing to protect investors, e.g., in one major Russian firm in which foreigners had purchased an apparently controlling interest, managers succeeded in doubling the total outstanding shares with the new shares being held by a wholly owned subsidiary. By diluting the equity holdings of outsiders the managers who controlled the subsidiary, thereby re-established control over the parent corporation. See 'Primorsky Shipping Makes Surprise Stock Sale to Unit', *European Wall Street Journal*, 24 April 1995.

start-up firms obtain bank finance before turning to public securities issues is evidence of efficient monitoring and suggests that in transition economies banks may be faster to finance new enterprises than would securities markets. Finally, under bank finance a firm faces a small number of creditors with whom it can negotiate. This suggests that if the firm is financially distressed the banks may be more effective in avoiding inappropriate liquidations of solvent firms than would be the creditors if the firm were financed through public debt issues.

Some of the disadvantages of bank-based finance were already implicit in our discussion of the advantages of markets. Since the banking sector emerged from the old socialist monobank there will be a tendency for banks to be dominated by the government. This may perpetuate practices of the past. In particular the same old banks may continue to lend money to the same old enterprises, even though these institutions may have changed name and legal status. Stated otherwise, it may be difficult to establish bank governance which orients them towards profits. The large banks may be owned by the State. Even if privatized, the government may retain a controlling minority interest. Also banks may be influenced by a variety of pressures from the central bank or other bank regulators. In particular, the experience in developed capitalist economies has shown that regulations aimed at assuring bank stability can invite problems of moral hazard, where banks make risky or otherwise ill-advised loans because they know that they will be bailed out in case of trouble.

In reality no capitalist financial system is based purely on banks or purely on securities markets. So the choice open to policy-makers in transition economies is not as stark as our discussion might suggest. Since they are starting with finance concentrated in banks, it is not conceivable that the financial development in transition economies could bypass banks. Even in the most market-oriented financial systems such as that in the USA banks continue to play a very crucial role. It might be easier to neglect financial markets. However, the experience in country after country has been that a modern financial sector requires at the least a liquid monetary market in which government securities are traded.

1.8.   *The Speed of Transition and the Sequencing of Reform*

Our discussion has shown financial transition involves a huge number of reforms reaching throughout the economy. How should this enormous task be approached? One of the most hotly debated issues in policy-making for post-socialist economies regards the speed at which reforms should be introduced. Some have pushed for rapid reforms, suggesting that the socialist economies could be brought to life only through the use of 'shock therapy'. Others have criticized such an approach as very misguided in that it imposes unnecessarily high adjustment costs on the population. Instead, reforms should be introduced step by step in a gradual manner. Closely related to the speed of reforms is the issue of the appropriate sequencing of reform. In this section we consider these issues as they apply to the financial sectors.

It should be remembered that in the past in order to overcome some obvious and chronic problems associated with planning most of the countries of Central and Eastern Europe experimented with partial reforms which shared some features of a market economy. However, these reforms were never anything but partial and in most cases reforms were undone in subsequent periods of retrenchment. Even Hungary and, to a lesser extent Poland, where the reforms proved somewhat more durable, the partial market reforms were difficult to make consistent with the basic functioning of the state planning mechanism (Balcerowicz 1988). Thus when in 1989 and 1990 when it was clear that the political support for the communist regimes had crumbled, this was perceived as the opportunity to introduce comprehensive changes throughout the system. Change was needed on all fronts. Simply changing the laws to allow market transactions would not be enough. The old institutions and habits were ill-adapted to the needs of the market place, so new institutions and, indeed, new mentalities were called for.

Other considerations make the case for rapid, comprehensive reform still more compelling. It was recognized that the transformation of the post-socialist economies would require significant investments in new plant and equipment as well as in human capital. If reforms were half-way, these investments would be based on signals that gave a false picture of what the conditions of supply and demand would be in the future. Furthermore, in order to bring about a change in habits and expectations of the population, it was important that the change be shown to be comprehensive from the beginning. In this way the credibility of the reform process would be enhanced. This line of argument was also made on clearly political grounds. The idea was that, after the almost simultaneous rejection of communism throughout Eastern Europe, there was an historical 'window of opportunity' to bring about fundamental changes to the system. It was important that this opportunity be used to effect the most important and durable reforms. While rarely stated in this way, the notion that there was a window of opportunity recognized that at the start of transition the democratic political systems were not yet in place. The development of democracy would make economic reforms more cumbersome to implement. Furthermore, as time would go on politicians would better define their constituencies and would learn how they could build support by distancing themselves from one or another aspects of the reforms.

Many convinced reformers might recognize some merit in these arguments in favour of rapid reform but would argue nevertheless that there are even more compelling reasons that the reform should not be too rapid. Our review of the main tasks of economic transition pointed out that economic liberalization often ran against efforts to stabilize the economy. Thus one important reason for slowing reforms is to avoid pushing the economy into either hyperinflation or depression. This is not just a vague fear of the unknown. It was clear early in the transition process that the CMEA trading regime would cease to operate and that all the former members would face terms of trade shocks of varying degrees. If in addition budget constraints would be immediately hardened for existing enterprises, there was a very strong likelihood of massive lay-offs and firm failures. This would mean that the economy would be submitted to a major fall in aggregate demand which if not countered could build into a major depression.[31]

A second line of argument in favour of gradualism emphasizes the costs of adjustment imposed on the population. Even if rapid reform could be shown to be the fastest path to the long-run growth of national income, some would oppose it because adjustment costs would be too high. In part, rapid change will create uncertainty for individuals which will reduce their welfare to a degree greater than that brought on by reduced consumption alone. Furthermore, the cost of adjustment would not be borne evenly. Among those laid off, the young will be able to adapt relatively quickly whereas the middle-aged will have a harder time adjusting or will find that the costs of retraining cannot be recovered in their remaining working life.

The case for gradual introduction of reforms can also be made on political grounds. In general terms the fear is that a radical approach to reforms would provoke a conservative backlash. In the context of Eastern Europe this would mean that if the initial experience of reforms was too harsh, the support for the former communist parties would be strengthened. In contrast, gradual reforms would allow time for some

---

[31] Coricelli and Milesi-Ferretti (1993) present a model where big-bang-type policies can induce larger output declines than gradualist policies. In this model rapid reforms may fail even if they promote large productivity improvements because they make the threat of hardening budget constraints incredible.

groups to perceive that they are better off, and for others that benefits of reform are becoming accessible to them. In this way pro-reform constituencies would be built up which would allow the reform effort to continue. A related argument recognizes that, in a democracy, reforms which impose costs can often be adopted only if many of those hurt by the reforms are given compensation. For example, if liberalization measures force labour shedding, those that are out of work will need income support. If reforms are gradual, much labour shedding can be accomplished on a voluntary basis as individuals perceive that they can obtain a higher wage in a growing sector. Thus income growth net of compensation costs may be maximized by moderating reforms.[32]

The debate on the speed of transition is related to that on the sequencing of reforms in transition. The advocates of a very rapid approach to reforms are apt to say that reform is needed on all fronts simultaneously. Furthermore, the transition process does not lend itself to careful planning so that it may be futile to determine an optimal sequencing of reforms. However, even radical reformers will recognize that not all the needed reforms can be accomplished at once and that in each dimension of reform there may be a natural maximum speed (Balcerowicz 1993). In particular, many of the needed reforms require the development of new institutions. The legal and organizational work required in these areas can be considerable so that the limitations of resources mean reforms will be at least somewhat time-consuming. These limitations will tend to establish a natural sequencing of reforms.

Still others have argued that policy-makers should voluntarily slow reforms in some dimensions while pushing hard to advance them in others.[33] In particular, reforms should be pushed early if they are clearly essential and beneficial and if they tend to make the reform process irreversible. Furthermore, high priority reforms should be advanced even though there may be uncertainty about the form the reform should take if such changes can be reversed later. An example of this might be exchange system reforms, where establishing a single exchange rate is an important part of liberalizing trade but where the exchange rate itself can be adjusted later if it is set at an inappropriate level. In contrast, policy-makers should delay reforms that would be difficult to reverse and where there is a risk of making a bad feature permanent. An example of this is privatization if the existing enterprises would be able to exert monopoly power within the economy. In such a case, a

---

[32] These arguments have been advanced by Dewatripont and Roland (1992a, b), who examine transition in a model which builds on recent developments of political economy.

[33] See Newbery (1991) for a statement of this position.

demonopolization policy (e.g. breaking up firms into smaller units) should precede privatization.

While stated in general terms, such precepts seem reasonable, but it is not always clear how they can be applied. For example, in the financial sphere which is our focus, separating central and commercial banking is one reform which has been accepted as a necessary fundamental step towards the introduction of the market. This was a priority for early reform and in some cases in Eastern Europe was already in effect when the political events of 1989–90 occurred. Most other issues of sequencing are much less clear. Should non-financial firms be privatized before or after banks? Should bankruptcy regimes be reinforced before or after privatization? Should banks be restructured before they are privatized or should the privatized banks be restructured by their private owners? The answers to these questions are not obvious. We will see that regarding these issues different countries have taken different paths. Part of our task will be to examine their experiences in order to identify the advantages and disadvantages of the approaches that they have followed. Only after having considered these cases in some detail will we attempt to state (in Chapters 7 and 8) our own conclusions on the proper sequencing of financial reforms.

1.9. Conclusion

Our review of the important conceptual problems posed by the transition of ex-socialist economies has been far from exhaustive. The unique historical circumstances created by the collapse of communism have stimulated economists to introduce new models of system-wide economic adjustment. However, we will not pursue these theoretical developments.[34] Instead, we turn to our main purpose: to analyse the main evidence regarding the financial aspects of transition in Central and Eastern Europe.

---

[34] A survey of the theoretical literature on transition is provided by Dewatripont and Roland (1997).

2

The Domestic Economic Context of Financial Transition

2.1. Introduction

The main task we have set for ourselves is to present and analyse the main features of the reform and development of the financial sectors of the Czech Republic, Hungary, and Poland. This comparison is prompted by the fact that these three countries have much in common. In particular for more than forty years they were under the direct influence of the Soviet Union which obliged them to organize their economies according to the logic of socialist central planning. This regime came to an abrupt end in 1989, and since then the three countries have been free to pursue their own separate paths towards the market. Almost inevitably there is a tendency to view this as something of a race which will establish the effectiveness of the policies chosen. Our comparative assessments in Chapter 7 of the financial development strategies are generally in this spirit. However, the analogy of transition to a race should not be pushed too far. There is no single, clearly defined end-point to transition. In addition, despite their common heritage of Soviet-Style communism, these countries did not start their transitions from exactly the same conditions. Furthermore, the non-financial policy approaches have differed across the countries, which means that the real economies have affected financial sectors in different ways.

The development of the financial sector cannot be understood in complete isolation of the rest of the economy or indeed of the political context. In this chapter we briefly review some of the main macroeconomic and political features of the three countries that we have targeted. Chapter 3 gives an overview of the international economic context. The rough sketch provided by these two chapters sets the context of financial development and is provided in order to make our study self-contained.[1] In addition, it will serve to remind us of the

---

[1] Readers interested in more details about the macroeconomic development of the region may consult the EBRD (1995) as well as the other studies that we cite in this chapter.

significant differences in the starting conditions of transition in the three cases. We will argue that some of these macroeconomic conditions have imposed different constraints on policy and have tended to introduce clear biases in the direction of financial sector reform.

2.2.   The Point of Departure

Despite being under Soviet influence since the early 1950s, there were major differences in the experience of socialism in Hungary, Poland, and Czechoslovakia. Something of these divergent experiences can be seen in the histories of the growth rates of industrial production in these three countries in the 1980s (Fig. 2.1). Czechoslovakia' growth rate from 1980 through 1989 was relatively constant at about 2.5 per cent. Hungarian growth rate was more variable and was negative in three years (1980, 1988, and 1989). The average growth rate for the decade was 1.4 per cent. Finally Poland's industrial growth averaged 1 per cent for the decade and was marked by a deep recession from 1980 through 1982. In Poland this history reflected significant political shifts brought about by mounting tensions between the State and organized labour.[2] Hungary's growth was marked by considerable experimentation with elements of market organization (Swain 1992).

Another view on these countries at the outset of transition is provided by measuring the relative size of their economies and the income level of the population. One difficulty of making such comparisons under socialism was that production and consumption were not measured at market prices. Table 2.1 reports estimates of gross domestic product for 1992, after prices had been liberalized and the economies had been opened to world trade. These data make the obvious but important point that Poland is a considerably larger economy than the other two implying a natural tendency for it to be relatively less open. Of the three Poland had the lowest income per capita in 1993, reflecting among other things the relatively larger fraction of the population living in rural areas. While these levels of income were quite high within the group of economies of Eastern and Central Europe undergoing transition, they were only between one-quarter and one-third of those of the advanced Western economies (EBRD 1994*b*). If the objective of transition is to draw closer to the West, this gap represents a considerable challenge which could only be closed by a period of sustained, high growth rates.

---

[2] The post-war history of Poland is discussed by Slay (1994).

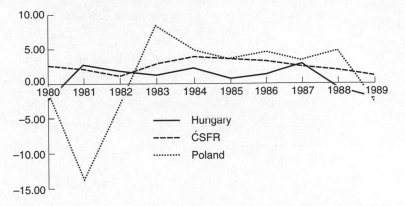

FIG. 2.1   Annual average growth rate of industrial production, 1980–9

TABLE 2.1   Income levels, 1992

	Gross domestic product (million & US calculated at PPP exchange rates)	Population (millions)	GDP per capita ($US)
Poland	187.392	38.4	4,880
Hungary	59.122	10.3	5,740
Czech Republic[a]	73.748	10.3	7,160
G-7		660.4	19,600

[a] Estimated from data on Czechoslovakia.

Source: EBRD (1994).

It is sometimes stated that the objectives of transition cannot be captured adequately by quantitative economic measures such as levels of national income and that instead transition involves a *qualitative* change in economic and social relationships. Under classical socialism economic activity was to be carried out predominantly within large state enterprises and administrations. At the outset of transition the Czech economy with 11 per cent of GDP and only 1.3 per cent of employment taking place in private enterprises corresponded closely to this model (Table 2.2). In Hungary earlier reforms has shifted a larger fraction of output to private firms; adding to this the output of cooperatives, almost 30 per cent of 1989 national income originated outside the state sector. In Poland the relatively high fraction of economic activity taking place in the private sector in 1989 in part reflects reforms initiated in the 1980s

TABLE 2.2 Share of the private sector in economic
activity, 1989

	Share of GDP	Share of employment
Czech Republic	11.2	1.3
Hungary	14.9	n.a.
Poland	28.6	45.7

Source: EBRD.

but also the fact that agriculture, which was quite important for Poland, had never been successfully collectivized. A large number of people worked on small private farms.

An additional factor which was of direct relevance to the reforms initiated after the collapse of communism was the underdeveloped nature of the financial sector. The consequence of rationing of consumer goods, especially durables, on the one hand, and of the limited forms of financial investment, on the other, was a tendency to accumulate monetary assets. The degree of monetary overhang was indicated by the ratio of money stock to gross domestic product which was 0.4 in Hungary, 0.7 in Czechoslovakia, and 0.9 in Poland.[3] The degree of monetary overhang was relatively less in Hungary in part because a number of prices had been liberalized but also because efforts had been made to develop the bond market in the 1980s.

2.3. Summary of Political Developments

While our central concern is the transformation in the organization of the economies of Eastern and Central Europe, the phenomenon of transition is fundamentally political in nature. At the end of the 1980s the communist system in Eastern Europe collapsed. The new political parties which participated in democratic elections competed with each other in proposing their own visions of how the economies should be transformed to be based on market principles. Even the socialist parties emerging from the remnants of the old communists expressed their commitment to market economics albeit while emphasizing state leadership and the importance of assuring social protection.

[3] M2 (currency, plus demand deposits plus savings deposits) divided by GDP in 1990 see Bruno (1993).

Despite an overall consensus in favour of transition, political instability is a potential threat to the success of economic policy reforms. In the unsettled situation of 1990 the outlines of the political landscapes were relatively unclear in Hungary, Poland, and Czechoslovakia. As a consequence, there was a risk that shifts in the political balance could give rise to stop-and-go in policy formulation. These fears have not been entirely borne out. The most politically stable country is the Czech Republic where economic policy has been dominated by the presence of Václav Klaus. In contrast Poland and, to a lesser extent, Hungary have been marked by significant political instability. Table 2.3 summarizes some of the main political developments in these countries since 1989.

In Hungary, the first democratic elections of March 1990 led to a three-party middle-right coalition government formed by the Hungarian Democratic Forum (MDF), the Christian Democrats, and the Smallholder Peasants Party. The prime minister was József Antall until his death on 12 December 1993. This government served its full four-year parliamentary term until the new elections in July 1994 in which the socialist party made significant gains. This led to the formation by the prime minister, Gyula Horn, of a coalition government with the young Democrats. The stability of this coalition has been difficult to maintain with political tensions focusing on the speed of privatization and fiscal discipline. The regime has been marked by instability in the important posts of minister of finance and the governor of the central bank.

In Poland, the first non-communist government which was formed in September 1989 launched the 'Balcerowicz' plan of economic transformation. Presidential elections were held in late 1990 and led to the victory of Lech Wałęsa. The same basic team was responsible for the economy until December 1991. In October 1991, the first democratic parliamentary elections led to the entry of twenty-nine parties in the parliament and the formation of the Bielecki Government. During 1992, three governments followed each other with four ministers of finance, three of them whom resigned. The Suchocka Government, formed in July 1992, faced increasing social unrest expressed by huge strikes, and in May 1993 a vote of no confidence from the parliament. President Wałęsa then decided to dissolve parliament and to keep the government in office up to the September elections. In these elections the Left made significant gains, and a new government formed by the prime minister Pawlak took office in October 1993. Tensions appeared quickly emerged between this government on the one side and President Wałęsa and the president of the National Bank on the other. Finally, in January 1995 the prime minister resigned after the refusal of the president to sign the budget law. A new government was formed in March

TABLE 2.3   Political developments

Hungary

March–April 1990	First democratic elections: middle-right three-party coalition with Antall as prime minister.
March 1991	'Programme of conversion and development for the Hungarian economy.'
July 1994	Second democratic elections: socialist and young democrats coalition with Horn as prime minister.

Poland

September 1989	First non-communist government formed with members of the Solidarity movement and with Mazowiecki as prime minister.
January 1990	'Balcerowicz' economic plan.
December 1990	Wałęsa elected as president.
October 1991	First Parliamentary elections: 29 parties earned seats, new government with Bielecki as prime minister.
1992	New government with Olszewski as prime minister.
July 1992	New government with Suchocka as prime minister.
May 1993	Dissolution of parliament.
September 1993	Parliamentary elections: left government with Pawlak as prime minister.
March 1995	New left-wing Democratic Alliance government with Oleksy as prime minister.
December 1995	Alexander Kwaśniewski former member of the Communist Party defeats Wałęsa in the presidential elections.
January–February 1996	Resignation of Oleksy, charged with spying. Cimoszewicz named prime minister.

Czech Republic

November 1989	'Velvet Revolution' in Czechoslovakia: Democratic Forum forms government.
June 1990	First democratic elections, government with Klaus as minister of finance.
June 1992	Havel elected as president, Conservative parties win elections, Klaus as prime minister.
1 January 1993	Separation from Slovakia. Klaus is prime minister and Havel is president of the new Czech Republic.
June 1993	Parliamentary elections. Klaus returned.
June 1996	Parliamentary elections. Klaus weakened but continues as prime minister.

1995 with Olesky as prime minister. The presidential elections of December 1995 saw Wałęsa turned out by Kwaśniewski, a young former communist, who projected an image of moderation and managed to unify the Left. In the aftermath of this vicious election campaign, the prime minister was accused of having spied for Russia and was forced to resign. This led to the formation in February 1996 of a new government under Cimoszewicz. However, political tensions within the ruling coalition continued. The political history of Poland is thus characterized by a high instability which made it difficult to define a clear path for reforms.

Political tensions within Czechoslovakia were concentrated in the divide between Czech and Slovak parties which led to the establishment of two separate republics on 1 January 1993. The political team that initially set the path of reform for the federation continued in power in the Czech Republic after separation so that this country has benefited from several years of effective political stability. Since late 1989 the 'Velvet Revolution' has been marked by a successful effort to articulate a consensus among the main opposition groups and resulted in the replacement of the communists by a government of Democratic Forum. In June 1990, the first free elections for parliament were organized resulting in a government in which Václav Klaus was finance minister. In June 1992, Václav Havel was confirmed as president of the federation and the parliamentary elections were won by the conservative parties. The president designated Václav Klaus, formerly minister of finance, as prime minister of the Federation and leader of a four-party coalition government. The parties' members of the Government are the Civic Democratic Party, the Civic Democratic Alliance, the Christian Democratic Union, and the Popular Party. Klaus became the prime minister of the Czech Republic Government after the splitting of the Federation at the beginning of 1993. In the elections of June 1996 the right lost ground and forced Klaus to form a government with an expanded and potentially more unstable coalition.

2.4.   Liberalization and Stabilization

A clear sign of the broad consensus in favour of moving towards a market economy in the countries of Central and Eastern Europe was the speed with which they moved to liberalize the economies. The experiments with market socialism of the past had never altered the fact that the State intervened directly in the interactions among economic agents. The heart of liberalization was to enormously expand the scope for exchanges to take place under conditions freely negotiated by the parties concerned.

Hungary was the first of the three countries to implement economic reforms with the introduction as early as 1968 of the New Economic Mechanism abolishing the centrally fixed quantitative targets of production. Value indicators (including profits) of enterprise performance were used and managerial incentives were introduced and linked to these performance criteria.[4] In the following years, different measures of liberalization were taken in the fields of prices determination, international trade, and private ownership.[5] However, the end objective of these measures was not a market economy. Instead, the aim was to offer a higher living standard in order to mitigate discontent with socialism expressed in the widespread uprising of 1956. Despite the changes the government's interventions in the allocation of resources were frequent and arbitrary. Following the same pattern though to a lesser extent, Poland also introduced liberalization measure culminating in the abandonment of the central quantitative plan in 1982. In contrast, Czechoslovakia remained an 'orthodox' centrally planned economy until the political liberalization of 1990.

Since mid-1990, Hungary has accelerated its gradualist liberalization reform process now redirected towards the creation of a market-based economy. One year after the political shift of 1989, Poland launched a more radical programme of liberalization combined with stabilization, the 'Balcerowicz' plan named after its architect, Leszek Balcerowicz, the Polish finance minister from 1989 to 1991. In 1991 Czechoslovakia also implemented a radical programme of transformation resembling the Polish plan. These programmes included broad trade and price liberalization and a substantial reduction in subsidies through the budget or prices.

Liberalization quickly led to significant changes in relative prices, thus demonstrating the fact that previously prices had been effectively controlled. It has been argued the changes in relative prices brought on the subsequent sharp decline in aggregate output (Gomulka 1994; Winiecki 1993; Bruno 1993). This is evidence of an asymmetric production response whereby firms facing declines in relative output prices cut output more rapidly than firms facing increases in output prices increased theirs. The reason for this may be that expansion in the productive capacity of an enterprise requires time for planning and

---

[4] For more details on Hungarian first round of transformation see Boote and Somogyi (1991).

[5] These measures included the 'self-governing' statute granted to most enterprises.

TABLE 2.4　Inflation rate (December to
December change in the consumer price index)

	Czech Republic[a]	Hungary	Poland
1980–5[b]	2.0	6.7	30.6
1986	0.6	5.4	15.8
1987	0.0	8.6	27.3
1988	0.2	15.5	57.1
1989	1.5	18.9	251.1
1990	18.4	33.4	585.8
1991	52.0	32.2	60.4
1992	12.7	21.6	44.4
1993	18.2	21.1	37.7
1994	10.2	21.2	29.5
1995	10.0	28.0	23.0

[a] Czechoslovakia before 1990.
[b] Geometric average of annual rates.

Sources: Czech Republic from 1990: CNB (1993) and
before: IMF; for Hungary from 1988: NBH (2/1995) and
before: IMF; for Poland since 1990: Warsaw School of
Economics (1994), and before: IMF.

investment while the reduction in production can be implemented almost immediately.[6]

The liberalization of prices proceeded at different paces in the three
countries. Although no country fully liberalized prices in one step,
Poland implemented large adjustments at the beginning. Czechoslovakia moved somewhat slower than Poland and maintained controls on
more goods considered necessities. Hungary operated its liberalization
more gradually.[7] The effect of price liberalization on the overall price
level can be judged from the consumer price inflation rates reported in
Table 2.4.

In each country price liberalization was followed by an upsurge of
inflation that was greater than had been anticipated. Of the three Poland experienced the highest inflation rates as one might expect from
the facts that it had the highest degree of monetary overhang and that

[6] However, Rosati (1994) suggested that the change in relative prices was not the major
factor behind the fall in output in 1990–2 as this contraction affected all major sectors.

[7] In Hungary, by 1982 over 50% of consumer goods were free of control, the percentage
gradually increasing to 80% by 1990; for more details see Bruno (1993).

almost all prices were liberalized in one step in 1990. Czechoslovakia went through a similar but more moderate inflation when prices were liberalized in 1991. In both cases inflation rates decline precipitously after the initial liberalization shock. This differs from the experience in Hungary in which inflation rates were already rising in the latter half of the 1980s reaching a peak in 1990–1 since which time inflation has persisted at relatively high levels. This points out one of the dangers of gradual liberalization, namely that by spreading the impact of freeing prices over several years there is a constant pressure on prices which will tend to be perceived as a chronic condition and will be translated into expectations of high inflation rates in the future.

The high inflation rates associated with price liberalization had a direct impact on the health of the banking sector. In many cases banks had extended loans to state-owned enterprises that were routinely rolled over so that they were effectively long-term credits. Some of these loans carried administratively fixed rates which were not allowed to follow the general rise of deposit rates. Thus inflation tended to inflict a substantial loss on these banks. As we will discuss at some length in our treatment of the financial sectors of the individual countries, many of the traditional borrowers failed to service their loans as the transition got underway. However, it should be noted that to the extent that the principal on these loans was fixed in nominal terms, i.e. so long as no additional credits were granted, inflation tended to reduce the real value of these loans. Thus high inflation early in transition tended to eliminate the stock of old bad loans. Despite this, we will see that the bad loan problem has proved to be difficult to solve and has had a considerable impact on financial policies adopted in transition.

Poland adopted strong policy measures to stabilize the economy following price and trade liberalization so that it become the first prominent exponent of 'shock therapy' in the early stage of transition.[8] One important part of this policy was the decision to fix the exchange rate against the US dollar in an effort to give a 'nominal anchor' to the economy (see Table 2.5). Setting the exchange rate target at 9,500 zloty per dollar in 1990 constituted a very substantial devaluation, and in retrospect it seems clear that this provided a strong boost to Polish exports and to domestic inflationary pressure. A second important part of Polish stabilization policy was the adoption of an excess wage tax (called the *popywek*) which imposed a substantial penalty on state-owned enterprises awarding wage increases in excess of an official norm. From Table 2.5 we see that the inflation of real wages has been

[8] See Berg and Sachs (1992) for a sympathetic presentation of the Polish stabilization programme. A more critical view can be seen in Bruno (1993).

TABLE 2.5 Annual average exchange rate of the currency against the $US

	Czech Republic (korunas)	% of change	Hungary (forint)	% of change	Poland (old zloty)[a]	% of change
1989	15.1		59.1		1,450	
1990	18.0	19.2	63.2	6.9	9,500	555.2
1991	29.5	63.9	74.8	18.4	10,580	11.4
1992	28.3	−4.1	79.0	5.6	13,630	28.8
1993	29.2	3.2	91.9	16.3	18,120	32.9
1994	28.8	−1.4	105.2	14.5	22,720	25.4

[a] The new zloty was introduced in early 1995 at the conversion rate of 10,000 old zlotys for 1 new zloty.

Source: EBRD (1995) and own calculation.

quite moderate in Poland. As we will discuss in Chapter 6, these measures were accompanied by an initially very tight monetary policy. The combined effect of these policies was to prevent Poland from falling into an inflationary spiral following the initial price liberalization.

Hungary adopted a programme in January 1991 involving small devaluation (15 per cent), a further liberalization of prices (90 per cent of consumer basket), and restrictive fiscal, monetary, and incomes policy.

In Hungary, inflation accelerated at the end of 1990 following the extension of price liberalization. Subsequently, inflation rates have tended to subside, although they received an additional push with increase in the VAT rate and in public sector prices in 1992. An attempt to stabilize the economy was made in 1991 with the introduction of a tax on wage increases in excess of 28 per cent. During this year, the real consumer wages slightly declined (see Table 2.5), and for most firms wage increases did not attain this allowed ceiling. In 1993 the tax was abolished.

Czechoslovak prices remained fairly stable throughout 1990 and then jumped in the first quarter of 1991 following the liberalization. Stabilization measures quickly ensued including the introduction of a tax on excess wage increases. This tax was again applied in 1992 for local authority enterprises. Also prices were not fully liberalized as the government stipulated maximum prices or trade margins on some key commodities. Furthermore, price increases were braked by requiring prior notification of price increases in some monopolistic sectors (Bruno 1993). In 1993 inflation accelerated in large part due to the introduction

TABLE 2.6   Annual average growth of rate of nominal and real wages

	Czech Republic		Hungary		Poland	
	Wages in industry		Gross monthly earnings		Wages and salaries	
	Nominal	Real			Nominal	Real
			Nominal	Real		
1990	4.5[a]	−5.7	27.2	−1.3	398.0	−27.4
1991	16.7	−25.5	33.4	−1.2	70.6	0.2
1992	19.6	7.7	24.7	1.4	39.2	−2.7
1993	23.8	2.5	22.0	−0.4	33.6	−1.3
1994	15.7	5.2	24.7	5.0	37.0	3.6

[a] The Czechoslovakia Federal Republic.

Note: Real wages are calculated by deflating the nominal wages with the CPI annual average.

Source: EBRD (1995).

of VAT. The tax on excessive wages increases was then reintroduced in July 1993 and applied to all enterprises with more than twenty-five employees. In July 1995 the government abolished this tax.

In all three countries, the inflation rate measured for consumer goods has been systematically above that for producer goods, although differences between the two rates appear to be narrowing.[9] There are several explanations for this. The most frequently given is the improvement in the quality of consumer goods not taken into account in the calculation of the CPI. This was evident at the outset of transition with the influx of relatively high-priced imported consumer goods which were of a much higher quality than the domestic counterparts at the time. Beyond this, the introduction of VAT and the subsequent rate increases had a positive effect only on the CPI. It also appears that retail trade margins were allowed to widen significantly following the privatization of this activity. In all three countries, the indicator monetary policy has been measured against the CPI and it is likely that this has introduced a bias towards a more restrictive monetary policy compared to a policy based on the PPI.

In summary, price liberalization translated into an acceleration of inflation in all three countries. The initial inflationary burst was rapidly brought under control in Czechoslovakia. The same was true of Poland

[9] See on wage increases in excess of 28% Estrin *et al.* (1993).

although the levels of inflation have been higher. Inflation rates have evolved more gradually in Hungary reflecting the progressive waves of partial price liberalization. Despite these differences, all three countries may be considered as having stabilized the initial inflationary shocks associated with the onset of transition.

In all three countries, price and trade liberalization were accompanied by other measures aimed at reorienting the economy away from the dominance of traditional state-owned enterprises. These included the substantial reduction or elimination of subsidies to (loss-making) state enterprises. This provoked a sharp reduction in their production and fed the tendency for consumers to shift to the recently liberalized import markets (Kornai 1995). High unanticipated price increases tended to reduce consumers' real purchasing power thus creating a negative demand-side effect on economic activity (Gomulka 1994; Bruno 1993). This was reinforced by sharp reductions in government spending which were included in the stabilization programmes of all three countries. The overall fiscal adjustment in the first year of stabilization was in the range of about 5 per cent of GDP for Poland and of about 7 per cent for Czechoslovakia in 1991 (Rosati 1994). The contraction recorded in Hungary was smaller but more persistent.

A central feature of the transition to the market economy is a complete reorientation of the activities of the State. Among other things this meant that the structure of public finances needed to be changed. Previously, state income was derived from enterprises' profits and turnover.[10] Generally, this system was characterized by high rates of tax applied to a narrow base. In all three countries, the main reforms consisted of the replacement of turnover taxes by a VAT system, the introduction of or the increase in the international trade taxes, and the adoption of a comprehensive system of personal income taxes and social contributions. The difficulty during this period of transformation was for the State to assure both an adequate revenue flow and that the new tax system would promote, or at least not impede, private sector development. Meeting these two objectives in a politically acceptable manner is not an easy matter, and as a consequence reform of the tax system has proceeded in a rather piecemeal manner. Another factor contributing to the exceptional character of public finances during transition is the sporadic receipt of large revenues from privatization.

The state expenditures have also been deeply modified. The direct public subsidies and public investment have been drastically reduced.

---

[10] For the theoretical exploration of the consequences of such a tax system on the transition process see Lane and Dinopoulos (1991).

TABLE 2.7   General government balance[a] and general government
expenditures in % of the GDP

	Czech Republic[b]		Hungary		Poland	
	Balance	Expenditures	Balance	Expenditures	Balance	Expenditures
1989	−2.8	64.5	−1.4	61.0	−7.4	48.8
1990	0.1	60.1	0.5	57.5	3.1	39.8
1991	−2.0	54.2	−2.2	58.3	−6.5	48.0
1992	−3.3	52.8	−5.6	63.4	−6.7	50.7
1993	1.4	48.5	−7.4	60.5	−2.9	48.4
1994	1.0	49.0	−8.2	n.a.	−2.5	50.2

[a] including state, municipalities, and extra-budgetary funds.
[b] Czechoslovakia through 1992.

Source: EBRD (1995).

At the same time, new kinds of expenditures have emerged. The transition process has led the State to take over some social services previously assumed by the state-owned enterprises in fields such as health or education. Increases in unemployment have raised the bill of social transfers to households. Exceptional expenditures have also been linked with the transition as it became obvious that state-owned enterprises and banks needed public intervention to help their restructuring process.

Since 1991 the Hungarian government has stopped the direct financing of investments in industry and has reduced public subsidies. According to OECD estimations (OECD 1993), the public subsidies decreased from 12.9 per cent of GDP in 1988 to 4.3 per cent of GDP in 1993. However, it is worth noting that these figures concern only direct subsidies. Implicit subsidies through, for example, lower interest rates are not taken into account. The share of GDP devoted to public investment expenditures decreased. Despite these reductions, the overall level of public expenditures has not declined (see Table 2.7). This is due to increases in current expenditures, in particular the wages of public employees and in social outlays caused by the jump in unemployment. The level of social security benefits is relatively high in Hungary and despite widespread calls for reform no strong steps have been taken to control costs. The result has been a constant drain from the state budget in order to shore up the social security funds. Another important reason for increasing public expenditures is the high level of the interest payments on the government debt. The stock of these government securities, excluding treasury bills, increased from 309.3 billion forint (or 10.5 per cent of GDP) in 1992 to 1,018.1 billion forint (or 23.5 per cent of GDP) in 1994.

At the same time, public sector revenues have fallen from 48.5 per cent of GDP in 1989 to 47.5 per cent in 1993 (EBRD 1994). The recession and the associated decrease in tax revenue, explain part of this reduction. Beyond this, structural factors have also tended to reduce the inflow of taxes. The transition process has squeezed profits of state-owned enterprises, especially banks, implying a reduction of taxes from this source. Furthermore, the rapidly growing private sector includes numerous small firms which have proven adept at reducing their tax burden through legitimate means or otherwise. Furthermore, the association agreement signed with the European Union and the free-trade agreement concluded with the Visegràd[11] group of countries have implied a progressive reduction in customs duties.

As a consequence of these developments, the public deficit has deteriorated sharply since 1990. This large public sector borrowing requirement has been a persistent heavy drain on domestic savings. Banks, favouring low-risk lending, have thus massively channelled the collected savings to the State. Since 1992 the share of the governments, national and local, has represented more than half of annual domestic credit.[12] In our detailed discussion of the Hungarian financial sector we will see the fuller implications of this tendency of the State to crowd out private sector development.

Poland has also implemented far-ranging reforms of taxation and public expenditures. In 1989 enterprise income taxes were unified. Personal income taxes were introduced in 1992. VAT replaced the turnover tax in 1993. On the social security side, a Labour Fund designed to provide unemployment insurance was created in 1990 and financed by a payroll tax. In contrast with Hungary, these modifications have led to an increase in state revenue from 41.4 per cent of GDP in 1989 to 44.0 per cent in 1992 (EBRD 1994). Despite this income increase, the public deficits have strongly increased under the pressure of the expenditure growth. As in other countries in transition, the size of investment expenditure and subsidies has been drastically reduced. The public subsidies have decreased from 12.9 per cent of GDP in 1989 to 3.3 per

[11] Visegràd group is the usual name of the 'Central European Free Trade Agreement' (CEFTA) between Hungary, Poland, and the Czech and Slovak Republics which includes a symmetric trade liberalization of all industrial and agricultural products.

[12] Excluding the share of domestic credit allocated to large state-owned enterprises; for more details see Ch. 4.

cent in 1992 (EBRD 1994). However, at current expenditure and the social outlays brought on by high unemployment rates have dramatically increased. This has created constant pressure on the state budget. Despite these pressures, the Polish government has managed to keep its deficits under control, and since 1993, the budget deficit has been reduced in large part by the effect of the economic revival.

After some initial tentative measures, the Czech Republic implemented a comprehensive tax reform in January 1993. The main changes involved the introduction of the VAT system, a lowering of the corporate income tax rate, and the introduction of a personal income tax with progressive rates and a top marginal rate of 43 per cent. At the same time, the social security financing was also reformed with its transfer from the general taxation to an insurance-based system.

In contrast with Poland and Hungary, the Czech Republic has managed to reduce sharply public expenditure as a share of GDP. It decreased from 64.5 per cent in 1989 to 48.5 per cent in 1993 (see Table 2.7). In particular, the direct budgetary subsidies which represented almost 17 per cent of GDP in 1989 had been reduced to zero by 1994. Beyond this, surprisingly low unemployment rates have meant that social expenditures have been kept under control. The separation of the Czech Republic from Slovakia in 1993 proved to be net beneficial to the public finances of the former. In addition to these factors, we will see in Chapter 6 how privatization which has proceeded rapidly in the Czech Republic has helped to relieve the state budget. A variety of expenditures has been effectively taken off the state budget and made the responsibility of a separate privatization budget. In particular, the costs of restructuring the banking system have been covered in this way.

2.5.   Macro-trends in Transition

Our discussion has identified several major internal shocks to the economy brought on by the reforms starting in 1990 in Hungary, Poland, and Czechoslovakia, namely price liberalization, tax reform, and stabilization policies. In addition to these came an equally major shock to foreign trade of these countries as the Council for Mutual Economic Assistance (CMEA) which was a rouble trading system within the Soviet bloc collapsed in 1991. As we will discuss in the next chapter, this has caused these countries to undertake a fundamental reorientation of their trading relationships. Furthermore, these countries faced a drastic increase in energy prices as Russia sold its petroleum for hard currency at world prices. According to IMF estimates (Bruno 1993; Rodrik 1992), these external shocks were particularly severe for Hungary; however, Poland and the Czech Republic have felt them as well.

These factors tended to reduce either aggregate demand or supply or both. At the outset of transition many analysts optimistically anticipated that these factors would not be so severe or that they would be offset by investment brought on by profit opportunities created by liberalization or by productivity gains as firms adopted efficient techniques. Thus the hope was that the transition countries of Eastern Europe would quickly settle on to a path of rapid growth. In fact, the negative shocks overwhelmed the positive shocks and all three countries entered a steep recession at the outset of transition (see Table 2.8). Between 1988 and 1992 the cumulative decline of Hungarian industrial production amounted to 33.9 per cent. In 1991 Polish industrial production was 35.2 per cent below its level of 1989 and Czech industrial production in 1993 was 40.7 per cent below its level in 1990. It is possible that these figures may overstate the degree of economic decline. For example, the massive shifts of relative prices may not have been adequately controlled in constructing indices of quantity of output. Perhaps more important was the fact that quality changes are not taken into account in the construction of output indices, whereas numerous enterprises have made dramatic strides in quality improvement.

State-owned enterprises in transition economies play a dominant role in industrial production. So it was perhaps to be expected that industrial output would be seriously disrupted as these enterprises were forced to restructure. At the same time, liberalization created enormous scope for

TABLE 2.8   Industrial production
(annual rate of growth %)

	Czech Republic[a]	Hungary	Poland
1989	1.1	−2.1	−2.9
1990	−3.3	−10.2	−23.3
1991	−24.4	−16.6	−11.9
1992	−10.6	−9.9	4.2
1993	−5.3	4.0	5.6
1990–3[b]	−11.3	−8.5	−7.1

[a] Czechoslovakia in 1989 and 1990.
[b] Geometric average of annual rates.

Sources: Before 1990: IMF various issues; since 1990: Kopint-Datorg (1995), NBH (1995), and ČNB (1995).

TABLE 2.9   Growth rate of gross domestic product in constant prices

	1989	1990	1991	1992	1993	1994	1995
Czech Republic[a]	1.4	−1.2	−14.2	−6.4	−0.9	2.6	4.0
Hungary	0.7	−3.5	−11.9	−3.0	−0.8	2.0	3.0
Poland	0.2	−11.6	−7.0	2.6	3.8	5.0	5.5

[a] Czechoslovakia in 1989.

Sources: OECD (1995), EBRD (1995), and NBH (1994).

the service sector to expand. Indeed, as gauged by gross domestic product which incorporates services, agriculture, and the public sector, the overall output decline in all three countries has been less than for industrial output alone (Table 2.9). These aggregate measures mask important differences in the responses of different sectors or categories of enterprises to the new economic environment. In particular, a basic premiss of those wishing to introduce a market economy was that the private sector would become the engine for economic growth. There are ample signs in all three countries that this has proven to be the case. For example, the fast-growing service sectors of these economies are largely private. Furthermore, private enterprises are accounting for an increasing share of GDP. At the end of 1993, the private sector[13] accounted for 52.8 per cent of total employment in the Czech Republic, 59.4 per cent in Hungary, and 57.6 per cent in Poland (EBRD 1995). Output is thus more and more produced by the private sector, including thousands of small enterprises, rather than the large state-owned firms.[14] In part, these trends reflect the fact that the old state enterprises are being privatized. However, as underlined by Fan and Schaffer (1994), for Poland most of the recovery in industrial output has taken place in the emerging private sector rather than via the reclassification of privatized industrial enterprises.

In 1992 Poland was the first transition country to emerge out of the recession with an increase in industrial production at a rate slightly above 4 per cent and an expansion of the real GDP estimated to be 2.6 per cent. The Czech Republic and Hungary took two years more to take off and the rate of growth remains somewhat below that recorded in Poland. This faster turnaround of the Polish economy has been taken by some to provide proof that 'shock therapy' is more effective than

[13] Including cooperatives for the Czech Republic and Hungary.

[14] The difficulties in capturing accurately activities of the private sector could lead to an overestimation of the deepening of the recession through the recorded GDP. For more information about the biases in the activity estimations see EBRD (Oct. 1994) and Berg (1993).

TABLE 2.10   Unemployment rate at year-end
(% of workforce)

	Czech Republic	Hungary	Poland
1989	0	0.3	0.1
1990	0.8	2.5	6.1
1991	4.1	8.0	11.8
1992	2.6	12.3	13.6
1993	3.5	12.1	15.7
1994	3.2	10.4	16.2

Sources: Before 1993: EBRD (1994); since 1993: Kopint-Datorg (1995) and ČNB (1995).

'gradualism' in setting an ex-socialist economy on to a path that will lead to convergence with the West. Such a simplistic assessment does violence to the several important dimensions of policy choice in which these countries have differed but for reasons that cannot ascribed simply to the speed with which reforms have been adopted. Our detailed discussions of the individual countries will show that there have been important differences in the monetary policies adopted in the countries and that there have been even more significant differences in the approaches taken to building the institutions of the financial sectors and to enterprise restructuring. These factors can have important bearing on the ability of the financial sectors to mobilize savings and to fuel growth through productive investments.

The sharp decline might be expected to translate into high unemployment rates. In Poland and Hungary this certainly has been the case (Table 2.10). Again the interpretation of these aggregate figures is made difficult by the nature of the great changes that have been taking place in the organization of the economies. Previously, registered unemployment was virtually unknown; however, workers maintained in unproductive occupations through enterprise subsidies constituted a form of disguised unemployment. Furthermore, in the absence of Western-style unemployment insurance, unemployment statistics of the 1980s are difficult to compare with those of the 1990s. Nevertheless the high levels of registered unemployment in Hungary and, especially, Poland are a clear manifestation of the important industrial restructuring underway. Overall, the expansion of the private sector has not been sufficient to compensate for the loss of jobs in state enterprises.[15]

---

[15] For a theoretical explanation of the role of unemployment in the transition process see Chadha *et al.* (1993).

Surprisingly, in the Czech Republic unemployment has risen during the transition but has stayed at relatively moderate levels. The unemployment rate even decreased in 1992 while production continued to contract. This paradoxical situation can be partly explained by the stricter eligibility rules for unemployment benefits applied since the beginning of 1992. More generally, the low level of unemployment can be explained by a political effort to maintain a social consensus in favour of the transition to the market. This resulted in labour hoarding (OECD 1994: 15) in state-owned enterprises and wage subsidies to employers hiring unemployed people. Furthermore, the Czech Government has de-emphasized bankruptcy as a solution of financial distress. This has allowed distressed firms to continue to operate, thus maintaining employment. Therefore, the low level of unemployment in the Czech Republic since the start of the transition might be interpreted as a result of the lack of adjustment at the enterprises level. However, the study of Layard and Richter (1995) shows that while the rate of inflow in unemployment is quite equal in the three countries (0.7 per cent in Poland and the Czech Republic and 1.5 per cent in Hungary), outflow rate from unemployment is clearly higher in the Czech Republic than in other countries (20.5 per cent in comparison with 6.2 per cent in Hungary and 4.9 per cent in Poland). This explanation is supported by the OECD study (1994) which emphasizes the fact that unemployed Czechs have been able to find new jobs in neighbouring countries such as Germany and Austria or in the newly developing service activities, especially tourism.

Behind the aggregate employment statistics, major changes in the composition of employment are underway. In general, industry and, to a lesser extent, agriculture are losing their importance and services are gaining. The rapid development of the tertiary sector has been apparent from the outset of transition reflecting the opportunities created by liberalization and the previously underdeveloped nature of services in these countries.[16] This development was mainly due to the creation of a huge number of new private enterprises, most of which are very small and began operations with little capital.

Within all three countries, employment trends have differed greatly from one region to another. In each case unemployment in the capital is low relative to the rest of the country. North-eastern Hungary, north-eastern Poland, and Moravia and the north of Bohemia in the Czech

---

[16] e.g. in the Czech Republic which had one of the most developed services sector before the transition, the tertiary sector employment increased from 37% of total employment in 1970 to 44% in 1991/2. The same figures for the USA are respectively 57 and 69%. For more details see Rask and Rask (1994).

Republic have all been hit by very heavy unemployment. Discrepancies in regional unemployment rates persist in part because of the limited geographic mobility of workers. In particular, housing tends to be in short supply in growing areas, especially the capitals. The governments have attempted to respond to this problem through regional development policies. We shall see in our discussions of the financial sectors of each country that the banking system has been involved in this through the provision of long-term, refinance credit which has maintained employment in selected, distressed regions.

2.6. Conclusion

Despite some past experimentation with elements of the market, the economies of Czechoslovakia, Poland, and even Hungary were in 1989 still deeply tied to the institutions and the logic of socialism. In the political breach left by the withdrawal of Soviet dominance in Eastern Europe there was a rush to embrace the market economy at least in some form. This change of political will was rapidly confirmed by a series of strong policy measures aimed at the liberalization and stabilization of the economies and which have made a return to the socialism of the past hardly imaginable. In all three countries most prices have been freed from state controls. As a result there was a sharp increase in inflation which served to wipe out monetary overhang. Even more important for the long-term direction of the economies there have been major changes in relative prices which, given a new openness to hard currency trade, reflect patterns seen internationally in the West. Stabilization measures have prevented inflation from getting out of control, although inflation levels have stayed above those of the West generally. Price and trade liberalization, fiscal reforms including the removal of direct subsidies to enterprises, the break-up of CMEA trade, the increase in energy prices were major economic shocks which combined with stabilization measures had the consequence of throwing the economies into a sharp recession especially in industrial output.

These were the conditions under which Hungary, Poland, and the Czech Republic undertook the deep reform of their economic institutions in order to greatly expand the scope of the market and to produce sustained high growth rates that can close the large income gap with the mature capitalist economies of the West. Poland's economy was the first to turn around, and by 1995 all three economies registered strong real growth rates. Furthermore, aggregate measures of the relative size of the private sector show that the private economy has expanded greatly in all three countries. Thus by the crudest of indicators, it appears these countries are achieving some success in meeting the goals of transition as we have stated them. Behind these figures are major differences in the way that policies have been implemented and in the directions taken in institutional reform. Some of the most interesting are institutional developments that have taken place in the financial sectors. Perhaps more than other sectors, the institutions of the previous regime were manifestly not capable of carrying out the tasks that are required to operate in the market economy. The initial inadequacy of these institutions may have played a role in causing the initial shocks to the economies and thus in aggravating the initial transition recessions. The speed and manner of introducing financial reform may have played a role in bringing the recessions to an end. And the efficiency of the new financial institutions channelling funds to high-productivity investments will determine the long-term growth rates for years to come. In order to explore these issues and many others we present in some detail the separate stories of financial development in Hungary, Poland, and the Czech Republic in Chapters 4 through 6 respectively. Before doing so we briefly describe the international context in which these changes have taken place.

3

The International Setting

3.1. International Economic Relations under Communism

In the post-war period the international trade relations of Czechoslovakia, Hungary, and Poland were moulded to fit the design imposed
by the Soviet Union. The Council of Mutual Economic Assistance
(CMEA)[1] was the international trade bureaucracy of the Soviet bloc. It
applied the principles of quantitative economic planning to the sphere
of international trade. Multilateral trade flows were agreed upon collectively within the organization. Monetary values of trade flows used the
rouble as the unit of account at administratively determined exchange
rates.[2]

Large as it was, the Soviet bloc was not economically self-sufficient.
To varying degrees all of the members of the CMEA had economic
relations with the non-communist world. Typically they had a foreign
debt contracted with Western banks or governments, and they had
commercial relations with Western countries. Czechoslovakia signed a
trade agreement with GATT in 1948. GATT agreements for Poland and
Hungary followed in 1967 and 1973 respectively. These agreements
gave these countries the status of centrally planned economies with the
consequence that most of the GATT's regulations did not apply to them
(Anderson and Tangermann 1991). They had no GATT obligations
regarding the nature of their border measures and at the same time
other GATT countries were allowed to impose quantitative restriction
on imports from them.

As Hungary and Poland experimented with economic decentralization during the 1970s and 1980s, economic contacts with the West increased (Portes 1993). At times both countries ran significant trade
deficits which were financed by borrowing from the West. In both cases,
the origins of these deficits were similar: mounting dissatisfaction with

---

[1] The CMEA was founded in 1949 and was originally composed of the Soviet Union,
Albania, Bulgaria, Czechoslovakia, East Germany, Hungary, Poland, and Romania.
[2] From 1963 onwards the rouble was made convertible for intra-CMEA trade. A variety of
conversion rates were negotiated within the organization.

the inability of the system to deliver an adequate supply of consumer and producer goods of decent quality provoked a political response in the form of increased level of imports. These deficits were never compensated by correspondingly large surpluses so that by the end of the 1980s both countries had accumulated substantial external debts. The policies that these countries have adopted with respect to these debts have had important bearing on the courses they have taken since the transition to the market began.

3.2.   Trade Reorientation since 1989

In all three countries, trade liberalization was one of the central elements of the transformation programmes. In contrast with developing countries in Latin America and elsewhere, trade liberalization was implemented at an early stage of economic reform. The decision to liberalize trade quickly was probably in part motivated by political considerations: rapidly reoriented trading relations away from the CMEA would serve as a commitment to permanent, close relations with the West. This has been confirmed by the decision of all three countries to seek membership in the European Union.

The speed with which these three countries liberalized trade was also a matter of dire necessity. After the fall of the Berlin Wall trade relations within the Soviet bloc deteriorated with astounding suddenness. One possible cause of this collapse was that once it was clear that the countries of Eastern Europe would no longer be directly subservient to Moscow, Russia and the other oil-rich countries of the former Soviet Union decided to abandon the trade system in order to promote their hard-currency export earnings. Whatever the causes, the CMEA was dismantled in 1991, leaving the countries of Eastern Europe to fend for themselves on the world markets as best they could. Hungary had begun to modify its trading system as early as 1968 followed by Poland in the 1980s. In contrast, Czechoslovakia had retained most of the archetypal characteristics of a central planning economy. Despite the differences in initial conditions and in the timing and speed of reforms, the trade systems of these countries looked quite similar by the end of 1991. The trade activity was decentralized and the licence procedures limited to a restricted number of products. The quantitative restrictions were replaced by Western-style trade control instruments, mainly tariffs and exchange rate policy. Initially (1989–91), tariffs were set at very low levels; however, subsequently they have been increased to correspond approximately to those prevailing in the West.

Quantitative import restrictions have been eliminated on all but some agricultural products, textiles, steel, and coal in the Czech Republic, and on wheat, cars, alcohol, tobacco, engine, oil, and petroleum in Poland. About 8 per cent of imports continue to be submitted to licensing or quota in Hungary. Overall, in all three countries, import regimes have become highly liberal by international standards. On the export side, the situation tends to be more restrictive in the Czech Republic, with 20 per cent of the exports requiring licensing, and in Hungary with license procedure for little less than 25 per cent of the exports.

The effects of trade liberalization and the collapse of the CMEA can be seen in Table 3.1. Both exports and imports have been rapidly reoriented from the rouble area to the Western markets. The speed of change has been very dramatic for Poland and especially the Czech Republic. In contrast, Hungary which had developed Western trade earlier has shifted its trade relations relatively gradually since 1989.

The change in the composition of trade in Table 3.1 could have come about either because CMEA trade collapsed or Western trade expanded. Table 3.2 shows that indeed there has been a significant growth in the total value of trade in all three countries since 1988. These data indicate that the rapid reorientation of trade by Poland and the Czech Republic is explained by their relative success in developing trade with the West. This performance is surprising given that this period coincided with a period of relatively slow growth for Western economies.

TABLE 3.1   Trade share of the former CMEA countries
(% of total exports or imports)

	Czech Republic[a]		Hungary		Poland	
	Exports	Imports	Exports	Imports	Exports	Imports
1989	62	64	47	44	60	50
1991	30	31	24	24	n.a.	n.a.
1993	15	19	26	30	16	13
1994	n.a.	n.a.	23	24	n.a.	n.a.

[a] Czechoslovakia in 1989.

Sources: For Hungary NBH (1995); for the Czech Republic, ČNB (1994), before 1992, IMF; for Poland since 1990, Warsaw School of Economics (1994).

TABLE 3.2 Evolution of convertible currency exports and imports ($US billion)

	Czech Republic[a]		Hungary		Poland[b]	
	Exports	Imports	Exports	Imports	Exports	Imports
1988	5.0	5.1	5.5	5.0	7.7	6.9
1989	5.4	5.0	6.4	5.9	8.3	8.4
1990	5.9	6.5	6.3	6.0	10.9	8.6
1991	8.3	8.8	9.3	9.1	12.8	12.7
1992	11.5	13.3	10.0	10.1	14.0	13.5
1993	13.0	13.3	8.1	11.3	13.6	15.9
1994	14.0	15.0	7.6	11.2	17.0	17.8

[a] Czechoslovakia through 1992.
[b] The data are based on payments statistics of the NBP and differ from data based on customs documents.

Sources: For Hungary after 1988, NBH (1995); for the Czech Republic, ČNB (1994), before 1992, IMF; for Poland since 1990, Warsaw School of Economics (1994) and NBP (1995), and before 1990, IMF.

In 1993 Hungary and Poland recorded reductions in export earnings while the Czech Republic continued to be successful in extending its export markets. This has been attributed by some to the consequences of relatively low levels of wages in the Czech Republic.[3] More generally there has been a constant real appreciation of Polish and Hungarian exchange rates causing a deterioration in their competitiveness. Their real effective exchange rate appreciated by 77 per cent and 31 per cent respectively between 1990 and 1993 (EBRD 1994). The situation continued to deteriorate in Hungary during 1994. This deterioration justified the devaluation of the forint and the shift to the crawling-peg exchange rate mechanism at the beginning of 1995 in an attempt to restore the external competitiveness of the country.

As might be expected given the scarcity of high-quality domestic products, imports have grown significantly in all three countries since trade liberalization. This trend is likely to be reinforced as these economies begin to grow again following the recession of the initial transition. However, the improvement in the quality of domestic products will help to counterbalance this tendency.

[3] In 1992 the average monthly wage was $US169 in the Czech Republic, $US188 in Poland, and $US280 in Hungary. See OECD (1994).

TABLE 3.3   Trade balance and current account ($US billion)

	Czech Republic[a]		Hungary		Poland	
	Trade balance	Current account	Trade balance	Current account	Trade balance	Current account
1988	0.08	−0.06	0.49	−0.81	0.85	−0.22
1989	0.42	0.44	0.54	−1.44	−0.11	−1.38
1990	−0.65	−0.95	0.35	0.13	2.21	0.72
1991	−0.48	0.33	0.19	0.27	0.05	−1.36
1992	−1.83	−0.03	−0.05	0.32	0.51	−0.27
1993	−0.30	0.68	−3.25	−3.46	−2.29	−2.33
1994	−0.92	−0.81	−3.64	−3.91	−0.84	−0.94

[a] Czechoslovakia through 1992.

Sources: For Hungary NBH (1995); for the Czech Republic IMF; for Poland since 1990 Warsaw School of Economics (1994), NBP (1995), and before 1990 IMF.

The market increase in imports inevitably caused a deterioration of the trade balance in all three countries (see Table 3.3). The fact that all three countries ran current account deficits in 1994 is perhaps to be expected given that rapid growth in these countries will probably mean that they will receive capital inflows. However, the deterioration of the trade balance has been particularly sharp in Hungary. Hungary has reacted by strengthening anti-dumping measures and countervailing duties, chiefly against imports from former CMEA trading partners in order to limit its imports. The new Hungarian government formed in July 1994 aimed at reducing the external imbalance, initially through a devaluation of the forint, but ultimately through fiscal action. This action was viewed as essential for the strategy of fully servicing its external debt. However, the only effective measure taken at the time was the devaluation of the forint. Only Poland raised its tariffs in 1992. However, it has taken the view that the trade deficit is closely linked to the state budget deficit which was reduced dramatically in 1993.

Given the geographical position of Poland, Hungary, and the Czech Republic, the potential for trade with the European Union is particularly great. All three countries moved aggressively to realize this potential by concluding three separate Association Agreements with the European Union on 16 December 1991. They are explicitly designed as a step to their future membership of the European Union. While the details of the agreements differ slightly from country to country, they all cover five substantive elements: free movement of goods; movements of workers; establishment and supply of services; payments; competition and the harmonization of laws; economic and financial cooperation.

On the economic side, each of the three agreements provides for the creation of a free-trade area between the countries and the European Union by 2002. To prepare for this, they stipulate from the outset of the Association Agreements the elimination of quantitative restrictions on the trade between the country and the EU. However, certain sensitive goods, notably agricultural products, are exceptions to this. Furthermore, the associated countries have retained the right to reimpose tariffs in cases where they can demonstrate a threat to an emerging industry. They provide for the progressive reduction of customs duties. Reduction of duties on industrial products is asymmetric: duties on products entering the EU are to be eliminated by the end of 1997 while those on products entering the three associated countries only by 2002.

The efforts to increase trade between these countries and the EU have been very successful. The countries of the European Union represented 63 per cent of Polish exports and 57 per cent of its imports at the end of 1993. The figures were 47 per cent and 41 per cent for Hungary, the Czech Republic's trade reorientation being between the performances of Poland and Hungary.

Following the logic of the single European market, the agreements call for freedom of movement for services, capital, and persons as well as goods. However, there are some major qualifications in particular with respect to movement of persons. This reflects the pragmatic realization that high unemployment and much lower wage rates in the East are likely to persist for years to come so that it is virtually inconceivable that all restrictions to labour mobility will be lifted in the foreseeable future.

As a complement to these economic measures, the EU has provided a significant amount of grant assistance to the countries of Eastern Europe. Most of this has been channelled through the PHARE programme (Poland and Hungary Assistance in Restructuring Economics programmes) initiative which has been extended to Bulgaria, Romania, Czechoslovakia, and Yugoslavia. In 1995 this programme received budget allocations of over 1 billion ecu per annum. The programme has five targets areas: the abolition of state monopolies, restructuring and privatization of public enterprises, modernization of financial services, promotion of the private sector, particularly small and medium-sized enterprises, and development of the labour market and the social sector.

The countries have also signed other free-trade agreements such as that with the European Free Trade Association which aims at abolishing all customs duties, quantitative restrictions and measures having equivalent effect on trade between partners, and the Central European Free Trade Agreement between Hungary, Poland, and the Czech and Slovak Republics which includes a mutual trade liberalization of all industrial and agricultural products.

3.3. External Debt

It is clear that for a country to attain high growth rates during transition it would be aided greatly if it could draw upon large inflows of capital from abroad. Its ability to do so is directly affected by its capacity to borrow on international financial markets. We have already remarked that during the course of the 1970s and 1980s both Hungary and Poland accumulated a large external debt whereas Czechoslovakia had not. As a consequence, these countries faced very different conditions at the outset of their transitions to the market. As can be seen in Table 3.4, in 1988 Hungary had a foreign debt equal to about 70 per cent of its GDP while Poland's was 60 per cent. These high levels of foreign debt meant that they would find it difficult to take on and service additional debt. The Czech Republic, on the other hand, had considerably more latitude to borrow on international markets.

TABLE 3.4   Total gross foreign debt in percentage of GDP

	Czech Republic[a]	Hungary	Poland
1985	11.7	70.6	48.7
1986	12.1	74.3	51.5
1987	12.8	78.1	69.9
1988	14.2	70.7	63.9
1989	15.7	73.1	54.6
1990	18.4	64.7	83.8
1991	29.7	72.5	72.0
1992	28.8	58.7	65.9
1993	28.1	64.2	61.5
1994	29.7	69.1	48.6

[a] Czechoslovakia through 1992.

Sources: NBH (1995), ČNB (1995), World Bank (1994), and EBRD (1994, 1995).

The composition of the foreign debts also has had an important bearing on the debt strategies adopted by these countries. The bulk of the Hungarian debt, more than 80 per cent, is made up of credits from private creditors and takes essentially the form of bonds and syndicated loans contracted by the NBH on behalf of the Hungarian State. In recent years, Hungary has relied primarily on bonds to raise new funds. The ability to issue bonds on the international market is a matter of some pride for Hungary; however, to do so it has committed itself to fully servicing its external obligations. Through 1995 it was successful in this policy. Despite the burden of this debt, Hungary never rescheduled its external loans neither with the Club of Paris (official debt) nor with the London Club (private debt). In order to lighten debt service the authorities have tried to improve debt management. They have diversified currencies and increased debt maturity. Despite the importance of the external debt owed to private creditors, it is worth noting that between 1987 and 1991 the main providers of external financing were the multinational institutions and Western governments. During this period, the convertible external debt increased by $2.8 billion of which 97 per cent was provided by the IMF, the World Bank, Japan, and others governments. The financial support of international institutions has in fact allowed it to avoid the potential debt crisis of failing to attract sufficient private capital to maintain its solvency.

The main providers of Poland's external financing are the governments, members of the Paris Club, which as of 1990 owned 61 per cent of the total foreign debt. Among them, France and Germany are the two largest creditors, followed by Brazil, Austria, Canada, the United Kingdom, and the USA. The other large group of creditors are the commercial banks, essentially German and American banks associated in the London Club, which hold 28 per cent of the convertible currency debt. Russia and banks of the former CMEA constitute the third group of creditors with 5.7 per cent of the entire debt. Given a debt burden roughly comparable to Hungary's, Poland has pursued a strategy that is the exact opposite of that pursued by Hungary. During more than ten years, Poland accumulated arrears on principal as well as on interest payments. During this time it sought to reduce its debt burden and managed to get creditors to reschedule debts several times. The consequence of this strategy was that Poland was unable to get new private loans, requiring a net outflow of financial resources even though the external debt continued to increase. The tensions between Poland and its creditors reached a peak in 1990 when the country decided unilaterally to reduce its debt service to a very low level, in effect, breaking the relations with its creditors. Poland resumed negotiations with its different creditors in 1991. After long and difficult negotiations and only after it obtained a three-year IMF Extended Fund Facility, Poland reached a debt reduction agreement with the seventeen members of the Paris Club in April 1991. The first stage of the debt reduction package provided for limiting debt service to 20 per cent of interest due during the first three years of the agreement (between April 1991 and April 1994). The principal repayments resumed in 1995 but will remain at low levels until the end of the decade. In this second stage the total debt burden was reduced by 20 per cent.[4] The agreement also imposed on Poland the obligation to negotiate similar debt reductions with other creditors in order to maintain an equal treatment between official and private creditors. A debt reduction agreement with the commercial banks associated in the London Club was signed on March 1994. This agreement differs from that reached with the Paris Club due to different financial mechanisms applied in both cases.[5] However, it provides for a reduction of 45.2 per cent of the debt which is a percentage comparable to the total debt reduction obtained from the Paris Club. The reduction package comprised all components of the debt including interest and principal payments and liabilities related to revolving credits.

Poland's debt strategy ran the risk of damaging its reputation among international creditors. The hope was that the international community would understand that these measures were necessary for the success of reforming the economy and that Poland would be able to normalize financial relations with main countries active in trade and international capital markets.[6] By reducing the debt service to sustainable levels, the debt reduction agreements were viewed as instrumental in restoring creditworthiness. This would open the way for foreign direct investment and access to international capital markets. In the short term, however, the debt reduction agreements have had a negative impact on Poland's

---

[4] In order to reach this reduction in the burden of Debt, creditors had to choose among three options: (*a*) partial principal write-off with a repayment period from 1997 to 2009; (*b*) lowering the interest rate below the market rate with a repayment period from 1995 to 2009; or (*c*) lowering the interest rate below market rate coupled with partial capitalization of interest payments due in the grace period to be payable together with principal and involving no new interest and a repayment period from 2003 to 2014.

[5] As far as the medium- and long-term debt are concerned, banks had the option to convert it into: (i) 30-year bonds at a 45% discount with a variable interest rate related to the market level (LIBOR + 13/16 on 6 months' basis); (ii) 30-year parity bonds with a fixed interest rate of 2.75% during the first 2 years and rising to 4% from the 10th to the 20th year and finally to 5% from the 21st to the 30th year; or (iii) new credit consisting of debt conversion into 25-year bonds with a 20-year grace period for principal repayments and fixed interest of 4.5% in the first year and 7.5% in the remaining years. Moreover, the terms of the agreement provided for the possibility of debt-equity swaps (Warsaw school of Economics 1994).

[6] See Warsaw school of Economics (1994: 201–7) for the detailed point of view of both Polish officials and creditors, representatives.

foreign currency since they call for increased payments in order to reduce accumulated arrears.

Towards the end of the 1980s Czechoslovakia had a foreign debt of moderate size held mainly by commercial banks. Since 1988 the country has issued significant amounts of international bonds. In 1991 the Czechoslovak Republic concluded standby loans with the IMF which explained the increase in its external debt recorded that year. As a consequence of the division of the country on the 1 January 1993, the newly created Czech Republic received its part of the external debt, amounting to $US7.5 billion. During that year, the external debt was increased by bond issues and reached $US8.5 billion at the end of 1993. Given that these new credits were used to replenish the Czech Republic's international reserves, the net indebtedness of the country actually decreased in 1993. The same external financing policy was followed during 1994 and the foreign debt reached $10.7 billion at the end of the year.

The consequences of the these debt strategies can be judged partially from the evolution since 1990 of outstanding foreign debt (Table 3.4). Despite passing through a very severe recession Poland's debt had fallen from more than 80 per cent of GDP to about 50 of GDP by 1994. During the same period Hungary's debt remained relatively unchanged at approximately 65 per cent of GDP. The Czech debt rose noticeably in 1991 when it used IMF credits to cushion the economy from some of the effects of the recession. Since then it has stayed at the same moderate level—less than 30 per cent of GDP. The burdens that these debt levels have meant for the three economies can be judged by the three indicators presented in Table 3.5. Here total effective debt service, i.e. principal and interest payments actually paid, are expressed as a fraction of export earnings and of GDP. Another measure of debt burden is interest actually paid expressed as a fraction of export earnings. It is important to realize actual debt service is reported in Table 3.7 and that for Poland during the late 1980s and early 1990s the figures for contractual debt service were much higher. For example, in 1990, when the Polish debt crisis reached a peak, the contractual services represented 78.6 per cent of export earnings of which interest payments represented 36 per cent.

Table 3.5 clearly shows the heavy burden of debt that has been carried by Hungary over a sustained period of time. In the mid-1980s its total debt service amounted to 18 per cent of GDP and some 40 per cent of export earnings. These debt burdens were among the heaviest borne by any highly indebted, middle-income country. Since then it has managed to work its debt burden down somewhat, but in 1994 it was still running at more than 12 per cent of GDP. In contrast, during the same period, Poland which had contracted a debt of about the same magnitude relative to the size of the economy, had an effective debt service that was about one-sixth that of Hungary's. This meant that out of the 18 units of GDP that Hungary channelled into debt service, Poland devoted only 3 units thus leaving 15 units for capital investment or other purposes. The amount devoted to debt service was reduced even more between 1989 and 1992, implying that additional resources could be devoted to productive investments which would allow the economy to grow again. By comparison, the Czech economy, which had a much smaller contractual debt burden than either Poland or Hungary, has had effective debt service that is significantly greater than Poland's in terms of the share of GDP. However, given the high level of Czech exports, this represented a relatively light demand on foreign exchange earnings.

Another perspective on foreign debt is provided by total net transfers defined as the total loans received by the country minus the total debt service payments. In 1992, the net transfer on Hungarian debt amounted to –$US1.988 billion. This negative transfer represented a net outflow of wealth from the country. In the same year, Polish net

TABLE 3.5   Foreign debt indicators (%)

	Czech Republic[a]			Hungary			Poland		
	TDS/ XGS	INT/ XGS	TDS/ GDP	TDS/ XGS	INT/ XGS	TDS/ GDP	TDS/ XGS	INT/ XGS	TDS/ GDP
1985	8.6	3.0	3.1	39.3	10.8	18.7	15.5	12.0	3.0
1986	8.2	2.7	2.9	41.0	11.9	18.4	12.8	7.8	2.5
1987	7.8	2.4	2.8	33.5	10.9	14.9	14.3	7.5	3.4
1988	8.8	2.8	3.1	31.1	11.6	12.7	10.6	5.6	2.7
1989	9.6	3.0	3.3	29.7	13.4	12.8	9.4	5.3	2.0
1990	9.1	4.3	3.0	49.0	19.4	12.6	4.9	1.7	1.6
1991	10.8	3.9	4.6	32.2	14.0	12.0	6.0	3.3	1.3
1992	11.4	3.4	5.1	31.2	12.3	11.4	9.2	6.0	1.7
1993	9.1	3.1	3.7	38.6	14.6	11.0	10.4	n.a.	n.a.
1994	n.a.	n.a.	n.a.	48.7	18.2	12.6	12.2	n.a.	n.a.

[a] Czechoslovakia through 1991.

Note: TDS: effective total debt service; XGS: exports of goods and services; INT: effective interest payments.

Sources: World Bank (1994), NBH (1995), and EBRD (1994).

transfers were –$US0.818 billion; whereas, Czechoslovak net transfers were –$US0.937 billion. Net transfers on Hungarian debt have been consistently negative since 1987. This reflected the difficulties Hungary encounted in raising new funds and the major effort starting in 1992 to decrease external indebtedness. Thus there has been a large drain on Hungarian wealth for an eight-year period during which the country has attempted to initiate a major rebuilding of its economy. The benefit of this policy is that Hungary has been able to maintain its credit standing in the international economy. This has undoubtedly contributed to the confidence of foreign investors that has spawned foreign direct investment in Hungary. Moreover, the good rating of the country has created the scope to issue private non-guaranteed debt by Hungarian companies borrowing from abroad. Between 1990 and 1994, the corporate sector gross foreign debt increased from $US1.23 billion to $US3.69 billion. Much of this debt has been extended by foreign parent companies to their Hungarian subsidiaries. The strong growth of this form of private lending is a reflection of the growth of the private sector and the relative success of Hungary in entering into joint ventures. However, as we shall see in Chapter 4, this also probably reflects the difficulty Hungarian enterprises, even those with good credit ratings, have had in obtaining credit from domestic banks.

The large external debt combined with the strategy of fully servicing it has clearly been a drag on the transition process in Hungary. The need of foreign exchange and the difficulty of borrowing it on international capital markets was probably instrumental at the beginning of transition in directing the privatization process towards foreign investors. The inflow of foreign direct investments has become critically necessary for the full service of the foreign debt. Exchange rate policy has been constrained by the consequences of the debt. Since the foreign debt is denominated in foreign currencies, a devaluation of the forint leads to an increase in the domestic value of the foreign debt. As we will see in Chapter 4, these devaluations generate an increase in government domestic debt held by the central bank. In 1992 the state debt generated by the forint devaluations represented 40.5 per cent of the total Hungarian state domestic debt. Thus the desire not to increase this source of debt too much has served to restrain forint devaluations, so the real exchange rate has been allowed to rise which has tended to hurt Hungarian exports. Since 1993 the trade balance has become increasingly negative, leading to a large current account deficit no longer covered by foreign direct investment. Given the restrictive monetary policy which limits the growth of money, the diminution in net foreign assets generated by the current account deficit has led the central bank to limit the growth of domestic credit. As the State has increased its borrowing on domestic markets, this has caused a sharp contraction of the credit available for the productive sector. In short, the large foreign debt in Hungary has contributed to a crowding-out of private sector investments. In Chapter 4 we will attempt to trace in detail the consequences of this crowding-out of the development of the financial sector.

In contrast, Poland was able to find effective debt relief at the outset of transition and therefore was able to channel more resources into rebuilding the economy. Total net transfers were positive in 1990 and 1991. Following the restructuring of official debt in 1991, debt service has risen so that net transfers have become negative since 1992. Poland must pay more to its creditors but at the same time its external indebtedness is reduced. This has allowed Poland to return to international capital markets. However, it should be remembered that the restructuring of the debt will require heavy service levels starting from 2000. The gamble is that the Polish economy will be large and dynamic enough to carry this burden without impairing its growth.

To summarize, Hungary has inherited of a large external debt whose full service has constituted a heavy burden for the economy. After making large efforts to reduce this debt in 1992, debt service ratios were again rising in 1994, implying a direct threat to the solvency of the country. In contrast, after a period of difficult relations with its creditors, Poland has managed to obtain significant debt relief. The country may have been less able to attract foreign capital during this period; however, given the comparatively light effective debt burden, it did not need capital inflows. However, in the long run it needs to import capital as well. However, its policy has shifted some of the costs of the debt to the future when the effects of damaged creditworthiness and an increasing debt burden may begin to be felt more acutely. Finally, the Czech Republic has inherited a comparatively low level of foreign debt. This has given it more freedom to implement its chosen course of transition.

3.4. Relations with Multinational Financial Institutions

The dramatic collapse of the Soviet order was immediately recognized as opening the way for closer cultural, political, and economic relations between the countries of Eastern Europe and the West. This has motivated a great many countries to attempt to aid transition countries. While some of the national efforts at aid have been very considerable, the largest scale and most systematic forms of economic assistance have been channelled through multinational financial institutions. In particular, the International Monetary Fund (IMF) and the World Bank have made major efforts to assist the governments of Eastern Europe in developing their transition strategies. Furthermore, the European Bank for Reconstruction and Development (EBRD) was created with the special aim of helping the private sector in the transitional economies. These organizations have all been active in Poland, Hungary, and the Czech Republic.

A major responsibility of the IMF is to provide short- and medium-term financial assistance to countries exposed to shocks which potentially could destablize their economies. Thus it is natural that the IMF was particularly active at the outset of transition when stabilization was the highest priority. Given their relatively early involvement with Western creditors it is not surprising that Hungary joined the IMF in 1982 and Poland joined in 1986. Czechoslovakia joined only in 1990 after the 'Velvet Revolution' had taken place and many of the main players of the Czechoslovak transition were already in positions of influence.

Besides the ordinary mechanisms of short-term finance such as standby agreements the IMF developed two facilities specially designed for countries in transition (the facility for systemic transformation and extended structural adjustment funds). One of the important and sometimes controversial aspects of IMF aid is that it imposes conditions on recipients of funds which can constrain severely the economic policies pursued by a country. Advocates of this approach argue that this helps to assure that the country has a coherent macroeconomic programme which will effectively stabilize the economy. Critics claim that the IMF can virtually dictate economic policy for the dependent country and that

TABLE 3.6   Assistance from multinational organizations since 1990
(loans authorized in $US million)

	IMF (4/94)[a]	World Bank (4/94)	EBRD (12/93)	Total loans received
Czechoslovakia	1,032 (445)	450	249	699
Hungary	1,613 (741)	2,042	552	2,594
Poland	2,245 (791)	3,390	591	3,981
Total loans given	4,890 (1,977)	5,882	1,392	

[a] Amount of loans actually used in parentheses.

Sources: Dabrowski (1995) and Conseil central de l'économie (1995).

this leads to a conservative economic policy which stresses fighting inflation, possibly at the cost of growth or distributional objectives. Both Poland and Hungary, which received extended fund facilities in 1991, were prevented from borrowing the total amount authorized because they failed to meet the IMF's performance criteria. The power of the IMF is enhanced by the fact that other lenders both private and public make their loans contingent on IMF involvement in the country. Thus the IMF can be a catalyst in stimulating external finance for a country. The scale of IMF lending to Poland, Hungary, and the Czech Republic is indicated in Table 3.6. The Czech Republic did obtain an IMF loan early in its transition. However, the scale of this assistance was considerably less than that to Hungary or Poland. Subsequently, the favourable development of its current account and a substantial inflow of private foreign capital has meant that the Czech Republic has not had great need for official assistance. The corollary of this is that IMF conditions have had little influence in framing Czech policies towards transition.[7]

The IMF approach has changed as it and its partners gained experience with transition. At the outset, the IMF was particularly concerned with macroeconomic stabilization and especially the external balance and exchange rates. There was a great stress on tight monetary and fiscal policies, on wage control, and on the management of the public debt. More recently, the IMF has oriented its action through more structural aid by including support for the privatization of the productive structure and the creation of a modern banking system.

World Bank aid is channelled through comparatively long-term loans and is aimed at facilitating sustained economic development. It has long provided loans for specific projects in various economic sectors such as agriculture, energy, education, and transport. More recently it has relied on structural adjustment loans which provide general finance to facilitate major adjustments in the organization of the economies. Such finance has often been granted to countries which wished to move away from state planning and to liberalize the economy. As with the IMF, World Bank funds are granted only if certain conditions, negotiated on a case-by-case basis, are fulfilled. Not surprisingly, it too has been viewed as undermining the autonomy in policy-making of the countries needing its assistance. It has been criticized for promoting a particular, pro-market line of economic policy. However, there are also many, including banks and other private lenders, who welcome its involvement

---

[7] All three countries have received IMF technical assistance. This covers a wide range of fields from the establishment of national accounts to the development of indirect instruments of monetary policy.

as an influence tending to promote a coherent, long-term approach to development.

Table 3.6 indicates the total amounts of assistance that Poland, Hungary, and the Czech Republic have received since the outset of transition. It is clear that the World Bank has made major efforts in Poland and Hungary. Lending at this scale has brought with it comparable amounts of technical and policy asisstance. World Bank advisers have had clear impact on a variety of policies that have been implemented in these two countries. World Bank assistance to the Czech Republic has been noticeably less. Given the role of the bank in long-term assistance and in structural adjustment, its relatively smaller involvement in the Czech Republic is not entirely explained by the favourable macroeconomic conditions of that country at the start of transition. In Chapter 6 we will explore in detail the course taken by the Czech Republic which will suggest reasons that its involvement with the World Bank has been somewhat different from those of Poland and Hungary.

The European Bank for Reconstruction and Development (EBRD) was created at the beginning of 1990 for the specific purpose of assisting the former socialist countries seeking to develop market economies and to join the mainstream of the West. In contrast with the IMF and the World Bank who deal with governments, the EBRD devotes 60 per cent of its assistance to the promotion of the private sector and 40 per cent to the development of public utilities. The EBRD has particularly emphasized financial sector development.[8] Usually, the EBRD finances the projects in collaboration with other sources of financing, and at times it will make equity investments as well as grant loans. We will see in what follows that the EBRD has been deeply involved in a number of large bank privatizations in Eastern Europe.

The total assistance figures in Table 3.6 show that despite being the multinational financial institution specializing in transition economies, the EBRD's assistance to Poland, Hungary, and the Czech Republic has been much less than that of the IMF and the World Bank. Indeed, early on it was criticized for being slow to become involved in transition; however, more recently the level of its activities has increased significantly. It is noticeable that Hungary has received a large share of EBRD aid when compared to the size of the country. We will see in Chapter 4 that Hungary has done much to build the institutional infrastructure of the market economy, so that it is likely that the EBRD has found that it fulfils the preconditions for fruitful lending to the private sector.

[8] In 1993 22.4% of the expenditures of the EBRD were devoted to the financial sector see Conseil Central de l'économie (1995).

The aggregate assistance figures of Table 3.6 show that Poland has received a significantly larger amount of multilateral assistance than either Hungary or the Czech Republic. Indeed, when estimates of bilateral assistance are included, Poland appears to lead all others in the world for total assistance received per unit of GNP. Overall, in recent years it has received about 17 per cent of total world economic aid, and this figure rises to 31 per cent if the official debt cancelled by the Paris Club is taken into account (see Espa 1992). Hungary, although a significant recipient of the IMF and World Bank lending, has received less bilateral assistance. The Czech Republic has received considerably less aid from all sources. This means that it has had less assistance but a freer hand in pursuing its transition policy.

3.5. *Exchange Rates and Capital Flows*

Exchange controls have often been used as a major policy tool by developing countries. In particular, many Asian and Latin American countries have promoted their development by following protectionist exchange policies and have only gradually made their currencies convertible. In contrast, Poland, Hungary, and the Czech Republic have all attempted to move rapidly to currency convertibility. It is not entirely clear why they have made convertibility such a high priority. It may reflect optimism about their development prospects so that they expected capital to flow into their country so long as they could convince foreign investors that they could withdraw their earnings and their investments when desired in the future at fair rates; it may have been motivated by the desire to expose the financial sector to competition from abroad; or it may have been viewed as instrumental in preparing for membership in the European Union. Whatever the reasons may be, this strategy has had important implications for the exchange rate regimes that they have adopted and has imposed clear constraints on their monetary policies.

After three successive huge devaluations recorded during 1990, the Czech Republic followed a policy of fixed exchange rates. Daily fluctuations in the interbank foreign exchange market are contained within a band around the official exchange rate against a basket of currencies composed of 50 per cent German marks and 50 per cent US dollars. The fact that the exchange rate was fixed over an extended period of time during which the country was undergoing major changes contributed significantly to the macoreconomic stabilization of this country. One reason the country was able to do this was that the initial devaluations left the currency clearly undervalued on a purchasing-power parity basis. Subsequently, Czech inflation rates have been above those of the USA and Germany so that the real currency value has eroded. However, the inflation differentials are relatively moderate (about 7 per cent per year) so that increase in competitive pressures felt by Czech firms has been relatively gradual. There is no strong pressure to devalue the currency. Indeed, the large volume of capital inflows into the Czech Republic has created pressure to revalue the currency. Prime Minister Klaus has declared his intention to maintain exchange rate stability until the country joins the European Union (Kopint-Datory 1995).

From the late 1980s until 1995, Hungary maintained a regime of fixed exchange rates. At various times the target basket has been composed of the dollar and either the ecu or the German mark. The forint has undergone relatively frequent devaluations in light of the large differential between Hungarian inflation rates and those of the Germany and the USA. Devaluations were designed to prevent the deterioration of the competitiveness of the domestic economy. According to Hungarian Central Bank calculations based on industrial wholesale prices, this objective was achieved in 1990 and in 1992, but not in 1991 and 1993. Since 1993 the country had been running large trade deficits and at the beginning of 1995 the rating agency Standard and Poors downgraded the country to BB+. This led to strong speculative selling of the forint. The authorities reacted by raising short-term interest rates significantly. Finally, in March 1995 the forint was devalued by 9 per cent against the dollar, and Hungary shifted to a crawling-peg exchange rate mechanism. This decision was linked with the introduction of a supplementary tariff on imports for a period of eighteen months and the adoption of an 'austerity' package by the Government.

Poland adopted a fixed exchange rate of 9,500 zlotys per $US, a rate which in retrospect left the zloty highly undervalued in terms of purchasing power. This was one of the famous 'nominal anchors' that were crucial to the Polish stabilization package. This helped in bringing inflation rates down, but not so much to prevent the zloty from becoming overvalued by early 1991. After a devaluation of the zloty by about 14.5 per cent in May 1991, Poland also has adopted a crawling-peg mechanism of monthly devaluation in relation to a basket of composed of the dollar, the mark, the French franc, the Swiss franc, and the British pound. The constant adjustment of the exchange rate reinforced inflationary pressures; however, it helped to ease the pressure on the international reserves of the country. At the beginning of January 1995 the monetary authorities adopted a currency reform, introducing the 'new' zloty. All pre-1995 values were divided by 10,000 and new coins and notes were issued which circulate with the old zloty. The crawling-peg mechanism was maintained with monthly devaluation of 1.2 per cent.

Each of the three countries we cover moved quickly to make current transactions of the business sector fully convertible. Since 1989 in Hungary, 1990 in Poland, and 1991 in the Czech Republic, enterprises can obtain foreign currency at the official exchange rates in order to pay for their import of merchandise and services related to international trade such as transport and insurance. In contrast, the foreign exchange dealings of households have been liberalized more gradually. In 1988 the Hungarian Government made an attempt to partially liberalize the supply of foreign exchange to the population for travel and other purposes. This resulted in strong foreign currency demand and a current account deficit exceeding $US1.3 billion. Following these problems, quotas on foreign currency supply to the household sector at the official exchange rate have been reintroduced. The Czech Republic initially maintained strict controls on the foreign exchange dealings of individuals; however, these restrictions were liberalized completely in October 1995. In Poland, households have free access to foreign currencies for tourism; otherwise they have the right to $2,000 per person per year for all other current operations. Thus in effect there is full internal convertibility of the zloty and the Czech crown.

In an effort to control reserves of foreign exchange, all three countries have required enterprises to deposit all their foreign currency proceeds in commercial banks. In this way they have effectively given the commercial banks a dominant position in the emerging foreign exchange market. Recently, Poland has relaxed this restriction. The first and probably the most sophisticated foreign exchange market is the Hungarian which started its activities on 1 July 1992. On 1 January 1994 the National Bank of Hungary discontinued its daily fixing at which banks could buy or sell foreign currencies. Instead, it intervenes on the interbank market in order to maintain fluctuations in the range of 0.5 per cent around the official exchange rate. The Czech Republic still determines foreign exchange rates in a fixing.

In the three countries, citizens are allowed to legally deposit foreign currencies with domestic banks without being required to reveal their source. Moreover, they are authorized to take and carry out of the country any amount of foreign exchange from their accounts. This liberal regime was intended to avoid problems of capital flight and to assure that households' savings would be channelled to domestic banks. This policy poses a potential, destabilizing drain on the countries' international reserves in case of unforeseen shocks. At the end of 1993, the foreign exchange deposits of the Hungarian household sector amounted to $3.2 billion in Hungary or 47.8 per cent of international reserves. In Poland these figures were $7.5 billion in Poland or 174 per cent of the international reserves, whereas in the Czech Republic the figures were 1.6 billion or 43.2 per cent of the international reserves.

Generally, capital account transactions of the domestic residents have been subjected to severe restrictions. In particular, portfolio investments abroad·by residents were not allowed. In December 1992, Poland was the first to relax this rule slightly by allowing mutual funds to invest up to 10 per cent of their capital in foreign assets. The Czech Republic in October 1994 and Hungary in April 1995 allowed unrestricted access to foreign exchange for direct foreign investment of domestic firms. Such operations are restricted in Poland, but authorization is easy to obtain. Domestic enterprises can also borrow freely abroad via domestic commercial banks in the three countries.

There are still important limits to exchanges by foreigners of forints, Czech crowns, and zlotys. Thus the currencies are not yet fully externally convertible. The main exception to this consists in the favourable treatment offered to foreign direct investment. In all three countries, foreign investors can transfer profits and capital in convertible currencies. However, because joint-ventures and foreign-owned but domestically registered companies are usually considered as residents by exchange regulations, the exception does not mean *de facto* external convertibility. This favourable treatment is designed to encourage inflows of capital which are considered as useful and stable. Hungary was the first of the countries to attract large amounts of foreign direct investment (Table 3.7). In part, this was the consequence of Hungary's initial privatization strategy which favoured foreign buyers. There was an upsurge in FDI in the Czech Republic starting from 1992. Following the signing of its debt restructuring agreements and the upturn in economic growth, FDI has begun to flow into Poland so that in 1994 it was the largest recipient of the three.

TABLE 3.7   Foreign direct investment ($US million)

	1989	1990	1991	1992	1993	1994
Czech Republic	10	166	200	1,210	1,100	800
Hungary	120	311	1,538	1,471	2,339	1,100
Poland	60	88	470	830	1,100	1,300

Source: Koping-Datorg (1995).

The countries have moved more slowly in extending full convertibility to other capital account transactions. However, more recently, there has been a recognition that portfolio investments by foreigners can bring benefits without being destabilizing. In Hungary and Poland the long-term segment of the securities market has been made freely available to foreigners who can repatriate both interest and principal in convertible currencies. However, there remain restrictions on short-term portfolio investments. In the Czech Republic since the beginning of 1994, there are no longer any effective restrictions on portfolio investments. Perhaps because of this, the country enjoyed an inflow of funds amounting to $2 billion in 1994.

3.6. *Conclusion*

In Chapter 2 we summarized the recent macroeconomic situation in Hungary, Poland, and the Czech Republic, and in the present chapter we have described the international economic relations of these countries over the same period. We have done this in preparation for our more detailed analysis of their development of banking and financial markets in the first years of the transition to market economies. This background is important because we will see repeatedly that macroeconomic and international considerations can impinge on the course taken in the financial sector. This is not to say that micro-economic development and institution building are not of great importance for a transition county's strategy. Indeed, we will argue that differences in the approaches to building financial institutions in the three countries are likely to have important consequences for subsequent developments. Nevertheless, the overall tasks that the financial sectors are expected to accomplish depend importantly on whether the country has a large foreign debt, whether it is running a current account deficit or surplus, whether inflation is under control, or whether the government's budget is in balance or not.

4

Hungary

4.1. Introduction

Among the communist countries directly dominated by the Soviet Union between 1950 and 1989, Hungary stood out as one which departed significantly from the Soviet model and managed to make reforms stick. Starting with the New Economic Mechanism adopted in 1968 Hungary eliminated quantitative planning and in other ways allowed a degree of decentralization of the economy. Managers of large enterprises obtained considerable scope for independent decision-making, but they never cut themselves off from the State. Indeed, maintaining good relations with high ministerial officials was important in ensuring that, in case of need, the enterprise had access to budgetary subsidies or soft loans. While bankruptcy laws were put into place, they were not brought to bear on large state enterprises, which if they were loss-making, were kept alive though the workings of the soft budget constraint. Furthermore, even if decision-making power was more widely distributed in the Hungarian system, this did not mean that the influence of the State receded very much. Indeed, in the late 1980s government expenditure as a share of GNP was about 64 per cent in Hungary as compared to 46 per cent in Western Germany and 37 per cent in the USA (Kornai 1992).

By 1989–90 when free elections established a clear political break with the past, in the economic sphere many aspects of the traditional socialist system had already been dismantled. Despite the fact that some of the reforms had borrowed institutions from market economies, the result was decidedly not capitalism.[1] In Hungarian market socialism most productive assets were still owned collectively and control of these assets was determined not as a matter of property rights but on the basis of the distribution of power. A decision-maker's power was not necessarily derived from the party but rather from the fact that others could not mount an effective challenge against his position. Thus the collapse of the Communist Party's political monopoly did not necessarily disrupt a decision-maker's power base. Perhaps partly for this reason, even in

[1] For a sympathetic account of the development of Hungarian socialism see Swain (1992).

the momentous times of 1989–90 no political consensus formed in support of a radical dismantling of Hungary's existing institutions. If a consensus existed for anything, it was that the reforms should proceed in a gradual, step-by-step manner. Beyond this it is probably true that after 1990 most Hungarian decision-makers took it for granted that the end-point of the reforms would be 'capitalism'—at least in the sense that there would be much greater scope for private property.

Our task in this chapter is to explore in some detail what the gradualist approach to economic transition has meant for the development of the financial sector in Hungary.

4.2. The Organization of Banking

The reforms of the Hungarian economy after 1968 initially did not alter the highly concentrated and specialized banking system which was left subordinated to financing the national economic plan. The separation of household finance from enterprise finance which had been established in the late 1940s remained almost unchanged. The National Bank of Hungary (NBH, Magyar Nemzeti Bank) performed central banking functions and the financing of enterprises through its credit department and branch offices. In addition, the State Development Bank (Állami Fejlesztési Bank) monitored and financed state investment projects and the Hungarian Foreign Trade Bank (Magyar Külkereskedelmi Bank) specialized in foreign-currency trade financing. Domestic banking for individuals was handled by the National Savings Bank (Országos Takarékpénztár és Kereskedelmi Bank) supplemented by 260 savings cooperatives.

At the end of the 1970s and the beginning of the 1980s, the first changes took place in the financial sphere. In 1979 the Central European International Bank Ltd was established as an 'offshore' bank in a joint-venture of the NBH and six Western banks. Starting in 1983 the authorities set up small financial institutions in the form of specialized funds mainly to finance research and development and venture capital for risky projects. The first effective step in the transformation of the banking system into a two-tier system was accomplished in 1985 by the introduction of institutional modifications. The central bank and commercial banking functions were separated within the NBH and its Budapest branch was converted into an independent subsidiary. At the same time, enterprises were allowed greater freedom to place their time deposits and the savings cooperatives were authorized to provide the same services as the National Savings Bank. In 1986 the Citibank Budapest was established as a joint-venture of the Citibank, holding 80 per cent of the bank's capital, and the NBH. The same year, the lending institutions were free to set loan rates to enterprises under a ceiling rate equal to the refinancing rate plus 1.5 per cent.

Finally, in January 1987 a two-tier banking system was effectively created when the commercial activities of the NBH and the State Development Bank were taken over by three newly created banks—the Hungarian Credit Bank (Magyar Hitel Bank), the Commercial and Credit Bank (Kereskedelmi és Hitel Bank), and the Budapest Bank. The new banks were set up as joint-stock companies owned directly by the State and the state enterprises. They took over the deposits and the loan portfolios of their predecessors. The Hungarian Foreign Trade Bank and the National Savings Bank were also authorized to function as full-service commercial banks. The requirement for enterprises to keep their current accounts with a particular commercial bank was also lifted. In addition, the authorities also granted banking licences to new entrants.

Despite these steps towards liberalization, the size of the banking system changed only gradually through 1989. After 1989 a spectacular increase in the number of financial institutions took place, reflecting mainly the entry of privately owned and foreign banks. In 1992 the strengthening of the banking regulations and the consequences of the recession caused both the closure of several institutions and a decrease in the demand for new licences leading to a diminution in the number of active financial institutions. The same pattern characterized the following years but the number of new licences increased partly due to foreign interest, and the number of institutions reached forty-two. In addition, there is one Hungarian bank offshore and 251 savings cooperatives.

TABLE 4.1   Number of financial institutions in the Hungarian banking system

	1987	1988	1989	1990	1991	1992	1993	1994	1995
Commerical banks	15	16	16	23	32	30	37	37	35
Specialized-financial institutions	6	8	8	8	5	5	5	5	7
Joint ventures and foreign owned	3	3	8	9	15	15	18	23	23
TOTAL	21	24	24	31	37	35	42	42	42

Sources: Ábel and Székely (1993), NBH (1992, 1993, 1994*a*, 1996).

At the outset of the two-tier banking system, the State was the main shareholder of the newly created banks either directly or indirectly through the participation of the state-owned enterprises. While many of the new entrants since 1989 have been privately owned, banks with state involvement tend to be the largest within the system. Table 4.2 gives the ownership composition of the five largest banks in 1991. Also listed is the average direct and indirect state share in other commercial banks, but excluding the specialized financial institutions and the savings cooperatives. The five largest banks as a group dominate the medium-sized banks—their total capital of 66 billion forint was almost twice the total capital of the medium-sized banks. By 1991 the State was the largest shareholder in the five largest banks. When the share of state-owned enterprises was added, the State had an absolute majority of shares in four of the five largest banks. In most cases the State was not directly involved in the medium-sized commercial banks. However, these banks were often owned at least in part by state enterprises. Thus state involvement in these banks is reduced only to the extent that their owners are themselves privatized.

It is commonly the case that firms (either state-owned or privately owned) which own shares in a bank receive credits from that bank (Várbegyi 1993: 13). This ownership pattern potentially creates a conflict of interest which could lead the bank to apply weaker credit standards on insider loans than on normal loans. We will see that this may

TABLE 4.2 Ownership structure of the Hungarian large banks at the end of 1991

	Share capital (billion forint)	Direct state ownership (%)	Indirect state ownership (%)	State ownership total (%)
1. National Savings and Commercial Bank	23.0	100.0	0.0	100.0
2. Hungarian Credit Bank	14.682	49.3	50.6	99.9
3. Hungarian Foreign Trade Bank	7.155	44.6	42.9	87.5
4. Commercial and Credit Bank	13.663	34.1	10.10	44.2
5. Budapest Bank	7.593	52.0	36.0	88.0
Average 1–5	66.0	63.6	22.1	85.7
Middle sized banks	36.34	3.67	36.79	40.4

Source: Várhegyi (1993).

TABLE 4.3   Market shares of Hungarian large banks
as measured by the share in the total balance sheet of
the financial system excluding the savings cooperatives

	1987	1990	1994
Large banks[a]	58.2	48.2	39.5
National Savings Bank	35.6	34.4	30.7
TOTAL	93.8	82.6	70.2

[a] Hungarian Credit Bank, Commercial and Credit Bank,
Budapest Bank and Hungarian Foreign Trade Bank
and Postabank since 1994.

Sources: OECD (1993) and NBH (1991, 1995c).

explain some of the bad loans problem in Hungary. In addition to the
National Savings Bank which it holds fully, the State has a major stake
in the four large commercial banks. Since 1992 the strengthening of
legislation concerning bank ownership has led to a significant decrease
in the share of the state-owned enterprises in the capital of the banks.
This has been reinforced by the actions of state-owned enterprises
which responded to liquidity problems by selling their shares directly on
the Stock Exchange. However, this tendency has been counteracted as
a result of bank debt consolidation schemes introduced by the authorities which we discuss below. As a result, the direct participation of the
State has increased to between 75 and 90 per cent of their capital in the
banks involved. In principle, bank privatization should reduce this involvement. However, by the end of 1994 only the Hungarian Foreign
Trade Bank had been privatized and only partly so.

By other criteria it can be seen that despite the sharp increase in the
number of financial institutions the majority of banking activities are
handled in banks which emerged out of the old monobank. Table 4.3
shows the share of the large banks and the National Savings Bank in the
balance sheet of the financial system.[2] This share has fallen significantly
since 1987, but still amounted to some 70 per cent of total banking-
sector assets in 1994. Furthermore, the separation of household and
enterprise banking has tended to persist. Even after the reform implemented in 1987, household and enterprise finance were separated by
law. The financial relations with households continued to be in the

---

[2] In 1993 the large banks even increased their share in comparison with the previous year,
but this increase could be attributed primarily to the impact of the bank consolidation scheme
which increased total assets.

hands of the National Savings Bank and the savings cooperatives, while the newly established commercial banks concentrated their activities on the corporate sector with sectorial specialization (the Hungarian Credit Bank in chemical and mechanical industry, the Commercial and Credit Bank in agriculture, the Budapest Bank in coal and buildings, and the Hungarian Foreign Trade Bank in import–export activities). The commercial banks were effectively allowed to deal with households from January 1989. However, the interest rate ceiling on household deposits remained an instrument of monetary policy until 1991, limiting the opportunities of competition between financial institutions. As a consequence, the State Savings Bank has maintained its dominant position in the business of personal banking.

Table 4.4 presents information on the concentration of deposits within the banking system. The National Savings Bank has some 38 per cent of total deposits and 20 per cent of the capital of the forty largest banks. Thus it has continued its role as a major recipient of personal savings for the Hungarian financial system. At the end of 1993, over 60 per cent of bank deposits of households was concentrated in this single bank (NBH 1994*a*).

The pattern that emerges from looking at bank size measured by total assets, total deposits, and bank capital is that Hungarian banking activity remains highly concentrated. Furthermore, the large institutions have direct ties to the State in that they emerged from the old monobank or that the State is directly or indirectly a large shareholder. One important question that this structure raises is whether Hungarian banking is competitive. The fact that there has been a significant growth in the number of the banks in Hungary may well indicate that in the late 1980s banks were earning a degree of monopoly profits. In principle, new entries should tend to reduce such profits.

In Table 4.5 we report the average prevailing interest rates on bank

TABLE 4.4   Capital and deposits in Hungarian banks, December 1993
(% of total of forty largest banks)

	5 large banks[a]	National Savings Bank	6 largest banks
Capital	25.1	19.8	44.9
Deposits	31.9	37.9	69.8

[a] Hungarian Credit Bank, Commercial and Credit Bank, Budapest Bank, Hungarian Foreign Trade Bank, and Postabank.

Source: *Wall Street Journal Europe* (1994).

TABLE 4.5   Hungarian interest rates and average intermediation margins
(December to December in %)

		1989	1990	1991	1992	1993	1994
Nominal interest rates							
Credits	S.T.	22.8	32.1	35.5	28.8	25.6	29.7
	L.T.	19.7	27.5	34.3	25.4	25.2	26.7
Deposits	S.T.	19.0	28.5	31.1	17.6	17.2	23.6
	L.T.	20.6	29.3	33.0	19.5	18.7	22.3
Spread	S.T.	3.8	3.6	4.4	11.2	8.4	6.1
	L.T.	−0.9	−1.8	1.3	5.9	6.5	4.4
Interest margin[a]		n.a.	5.3	8.1	3.4	3.8	n.a.

[a] Interest margin is defined as Total interest received less total interest paid/Total balance assets

Sources: NBH (1992, 1993, 1994a) and Várhegyi for the interest margin in 1990 and 1991.

loans and bank deposits. From this we are able to calculate the marginal intermediation spread, that is the spread between the lending rate and the deposit rate for contracts of similar maturity. We see that both the short-term and the long-term spreads rose from 1989 to 1992, a period during which there was considerable entry of new banks. Subsequently, these spreads have fallen. We also report the average intermediation margin for 1990 to 1993. This rose until 1991 and dropped off subsequently. Thus this indicator does not indicate a clear increase in competition since 1989. However, this indicator is crude at best since it does not take into consideration other factors which affect costs of banking and thus enter into the determination of profits. The Hungarian National Bank has estimated the profitability of commercial banks as a whole. Their aggregate results are reported in Table 4.6. When measured either by return on assets or return on equity, bank profitability fell steadily from 1989 to 1993. The reason that bank profits have fallen even as interest spreads have increased may be due to the failure of bank borrowers to meet their contractual obligations. We would expect that, both because of the removal of direct subsidies and because of the disruption of CMEA trade, many Hungarian enterprises would become financially distressed. As we will see later this did in fact occur and thereby created a very significant bad loan problem. Thus, one plausible interpretation of Tables 4.5 and 4.6 is that in the face of a rising share of non-performing loans, banks tended to increase the spread of lending

TABLE 4.6   After-tax profits (in billion forint), return on equity and return on
assets (%) of the Hungarian banks

	1989	1990	1991	1992	1993	1994
After-tax profits	50.3	63.2	35.0	−1.0	−159.7	23.6
ROE	51.7	16.9	14.8	−0.5	n.a.	n.a.
ROA	4.0	3.9	1.7	−0.1	−5.9	0.8

Sources: NBH (1991, 1992, 1993, 1994*a*, 1995*c*).

rates over their deposit rates. This increase, however, was insufficient to
compensate for loan losses and as a consequence the banking sector as
a whole began to make losses from 1992. The fact that the interest rate
spread on short-term contracts fell in 1993 despite the fact that the
losses of the banking sector as a whole increased might indicate increasing competitive pressures.

4.3.   Instruments of Monetary Control and Monetary Policy

Having described the structure of commercial banking since the creation of two-tier banking we now turn to the parallel development of
central banking. In doing so we will be concerned in part to see to what
extent the central bank has withdrawn from the equilibration of saving
and investment, that is, from direct involvement in the allocation of
credit. In addition, we will try to understand the monetary policy that
has been pursued and in this way see how macroeconomic conditions
have created the environment in which the deep financial institutional
development of the economy has taken place.

The National Bank of Hungary (NBH) was established by an Act of
parliament on 26 April, 1924 in the form of a joint-stock company. Thus,
the NBH is a venerable institution with a tradition of at least formal
independence from the administration of the State. However, the shares
held by Hungarians were nationalized in 1947. On January 1985 a
government resolution separated the commercial and central banking
functions of the NBH and in January 1987 the NBH delegated almost all
of its commercial banking functions to the commercial banks. The Act
LX of December 1991, amended by the Act IV of 1994, set out the main
responsibilities of the NBH and affirmed its independence in determining monetary policy. However, the independence of the central bank is

limited, since the law provides explicitly that monetary policy and the credit controls of the NBH must promote the economic policy of the government. The governor is appointed by government but theoretically is accountable to parliament as a whole. However, the law does not provide clear criteria which justify his dismissal and a governor has already resigned under pressure from the government.

Hungarian bank laws give the NBH the exclusive right to handle the gold and foreign exchange reserves of the State and to issue banknotes and coins. The NBH is charged with conducting a sound monetary policy in order to maintain the value of the national currency through prices stability. The NBH is also in charge of the management of the external debt on the behalf of the State. We might expect that given the huge size of the Hungarian external debt this last responsibility has been an important constraint on policy. We will see that this has in fact been the case.

At the outset of two-tier banking, the NBH employed a variety of tools for direct credit allocation which effectively limited the role played by commercial banks. Since 1987 the instruments used by the NBH in order to guide credit creation have become progressively more indirect. Interest rate ceilings imposed on household deposits have been progressively removed, and the restriction on the interest rate of deposits of more than six months' maturity was abolished in January 1991. The most important interest rate in the conduct of monetary policy is its base lending rate which serves as a basis for settings a variety of the NBH's lending rates, and thus is a major determinant in the funding cost throughout the banking system.

A system of mandatory reserves was introduced in early 1987. This became a binding constraint for banks in 1990 when the NBH extended the system to all external liabilities thus eliminating the ability of banks funding themselves from sources not subject to reserve requirements. A uniform mandatory reserve rate was applied to all banks. The reserve rate for forint deposits stood at 12 per cent at the beginning of 1994. There are separate reserve requirements for foreign currency deposits. Since 1992 a bank's foreign exchange deposits at the NBH are deducted from its customer's foreign exchange deposits in calculating reserve requirements. The NBH pays interest on both mandatory and voluntary reserves with different rates applying to each category. At the end of 1994 the rate paid on a reserves required for forint deposits was 8 per cent, while reserves held against foreign exchange deposits earned 18 per cent. The higher rate paid on the latter type of reserve allows banks to be competitive in the rates paid on foreign currency deposits. The penalty rate for a deficiency of mandatory reserves is the base rate plus

10 per cent. Since the level of reserves is relatively high, bank profitability is relatively sensitive to changes in reserve ratios and to changes in rates paid on reserves.

The NBH's refinancing of credits granted by commercial banks is an instrument inherited from the socialist system. To the extent that the central bank applies credit quotas or preferential rates for credits to different classes of borrowers, it tends to perpetuate its direct involvement in credit allocation. Most developed capitalist banking systems have tended to rely more on open-market operations in which the central bank operates on the secondary market for treasury securities. This indirect policy by its nature leaves to the commercial banks the decision on how to allocate increases or decreases of credit within the system.

In recent years Hungary refinance credits have been drastically reduced for short-term loans, but they remain significant for long-term loans. At the end of July 1994, 98 per cent of outstanding refinance credits were to mature over one year. These refinance credits are allocated for specifically defined programmes and carry preferential rates far below the base rate of the NBH. Such programmes are designed to promote either investment in specific economic sectors or such activities such as exportation or privatization. At the end of June 1994 the long-term refinancing amounted to approximately 31 per cent of the long-term credit granted to the private sector.

The rediscount mechanism is a tool of short-term monetary control, but has played a minor role in setting monetary policy since 1992. The rediscount rate is revised by the NBH once every three months and is in line with the rate of the three-month treasury bills.

The NBH also grants credits to banks when secured by foreign exchange deposits and when the funds are destined for investment purposes. Such loans pay interest equal to the base rate. This kind of refinancing allows the NBH to attract foreign currencies deposited with the commercial banks and at the same time to promote the financing of investment. When taken together with the favourable reserve treatment of foreign currency deposits, this constitutes a significant effort to ensure a regular inflow of foreign exchange into the central bank. At the end of June 1994 this kind of refinancing credits amounted to almost 13 per cent of long-term credit granted to the private sector.

Increasingly monetary policy has been guided by the use of open-market operations, repurchase agreement (repos) and foreign exchange swaps. As far as the open-market transactions are concerned, the central bank influences the liquidity of the banking sector by purchasing or selling securities which are primarily government bonds including consolidation bonds. Since 1993 the short-term refinancing of the commercial banks has largely taken a securitized form. In repos the underlying securities are treasury securities. Alternatively, much the same can be accomplished through foreign currency swaps. The repo operations were already used in the previous years but generally with central bank certificates of deposit and not with treasury bills given the insufficient stock held by the central bank. Since 1992 most increases in the internal public debt have been in the form of treasury bills or bonds thus increasing the flexibility of the NBH's monetary operations. At the end of October 1994 31.1 per cent of the forint loans to the government took the form of bonds.

In order to gain an overview of the factors that shape monetary policy in Hungary it is useful to study the balance sheets of the central bank. Table 4.7 gives the year-end balance sheets for 1990, 1992, 1993, and 1994. The central bank has been given the responsibility of managing the government's foreign debt. This means that the most striking thing about the assets and liabilities of the NBH is that its major asset is the forint debt owed by the State while its major liability are 'deposits from non-residents' which is the foreign debt, including international bond issues, bank loans, and official credits. These liabilities are in foreign currencies implying that the NBH is exposed to the risk of depreciation of the forint. That is, a fall in the forint would increase the liabilities of the bank but not the assets of the bank. In order to take this into account, since the late 1980s the increases in the forint value of foreign debt automatically give rise to a creation of a new state debt held by the NBH. Through the decline of the forint since 1990, this latter form of government debt has grown to exceed the ordinary government debt. The government debt originated because of currency depreciation does not pay interest. Thus while this convention protects the NBH from some foreign exchange risk, the protection is not complete.

In the period 1990–4 the NBH's assets and liabilities underwent some important changes which reveal something of the macroeconomics policy pursued in Hungary. The foreign debt as a fraction of the total balance sheet fell from 1990 to 1992 after which time it rose. This reflected the repayment of principal in 1992 which led to a reduction in the dollar value of foreign debt outstanding. On the asset side, there was a sharp fall in the share of credits destined for the banking sector. In part, this reflected the declining importance of the refinance mechanism. This decline has been compensated in part by the increased share of government debt and even more so by the increase in the fraction of assets held in the form of foreign exchange, gold, or IMF quotas. This latter development reflected the very high priority placed on maintain-

TABLE 4.7   Structure of the balance sheet of the National Bank of Hungary, in billion forint and %

	1990	1992	1993	1994
Assets				
Gold, foreign exchange, and IMF quota	8.8	16.9	22.2	21.1
Government	54.8	68.5	62.5	63.6
(a) Loans	27.4	35.4	28.4	27.8
(b) Debt from exchange rate changes	27.4	33.1	34.1	35.8
Loans to financial institutions	32.5	10.7	10.7	10.2
Other loans	0.1	0.1	0.0	0.0
Advances and loans to non-residents	0.5	0.3	0.2	0.8
Other	3.4	3.6	4.4	4.3
Liabilities and capital				
Capital and provisions	1.3	1.5	1.3	0.8
Deposits and other liabilities				
(a) Government	5.0	9.5	9.8	7.7
(b) Financial institutions	15.8	19.4	17.4	18.0
(c) Other	0.0	0.5	0.5	1.1
Deposits from non-residents	56.6	46.8	50.1	52.8
IMF deposits	3.4	6.4	5.7	5.3
Banknote and coins	12.2	13.0	11.6	10.9
Other	5.7	2.9	3.6	3.4
TOTAL	1,892.5	2,688.9	3,468.8	4,024.2

Sources: NBH (1990, 1992, 1993, 1995*b*, 1995*c*).

ing the confidence of the world investment community in Hungary's ability to service its foreign debt.

It will be noted that the NBH's holdings of government debt rose faster than did the value of the bank's foreign debt. This shows the importance of the central bank lending in financing the general government. There have been some efforts to establish the independence of the NBH from the government; however, these have not been entirely successful. The Act LX of December 1991 provided a limit to the financing of the budget by the NBH as a percentage of annual budgetary income: 5 per cent in 1993, 4 per cent in 1994, and only 3 per cent starting in 1995.[3] This was to serve as a brake on the monetization of the deficit, one of the conditions imposed by the IMF. However, this Act was amended by parliament in 1993 to set a maximum increment not

[3] This last limitation is even stricter than limitations applied in Germany before 1994. For more details see Hochreiter *et al.* (1996).

exceeding 80 billion forint of the stock of loans that could be granted to the budget in 1994. In effect this increased the share of debt finance from 4 per cent previously authorized to more than 6.1 per cent of the revenue of the 1994 central budget. In addition, until the ceiling on the growth of the loan stock referred to is reached, the central bank is obliged to underwrite government papers to be issued for the central budget. The government has found it increasingly difficult to market its forint debt and thus has continued to rely on the central bank for its financing.

The picture that emerges from these accounts is that, despite its nominally independent status, the NBH has been forced to be the direct agent of the government. In this role it has developed its policy in the face of a major constraint imposed by the high level of foreign debt and by the developments of the government budget. To gain a further perspective on this problem, Table 4.8 summarizes the important trends in the major components of Hungary's balance of payments and its foreign debt, all expressed in dollars. Through the 1980s Hungary had financed its growing burden of debt service largely through the issue of new foreign debt. Thus in 1988 interest on the external debt of some $1 billion more than wiped out a trade surplus and led to a current account deficit. This was covered by increased foreign borrowing. This pattern repeated itself in 1989. In 1990 despite a smaller trade surplus and increased interest charges, favourable developments in other inflows allowed Hungary to run a small current account surplus. Two additional factors emerged in 1991 to ease the burden of the foreign debt. The first was the decline in interest rates paid on the debt, and the second was the significant increase in foreign direct investment related in part to privatization of Hungarian state-owned enterprises. The combined effect of

TABLE 4.8   Hungary's external flows and foreign debt ($ million)

	1988	1989	1990	1991	1992	1993	1994
Trade balance	489	537	348	189	−48	−3,247	−3,537
Interest	−1,077	−1,387	−1,414	−1,331	−1,216	−1,130	−1,275
Current account	−807	−1,437	127	267	324	−3,455	−3,713
Foreign direct investment	14	187	311	1,459	1,471	2,328	1,136
Net convertible debt	13,966	14,900	15,938	14,554	13,276	14,927	18,476

Sources: NBH (1991, 1992, 1993, 1994*a*, 1995*b*).

this was to permit a reduction in Hungary's net foreign debt by more than $1.3 billion. This was roughly equal to foreign direct investment so that Hungary was effectively substituting public debt owned by foreigners with direct foreign participation in Hungarian firms. Whether or not this policy was short-sighted, it did appear in 1992 that the growth of the external debt was under control. These hopes were dashed in 1993 by the sharp reversal of Hungary's trade balance as the rate of growth of its exports declined and that of its imports rose. This meant that despite the continued increase in foreign direct investment, the official foreign debt increased. In 1994 there was no improvement in the trade balance while interest charges rose. Furthermore, foreign direct investment fell off sharply partly reflecting the slowdown in the privatization programme. Again the shortfall was met by borrowing abroad with the result that the dollar principal of Hungary's net foreign debt increased by nearly one-quarter in one year.

These developments in Hungary's foreign balance had important implications for its monetary policy.[4] A basic fact captured in balance-of-payments accounting is that, abstracting from official reserves transfers, a current account deficit must be met by the combination of foreign direct investment and an increase in net foreign debt. On the assumption that all foreign debt is held within the banking sector, this means that current account deficit not covered by foreign direct investment must equal the increase in domestic credit less the growth in the money supply. The growth in domestic credit in turn is composed of growth in the government's debt on the one hand and of enterprises and households on the other. Summarizing in an equation we have,

$$c = f + l_g + l_e - m,$$

where c is the current account deficit, f is foreign direct investment, l_g is the growth of the government's domestic debt, l_e is the growth of credit to enterprises and households, and m is the growth of the broad money stock and where all variables are denominated in forint. This suggests that in face of a given current account deficit the monetary authorities may have some policy options. With a negligible inflow of direct investment ($f = 0$) and a balanced budget ($l_g = 0$), the authorities might try to allow for a greater expansion of enterprise credit through the expansion of the money supply (an increase of both l_e and m). However, the foreign exchange market may make it difficult to pursue a rapid monetary expansion. That is, an excessive growth of the money stock will give rise to forint depreciation and therefore an increase in the current

---

[4] These are elaborated by Obláth (1992).

TABLE 4.9 Hungary's government deficit (million forint)

Year	1988	1989	1990	1991	1992	1993	1994
Government deficit	19,736	54,008	1,369	114,156	197,140	199,667	321,702

Source: NBH (1995c).

account deficit in forint terms. Thus considering money growth to be determined by this foreign exchange objective, there is a basic trade-off between the government deficit and the growth of enterprise credit. Stated otherwise, government debt can be expanded at the cost of crowding out enterprise credit.

Table 4.9 presents the evolution of the government deficit. After reaching low levels in 1990 it has progressively increased so that by 1994 it stood at some 321 billion forint which was approximately 9 per cent of the GDP.[5] This very sharp increase in the deficit was due essentially to two factors—the increase in social benefits and the increase in interest charges on the domestic debt with the latter in part being the result of earlier debt consolidations of the banking sector.

Thus trying to maintain control on the debt service burden has been a high priority for the Hungarian government, and to this end a variety of techniques have been adopted which do not involve reducing the non-interest government deficit. The interest rate on the public debt incurred before 1991 is fixed by the law at a very low level. At the end of 1994 this interest rate amounted to 8.72 per cent at a time when the base rate of the NBH was fixed at 25 per cent. Furthermore, no interest is paid on the component of the public debt owed by the central bank in compensation for increase in the foreign debt due to forint depreciation and which has not been securitized.[6] For other, non-securitized public debt contracted after 1991, the interest rate is equal to the base rate. For security issues the treasury pays the rate determined in the initial public sale.

Despite the fact that this exposes the government to market-determined interest rates the government has increasingly relied on the securitization of the government debt. This was the policy adopted in the budget law of 1991. The stock of discounted treasury bills rapidly

---

[5] By way of comparison the norm of the Treaty of Maastricht calls for a maximum deficit of 3% of GDP.

[6] Under the budget law in effect in 1994 about 5% of the then-outstanding government debt from depreciation of 59 billion forint was replaced by treasury securities sold at market rates.

increased from 27.1 billion forint at the beginning of 1992 to 267.1 billion forint at the end of 1994 and to more than 400 billion forint at the end of 1995. The maturities of these bonds range from one, three, six, and twelve months. The basic denomination of 500,000 forint and 100,000 forint have given way to 10,000 forint just as in the case of government bonds. These bonds serve as collateral for the repurchase operations. Since 1992, however, the trends in government debt management has been to issue bonds with longer maturity from two to five years.

4.4. Credit Allocation

We have seen that monetary developments in Hungary since the late 1980s have been the product of several distinct and conflicting tendencies. First, Hungary has attempted to assure monetary stability by endowing the central bank with increased formal independence of the government. Second, an overriding objective of policy has been to respect all its external financial obligations and in this way assure continued access to international credit markets. Third, the inability of the government to control its deficit has meant that it has continued to rely in part on the central bank for credit. We now trace through the consequences of these circumstances for the allocation of credit within the financial system.

Some of the story is told by the interest rates reported in Table 4.5. Perhaps the most surprising aspect of this table is that during the whole period, the yield curve of loans had a negative slope. Long rates lying below short rates could reflect the expectations of a decrease in the inflation in the future. However, this explanation is not very plausible in light of the fact that the long deposit rates were greater than short deposit rates. The rates reported in the table are averages received or paid over all banks and all types of credits. Thus a more likely explanation is that a large amount of long-term credits were granted through the refinance mechanism and therefore benefited from state support in the form of reduced interest rates. This would be compatible with the fact that the spread between long-term loan rates and deposit rates was negative in 1989 and 1990 at a time when the quantity of refinance credits was still relatively great. Thus it can be assumed that access to these long-term credits was rationed and that other investors were obliged to borrow at higher rates or short term.

The other striking feature of Table 4.5 is the dramatic increase in the interest spreads recorded in 1992 and the high level maintained in the following years. In part this reflects the New Banking Act of 1992 which required banks to satisfy at the year end the international capital standards established by the Cooke committee. As a consequence of this, banks sought to shift away from enterprise lending which carries full weight in the calculation of risk-adjusted capital requirements to assets such as treasury securities which have a more favourable treatment. More generally the increased spread may have reflected an increase in the risk-premium banks required on loans.

Regarding the level of interest rates, to varying degrees all rates rose from 1989 to 1991 and have fallen subsequently. These developments can be best understood in relation to the inflationary pressure during this period. Table 4.10 presents Hungarian annual inflation rates measured by both consumer prices and producer prices. This table also combines the interest rates of Table 4.5 with the inflation rates of the subsequent year to give a measure of the realized real interest rates. We see that in 1989 and 1990 monetary policy was relatively loose so that interest rates on deposits and loans lagged behind inflation. These negative real rates plus increasing liberalization of prices contributed to the doubling of inflation rates between 1989 and 1991. In light of this loan and deposit rates increased very sharply in 1991. These rates proved to constitute real rates in excess of 20 per cent. These onerous rates proved sufficient to bring down inflation rates in 1992 and again in 1993. Interest rates followed this decline. In 1994 the rate of consumer price inflation remained at 21 per cent through the year; whereas the rate of producer price inflation rose significantly. Thus the monetary history since the late 1980s has been one of stimulus feeding inflationary ten-

TABLE 4.10   Hungarian inflation and real interest rates
(December to December, %)

		1989	1990	1991	1992	1993	1994
Inflation							
Producer prices		15.4	22.0	32.6	11.5	10.3	14.8
Consumer prices		17.0	28.9	35.0	23.0	21.1	21.2
Ex post real interest rates (PPI)							
Credits	S.T.	0.7	−0.4	21.5	16.8	9.4	n.a.
	L.T.	−1.9	−3.8	20.4	13.7	9.1	n.a.
Deposits	S.T.	−2.5	−3.1	17.6	6.6	2.1	n.a.
	L.T.	−1.1	−2.5	19.3	8.3	3.4	n.a.

Sources: NBH (1991, 1992, 1994*a*, 1995*b*, 1995*c*).

dencies, followed by a period of monetary tightness and declining inflation rates.

We now turn to the issue of the distribution of credit within the
Hungarian financial sector. Here we will be interested to see the trade-
offs at one level between government and enterprises and at another
between large enterprises which at least at the outset of the period were
state-owned and small enterprises most of which are private. Table 4.11
reports the growth rates of bank credits since 1990 to various categories
of non-financial borrowers. The overall tightness of monetary conditions is reflected in the fact that the growth of total domestic credit
lagged behind consumer price inflation during the period 1990–3. When
compared to producer price inflation we see that there was a real expansion of credit in 1993 and again in 1994. This points to the fact that in the
Hungarian context the large gap between consumer price and producer
price inflation makes it somewhat difficult to judge the tightness of
credit conditions.

Since 1990 credit to the public entities, local and national governments, has increased rapidly. In contrast, credit in enterprises has not
kept pace and actually fell in nominal terms in 1992 and 1993. This
demonstrates that the government has indeed crowded out the enterprise sector. This reflects the combined effect of high real rates and of
constraints placed on the use of subsidized refinance credits. In particular, refinance credit for investments was particularly affected by this
contraction, decreasing by 5.2 per cent in 1992 and 1.5 per cent in 1993.
Since the beginning of 1994, a slight improvement in investment

TABLE 4.11   Growth rate of Hungarian domestic
credit (% preceding year's stock)

End of period	1990	1991	1992	1993	1994
Domestic credit[a]	11.1	7.2	10.3	18.0	16.8
Public credit	1.3	16.4	20.5	32.7	18.2
Enterprise credit	25.0	18.7	−1.4	−2.8	16.2
Small enterprises	135.3	39.5	24.1	12.5	4.2
Household credit	5.3	−35.3	6.7	14.6	14.2

[a] Domestic credit includes all credits granted by
financial institutions to Hungarian non-financial agents.
The rate of growth is measured in forint terms from
December to December.

Source: NBH (1995c).

financing has been recorded in line with the economic recovery. Small enterprise credits grew substantially from very low levels initially. This reflects the general expansion of the private sector and, since 1992, the existence of the Fund of Guarantee for small and medium enterprises.

As a consequence of this evolution, the share of the State and local and national governments in domestic credit increased and represented after 1992 more than half of the credit granted (see Table 4.12).

This crowding-out of the private sector by the increasing needs of financing of State is quite difficult to prove in a context of sharp contraction in economic activities. Indeed, the decrease in the share of banking credits allocated to the business sector might be due to a reduction in the demand for loans by enterprises. However, between 1990 and 1994 the business sector rapidly increased its foreign borrowing. The gross foreign debt of this sector had increased from $US1,230 million (77.7 billion forint) in 1990 to $US3,693 million (386.6 billion forint) at the end of 1994. This amount represents 34 per cent of the total credit granted to enterprises at the end of 1994. This is an indication that the dynamic private sector, even in the context of recession, needed external financing and was not able to obtain it from the Hungarian banking system.

Not only was the State obliged to borrow heavily, but the banking system was willing to accommodate it. This willingness is explained partly by the banks' desire to improve the quality of their assets by reducing their riskier activities and by the necessity of meeting capital standards. At the same time, the public sector borrowed directly through the issue of securities.[7] Table 4.12 also shows that despite its strong growth the share of domestic credit destined for small enterprises remained relatively insignificant.

A somewhat broader view of credit patterns can be seen in the evolution of the consolidated balance sheet of the banking system. Unfortunately, because of several changes in data definition this is not available on a consistent basis over the entire period. Table 4.13 reports the consolidated balance sheet of the banking system including savings cooperatives but excluding the central bank for year-end 1992, 1993, and 1994.

The most important fact that can be observed from this table is the

---

[7] According to the survey conducted by the National Bank of Hungary in June 1993, the outstanding government securities in circulation amounted to 497 billion forint or 21.4% of the total balance sheet of the banking sector (see Kopint-Datorg 1993). This amount excluded bank credit, consolidation papers, compensation coupons, and bonds issued by the Social Security Administration under state guarantee.

TABLE 4.12   Distribution of the Hungarian domestic credit creation
(% of the total new credits)

End of period	1989	1990	1991	1992	1993	1994
Public entities	47.9	43.7	47.4	51.8	58.3	59.0
Enterprises	30.7	34.5	38.2	34.2	28.2	28.0
Small enterprises	1.2	2.6	3.3	3.7	3.6	3.2
Households	20.2	19.2	11.0	10.3	9.9	9.8
TOTAL (billion forint)	1,550.4	1,721.8	1,846.4	2,035.7	2,401.7	2,804.6

Sources: NBH (1993, 1995*b*).

importance of the central bank on both sides of the balance sheet of the
banking system. On the assets side, the banking system carried between
15 and 20 per cent of its assets in reserves. This is a very high level of
reserves by international standards. In part this reflects the mandatory
reserve requirements which in Hungary have been set at very high
levels. At the end of 1994, the mandatory reserves amounted to 16 per
cent for most deposits but excluding foreign currency deposits. Already
in 1992 this exceeded mandatory reserves by a wide margin. The high
level of excess reserves may reflect imperfections on the interbank
market and the relatively heavy penalties for violations of reserve standards. Most of the excess reserves are foreign currencies deposited by
banks at the NBH. Thus the high reserves demonstrate the attractive-
ness of the inducements that the NBH has introduced to build up its
holding of foreign exchange. Given the high level of reserves carried by
banks, variations of the interest rates can generate large swings in their
profitability. On June 1994 in the face of the rapidly eroding financial
position of the banking sector, the central bank was thus obliged to
increase from 2 per cent to 6 per cent the interest rate on reserves held
against forint liabilities and from 11 per cent to 18 per cent on forint
reserves held against foreign exchange liabilities. The same evolution
was observable during 1995 when the interest rates at year-end reached
15.5 per cent on mandatory reserves held against forint deposits and 28
per cent on reserves against foreign exchange deposits.

On the liabilities side, the central bank intervention takes the form of
refinancing credits. At the outset of the two-tier banking system, the
newly established banks did not have a large deposit base and were thus
dependent on refinancing through the NBH. The importance of the
refinancing credit as a funding source has been reduced progressively,
especially for short-term maturity. From January 1991 to December

TABLE 4.13 Consolidated balance sheet of the Hungarian banking system at the end of the year including savings cooperatives (in billion forint and % of total assets)

Assets	1992	1993	1994	Liabilities	1992	1993	1994
Credit to enterprises and households of which	40.8	36.9	36.4	Deposit from non-financial sector	54.1	60.5	60.3
classified	7.5	15.7	11.0	Deposits from financial institutions	4.8	4.9	4.4
Credit to government	14.7	23.5	22.7	Credits from NBH	11.7	13.3	12.9
of which consolidation bonds	0	10.1	n.a.	Bonds issued	6.5	7.6	7.3
Credit to financial institutions	4.1	4.2	3.6				
Reserves at NBH of	19.8	14.6	17.6				
which mandatory	8.2	6.7	n.a.	Other liabilities	12	6.8	6.3
Non-loan	4.3	5.0	4.6	Provisions	3.6	-4.3	-4.5
Liquid and other assets	16.4	15.8	15.1	Equity	7.3	11.4	13.3
TOTAL	2,476.3	2,691.4	3,126.5	TOTAL	2,476.3	2,691.4	3,126.5

Sources: NBH (1994a, 1995c).

1993, the refinancing credits as a percentage of the total loans of the financial system was reduced from 51 per cent to 7.4 per cent. Almost all of the remaining refinancing credits were long term. The majority of these long-term refinancing credits were granted with a preferential interest rate as low as 70 per cent and 75 per cent of the NBH base rate. These preferential rate refinancing credits are in fact a survival of the old practice of direct intervention of the NBH in the lending decisions of the banks. Thus while it is true that refinance has become less important as a means of monetary control, the refinance credits which remain represent a significant source of subsidies to the enterprises which have access to them.

In light of our discussion concerning the fact that the central government has received a very large share of Hungarian domestic credit creation, the level of credit to the central government by the banking sector may seem surprisingly low. The reason for this is that the central government has turned to a great extent to the central bank for its finance. This was seen in Table 4.7. It is true that the share of banking system assets devoted to the government did rise from 1992 to 1993; however, this is more than accounted for by the consolidation bonds which the government issued as part of the recapitalization of the banking sector (to be discussed below).

In Table 4.13 the low level of assets in the form of credit issued to other financial institutions suggests that the interbank funds market in Hungary may be relatively underdeveloped. This is explained in part by examining Table 4.14 which reports the consolidated balance sheet of commercial banks but excluding savings cooperatives and specialized banks. Here the level of interbank assets is of the order of 20 per cent of total assets which is comparable to levels in Western Europe. Another fact that can be observed from this table is that reserves were relatively low (6.7 per cent and 4.4 per cent for the two years reported). Thus most of the excess reserves reported in Table 4.13 are accounted for by savings cooperatives and specialized banks.

To summarize, during the period 1991 through 1994 the Hungarian authorities raised real interest rates to very high levels. During the same period the credit conditions for enterprises and households were tight— real credits to these borrowers fell much of the time and sometimes declined in nominal terms as well. This not only reflected the tight monetary conditions. It also was the result of renewed growth in the public sector borrowing requirements and of changes in capital standards applied to the banks. The data do not allow us to distinguish the flows to private and state-owned enterprises with any precision. Credits to small enterprises which are generally private did grow substantially;

TABLE 4.14 Consolidated balance sheet of the Hungarian banks (excluding specialized financial institutions and savings cooperatives)

Assets	12/1993	9/1994	Liabilities	12/1993	9/1994
Credit to enterprise and households	40.9	39.5	Deposit from enterprise and households	55.6	54.0
Credit to government	23.5	22.6	Deposit from government	4.9	5.8
Credit to financial institutions	18.8	21.5	Other deposits	26	24.8
Reserves at NBH	6.7	4.4	Other passive settlements	6.7	7.0
Non-loan	1.0	0.9	Ordinary resources	6.8	8.3
Liquidity and other assets	9.1	11.0			
TOTAL	2,524.8	2,793.3	TOTAL	2,524.8	2,793.3

Source: NBH (1994*b*).

however, given their very low starting level, such credits are still relatively insignificant within the Hungarian financial sector generally.

4.5. Bank Supervision and Deposit Insurance

The New Banking Act of December 1991 placed the supervision of the Hungarian banking system in an independent institution, the State Banking Supervision Agency (SBSA). This agency is a state administration operating under the government's supervision. The task of the SBSA is to license financial institutions and to ensure the application of banking operational and competition rules. The SBSA has power to audit banks and otherwise obtain all information judged as useful and, in cases of rule violations, to impose sanctions ranging from fines to withdrawal of licence.

Since a wave of bankruptcies was recorded in 1992, the NBH has also developed a bank supervision division in order to perform on-site audits and to exercise central bank control based on data collected jointly with the SBSA. As a consequence of this new collaboration between the two institutions, the effectiveness of the banking supervision has been reinforced and the number of sanctions has increased.

The most important rules enforced by the SBSA are the capital adequacy standards, the assets classification and provisioning, the lending limits, and the liquidity ratio.

According to the New Banking Act, the capital adequacy ratio was to reach the Cooke Committee standard of 8 per cent by January 1993. This would have proved extremely difficult if not impossible for many banks. Consequently, the law allowed some exceptions for the period until 31 December 1994. Given their low level of capitalization and the poor quality of their portfolios, the large banks used this exemption. As time went on it became clear that the banks would not be able to reach this ratio without external help. Therefore, the State embarked on an extended consolidation effort aimed at cleaning up bad loans and raising bank capital. The main beneficiaries of these efforts have been the large state-owned banks.[8]

The law also imposed standards for the classification of bad loans and for providing loan loss reserves. Three categories of non-performing assets are defined by the law. Institutions must provide loss reserves equal to at least 20 per cent of the assets qualified as substandard, 50 per cent of the assets qualified as doubtful, and 100 per cent of the assets qualified as bad debts. Reserves are built up from bank net nevenues before tax and are deducted in calculating taxable profits. In accordance with regulations, over and above these provisions, before paying dividends or profit-sharing, financial institutions must set aside a general reserve from after-tax operating profits against which losses arising from banking operations may be written off once specific provisions are exhausted. These procedures were quietly amended in January 1994 to allow the reserve requirement for the various categories of classified credits to be determined by the NBH on a case-by-case basis. During 1994 average provision for loans categorized as bad was 86 per cent. Thus the effect of the rule change was to weaken the loan loss provisioning requirements.

In order to assure a minimum of diversification, the law limits the lending to a single customer to a maximum of 25 per cent of the financial institution's adjusted capital. Interlocking financial relations effects are partly restrained by limiting lending to shareholders to a maximum of 5 per cent of the financial institution's adjusted capital. There are also rules which enforce a separation between commercial banking and investment banking. In particular, commercial banks may not own more than 51 per cent of the common stock of a non-financial enterprise, and

[8] As of May 1994 the five largest commercial banks held 75% of all consolidation bonds (NBH 1994*b*).

the bank's total equity holdings in non-financial enterprises cannot exceed 60 per cent of the bank's risk-adjusted capital. A bank's holding in any single enterprise cannot exceed 15 per cent of the bank's adjusted capital. On the other hand investment banks cannot issue deposits for maturity of less than one year, and their deposits are not covered by deposit insurance. Thus in Hungary there are significant obstacles to universal banking.

These prudential rules are designed to reinforce the stability of the banking system and to promote sound financing of the economy. However, their effective implementation is often hampered simply by lack of managerial capabilities of the financial institutions' staffs or by the limit of the effective supervision exercised by the SBSA and the NBH.

The New Banking Act also called for the creation of a deposit insurance fund by January 1993. In fact, the Act XXIV of 1993 on the establishment and the detailed rules of operation of the National Deposit Insurance Fund (NDF) came into force on 30 June 1993. The objective of this new system was to provide sufficient insurance to deposit holders in case of insolvency of financial institutions. By the establishment of the NDF, the law extends protection to a much wider range of deposit holders than before. It insures deposits, in forint and convertible foreign, held by insolvent financial institutions up to the amount of 1 million forint per deposit holder. The Fund participation fee is 0.5 per cent of the bank's capital plus a percentage of the deposits insured by the Fund. If the activities of a bank are judged as too risky, the Fund with the agreement of the NBH and the State Banking Supervision, can decide to increase the participation fees of the bank with an upper limit of 1/1,000 of the guaranteed deposits. For the large banks created from the monobank system, the government had already guaranteed deposits placed before 30 June 1993 and this guarantee remains in force.

4.6.   Bad Loans and Bank Recapitalization

Bad loans were the by-product of the economic changes in Eastern Europe during the late 1980s and early 1990s. In Hungary, the burden of bad loans from the late 1980s was concentrated in the large commercial banks. In 1987 when the two-tier banking system was created, the National Bank of Hungary transferred its assets to the newly established commercial banks. The majority of these loans were in fact substitutes for direct government subsidies and had not been submitted to a credit analysis. With the suspension of direct subsidies, many large debtors, most of which were state-owned enterprises, became insolvent. The undercapitalization and the lack of reserves of the newly created banks hampered a direct write-off of these loans. Furthermore, since in case of a borrower's bankruptcy the banks would be forced to take the loss on their books, banks were slow to initiate bankruptcy proceedings. Instead banks rolled over the principal and interest due. Furthermore, owing to the concentration of their loan portfolio, the banks were dependent on the interest income from a small group of clients among whom most of the substandard loans could be found. In 1988, fewer than 1 per cent of all Hungarian enterprises had between 40 and 50 per cent of the total amount of loans outstanding in the corporate sector.

After 1987 the problem may well have been worsened in part by the risky lending policy followed by some financial institutions. As discussed in Chapter 1 this is precisely the type of behaviour expected of a severely undercapitalized bank. Furthermore, risks increased generally as Hungary embarked on a more rapid transition towards a market. Indeed, the recession of the Hungarian economy did lead to the deterioration of the quality of bank portfolios. As a result the bad loans problem spread throughout the banking system, hurting also the middle-sized banks and the specialized financial institutions. The risk of greater loan losses was surely one explanation of the increase in Hungarian intermediation spreads observed through 1992 (see Table 4.5).

The development of the bad loan problem in Hungary is hard to document quantitatively for several reasons. Prior to 1991 when the Accounting Act was introduced, legislation allowed banks to classify their loans based on their own subjective assessment of the borrowers' position which thus varied across banks. At the same time, the definition of the subcategories of non-standard loans had changed since 1987. Furthermore, the large banks created subsidiaries or joint ventures with other Hungarian financial institutions to handle part of these loans. As a consequence the balance sheet of some large banks improved without an improvement in the loans quality.

According to the New Banking Act of 1991, the non-performing assets have to be classified into three categories: substandard loans defined as the assets with large economic sectorial risks but otherwise performing; doubtful loans corresponding to debts of a borrower who is in default in servicing the principal and the interest for more than sixty days, or has incurred losses in each of the two years preceding the period of closing the balance sheet; and bad loans defined as debts of a borrower who is in default in servicing the principal and the interest for

TABLE 4.15   Non-performing loans in the Hungarian banking system
1987–1992 excluding savings cooperatives

	Category of bank				
	Four large	Medium-sized	Retail	Specialized	Banks total
In billion forint					
1987	2.7	0.1	0	0	2.8
1988	6.5	0	0	0	6.5
1989	21.2	1.1	0	0.3	22.6
1990	38.8	3.2	0.6	0.7	43.3
1991	45.0	14.2	26.6	1.7	87.5
1992	n.a.	n.a.	n.a.	n.a.	262.0
As a percentage of total assets					
1987	0.5	0.2	0	0	0.3
1988	1.2	0	0	0	0.6
1989	3.3	0	0	1.1	1.8
1990	5.0	1.4	0.1	2.0	2.6
1991	5.0	3.0	3.6	10.6	4.1
1992	n.a.	n.a.	n.a.	n.a.	11.4

Source: OECD (1993).

more than 360 days, or against whom restructuring and liquidation procedures have been initiated.

The amount of problematic loans increased from 2.8 billion forint in 1987 to 43.3 billion forint in 1990 and 262 billion forint or more then 11 per cent of total assets at the end of the third quarter of 1992 (see Table 4.15). This rapid increase in the amount of problem loans reflected the deterioration in the quality of banks' portfolios but also an improvement in the accounting standards and loan classification methods. In all likehood the estimates of bad loans prior to 1991 were too low. It is clear that the problem loans level of 11 per cent constituted a banking crisis. By way of comparison at the peak of the crisis of the savings and loans associations in the USA in the 1980s, problem loans reached 1.8 per cent of the total assets and 3.1 per cent of the total loans. The Hungarian situation is more comparable to the banking crises in Norway and Sweden in the early 1990s where the bad loans reached 9.3 per cent of total assets and 11.5 per cent of total loans. Table 4.15 also supports the view claiming that at least at the outset the bad loan problem was concentrated in the large banks; however, it is possible that in the 1980s reporting standards were lower for the smaller banks. This certainly seems likely, given the sharp increase in problem loans for banks other than the top four in 1991 when accounting standards were tightened.

While the first reaction of the Hungarian authorities to the bad loans was to ignore the problem and to adopt a wait-and-see attitude, the negative effects of the banks 'portfolios' deterioration forced public intervention. Even if at each stage the public intervention was presented officially as a once-for-all clean-up, in fact, the measures taken proved inadequate and the State was forced to intervene again at a later time. Table 4.16 presents the history of state interventions in the bad-loan problem. The fact that Hungarian banks have been recapitalized many times creates doubt about claims that the state will not bail out the banks if they fall into trouble in the future. If so, it creates incentives for poor bank management which could in turn burden the public finances for some time to come. In light of the official view that the bad-debt problem was concentrated in loans inherited by the commercial banks split off from the national bank, public intervention has mainly concentrated on large banks and large state enterprises.

The first step towards cleaning up the balance sheets of banks was taken at the end of 1989.[9] A special audit assessed the total stock of bad debts in the portfolio of the large banks. The essential goal of this audit was to restructure the banks on a strictly once-and-for-all basis and as a final adjustment to the two-tier banking system. Such an audit was designed to avoid the creation of an additional moral hazard situation for the banks and their customers by stating that all loans after a given date would not become candidates for intervention. Specifically, only those bad loans clearly identified as the consequence of the credit decisions taken by the National Bank of Hungary before the 1987 reform could enter into consideration in the government plan.

The audit identified 43.3 billion forint of bad loans (see Table 4.15). After prolonged negotiations with the banks involved, 21 billion forint of the non-performing debt was accepted by the National Bank of Hungary as outstanding from the long-term credits it extended before 1987. In the summer of 1991 the government finally decided to provide its guarantee to cover half of these inherited receivables (10.5 billion forint), the other half to be covered by existing and future reserves of the banks. The state guarantee was for five years and could be called upon only in case of liquidation proceedings against the debtors. The scheme therefore linked the recapitalization of banks to bankruptcies. This may have been intended for banks to become active creditors;

---

[9] An earlier programme was limited to the resolution of the problem of housing loans. The National Savings Bank received government bonds instead of low-interest housing loans granted before the transition. This programme was completed in 1989.

TABLE 4.16 Summary of public interventions in the Hungarian
bad-loan problem

Date	Name	Amount (billion forint)	Type of intervention
Summer 1991		10.5	State guarantee
1992	Bank-oriented loan consolidation	80.0	Bad loans swapped to consolidation bonds. Bad loans transferred to specialized, state-owned financial institution.
July 1992	Company-oriented clean-up of bank's portfolios programme	57.0	Consolidation bonds
April 1993	First stage of bank recapitalization programme	114.0	Consolidation bonds
		1.9	Purchase of shares from SOEs
		5.0	Subordinated debt in the form of consolidation bonds
		8.6	New shares acquired against consolidation bonds
May 1994	First round of the second stage of bank recapitalization programme	18.0	Consolidation bonds
December 1994	Last round of the second stage of bank recapitalization programme	15.0	Consolidation bonds

however, it may have also had the effect of provoking bankruptcies even in cases when this would not have been the course that maximized the payoffs to the existing loans. The guarantee also exempted from income tax any additional provisions that banks might need in order to write off the non-performing loans and allowed the large commercial banks to carry out debt-for-equity swaps with the inherited stock of non-performing loans. The main failure of this first plan was that it was too small given the magnitude of the problem. It still left some 30 billion forint of bad loans to be covered by the banks' own capital. However, this left the large banks in a very weak position to confront future loan losses or to meet the soon-to-be-implemented capital standards. Furthermore, modifications of the bankruptcy law (discussed below) provoked an immediate worsening of the quality of the loan portfolio. As a consequence, the bad-loan problem re-emerged almost immediately as a high priority for action by the State.

A second stage of the bad-loan remedies came at the end of 1992 with the adoption of a consolidation programme. This second step like those which have followed was financed by the issue of consolidation bonds. Thus, unlike the first set of state guarantees, the expected financial consequences of the clean-up were reflected in the increase of the state debt-service requirement. The bank-oriented loan consolidation programme gave to the banks, whose capital adequacy ratio did not reach 7.25 per cent, the possibility of swapping the bad debts which predated 31 December 1992 into twenty-year government bonds. The bond/debt swap ratio was fixed at 50 per cent for the bad debts made before 1992 and 80 per cent for the bad loans made during 1992. In this way, the State deviated clearly from its earlier stance that only old bad loans would be given support. The State sold a part of these bad debts (40 billion forint) at a discount (between 0 and 50 per cent) to the Hungarian Investment and Development Bank which is a state-owned financial institution created in 1991. This new institution had neither experience of managing non-performing credits nor information on the borrowers. With a staff of eighty to deal with 1,885 borrowers, the Hungarian Investment and Development Bank was obliged to ask the banks responsible for the bad debts to continue managing the loans carved out until the middle of 1993 (Aghion *et al.* 1994). The remaining part of the claims was managed by the seller banks. The consolidation government bonds of 1992 were issued in two varieties. The A bonds for principal claims yielded a variable rate equal to that of the three-month treasury bills. The B bonds for interest arrears were to carry an interest rate equal to 50 per cent of interest rate on the A bonds.

In all fourteen banks and seventy-eight savings cooperatives took part in the 1992 consolidation plan. Altogether they submitted 102.5 billion forint and in return received government consolidation bonds worth 80 billion forint. As a result of this consolidation plan, the capital adequacy ratio of financial institutions improved; however, after the programme had been negotiated the banks complained that the conditions were not sufficiently helpful to them, in particular because reasonably heavy consolidation fees were deducted from the interest the banks received. In June 1993 the government agreed to remove the consolidation fees and to increase the rate on B bonds to be equal to that on A bonds. Thus despite the appearance provided by the issue of securities, the terms of the bank bailout proved to be negotiable after the programme was supposedly closed. Again, this hardly contributed to the State's credibility in saying that future bailouts would be impossible. Furthermore, it clearly illustrates the continuation of old socialist practices. As a consequence of this consolidation scheme, the stock of all problem loans declined from 288 billion forint to 186 billion forint at the end of 1992. The stock of bad loans fell from 186 billion forint to 84 billion forint. If the consolidation programme to some extent helped the banks, it did not resolve the bad-loan problem. Furthermore, no institution was given continuing responsibility for addressing. In particular, the Hungarian Investment and Development Bank which received many of the non-performing assets did not develop a clear mission for recovering the bad debts. Subsequent to the 1992 programme bankruptcy proceedings were intensified, and the amount of substandard, bad, and doubtful loans increased. Thus once again the measures taken were not equal to the task, and further state action were soon called for.

The third step of the clean-up was aimed at specific debtors. In July 1992 the government classified thirteen enterprises as being of 'national economic importance' in order to maintain the industrial employment level. To avoid bankruptcy of these enterprises representing more than 7 per cent of the total industrial labour force, the programme provided that the State would transform the dividends it was due to receive as full or partial shareholder into capital increases. Furthermore, it allowed the rescheduling or partial write-off of the debt arrears against public entities and the purchase by the State of a substantial part of their bank debt against consolidation bonds. Under the programme the firms submitted a strategic plan which required the approval of the ministry for industry and trade. The total cost of this programme was initially estimated to be about 12 billion forint. In September 1993 the ministry expanded the programme to include seventy-eight additional industrial companies. Ultimately, under this scheme, the Government issued consolidation bonds equal to a total of 57 billion forint to the financial institutions at the end of 1994. This does not include the costs of the programme in terms of ploughed back dividends and forgiven commercial credit. The was scheduled for completion by mid-1995. However, the privatization bill still pending in early 1995 provided that consolidation would continue in a modified form and would involve 12,000 loans instead of the 2,000 initially covered.

In April 1993 the Government also decided to perform the further consolidation of the banking system not by the way of portfolio clean-ups but by recapitalization of the banks financed by the State through the so-called 1993–4 bank consolidation scheme. Thus the banks kept the problem loans on their books. The recapitalization of the banks took place in two steps. As a first step, the State increased the capital of eight banks by an amount of 114 billion forint at the end of 1993. This enabled them to reach an adjusted capital adequacy ratio that was equal to zero. By adopting the principle of recapitalizing the amount of the bad loans, the State gave the perverse signal to the banking community that improving performance reduces the amount of state subsidy. Moreover, it is worth noting that no independent in-depth portfolio or operations reviews were completed by Government prior to the recapitalizations (Baer and Gray 1994). In addition, the Government bought shares worth an amount of 1.9 billion forint from the shareholders of the banks who expressed their intention to sell. They were essentially state-owned enterprises obliged by the law to decrease their bank participation or those suffering form illiquidity. The State also acquired 5 billion forint of subordinated debt issued by the National Savings Bank; in effect this was very close to an increase in equity. It also included savings cooperatives in the bank consolidation provided their capital adequacy ratio was below 4 per cent. This intervention amounted to 8.6 billion forint and was channelled through the National Savings Cooperatives Institution Protection Fund. The capital injection took the form of the state purchase of newly issued stock by the banks against credit consolidation bonds which were marketable and acceptable by auditors at face value. In order to create incentives for bank-led enterprise-restructuring, the capital injection banks had to waive, reschedule, or convert into equity part of their claims on the debtor according the debtor consolidation plan. Every debtor consolidation plan had to be accepted by the SPA, the finance, social security, and sectorial ministries. In 1993 fourteen enterprises were involved in a debtor consolidation plan and fifty-five enterprises were concerned in 1994. Moreover the banks benefiting from the state intervention had to undertake modernization of their management, organization, and operation systems in accordance with the consolidation agreements signed with the State. The financial institutions received consolidation government bonds to a total value of 127.6 billion forint.

The second stage of the consolidation programme proceeded in two steps, the first was implemented at the end of May 1994. The purpose was for the eight state banks included to be brought to a capital adequacy ratio of at least 4 per cent by the end of 1994. In addition to acquiring newly issued shares, the government also bought subordinated bank debt. These two kinds of intervention were implemented by placing 18 billion forint of consolidation bonds on the banks 'balance sheets. In December 1994 the second recapitalization programme continued for the three large banks that were considered by the government to be of strategic importance. These banks were brought up to the 8 per cent capital adequacy level. Via this operation, 15 billion forint of consolidations bonds were again injected in the banking system.

While the capital position of the banks was being improved, the dimension of the bad-debt problem continued to grow. Table 4.17 summarizes the evolution of problem loans during the period of intensive intervention by the State to reduce the bad-loan problem. Through the loan consolidation scheme of 1992, the capital adequacy ratios of banks improved for a while, but the continuation of the recession and the significant number of bankruptcy and liquidation procedures led to a situation in which no substantial improvement took place for the banks' clients in 1993. Consequently, the quality of the portfolio of banks continued to deteriorate. By the end of 1993 the banks' portfolio contained about 16 per cent of problem loans which was about the same level as before the consolidation scheme. Classified assets reached 11.0 per cent of the total assets of the banking system at the end of 1994. The financial situation of the large state-owned commercial banks remains fragile. Even after the 1993 recapitalization, it has been estimated that equity remained negative for five of the eight banks in the programme (Baer and Gray 1994). Thus as of early 1995, it is difficult to believe that state bailouts of the Hungarian banking system are at an end.

Not all the banking sector was touched equally by the bad-loan problem. At one extreme, the position of the banks with partial foreign

TABLE 4.17   Non-performing assets of the
Hungarian financial institutions after audit and
consolidation (billion forint)

	1992[a]	1993	1994
N-P assets	186.4	422.7	344.0
Total assets	2,476.3	2,691.4	3,126.5
Per cent	7.5	15.7	11.0

[a] Excluding specialized financial institutions and savings cooperatives.

Sources: NBH (1993, 1994*a*, 1995*c*).

ownership is generally good. Their corporate customers are generally solvent as they mainly finance joint-venture businesses. Therefore, the ratio of qualified loans in their portfolios is lower than elsewhere in the system. Nevertheless it had risen to 6 per cent by 1994. The group of large banks was in the worst situation at the outset of state intervention. Since the implementation of the consolidation schemes, the large banks have slightly fewer classified assets than the group of domestic small and medium-sized banks. Some of banks of this latter group have pursued highly expansive business policies under the pressure to grow because of their high fixed costs. The sources of this growth consisted substantially of short-term borrowing. At the same time, the quality of their loan portfolios is poor, as they frequently granted loans to clients that would not be financed by other banks because of their high-risk rating.

Overall, the various rescue plans led to an increase in bank capital from 4.9 per cent in 1992 to 8.8 per cent at the end of 1993. This has been accomplished through a significant increase in the total domestic debt of the government. At the end of 1994, the stock of consolidation government bonds held by the financial institutions including the NBH amounted to 332 billion forint or 7.7 per cent of the 1994 GDP. Furthermore, the consolidation schemes also had the consequence that the State's share rose to 75 per cent or more in seven of the largest banks. This high state shareholding is expected by some to be temporary. The recapitalization of banks was rationalized in part as a precondition to their ultimate privatization.

In early 1995 only one state-owned bank, the Hungarian Foreign Trade Bank (MKB), had been privatized and that one only partially so. The sale of 42 per cent of this bank was directly negotiated with two strategic investors, Bayerische Landesbank from Munich and the European Reconstruction and Development Bank. The privatization of the other banks was more difficult, given the reservations expressed by the potential investors, especially concerning the quality of their loans portfolio. This fear has been met at least partially by the State's debt consolidation. A further problem with bank privatization, especially of the large banks, was the reluctance to give up control of the major financial institutions, given the continuing heavy need of finance by the State. However under the privatization low of 1995, the State was to privatize most of its bank holdings. The State would retain a 25 per cent stake in the National Savings Bank (OPT) and would also retain control of several specialized financial institutions such as the Export-Import Bank. The first bank to be privatized after this law was Budapest Bank which was sold in early 1996 to a group involving foreign strategic investors.

4.7.   Enterprise Restructuring and the Treatment
of Financial Distress

One of the motivations of the New Economic Mechanism started in 1968 was to improve the performance of enterprises. However, given the possible consequences on employment and social peace, few concrete steps were taken towards enterprise restructuring. In fact, the large state-owned enterprises were protected against the possible actions of their creditors.

It was only in the 1980s that some serious efforts were made to harden Hungarian budget constraints. In 1983 new regulations took effect which were intended to accelerate the phasing-out of inefficient enterprises. Loss-making enterprises were required to draw up restructuring programmes that would restore profitability. However, these regulations were rarely effectively implemented. In September 1986 a bankruptcy law was adopted. This was directed at facilitating negotiations between creditors and debtors leading to an out-of-court settlement of claims. As a last resort, courts intervened to initiate liquidation proceedings. The provisions of the bankruptcy law were largely used to liquidate small enterprises on a modest scale. Between 1986 and 1991 there were about 1,000 bankruptcy filings only fifty of which involved state-owned firms. Very few of the cases resulted in liquidation (Frydman *et al*. 1993: 117). The large, chronic bad debtors were not really concerned by the bankruptcy threat. Given their low level of loss provision and capital, the banks were in practice unable to initiate the bankruptcy proceedings against the large enterprises which were usually their main customers. By the late 1980s these same debtors were often bank shareholders closely aligned with management so that creditor passivity tended to be reinforced. Suppliers were also often loath to pursue their claims. Under the 1986 bankruptcy law, the priority in liquidation was to pay first the State (both taxes and tax penalties), the employees, and the banks. Suppliers had a lower priority and therefore would have little to gain in initiating bankruptcy against a highly indebted firm. This was particularly true when credit had been granted to a large state firm which was one of its main customers. As a result large state enterprises may have been in a position to gain involuntary credits from suppliers.

The amount of trade credits increased drastically after 1988, a period in which bank financing became progressively tighter. At the beginning of 1992, the inter-enterprise debt was estimated to be as great as 240 billion forint including the claims 'kept in drawers' (Estrin *et al*. 1992).

TABLE 4.18   The payments queue in Hungary at year-end

	1987	1988	1989	1990	1991	1992	1993[a]
Queued payables (million forint)	14.0	45.5	72.8	90.5	158.6	104.0	103.0
Queued payables (% of GDP)	1.0	3.2	4.3	4.4	6.8	3.7	—

[a] Third quarter.

Source: Bonin and Schaffer (1995).

This was equivalent to 23.8 per cent of the banking credit to the private sector in 1992. A large proportion of these interenterprise arrears was caused by a handful of huge enterprises largely concentrated in heavy industry and coal mining. Other estimates were somewhat lower. Table 4.18 presents one indicator of interenterprise arrears. This is the bank payments queue, that is, amounts of payables submitted to banks awaiting payment. These figures suggest a somewhat lower level of interenterprise credit which nevertheless did rise very sharply through 1991. Such data were widely viewed as indicating that there was a dangerous expansion of involuntary trade credits as Hungary's transition proceeded.[10]

A new bankruptcy law was enacted on 1 January 1992 which altered radically the regime in force in Hungary for resolving financial distress. It applies to all business organizations and creditors excluding individual proprietorships. The new law continues to favour negotiation between creditors and the firms over liquidation. However, the procedure for negotiation was modified to take a form similar to chapter 11 of the US bankruptcy code. Specifically, the firm can obtain temporary shielding from its creditors thus allowing it an opportunity for restructuring and reorganization. Managers of bankrupt firms retain their jobs after filing for protections and have the first opportunity to present a reorganization plan. Creditors then vote on the plan and have the opportunity to present alternative plans. If an agreement cannot be reached, the procedure reverts to liquidation. Priority under liquidation was changed to give tax penalties a lower status than

[10] Bonin and Schaffer (1995) suggest that such an interpretation is unwarranted. They point out that the payments queue included taxes due as well as commercial credit and that the former may well have been much larger than the latter. Furthermore, comparing estimates of trade credit for Hungarian firms with levels observed in other countries, they suggest that Hungarian levels are not unusual and therefore cannot be considered involuntary.

taxes themselves. Given that tax penalties can be very large relative to other claims, this change improved the probable payoff to unsecured creditors including other firms and thereby increased their incentive to initiate bankruptcy.

A very controversial feature of the law was to make it a criminal offence for firm officials not to declare bankruptcy when they had an outstanding debt with scheduled principal or interest payment more than ninety days overdue, independently of the amount of the deficiency. By forcing the debtor himself to declare bankruptcy even in the absence of strong pressure from the creditors, the legislative intent was clearly to harden the budget constraints of the state-owned enterprises. In particular it was aimed at cutting off the expansion of forced inter-enterprise indebtedness. It seems likely that the threat of bankruptcy was an important reason why the payments queue fell significantly in 1992 (Table 4.18).

Another controversial provision of the bankruptcy law was the requirement of unanimous consent of creditors to implement the restructuring plan. This provision implied very long and complex negotiations to obtain the creditors' agreement and gave too much power to marginal creditors to stop the process.

The strict new bankruptcy code was not the only factor increasing the chances that a distressed firm would end up in a bankruptcy court. Starting in 1992 the Hungarian social security administration, one of the main creditors of bad debtors, started bankruptcy proceedings against these enterprises.

The effects of these changes were rapid and dramatic. Table 4.19 shows that in 1992 after the new law went into effect there were some 4,000 filings for bankruptcy (the temporary protection from creditors) and almost 10,000 for liquidation. While most of the firms involved were small, many were large so that the potential impact on Hungarian

TABLE 4.19   Bankruptcies and liquidations in Hungary

	1989	1990	1991	1992	1993	1994[a]
Bankruptcy filed	n.a	n.a.	n.a.	4,169	987	151
Bankruptcy closed	n.a.	n.a.	n.a.	2,703	1,924	340
Liquidations filed	n.a.	n.a.	n.a.	9,891	7,242	3,940
Liquidations closed	141	233	526	4,936	5,115	2,984

[a] First through third quarters.

Source: Bonin and Schaffer (1995).

national output was significant.[11] The National Bank of Hungary presents different figures for bankruptcies and liquidations given that the former concern only corporations whereas the latter also cover individual entrepreneurs. Between 1992 and the end of 1994, the central bank recorded 3,147 bankruptcies and 6,671 liquidations. Liquidations primarily affected limited liability companies and cooperatives. These accounted for 90 per cent of liquidated businesses.

In fact, most bankruptcies and liquidations ended up being settled administratively and did not generally involve closing the firm. Nevertheless, the feared consequences of this wave of bankruptcies on employment and on the portfolio quality of the banks led the Government to water down the law and to limit its scope of application. In July 1992 the Government launched the debtor consolidation scheme offering protection against bankruptcy for enterprises classified as of 'national interest', and in July 1993 the bankruptcy law was amended to remove the institution of mandatory self-declared bankruptcy and changed several other significant features of the law. The self-bankruptcy procedure can be initiated only when it is supported by the majority of the creditors. In order to accelerate the procedure, the amendment reduced the required majority for approval of a reorganization agreement from 100 per cent to a two-thirds (in value) and to one-half (in number) of mature claims plus one-fourth (in number) of not-yet-mature claims.

Despite these steps to moderate the force of the law, the Hungarian approach represented a very aggressive and bold attempt to force restructuring on Hungarian enterprises. It was motivated to a significant degree by the fear that uneconomic firms were surviving without restructuring because there were able to force creditors to extend further credits. The measures were effective in the sense that a very large fraction of the liquidation cases was initiated by creditors other than the banks or the tax authorities. It is difficult to say if Hungary went too far, that is, that many of the bankruptcies and liquidations were economically inefficient. However, the view that the measures were excessive tended to contribute to a feeling that the aggressive disruption of the economy was ill-advised.

4.8. *Privatization*

The privatization process in Hungary began in the middle of the 1980s and ten years later was still far from being finished. On the whole it can

---

[11] Bonin and Schaffer estimate that employment in firms declared bankrupt in 1992–3 amounted to 12 to 13% of enterprise employment.

be regarded as having been a gradual process. However, it has proceeded in fits and starts which resulted not so much from the measured
application of a single vision but rather from conflicting efforts to direct
the programme in one direction or another. In part, this was a by-
product of the 1980's attempts to reform the economy through the
decentralization of initiative to enterprises. This gave rise to a wave of
'spontaneous' privatizations initiated by the firms' managers themselves. Subsequently, the State attempted to take back control of the
process and to some extent has been successful. In 1990 its goals were
ambitious. From a state sector comprising 2,200 enterprises, valued at
1,900 billion forint, about 900 companies were expected to be rapidly
privatized representing a value of 700 billion forint. The priority was
given first to the maximization of privatization income, particularly in
foreign currency, given the lack of international reserves and the burden
of the external debt. However, the principles of the process were never
terribly clear. Furthermore, in response to criticisms that it was selling
too cheaply, the State slowed the process. Thus, in practice much privatization continued to be initiated by the firms or by investors. Also after
a period of selling essentially for cash, often to foreigners, the government attempted to grant access to small domestic investors. In this
section we summarize this somewhat complicated saga with particular
interest in those aspects that affect either banking activities or the
development of financial markets.[12]

Table 4.20 lists some of the major initiatives that have shaped the
privatization process in Hungary. Reforms implemented in the early
and mid-1980s tried to moderate the predominance in the economy of
large state-owned enterprises by allowing various forms of small businesses based on private initiatives. The reform started in 1984–5 also
introduced self-government to large enterprises. The 1984 amendment
to the Enterprise Act substantially increased enterprises' autonomy and
decision-making powers. In 1987 the legislation was modified to author-
ize the formation of joint-stock and limited liability companies by
domestic legal entities. Using this new opportunity, large enterprises
initiated substantial organizational changes. They transformed their
plants and factories into joint-stock companies while they organized
themselves into holding companies maintaining certain central functions and holding the majority of the shares of different newly created
companies. By this reorganization, the state ownership was not decreased but only modified by transforming former ownership of assets
into shares. This kind of transformation was accelerated by the provi-

---

[12] For additional discussion see Frydman *et al.* (1993) and OECD (1995*b*).

TABLE 4.20 Hungarian initiatives regarding private property ownership

Date	Initiative	Summary
1987–9	Company Law Acts	Established forms of private companies as alternatives to state-owned enterprise or cooperative forms. These include joint-stock companies and limited liability companies.
1990	Laws on state property	Created the Satae Property Agency (SPA) and established guidelines for the management of state properties including the means of privatization.
1990	First privatization programme	The purpose was to sell 20 large state-owned enterprises at the initiative of the SPA.
1990	Second privatization programme	Designed to privatize 22 state holding companies owning more than 115 companies.
1991	Pre-privatization	Privatization mainly by auction of more than 10,000 small-scale businesses mainly in the retail and service sectors.
1991	Compensation Act	Transfers compensation vouchers to individuals with claims to property nationalized after 1939. Vouchers are used in various SPA-organized privatizations.
1992	Laws on state property	Created the Hungraian State Holding Company (SHC) to take over some of the functions of the SPA.
1994	Small investor share ownership programme	Provides access to credit for small investors to allow them to participate in state-initiated privatization.
1995	New Privatization Law	Created APVRt by the merger of SPA and SHC.

sions of the New Company Law of January 1989 which allowed the formation of business associations with resident companies and individuals. At the same time, foreign direct investment was encouraged by the liberal provisions of the Foreign Investment Act of 1988 and generous tax relief granted to joint ventures.

In this environment, managers of large enterprises started to sell assets and shares in subsidiaries to raise capital. This first wave of ownership restructuring was called 'spontaneous privatization' as it was initiated by the enterprises themselves. In many cases the buyers were foreign investors. Given the lack of established accounting practices or clear guidelines for the fiduciary responsibility of management, there were often allegations that assets were being sold at below their true market value and that individuals were enriching themselves in the process. One method used was to transfer the most valuable assets to newly created enterprises, leaving the state-owned firms as empty shells.

The perceived abuses recorded during this period led to the creation of the State Property Agency (SPA) in March 1990 and the enactment of the law on the protection of state enterprises' assets. The SPA was given the responsibility of supervising the privatization of the public enterprises. In Hungary privatization involved two steps. The first step consisted in the commercialization of state enterprises by transformation into joint-stock or a limited liability companies. The law on transformation provides for this commercialization. Part of the process involves an external audit and the reassessment of the assets and liabilities of the firm. The second step is the sale of the majority of the shares to private investors.

Three types of privatization were permitted by law, the State initiating privatization of about 500 to 600 enterprises, the Enterprise initiating privatization for 300 to 400 firms, and finally, privatization initiated by external investors bidding for an entire enterprise. A wide range of privatization methods were allowed ranging from the public auction to leasing by the State. In cases where privatization was not directly initiated by the SPA, its agreement was needed for each of the two steps. By and large, Hungarian privatization has been on a case-by-case basis rather than processing many enterprises at once in a mass privatization programme.

The first action of the SPA was the 'First Privatization Programme' launched in September 1990 in which it intended to sell twenty companies with a total equity amounting to 33 billion forint and a total book value of 73 billion forint. At the end of 1993, only six of these enterprises were privatized and five were liquidated. The public offering of shares was successful only in the case of two enterprises, IBUSZ and Danubius Hotel. The privatization of other large companies failed for lack of investors willing to meet the price sought by the SPA. While this may have been the result of the poor functioning of the SPA, it also may have been the consequence of pressures on the SPA not too sell too cheaply.

The 'Second Privatization Programme' was introduced in December 1990 and focused on twenty-two state holding companies. These were companies where at least 50 per cent of the assets in the form of joint-stock companies or limited liability companies. The idea was that once the holding company was privatized, it could sell or keep the smaller companies it controlled so as to maximize its value. At the end of 1993 only two of these holding companies had been reorganized and sold. In the majority of cases, rapid privatization was taken off the agenda because of the deteriorating financial condition of the enterprises.

These first initiatives of the SPA were slow to produce results. In order to accelerate the process and to increase domestic participation, the government launched two other programmes. The first was 'pre-privatization' in 1991. In this, state enterprises which had been blocked from selling assets were allowed to sell off retail, catering, and service activities which could be operated as individual proprietorships or partnerships. A total of 10,816 small and medium-sized businesses were put up for sale. These sales were open only to Hungarian citizens. By the end of 1993, 9,065 had been sold of which 90 per cent were sold by way of public auctions. The second programme, the Enterprise Initiated Privatization Programme, was launched in October 1991 and affected companies with fewer than 300 employees and a book value less than 300 million forint. Later, the limits were increased to 1,000 employees and to 1 billion forint of book value. Some 749 small and medium-sized enterprises were eligible for privatization under this programme. By the end of 1993, 260 companies had been sold in full. Under this programme, most of the new owners of these companies were employees and managers. However, foreign investors were also active buyers of the larger companies.

In order to promote the employees' participation, the government also introduced an 'Employee Stock Ownership Programme' (ESOP) which allowed the transfer of state assets to employees at market value assisted by substantial loan preferences and allowances in the form of payment by instalment and profit tax concessions. The costs of subsidizing the employees' loans at below market rates is covered by the ESOP budget.

The government also took steps to increase the participation of small domestic investors who were not employees of the companies being privatized. It also introduced privatization loan facilities. In 1992 the interest rate on these loans was set at 60 per cent of current base rate of the NBH and in most cases carried a maturity of ten years. In 1993 the conditions of these loans was changed. Their maturity was extended to fifteen years, the interest level was reduced to 7 per cent, and a grace period of three years on the principal repayment was introduced. At the end of 1993 the stock of these loans amounted to 31.2 billion forint.

In 1991 the Compensation Law provided for the distribution of compensation to persons with claims on property nationalized after 1939. The maximum compensation for a single claim was 5 million forint per person. These compensation vouchers can be swapped for shares in enterprises or land being sold by the SPA. The introduction of this compensation voucher–equity swap technique increased the rate at which state assets were sold off. Vouchers can be sold on the secondary market. However, the demand on this market has fluctuated widely but has been generally quite low. The main reason was the limited number of enterprises selected by the SPA for which the conversion of vouchers was possible. At the end of 1993, the face value of the issued vouchers was estimated (NBH 1993) at 100 billion forint and only 13 billion forint were exchanged against state assets.

In August 1992 parliament passed new laws which changed the administration of state properties. In particular, it created the Hungarian State Holding Company (SHC) for the purposes of managing assets to be retained by the State in the long term. These are those presenting a strategic economic interest or those deemed as requiring a particularly long preparation before privatization is feasible. The government selected 163 enterprises in which it decided to keep partial or total ownership. These were put in the portfolio of the SHC. The assets remaining in the SPA were thus earmarked for relatively rapid privatization. The SHC is a legal entity independent of the budget. However, its activities are supervised by the minister of privatization. Parliament sets the maximum share of a firm that the SHC can hold (mostly between 25 and 51 per cent). As this percentage is generally below the current State's participation, the remained must be sold to private investors. Thus the SHC is also in the business of privatization. This division of authority for privatization in Hungary has created a certain amount of confusion and given rise to considerable intra-governmental turf-fighting.

In the spring of 1994 the government launched a new programme designed to widen the citizens' participation in the privatization process—the 'Small Investor Share Acquisition Programme' (SISAP). This reinforced the previous loans facilities and made instalment payments for shares accessible to the public (OECD 1995*b*).

In 1994 there were some 289 (OECD) enterprises still controlled by the State, and there were clear divisions within the government over the direction that should be taken in privatizing these. The prime minister created a minister of privatization, but the finance minister maintained that the privatization programme remained his responsibility. After a prolonged debate, a modified privatization law was voted by parliament in May 1995. The main changes introduced by this law was the creation of the State Privatization and Asset Management Company (ÁPVRt), which is the result of merging the SPA and the SHC. The management of the ÁPVRt is controlled by the minister of privatization. In addition, the law established three procedures for privatizing enterprises. The first category of firms is composed of thirty to forty large enterprises belonging to 'national interest' sectors. The privatization of these requires the agreement of the government and preferably would involve the participation of foreign strategic investors. The second concerns medium enterprises (with a capital of more than 600 million forint and more than 500 employees) which will be privatized by ÁPVRt. The last group refers to small and medium enterprises of which the sales will be organized with the management or the workers.

What has been the net result of all these efforts? Table 4.21 provides a summary of the Hungarian State's efforts since 1990 to restructure its business enterprises. The SPA was initially given the responsibility of 1,848 public enterprises with an estimated book value of 2,000 billion forint. Subsequently, a number of other state activities were grouped to form an additional 229 commercialized companies initially owned by the State. From this total of 2,077 entities to be disposed of, 533 were wound up directly or were liquidated after a privatization effort failed to find an interested buyer. Eighty-seven enterprises were not commercialized but were transferred to governmental authorities other than the SPA or the SHC to be run permanently as government enterprises, and 624 have been fully privatized so that the State no longer holds an interest in them. These actions plus a few miscellaneous disposals left 829 business in the portfolios of the SPA and the SHC as of November 1994. Of these there were a total of 147 commercialized enterprises held

TABLE 4.21   Summary of Hungarian privatization results, March 1990–October 1994, excluding pre-privatization

Total number of state enterprises held by SPA, 1 January 1990	1,848
plus new commercial enterprises created	229
less liquidated firms	533
less state enterprise and commercial enterprises transferred to other governmental authorities	87
less fully privatized compaines	624
less other disposals equals	4
Total business enterprises held by SPA and SPA in November 1994, of which	829
State-owned enterprises held by SPA	24
Commercial enterprises held by SPA	651
State-owned enterprises held by SHC	7
Commercial enterprises held by SHC	147

Source: NBH (1995c).

by the SHC to be operated as long-term commercial holdings of the State. The SPA had holdings in 651 commercialized enterprises. Some of these had already been partially privatized leaving the SPA with a minority stake. Given the stated responsibilities of the SPA, the State is to withdraw from all 651 by privatization, liquidation, or other means. Finally, thirty state enterprises have not yet been commercialized, including twenty-four held by the SPA and seven held by the SHC.

These figures show that despite the slow beginning and the numerous changes of direction in the State's active privatization efforts, a large fraction of state enterprises have at least been commercialized or closed down. Much of this activity has occurred since 1993. For example of the 1,200 state-owned enterprises that had been transformed by the SPA into joint-stock or limited liabilities companies by November 1994, 506 were transformed in 1993 alone. An important feature of the Hungarian privatization strategy up to now has been that the State conserves an important minority of the shares in the privatized enterprises (OECD 1995*b*).

Another view of privatization activity is given by Table 4.22 which reports the revenues of sales organized by the two institutions, SPA and SHC. The acceleration in the privatization process since 1992 is clearly demonstrated by the evolution of their total income. While through 1992 most of the income derived from foreign sales, these foreign sales dropped off sharply in 1993 and fell away almost entirely in 1994. During that year, foreign exchange sales amounted to 10.9 billion forint which was one-tenth of the corresponding figure for 1993. The drop in foreign exchange sales partly reflects the fact that some of the State's most valuable enterprises had been sold. Also it testifies to the existence of a significant political reaction to the initial government policy of selling to foreigners. The opening of the privatization process to domestic investors was accomplished largely through the use of credit and compensation vouchers. Thus the cash proceeds fell from 133.2 billion forint in 1993 to 36.1 billion forint in 1994. Furthermore, whether or not the institutions will ever actually receive cash for much of the 85.9 billion forint sales on credit remains somewhat in doubt. Should the value of the shares bought on instalment credit fall below their purchase price, investors may choose not to make their payments. The penalty for this would not be likely to be greater than relinquishing the claim on the shares not paid for.[13] Overall, the SPA and the SHC have sold assets for a total value of 415 billion forint. This is far short of the

[13] See OECD (1995*b*). In effect this means that the instalment credit facilities provide Hungarian investors with a call option on state assets.

TABLE 4.22   Composition of revenues from sales of state properties
(billion forint)

	1990	1991	1992	1993	1994	1990–4
Cash	0.67	30.37	66.74	133.19	36.06	267.03
E-loan	—	1.01	9.07	21.70	30.23	62.01
Compensation vouchers	—	—	2.64	19.54	63.68	85.86
TOTAL	0.67	31.38	78.45	174.43	129.97	414.9

Source: NBH (1994*a*)

700 billion forint in book value that the State set out to privatize in 1990. The reasons for the shortfall are that some assets proved to be worth less than their book value and that some of the properties still on the State's books are large with considerable value at least in accounting terms.

More than the half of the annual income of the SPA (55 per cent in 1992 and 67 per cent in 1993) was used to support the government budget via state debt amortization or funds outside the budget such as the Employment Fund and the Agricultural Development Fund. This budget support means that part of the privatization receipts is used to cover current expenditures of the State.

The Hungarian government has bealt with most of the state-owned enterprises it set out to reorganize in 1990, but in many cases this has meant that they have been shuffled into the State Property Agency and out again into the State Holding Company. Thus a key to understanding the true extent to which the State has withdrawn from industrial and commercial activities is to have a clearer picture of the SHC. Table 4.23 gives a quantitative breakdown of its assets in December 1992. The total equity value of the companies it held was more than 1,200 billion forint which was large compared to the estimated book value of 1,700 billion forint for the whole of the state enterprise sector in 1990. This high value placed on a subset of state enterprises might have resulted from the revaluation of these enterprises after January 1990. However, even allowing for revaluation this shows that the portfolio of the SHC included some of the very largest state enterprises. These big firms in many cases had great numbers of employees so that their rapid restructuring was viewed as politically risky. This was the case for the coal mines which are reflected in the large portion of the SHC's portfolio devoted to the energy sector.

TABLE 4.23   The portfolio of the Hungarian State Holding Company
at the end of 1992

Sectors	No. of enterprises	Total balance sheet (billion forint)	Equity (billion forint)
Energy	8	691.3	596.6
Infrastructure	11	275.9	195.0
Industry	13	291.0	187.9
Agriculture	25	50.6	34.6
Forestry	20	26.8	22.0
Research and development	33	15.6	10.1
Brand names	20	55.1	37.9
Culture	20	11.2	8.3
Bank and insurance	10	1,923.6	118.1
TOTAL	160	3,341.1	1,210.5

Source: HSHC (1993).

How are the firms in the SHC's portfolio administered? The SHC is a private company with the State as principal owner. The stated objectives of this institution are (i) to privatize the companies it holds to the maximum extent allowed by the law; (ii) to manage the assets entrusted to it so as to maximize their value, and (iii) to pay a dividend to its owner, the Republic of Hungary. The companies it holds are to be transformed into commercial enterprises. By the end of 1994 this had basically been accomplished. The maximum shareholding targets are set by parliament and are generally 25–50 per cent. As a private company the accounts of the SHC are off the budget of the State. However, parliament includes in the budget a planned fixed dividend that it expects to receive from the SHC.

At the outset of its activities, the SHC classified its enterprises into three groups on the basis of a series of strategic studies. The first group consisted in companies in the best position for immediate privatization which included pharmaceutical companies and the Hungarian Foreign Trade Bank. The second was composed of companies in the poorest condition whose the restructuring would incur prohibitive costs and for which the solution was quick privatization and/or downsizing. The third group consisted of companies that had good market potential but required restructuring to maximize their privatization value.

The SHC as the manager of the enterprises was an active partner in the bank and debtor consolidation schemes. However, the distribution of the main part of its income in the form of dividends to the State limited its ability to finance the restructuring of the enterprises that it managed. It also carried out the partial privatization of the best firms such as the Hungarian Foreign Trade Bank. There are managerial limits to how actively the SHC can monitor its investments. In late 1990 it had only 160 employees.

4.9. *Role of Banks in Enterprise Restructuring*

We have seen that despite ten years' experience in the development of private firms in Hungary, large segments of business activity continue to take place in state-owned enterprises or enterprises in which the State owns a significant share. Thus the privatization process on its own has not brought about a complete restructuring of Hungarian industry. Furthermore, this experience has sometimes revealed the lack of political will to pursue an active programme of state-initiated restructing. As underlined by Baer and Gray (1995), an interesting question is why one-half of Hungary's largest loss-makers in 1992 (603 firms) had still not entered into bankruptcy or liquidation by early 1994. In the face of incomplete privatization, other forces could potentially bring about the needed restructuring of firms. In particular, even if a firm is state-owned, so long as the State abstains from subsidies, the survival of an un-restructured, loss-making firm will depend on its access to credit or to the possibility of defaulting on its debt contracts without leading creditors to seize control of the firm. That is, if creditors impose hard budget constraints, firms (whether state-owned or not) are forced to restructure to achieve profitability or have restructuring forced upon them. In particular, in light of the experience of developed capitalist economies, it is expected that banks may be the most active creditors in monitoring firms and in guiding their restructuring. Table 4.24 shows that of total debt of the largest loss-making enterprises at the end of 1992, the largest fraction was owed to banks. Thus, seemingly banks should have been most active in initiating bankruptcy proceedings.

What is the evidence that Hungarian banks have developed into active monitors of firms? It is widely believed that in the first years following the creation of the two-tier banking system, Hungarian banks were not active in restructuring enterprises. On the contrary, they tended to grant credits to the large state-owned enterprises even though they may have failed to service their existing loans. Thus the banks allowed firms soft budget constraints and in so doing removed the incentives for them to adjust. At the same time, they limited the flow of

TABLE 4.24   Debt burdens of Hungarian firms, 1992

	57,000 firms	603 firms (loss-markers)
Total debt/Total assets	0.34	0.43
Percentage of debt owed to:		
Banks		0.45
Government		0.27
Suppliers		0.21
Other		0.07

Source: Baer and Gray (1995).

credits available for the newly emerging private sector so that the competitive pressures on the state-owned enterprises was reduced.

Since that time the changes in the structure of banking have been limited. In particular, in the period 1990–5 a disproportionate share of total bank assets were concentrated in state-owned banks. Nevertheless, there has been considerable discussion regarding the ultimate privatization of the large banks and in the case of one bank, partial privatization has already taken place. It is possible that in anticipation of their likely future as privately owned banks, the behaviour of these banks changed before they were privatized.

Something about the behaviour of banks can be learned from the financial accounts of firms. This is the approach taken by Bonin and Schaffer in their study of 2,871 medium- and large-sized firms in 1992. Some of their results are summarized in Table 4.25. They found that the least profitable firms accounting for 10 per cent of employment in their sample accounted for 18 per cent of total bank credits. Thus they found that the poorest performing firms tended also to be highly indebted. When they examined the growth of credits granted in 1992, they found overall that all firms tended to have total bank loans reduced but that the low-profit firms were cut back relatively more. Furthermore, when they deducted scheduled interest charges not paid in 1992 from credit creation in order to obtain a measure of fresh credits, they found that the worst-performing firms were those where new loans were most restricted. Thus by these indicators it appears that a certain amount of creditor discipline was operating on Hungarian firms in 1992. Their sample combined privately owned and state-owned companies, so that it does not tell us whether state-owned enterprises were treated in the

TABLE 4.25   Distribution of bank credit across Hungarian firms (%)

	Low-profit firms	All firms
Fraction of total bank credit	18.1	100
Real growth of bank credit, January through December 1992	−4.3	−3.6
Fresh credit growth as percentage of total bank debt	−18.1	−13.9

The set of low-profit firms is obtained by ordering firms with respect to return on equity and by taking lowest-profit firms that together account for 10% of the total employment within the set of all firms. Fresh credit is defined as growth of bank credit less accured interest charges unpaid.

Source: See Bonin and Schaffer (1995, table 2).

same way as their private counterparts.[14] Furthermore, the data set does not provide a breakdown by type of credit, and they were forced to construct a relatively crude approximation of bank credit. Thus, for example, it is conceivable that the cutback in credits felt by loss-makers in their sample may reflect the cutback in subsidized refinance credits (see Section 4.4). If so, this is not an indication of active monitoring by the commercial banks so much as a change mandated by the public authorities. These doubts suggest some amount of caution; however, the study is at least consistent with the view that banks had begun to exercise profit-maximizing credit practices by 1992.

Another measure of creditor activism is given by the behaviour of creditors of firms in financial distress. Some of the information available for Hungary in this area is shown in Table 4.26. This covers the period after the introduction of the radical bankruptcy reforms in 1992. The data on bankruptcies (i.e. the Chapter 11-style proceeding) show that most of filings were compulsory in the sense of being required of firm officials in order to avoid being liable to criminal charges. Voluntary proceedings would include cases where the firm sought protection from legal actions initiated by creditors. The data suggest that as regards bankruptcies the strict rules for compulsory bankruptcy in effect during 1992 and 1993 removed the need for banks and other creditors to force firms into bankruptcy.

[14] Bonin and Schaffer (1995) also exclude from their sample firms which data reports are incomplete. They do not consider to what extent this might bias their result e.g. as might be the case if state-owned enterprises were not subjected to the same reporting requirements as other firms.

Perhaps of more direct relevance to the question of creditor activism are the data on liquidation where Hungarian reports allow us to identify the type of organization which initiates liquidation proceedings. Table 4.26 indicates that banks have been relatively inactive in initiating liquidations. By far the largest number of cases was initiated by 'other creditors' which include commercial companies which may be suppliers to the firm. Liquidations initiated by tax authorities remained at relatively low levels despite the fact that a large portion of the delinquent credits were tax arrears.

What do these data say about monitoring activities of Hungarian commercial banks? Had these data shown that banks initiated most liquidations, it would have been clear evidence of bank activism. However, the fact that other creditors initiated most proceedings does not necessarily mean that banks have been 'passive creditors'. It might be argued that banks simply calculated that they were likely to earn less by liquidating a firm than if they allowed it to survive. This argument is reinforced by the fact that banks would be forced to provide full provision for bad loans once bankruptcy was declared. However, this view is not entirely convincing because under the priority rules in force for Hungarian liquidations, banks are treated at least as well as other general creditors. As a consequence, these data seem weak evidence of the relative passivity of Hungarian banks.

If most Hungarian commercial banks have not actively used bankruptcy and liquidation to pursue non-performing borrowers, it might be that this has been because they had less costly tools available to them. In particular, the some of the banks have been able to swap their bad loans

TABLE 4.26   Hungarian creditor activity in
bankruptcy and liquidation

	1992	1993	1994 (1q–3q)
Bankruptcy filings			
voluntary	1,016	137	102
compulsory	3,153	850	49
Liquidation fillings			
by debtor	1,760	1,359	722
by tax authority	900	608	539
by banks	60	159	69
by state enterprises	1,100	739	200
by other creditor	6,100	4,377	2,400

Source: Bonin and Schaffer (1995).

through the government's banks debt consolidation schemes. What has been the implication of these consolidations for the borrowers whose debts were treated? Some of them have been subjected to the government's efforts to restructure them. In other cases, these debts have remained on the books of the banks. To the extent that the banks expect to be bailed out of future financial difficulties they have little incentive either to take the bad loans off their books through a liquidation or bankruptcy, or to screen new loans very severely. Finally, some of the bad loans have been taken over by the Hungarian Investment Development Bank. However, this bank has not been given a clear mission as the collection agent for the commercial banking system. Instead, it is being asked to perform collection at the same time that it supports long-term investment and development.

The Government's changes in privatization proposed in late 1994 were motivated by the desire to see the banks play a greater role in the restructuring process. However, some conditions for having effective banks were not yet in place. In particular, recapitalization was still insufficient, the classified loans problem was not yet completely resolved, the big banks were still largely state controlled. It seems difficult to escape the conclusion that turning the banks into active agents of firms' restructuring will require at least a partial privatization of the large state-owned banks. Furthermore, the more active implication of banks in the restructuring process and the emergence of restructuring rather than the liquidation at the end of bankruptcy procedures require an easy use of debt-to-equity swaps. Currently, a bank can hold for only six months the equity participation resulting from a financial restructuring operation in excess to the ceiling fixed by the law (15 per cent of its adjusted capital). The other option consists in the rapid development of investment banks which are not yet present in Hungary.

4.10. Financial Market Development

Hungary made an early effort to create financial markets. At the beginning of the 1980s, Hungary was the first Eastern European country in which a bond market was organized. Initially, bonds were issued only by state enterprises and local governments. The bonds were purchased primarily by individuals and commercial banks. The main advantage for households was the higher return of these bonds compared to the bank deposits. The popularity of this financial asset was enhanced by government guarantee of the principal and interest which was practically automatic. In 1988 the success of this market was substantially reduced as a result of changes affecting the condition of bonds. In particular, state guarantees were no longer given and the new tax system introduced a withholding tax on interest income. Furthermore, increased inflation may have discouraged investors. Nevertheless, starting in January 1988, a secondary market grew up which allowed financial institutions to trade these bonds.

On 19 June 1990, forty-one banks, financial institutions, and securities trading companies with the support of the NBH opened the Budapest Stock Exchange (BSE) for the purpose of trading shares of joint-stock companies. During the first two years trading remained at a low level (see Table 4.27). Trading in Hungarian treasury securities was introduced in the Stock Exchange at the end of 1991. Since the end of 1992 there has been trading with compensation vouchers. Stocks of about forty enterprises have been offered to compensation voucher holders and sixteen of them were securities traded at the BSE.

Foreign portfolio investment is permitted in Hungary, and trading on the stock market has been dominated by foreigners. According to NBH estimates (NBH 1995c), some 50–70 per cent of investments in the Stock Exchange are due to foreign investors. In order of importance, Austrian, German, British, French, and American investors are the most active.

One factor that may explain this foreign dominance is that foreigners have an easier means of diversifying the risks associated with holding Hungarian shares. Stock prices in Budapest have indeed been volatile. The stock price index (BUX) which has been computed since the beginning of 1991 started at an initial value of 1,000 from which point it rose. Subsequently it dropped to 718 by May 1993 (−28 per cent) and then recorded a spectacular upswing to reach its peak of 2,255 (+214 per cent) nine months later. Between that point and the end of 1994, the index declined. According to the financial press this decline reportedly coincided with the departure of foreign investors disillusioned with the lack of progress in the privatization process.

The stock market is still underdeveloped because the lack of interest expressed by domestic savers in investment in shares is seen as being of higher risk than other papers. In addition, a high profits tax and withholding tax make dividend income relatively unattractive. Moreover, owing to the low liquidity of the secondary market, investors find it difficult to withdraw their investments. Furthermore, Hungarian stock mutual funds are not well developed. Pension funds on the other hand have been established but only since the second half of 1994. At the same time, a number of Hungarian companies are also listed in markets abroad, especially in the Vienna stock market and London

TABLE 4.27   The Budapest Stock Exchange

	1990	1991	1992	1993	1994
No. of Stock Exchange members	42	48	48	47	50
No. of securities listed	6	22	40	62	120
of which shares	6	20	23	28	40
bonds	—	2	5	17	28
treasury bills	—	—	10	10	31
Stock Exchange capitalization	16.4	53.6	201.9	457.0	883.8
(billion forint) of which shares	16.4	38.2	47.2	81.7	181.5
bonds	—	15.4	82.4	242.0	394.7
treasury bills	—	—	54.4	74.0	239.6
Turnover (in billion forint)	6.12	10.11	33.67	185.69	224.57
of which shares	6.12	9.81	6.01	18.26	58.67
bonds	—	0.30	12.36	73.38	55.31
treasury bills	—	—	15.06	85.00	90.94
Average number of transactions a day	27	58	34	94	302
Average daily turnover (million forint)	33.8	40.1	133.6	736.9	891.2

Source: NBH (1993, 1995c).

stock market. The Government's privatization initiative of 1994 envisages a greater role for the Stock Exchange with the sale of shares of ten to twelve enterprises and the promotion of investment funds for this purpose.

In contrast to the stock market, the market of government securities is dominated primarily by domestic investors and of these by financial institutions and mutual funds. Most government securities are not available to non-residents, a fact that establishes a segmentation of the markets for Hungarian domestic and foreign debts. Since 1992 the financing of the deficit has been principally based on bonds issues. The central banks buys the issues and then sells them on the secondary market. In so doing it promotes the development of that market. The NBH, commissioned by the ministry of finance, sells treasury bills by regular auctions and other longer-term bonds by occasional auctions. In order to make the market attractive to small investors, since 1993 individuals have been able to buy bonds for a period after the auction at the average price of the auction. At the end of 1994, twenty-five treasury bonds and thirty-one treasury bills were traded on the Stock Exchange representing 65.1 per cent of all trading on this market which is a marked decrease in comparison with the 85.2 per cent of 1993. The greater part of the total turnover of government bonds were at the two- to three- year maturity while the trading in bonds with maturity of four to five years was exceedingly low. Since May 1994 the ministry of finance and the NBH have gradually opened the government bond market to foreign investors, and since September 1994 foreign investors have been allowed to purchase government securities with shorter maturities, i.e. treasury bills.

The corporate bonds issues are partly public and partly private. For public issues, the licence of the Securities Supervision Agency is required. In this market, a few large public utility companies have been able to raise significant amounts of funds in recent years. The decisive part of the private issues is the papers issued by the domestic subsidiaries of large international corporations. Most of the buyers of these papers are financial institutions. In 1993 only one corporate bond was introduced on the Stock Exchange and only two others in 1994. The banks also issue papers which are essentially short-term certificates of deposit. Finally, a commercial paper market has emerged since 1992.

4.11. Evaluation

We have now examined, at least superficially, the main factors affecting the financial development of Hungary since the late 1980s. How do we evaluate this from the perspective of a transition towards the type of financial sector which might be found in a mature capitalist economy?

In a formal sense the progress on this path has been clear. Hungary was the first communist country of Eastern Europe to establish a two-tier banking system and to remove legal barriers to entry for new banks, including foreign ones. Furthermore, ownership of the type of the old socialist system has largely been replaced by joint-stock companies or other commercialized forms.

However, despite the many formal changes of institutions, there are signs that a fundamental reorientation of business and financial practices has not been brought about. For example, despite the apparent absence of barriers to new entry in banking, in many ways banking practice has been slow to change. The State, through the originally created large banks, retains its dominant position. Furthermore, the most credit is still channelled towards the public sector. Similar remarks apply to central banking. The central bank has progressively used credit control instruments comparable to instruments in other OECD countries, especially on the short-term section of the market. But persistence of certain practices of the NBH, e.g. provision of subsidized refinance

credits, has contributed to maintaining public influence on the allocation of savings. The independence of the NBH is still relative and the
recent modification of the law limiting the monetary financing of the
budget has reinforced its subordination to me government's goals.

The efforts to solve the bad-debt problem and restore the financial
health of commercial banks have also had mixed results. The government saw relatively early on that the development of good banking
would require a debt-restructuring with public sector assistance. In
practice, the initial efforts were far too small to resolve the problem, so
that a short time later it found it had to intervene again. This process has
been repeated several times, so that by now the government has established a precedent which invites banks to assume their mistakes will be
covered by future government bail-outs.

Privatization for some is the most important means of bringing about
the basic economic changes that will allow the market economy to
establish itself. In Hungary the growth of small, private sector in enterprises, especially in services, has been very dynamic. Undoubtedly, this
has done much to address some of the imbalances of the former socialist
system. However, large portions of economic activity still take place in
enterprises wholly or partially owned by the State. Those portions of
industry that have been privatized in many cases have ended up in the
hands of foreigners. Direct finance of investment, in the form of shares
listed on the stock market, has still not developed as a viable alternative
to bank finance or self-finance for most private sector enterprises.

What are the factors that have produced this pattern of market-
oriented reforms that are only half-implemented or are deformed
through the political process? Part of the explanation may lie in the fact
that market-oriented reform is an old story in Hungary. The partial
reforms of the 1980s may have already demonstrated that along the path
of reform there are both winners and losers, so that each reform initiative quickly created its own opposition. Stated differently, the political
breakthrough of 1989 was not so dramatic in Hungary as in the case of
its socialist neighbours. Consequently, it did not create the same window of political opportunity to bring about deep institutional reforms to
create the market. Furthermore, what political capital did exist to support transition was perhaps misused on reforms which were politically
costly and which in the end may have been addressed at the symptoms
of the problems and not their causes. An example of this was the radical
reform of bankruptcy laws which make bankruptcies compulsory for
many firms, thus provoking the disruption of a large number of enterprises without necessarily creating a positive contribution to enterprise-
restructuring on the part of creditors.

While this line of explanation seems to us to be at least partly true, it should not be pushed too far. At least as important for us is the fact that transition since the late 1980s has been undermined by the macro-context of the reforms, in particular the persistent and large external debt. We have found that many of the actions of the government and the central bank have been aimed at guaranteeing the ability of Hungary to service the debt and to maintain its access to international capital markets. Thus reserve requirements are distorted to ensure an adequate level of foreign exchange. The inability of the government to generate a budget surplus implies that it has continually been a heavy borrower on the domestic market, crowding out private borrowers in the process. Privatization is aimed at attracting foreign investors thus lightening the foreign debt burden, but also allowing the mechanism of domestic control of enterprises to languish.

Despite all these efforts, the external debt is as large in real terms in 1995 as it was in 1989. What is different in 1995 is that the cost of servicing this debt in terms of the failure to allow the private sector to take control of the economy is becoming increasingly clear. It remains to be seen whether the present and future government of Hungary will be willing to pay this price.

5

Poland

5.1. Introduction

The history of socialism in Poland is one in which the Communist Party's attempts to introduce Soviet style orthodoxy repeatedly met significant resistance.[1] In the face of clear challenges to its authority the party granted a variety of concessions which served to reduce the sacrifices that Polish consumers were called upon to make in support of the process of rapid industrialization. Thus socialism in Poland had been submitted to a series of reforms which meant that by 1989 the organization of the economy departed significantly from the model of central planning.

The most critical challenges to the party originated from labour which used strikes to protest against price increases on basic consumer products. This helped to determine the direction that economic reforms took in Poland. In particular, workers gained very significant powers of economic decision-making through the creation of worker management committees. This tradition of worker self-management is one of the prominent features of the Polish economy which has had important consequences for the direction that was taken during the transition since 1989.

A second notable feature of the Polish economy is the traditional importance of agriculture. In the 1950s agriculture accounted for more than 40 per cent of Poland's gross national product, and close to half the population lived in rural areas (Slay 1994: 31). Over time agricultural production has been outstripped by industrial production so that by 1989 the fraction of agricultural production was approximately 12 per cent (Govt. of Poland 1990). Nevertheless, nearly 40 per cent of the population still lived in rural areas, although in many cases commuting to jobs in a city. Also of importance is the fact that attempts in the 1950s to collectivize agriculture failed so that production in agriculture took place either in private farms or in large state farms. Through the large number of small private farms, a large fraction of the population

[1] The history of the Polish economy is presented in Slay (1994).

maintained some contact both with agriculture and with private enterprise.

A key part of the strategy to improve the lot of Polish consumers involved the opening of the economy to imports from outside of the Soviet bloc. Imports of consumer goods were to satisfy some of the consumer demands that domestic production was unable to meet at that stage, while imports of investment goods were to feed the technological change that was viewed as necessary to bring Polish productivity and product varieties up to the desired standards. The consequence of this strategy was that Poland ran very significant deficits in hard currency trade with the result that by 1980 the net hard currency debt stood at $23 billion.[2]

The events that led up to the democratization of Poland in 1989 can be traced to 1980 when worker protests led to the founding of the labour movement, Solidarity. Instead of simply acceding to wage concessions as had been the case in previous labour disputes, this time labour pushed the authorities to accept Solidarity as a legitimate expression of worker sentiment which was independent of the Communist Party. If allowed to develop further, this political pluralism would clearly have undermined the prevailing order in Poland, so the party responded by imposing martial law at the end of 1981. Subsequently, the activities of Solidarity were curbed, but the organization managed to continue underground. Solidarity was behind the large wave of strikes that took place in 1988 which led to a series of round-table discussions between Solidarity and the authorities. The upshot of these discussions was to allow free voting in June 1989 for a limited number of seats in parliament, with the rest being reserved for the Communist Party. The results of the election were decisive. Solidarity won virtually all of the freely contested seats, while the leaders of the Communist Party running without opposition failed to receive the minimal number of votes needed for their election to be considered valid. After several months of negotiation, eventually a new government was formed in August 1989 with Solidarity candidate Tadeusz Mazowiecki as prime minister and the economist Leszek Balcerowicz as vice-premier and finance minister.

From the outset, the new non-communist government faced a very difficult set of circumstances (Balcerowicz and Gelb 1994). The previous regime had made economic concessions which greatly increased de-mand pressures so that inflation was running at over 200 per cent in 1989. The service of the external debt was a heavy burden. The econo-

---

[2] This debt service ratio of 83% of GNP. This is the level of *contractual* debt service which is higher than the realized debt service reported in Ch. 2.

mies of Poland's main trading partners of the CMEA were in great flux. The success of Solidarity had bestowed the labour movement with considerable prestige, and labour had accumulated extensive power through the development of workers' councils in state-owned enterprises. Nevertheless, labour would be required to accept considerable sacrifices if the necessary investments and enterprise restructurings were to be made.

Perhaps because the large number of partial reforms of the past which were largely viewed as failures, the new government chose a strategy of rapid and extensive changes. All but a few prices were liberalized from 1 January 1990. There was a radical opening of foreign trade with most quotas being eliminated and tariffs set at relatively low levels. Most direct subsidies of enterprises were cut off. The incipient hyperinflation was to be cut short by a severe monetary policy. These liberalization and stabilization measures were to set the stage for the deep institutional changes needed to promote the growth of the private economy. We now examine in detail how these institutional changes took place within the financial sphere.

5.2. The Organization of the Banking Sector

As in other socialist systems, the banking sector in Poland that was in place from the 1950s through 1988 was designed as an adjunct of the state-planning mechanism. Credits were allocated according to quotas related to the plan and were not related to the creditworthiness of borrowers. As in other spheres, banking was organized effectively as a monopoly dominated by the national bank, Narodowy Bank Polski. In addition there were a few specialized state-owned banks. The fundamental departure from this monobank system was initiated by the Banking Law of 1989 which, with some amendments of detail, has determined the structure of the banking sector until the present. This law established two-tier banking. Central banking became the responsibility of the National Bank of Poland (NBP). The branches of the state bank were organized in nine state commercial banks operating on a regional basis. The 1989 law and administrative changes made it possible to create private banks organized as joint-stock companies. The requirements for licensing were relatively light, with a minimal capital generally set at 6 million ecu.

Table 5.1 reports the number of banks in Poland excluding the some 1,600 agricultural cooperative banks and branches of foreign banks. It is seen that there was a huge increase in the numbers of banks in Poland

TABLE 5.1   No. of commercial banks in Poland

Year-end	1988	1990	1992	1993	1994	1995 (July)
Total banks	6	75	87	95	85	75

Sources: *The Banking System in Poland 1992–3*, *Poland International Economic Report*, 1993/4 and 1994/5, and the National Bank of Poland.

TABLE 5.2   Distribution of bank assets in Poland (million zlotys)

		Dec. 1992	Dec. 1993
1.	Specialized state banks	337,886,000	453,322,000
2.	Regional state banks	191,397,000	263,019,000
3.	1 + 2	529,283,000	716,341,000
4.	Others	123,427,000	199,989,000
5.	Total	652,710,000	916,330,000
6.	1/5	52%	49%
7.	2/5	29%	29%
8.	3/5	81%	78%

Sources: *Gazeta Bankowa* and NBP.

in 1990 when many banks were founded at the initiative of Polish enterprises. Subsequently the growth slowed, and since 1993 the total number of banks has dropped. This consolidation of the banking sector has taken place as a number of the start-up banks fell into difficulty. They were subsequently taken over by stronger banks or in some cases liquidated. Since early 1993 only one bank licence has been granted.

This rapid rise and subsequent fall in the total number of commercial banks gives the impression of openness of the banking sector to entry and exit. In fact, this dynamism is largely limited to the new banks which are generally small. Otherwise, the banking sector is still heavily dominated by the nine regional commercial banks created from the national bank plus the specialized state-banking institutions. Table 5.2 gives a breakdown of the total balance sheet of the banking sector excluding cooperative banks.[3] More than three-quarters of bank assets are in the hands of the commercial and specialized banks that have emerged di-

[3] In early 1995 Poland carried out a currency reform in introducing new zlotys which were equal to 10,000 old zlotys. All zloty amounts quoted in this chapter are for old zlotys. At the end of 1994 the exchange rate was approximately 24,000 old zlotys per $US.

rectly from the old monobank. About half of the total assets are in the hands of five specialized banks.

Table 5.3 gives an overview of the state-dominated banks ranked by share of total assets of all commercial banks in 1993. These constituted fifteen of the sixteen largest Polish banks as judged by asset size in 1993. The largest banks are PKO-BP and PKO-SA (the state savings banks) which were originally specialized in domestic currency deposits and foreign currency deposits respectively. Next in size is Bank Handlowy of Warsaw, a bank founded in 1870 which was allowed to exist under the communist regime as a bank specializing in foreign trade. BGŻ is a bank specializing in the agricultural sector of the Polish economy. Since its founding in the 1970s it has been the big brother to the large number of rural cooperative banks spread throughout the country. Unlike other banks which were owned directly by the state treasury, a large minority interest (46 per cent) is held by the cooperative banks which rely on it for funding. This interlocking control structure has arguably been the origin of the considerable problems with had loans in the agricultural sector and has impeded attempts at restructuring BGŻ. After these very large state banks rank the nine regional commercial banks which were spun off from the NBP plus two smaller development banks.

The remainder of the banking sector consists of about sixty 'private' banks which have been created since 1989. Calling these banks 'private' is somewhat misleading in that in most cases the original owners were Polish state-owned enterprises, many of which had not been privatized as of 1995. Thus the state dominance of banking is even greater than the concentration ratios in Table 5.2 would suggest. Foreign bank participation in Poland has been relatively limited. This may have partially reflected the reluctance of large international banks to invest in Poland while there were disputed debts outstanding. After the agreement in the spring of 1994 with the London Club of creditors, this obstacle was removed. However, by that time the Polish authorities were reluctant to grant new bank licences in part as a means of encouraging foreign banks to become strategic partners in banks being privatized. By early 1995 thirteen banks had a majority of foreign ownership, and this was concentrated in the smaller-sized banks.

In order to change the pattern of state dominance in banking, Polish authorities have initiated a programme of privatizing the major banks. The ministry of finance is in charge of the programme and declared its intention of privatizing the nine regional commercial banks by the end of 1996. By mid-1995 only three of the original nine regional commercial banks and two smaller development banks had been privatized so that the target was unlikely to be met. The strategy in privatization

TABLE 5.3   Large Polish banks 1995

Name	Type	Assets 1993 (billion zlotys)	Asset share	Privatized[a]
1. PKO-BP (Powszechna Kasa Oszczędności BP Warszawa)	Specialized state savings bank	140,219	15	no
2. PKO-SA (Pekao SA Warszawa)	Specialized foreign currency savings bank	124,858	14	no
3. Bank Handlowy w Warszawie	Specialized foreign trade bank	71,861	8	no
4. BGŻ (Bank Gospodarki Żywnościowej Warszawa)	Specialized agricultural bank	69,674	8	no
5. Powszechny Bank Kredytowy SA Warszawa	Regional commercial bank	41,154	4	no
6. Powszechny Bank Gospodarczy Lodz	Regional commercial bank	40,190	4	no
7. Bank Śtąski Katowice	Regional commercial bank	39,311	4	yes
8. Bank Przemystowo-Handlowy SA Kraków	Regional commercial bank	32,959	4	yes
9. Bank Gdański	Regional commercial bank	26,651	3	no
10. Pomorski Bank Kredytowy SA Szczecin	Regional commercial bank	24,148	3	no
11. Wielkopolski Bank Kredytowy Poznań	Regional commercial bank	21,558	2	yes
12. Bank Zachodni SA Wroclaw	Regional commercial bank	20,590	2	no
13. Bank Depozytowo-Kredytowy W Lublinie SA	Regional commercial bank	16,458	2	no
14. Bank Rozwoju Eksportu Warszawa	Specialized export development bank	7,307	1	yes
15. Polski Bank Rozwoju SA Warszawa	Specialized development bank	6,747	1	yes

[a] As of July 1995.

Source: *Gazeta Bankowa*.

employed in each case was similar. The bank was recapitalized either through a stake taken by the treasury or through the Financial Restructuring Act applied generally to the sector. Then a major foreign partner is found to purchase another significant stake. Additional shares are then sold through an initial public offering with employees bcing allocated a block at a price equal to half of the offering price.[4] The first two public issues were conventional fixed-price offerings. Since both issues were heavily oversubscribed and successful bidders realized very large gains, the finance ministry was severely criticized as having grossly underpriced the deals. In order to avoid this problem the third commercial bank offering was executed as an auction on the Warsaw Stock Exchange. So far the Polish authorities have not attempted to submit any of the large specialized banks to privatization.

Privatization of banks in Poland has been slowed by the same factors which have slowed privatization in other spheres, namely management and employee resistance and political opposition to rapid privatization. In addition, the strategy of seeking a strategic foreign partner has posed something of a dilemma for the authorities. In order to attract foreign partners, the offering price cannot be set too high. However, if, after the sale, the deal looks as if it is underpriced, the responsible officials are open to public criticism and possible loss of their job. In the face of this there is a natural tendency to got slow. Furthermore, there is a widely held view that Polish commercial banks are too small and regionally based to be attractive. As a result, there has been lobbying by some interested parties to consolidate some of the remaining state-owned commercial banks into large units before privatizing them.[5]

Many Polish reforms since 1989 have been aimed at creating competition. The emergence of a large number of new banks in Poland gives the appearance of competitive conditions. However, as judged by total assets or by other measures, banking activity is highly concentrated in a small number of large state-owned banks. Furthermore, the nine commercial banks that were spun off from the NBP were organized on a geographic basis. While there is no legal obstacle to their branching into other regions, the tendency has been to concentrate activities in the original region. Table 5.4 reports the three-bank concentration ratios

---

[4] The first major privatization was the Wielkopolski Bank Kredytowy which after its offering in 1993 had an ownership consisting of 28.5% EBRD, 30% state treasury, 14.3% to employees, and 27.2% public investors. This was followed in 1994 by Bank Śląski owned 25% by ING Bank (Netherlands), 34% by the state treasury, 10% by employees, and 30.1% by public investors. Bank Przemysłozo-Handlowy was privatized in early 1995 and had an ownership which was distributed: 46.61% state treasury, 15.06% EBRD, 5.31% ING Bank, 4.57% Daiwa, 9.24% large Polish institutional investors, 2.21% employees, and 13% public investors. See Zemplinska (1995).

[5] By late 1995 it appeared that these efforts were beginning to change the direction of Poland's bank privatization programme. In particular, parliament had approved a bill transferring the large minority stake the treasury had retained in a bank previously privatized (Bank Przemysłowo-Handlowy) to a large specialized bank which remained state-owned (Bank Handlowy of Warsaw). In this way it attempted to force a merger of the two banks. If such a merger were put into effect, the consequence would be a *de facto* renationalization of a recently privatized bank.

TABLE 5.4　Regional bank concentration in Poland (share of regional branches in three largest banks, excluding BGZ and cooperative banks, %)

North-east	South-east	South	West	North	Central
59	62	51	51	56	40

Sources: Jerschina (1995) and own calculations.

for the six major geographic regions of Poland. In the calculation we have excluded BGŻ and the cooperative banks which are exclusively devoted to the agricultural sector. Bank size is measured by the number of branch offices. With the exception of the central region (which includes Warsaw), in each region three banks account for at least 50 per cent of the total bank branches. This relatively dense branching by a few banks in any given region may mean the banks face weak competition in attracting depositors which in turn translates into low funding costs. At the national level much the same applies to the large specialized banks, PKO-BP, PKO-SA, and BGŻ, whose very large deposit base gives them a competitive advantage in funding.

Thus, despite administrative efforts to remove barriers to bank competition, the structure of Polish banking has tended to remain concentrated in a way that endows the commercial banks emerging from the ex-monobank with important competitive advantages. What of bank performance? Table 5.5 shows that the average intermediation margin for the Polish banking sector has declined steadily since 1990. There are at least two possible explanations for this. This may indicate that growing competition in Polish banking is squeezing profitability. Alternatively, this may reflect an increasing problem of bad debts as borrowers are subjected to systematic shocks not adequately compensated by the lending rates charged. Information on bad loans, to be discussed below, suggests that the latter interpretation is quite plausible. As a consequence, the decline in average intermediation margins cannot be taken as a proof that Polish reforms have created a competitive banking environment.

Another perspective on bank performance is provided by bank profitability. Recent data indicates that the profit rate for wholly Polish banks has been 6.7 per cent whereas that of foreign-owned banks has been 47.2 per cent.[6] Arguably, the foreign-owned banks which are start-up banks

---

[6] Profit rate is defined as net revenues divided by gross costs (= operating expenses + interest cost + provisions). So*urce*: NBP.

TABLE 5.5   Average intermediation margin (%)

	1990	1991	1992	1993
Margin	17	5.5	2.8	0.5

Definition: (Total interest received less total interest paid)/total balance assets.

Sources: NBP and OECD.

have relatively higher funding costs than do the large state banks. The lower profitability of the latter is very likely linked to the number of non-performing loans in their portfolio.[7]

To summarize, even though a large number of new banks have been created since 1989, the State continues to dominate the banking sector. Bank privatization is changing this picture only slowly. Banking remains highly concentrated in a handful of large institutions. Some of the largest are state-owned specialized banks which have inherited considerable competitive advantages. Nevertheless, these banks have been among the poorest performers. All this suggests that there remains considerable untapped potential for improving the efficiency of the banking sector.

5.3. Money Markets and Monetary Policy

Poland's stabilization policy has relied heavily on monetary tools. Given the background of socialist banking, this strategy staked much on one of the weakest links in the economic system. There was a clear need to develop a structure of monetary policy which would give the authorities an adequate control of the factors influencing inflation and economic activity while at the same time being consistent with the liberalization of the financial sector. The actions taken in 1990 made it clear how the Polish authorities intended to achieve this goal. There was to be a strong central bank operating at some remove from the political process and a modern monetary market built around the treasury securities. It is remarkable that despite the considerable political instability in Poland the progress towards this goal has been steady and perceptible.

---

[7] The unweighted average return on assets in 1993 for the 16 largest Polish banks was 1.75 per cent. During the same period the return was 0.33 per cent for PKO-BP and 0.04 per cent for PKO-SA, the two large savings banks. BGŻ did not report profits for that period but was generally viewed as running at a substantial loss.

The rules governing the central bank are set out in the National Bank of Poland (NBP) Act of January 1989. This specified that the fundamental objective pursued by the NBP is the strengthening of the currency. However, it also specified that the NBP must collaborate in implementing the government's economic policy. As in a number of OECD countries the independence of the central bank is to be promoted by the fact that the NBP is accountable only to parliament but its president is nominated by the President of the Republic.

The other role of the central bank is to regulate and supervise the banking system. The NBP has the power to liquidate a bank or impose a merger with another banking institution in cases where the bank's capital base decreases by half.

Prior to the establishment of two-tiered banking in Poland, the main instruments of financial control were directed lines of credit which were granted to state-owned enterprises (SOEs) on the basis of quota. There were no monetary and capital markets as they are known in developed capitalist economies. The centrepiece of financial liberalization is to establish freedom for negotiation of interest rates and other conditions between lenders and borrowers. To this end Poland has moved since 1989 towards the forms of monetary control used in mature capitalist economies. Controls on setting interest rates on credits and deposits were removed in October 1990. Since January 1993, the NBP has ceased the general use of credit quotas for banks, preferring instead more indirect instruments.[8] The instruments of monetary control are: (i) mandatory reserves, (ii) refinance credits, (iii) discount and Lombard credits, and (iv) open-market operations.

The requirement that banks maintain mandatory reserves was introduced in 1989. The mandatory reserve ratio to zloty deposits has been rapidly increased from 1.8 per cent in January 1990 to 23 per cent for demand deposits and 10 per cent for time deposits in 1994. Since February 1994 commercial banks are obliged to transfer to NBP obligatory reserves not only for deposits in zloty but foreign exchange deposits (0.75 per cent of demand deposits and 0.5 per cent of time deposits) as well. Since the beginning of 1992 banks' resources in current account in the NBP are interest-free. In accordance with the NBP Act, interest accruing on the mandatory reserves are assigned to the Agricultural Restructuring and Debt Restructuring Fund.

Refinance credits are a direct extension of the centralized credit

---

[8] Some of the actions of the central bank have gone against this general liberalizing tendency. Specifically, at the end of 1991 the NBP adopted strict rules which prohibited the 9 large regional commercial banks from increasing credits to state-owned enterprises which had fallen behind in servicing their existing loans.

allocation practices of the past. In this procedure commercial banks receive funds at the standard refinance rate on the basis of a proposed loan to a SOE. The lending rate is equal to the refinance rate plus a margin (usually around 3 per cent) that is negotiated with the NBP. Since the loans carry a state guarantee, the banks bear little risk on such loans.

Other monetary policy tools are linked to the market for Polish treasury bonds and bills. At the end of 1990, banks did not hold any government paper except for bills issued by the NBP which were available to all investors (both corporate and individual) and which became gradually a more attractive alternative to bank deposits. Since 1991 the NBP began weekly auctions of treasury bills, and sale of NBP bills was finally halted at the end of 1992. This has facilitated the use of the rediscount mechanism whereby a bank may receive reserves from the NBP using treasury securities as collateral. Since 1992 the NBP has used open-market operations, that is, purchasing and selling treasury securities as an important means of monetary control. Furthermore, there has developed an active interbank market for NBP reserves in which banks which fall short of required reserves may obtain them from other banks with excess reserves at market-determined rates. The Polish money market is a domestic market in which the participating banks must be registered in Poland. Beside treasury bills other short-term fixed-income instruments treated are certificates of deposit, bank bills, and commercial paper.

We now describe the development of the Polish monetary policy in quantitative terms. Table 5.6 reports the trends in Polish interest rates and inflation since 1990. We see that the incipient hyperinflation of 1989–1990 was effectively brought under control by 1991. Retail price inflation dropped steadily to the end of 1994. Producer price inflation also fell sharply from the very high levels of 1990. The high level of interest rates suggests that tight monetary policy was instrumental in this.[9] A measure of monetary tightness is the real rate of interest rate defined as the nominal rate less the *expected* inflation rate over the period covered by a loan. Measuring expected inflation is not a simple matter, but if we approximate this by the actual inflation rate of producer prices realized over the period of the loan we see that by this measure real rates in Poland have been positive since 1990 (Table 5.7).

The details of Table 5.6 tell us some interesting stories about the state of the Polish financial sector over the period covered. The term structure of interest rates on interbank deposits is generally positive and was

[9] Until the end of 1992 quantitative limits on credits were in force. Calvo and Coricelli (1993) report that during the initial period the credit limits were not binding.

TABLE 5.6   Inflation and interest rates in Poland (%)

	1990	1991	1992	1993	1994	1995 (May)
Inflation (percentage change over 12 months)						
Retail prices	249.3	60.4	44.3	37.6	29.5	32.3
Producer prices	192.8	35.7	31.5	35.9	27.9	29.7
Interest rates (year end)						
Refinance rate	55	40	38	35	33	31
Discount rate	48	36	32	29	28	27
Interbank rate						
0–1 month	54.3	36.7	35.8	31.4	24.8	26.1
3–6 months	53.5	44.0	38.4	35.7	26.1	24.1
6–12 months	55.2	45.7	41.0	36.5	29.4	26.6
12–24 months	57.7	50.3	43.1	43.4	31.3	28.2

Source: NBP.

very steep at the end of 1993 when very short-term interbank funds carried a rate of 31 per cent while one- to two-year deposits had a rate of 43 per cent. A steep yield curve could be the consequence of an expectation of future increases in real rates or inflation rates or of higher-risk premium assigned to longer-term loans. Given that inflation rates were moderating at this time, the latter is the more likely explanation. The fact that the term structure has flattened subsequently may be indicative of growing confidence in the solidity of Polish commercial banks.

The rediscount rate has been somewhat below the short-term interbank rate, a pattern which is consistent with the fact that these credits are backed by treasury securities. The refinance rate has been above the short-term interbank rate but through 1993 below the rate on one- to two-year funds which on the basis of maturity are more directly comparable. The spread at the end of 1993 was substantial, 35 versus 43 per cent. This spread represents a substantial indirect subsidy for borrowers who qualify for refinance credits.

Otherwise in Table 5.6 it is seen that the inflation rate measured for consumer goods has been systematically above that for producer goods, although the difference between the two rates appears to be narrowing. One plausible reason to expect this pattern in a transition economy is that liberalization of trade gives rise to an influx of higher-quality imported goods. Since the CPI does not correct for changes in the quality

TABLE 5.7   Realized real interest rates in Poland

	1990	1991	1992	1993
Refinance rate less CPI inflation	−5.4	−4.3	0.4	6.5
Refinance rate less PPI inflation	19.3	8.5	2.1	7.1
Interbank rate (12 m.) less CPI inflation	−5.2	1.4	3.4	8.0
Interbank rate (12 m.) less PPI inflation	19.5	14.2	5.1	8.6

of the goods, this introduces an upward bias in CPI inflation rates. The producer price index is based on relatively more homogeneous goods where quality changes are likely to have been less important so that the PPI does not reflect a similar upward bias.[10]

This raises the question of which inflation rate should guide monetary policy. Statements of the NBP suggest that it takes the CPI was reference. As can be seen in Table 5.7, by this measure commercial real interest rates were negative in 1990 and have risen since then. Furthermore, by this measure the real refinance rate was negative in 1990–1 and approximately zero in 1992. In our view the quality change bias of the CPI means that the PPI is a better indicator for judging monetary policy. When judged by PPI, realized real commercial interest rates were extremely high in 1990 and have been declining subsequently. Thus by this indicator monetary policy has tended to become more lax as the transition progressed.

This discussion may place unwarranted emphasis on interest rates. It must be remembered that under communism interest rates had served no real function in regulating credit. So it is quite possible that the interest rates prevailing over this period were not equilibrium rates. For this and other reasons it is important to examine monetary policy from the point of view of the quantity of credits as well as their price.

We start by examining the central bank's balance sheet. Table 5.8 reports the NBP's total assets and their breakdown since the beginning of 1992. We report data starting from January 1992, since in that month there were important changes in accounting definitions which make comparisons with earlier periods difficult. All figures are expressed as percentage of total assets. First, we note that the total asset growth from January through December of 1992 was 55 per cent annualized. For 1993 the bank's asset grew 31 per cent, which was consistent with the view that the NBP was using monetary discipline to reduce the inflation

---

[10] A VAT was introduced in 1991 and subsequently the VAT rates have been modified. This was likely to have induced greater distortions in the CPI than in the PPI.

TABLE 5.8   Balance sheet of the National Bank of Poland

	Jan. 1992	Dec. 1992	Dec. 1993	Dec. 1994
Assets (% of total assets)				
1. Foreign	25	26	35	40
2. Government	23	42	41	37
2.1 Loans	13	15	5	3
2.2 Treasury securities	10	27	36	34
2.2.1 Treasury bills	3	14	22	16
2.2.2 Treasury bonds	7	13	14	17
3. Loans to financial institutions	38	17	16	13
3.1 Refinance credit	16	12	12	10
3.1.1 Central investment	7	7	7	7
3.1.2 Current account	4	2	3	3
3.1.3 Rediscount	2	1	1	1
3.1.4 Other refinance	2	2	1	0
3.2 Other financial sector credits	21	5	4	3
4. Other assets	14	16	8	9
Liabilities and capital (% of total assets)				
5. Foreign liabilities	7	7	15	19
6. Deposits	25	22	18	16
6.1 Government	5	4	6	5
6.2 Financial institutions	16	14	12	11
6.2.1 Reserves	16	14	10	9
6.3 Non-financial sector	4	4	0	0
7. Banknotes and coins	35	32	32	28
8. Other liabilities	33	38	36	37
TOTAL (billion zlotys)	196,597	293,246	385,687	527,974

Source: NBP.

rate. This policy may have been relaxed somewhat in 1994 as total assets grew 37 per cent.

Over the period covered, there were very dramatic changes in the composition of the central bank's balance sheet which reflected important transformations in the institutions of the financial sector. Perhaps the most important was a very strong increase in the share of securities, especially short-term Polish treasury bills, and the correspondingly rapid shrinkage of the budget sector. In essence this represents transformation of the state deficit into a securitized form in line with the practice in most OECD countries. In gencral this permits greater transparency in the management of the public debt as the size of treasury issues and their effect on market rates are readily observed. In addition this has permitted the NBP to shift the emphasis of its monetary policy to the use of open-market operations. The increased emphasis on the use of treasury bills is directly related to the efforts to create a liquid monetary market. When government loans and securities held by the NBP are aggregated, we see that this total as a proportion of total central bank assets grew very sharply during the course of 1992, after which it fell somewhat.

The total loans to financial institutions expressed as a percentage of total assets fell sharply in 1992. In part this was the consequence of operations in that year to shift liabilities from state-owned enterprises onto the government account. However, it is also due to the overall reduced use of refinance credits.

The breakdown of refinance credits reveals some interesting trends. It will be noted that rediscount credits have declined from 2 per cent of total asset to only 1 per cent of total assets. Furthermore Lombard credits represent a negligible fraction of total central bank assets. Thus, while the discount and Lombard rates are represented by the NBP as significant tools of monetary policy, their direct impact on credit creation has been slight and declining.

Other forms of refinance credit are often overlooked, but, in fact, these remain quite sizeable. In particular, central investment credits have grown in step with NBP assets, representing 7 per cent of the total. These credits have been used to support the activities of designated large SOEs, for example in the mining sector. While current account refinance credits are smaller in scale than central finance credits they actually grew as a fraction of NBP assets in 1993. Much of this growth was destined for the BGŻ as a means of financing agricultural stock-holding. As will be discussed below, agriculture has been a major source of bad loans in Poland. In addition, current account refinance has been used as a means of support for certain commercial banks which risked failure after being hit by sizeable bad loans.

The continued heavy reliance on refinance is strong evidence of the persistence of state-directed credit allocation. Of course, we cannot judge from an aggregate balance sheet whether these have been destined for creditworthy borrowers. It is clear however that heavy use of refinance implies significant subsidies to qualified borrowers who come essentially from the state-owned sector. For example, if we assume a 3 per cent bank margin, the cost to an enterprise of refinance credits in 1993 was 38 per cent as compared to something over 43 per cent on commercial loans. Thus, if we consider this a 5 per cent subsidy applied to the 46.2 trillion (10^{12}) zlotys of refinance credits, this constituted an indirect subsidy of 2.31 trillion zlotys or approximately $115 million per year. Some might say that this does not reflect an active policy of the central banks because it is likely that a large fraction of the central investment refinance credit growth is simply capitalized amortization and interest for old loans that are not being serviced by distressed SOEs. Even if this is true, the tenacity of some forms of refinance means that the budget constraints faced by some major SOEs have remained soft five years into the transition process largely because of discretionary interest subsidies.

The finally we note the relatively high level of foreign assets held by the central bank. In part this is needed to serve as counterpart to the high level of foreign currency deposits within the banking system which provide Polish savers with a form of inflation hedge. The strong growth of these foreign assets in 1993 and 1994 also reflects foreign aid and capital inflows.[11] However, because of the increased importance of what has come to be known as cross-border trade, not all apparent capital inflows are real. Specifically during since 1993 increasing numbers of foreign consumers (especially German) were coming to Poland's border regions to make purchases in informal markets where they found large advantages. This trade is conducted in foreign currencies. Statistically, this is not captured in the trade statistics, rather the increase in currency holds is treated as a capital flow.

To have a broader view of Polish credit patterns we summarize in Table 5.9 the consolidated balance sheet of Polish commercial banks, excluding the cooperative banks. Again the data are available on a consistent basis only since January 1992.

Since 1991 there have been important changes in the make-up of the portfolios of commercial banks in Poland. The first thing to note is that loans to enterprises have declined relative to other assets. This indicates a significant credit contraction brought on by transition. Possible reasons for this are clear. Disruption of previous trade patterns and large changes in relative prices have meant that many previously strong SOEs have been making losses and are no longer creditworthy. New private enterprises have short track records that could be used to justify authorizing credits. Research based on a sample of Polish enterprises suggests that there was indeed a strong credit contraction in the early stages of Polish transition. This has been seen has one of the major causes of the sharp decline in aggregate income in Poland (see Calvo and Coricelli

---

[11] e.g. new foreign medium- and long-term loans during the first half of 1995 were $850 million compared to $173 million in all of 1994. Similarly, foreign direct investment rose from $291 million in 1984 to $336 million in the first half of 1995.

TABLE 5.9   Consolidated balance sheet of polish commercial banks

		Jan. 1992	Dec. 1992	Dec. 1993	Dec. 1994
Composition: (% of total assets)					
Asset					
1.	Foreign assets	14	16	14	16
2.	Financial sector assets	14	13	13	12
2a.	Interbank deposits	4	4	5	5
3.	Public sector assets	3	4	2	1
4.	Non-financial sector assets	42	38	36	34
4a.	Enterprise loans	40	36	34	32
5.	Securities	16	16	20	24
5a.	Treasury bills	4	8	9	11
5b.	Treasury bonds	10	7	10	11
5c.	Shares and other securities	0	0	0	0
6.	Other assets	11	13	15	14
Liabilities:					
7.	Zloty deposits	31	35	33	36
8.	Foreign currency deposits	13	14	18	18
9.	Capital and other liabilities	56	51	50	46
TOTAL ASSETS (billion old zlotys)		469,669	652,710	916,330	1,209,529

Source: NBP *Information Bulletin*, Jan. 1993 and Dec. 1993.

1993).[12] The data of Table 5.9 do not distinguish loans to state-owned enterprises and to private enterprises, and, as a result, they do not show whether the banking sector has tended to shift from lending to the state sector to the private sector as might be expected as part of the transition process. We return to this issue below.

A second fact to note in Table 5.9 is the increased proportion of bank assets held in the form of securities. The growth has been particularly marked with respect to treasury bills. This reflected several important developments. First, as has already been noted, the securitization of the Polish public debt helped to create a liquid money market. Commercial banks have naturally sought to use this opportunity to hold their assets in a more liquid form. Second, returns on government securities have been attractive because the continuing public budget deficit has forced the authorities to borrow heavily domestically. Finally, the banking sector has been pursuing safety by increasing holdings with good credit

[12] However, Berg and Sachs (1992) have argued that the growth of exports in exports in 1990 argues against the existence of a credit crunch.

ratings and short maturities. In part, they have been strongly encouraged in this by the public policy of bringing Polish banks up to the Basle capital standards.

Somewhat surprisingly, the share of interbank deposits has grown only slightly since 1991. One might have expected a strong growth in interbank lending as part of the development of financing patterns which bypass the central bank and the State. In particular, the commercial banks established in regions with relatively few growth opportunities would naturally be the suppliers of funds to banks in areas with relatively more growth opportunities. Alternatively, savings banks might supply funds to new private commercial banks with special expertise in evaluating borrowers in certain sectors. Judging from our aggregate data, there have not been major developments of this type.

A final point regarding the asset side of the ledger is that bank holdings of shares remains negligible. Polish bank law presents no obstacles to the creation of German-style universal banks, and such a development would be welcomed in many circles. The available data suggest that this is yet to be realized. We will see some of the possible reasons for this in discussions of enterprise-restructuring, privatization, and security market development.

Regarding the liabilities of commercial banks, Table 5.9 documents the steady increase in the share of bank funds coming from deposits (either in zlotys or in foreign currency). This is the parallel development of reduced reliance on directed NBP lines of credit.

The aggregated data of Table 5.9 do not allow us to approach the central issue of whether the Polish financial sector has modified substantially the pattern of credit flow. Fortunately, the NBP has also provided information on total bank credits outstanding at year-ends since 1990 by type of borrower and by type of lender. Table 5.10 presents the status of outstanding credits in 1994 after five years of transition. The category 'regional commercial banks' refers to the nine commercial banks split off from the national bank.

These data reveal immediately some important features of the Polish financial sector. The total credits outstanding of 415 billion zlotys less the 28 billion due the cooperative banks coincides with the 34 per cent of non-financial sector credits reported in Table 5.9. At the end of 1994, the commercial banks created since the beginning of 1990 still account for only 18 per cent of total bank credit outstanding. Nevertheless this represented a substantial increase from 1990 when these banks accounted for 3 per cent of outstanding credits. During this period the regional commercial banks share of credits fell from 43 to 32 per cent. The share of specialized banks has declined only slightly from 46 to 43

TABLE 5.10 Polish domestic, non-governmental credits outstanding,
31 December 1994 (%)

	Regional commercial banks	Specialized banks	Cooperative banks	New commercial banks	Total
1. State-owned enterprises	64	41	2	9	40
2. Privately owned enterprises	30	52	82	72	51
3. Bills of exchange	1	1	0	3	1
4. Households	4	6	16	16	8
5. Total 1–4	100	100	100	100	100
Total credits (billion zlotys)	133,972	178,366	28,206	74,843	415,387
As percent age of grand total	32	43	7	18	100

Source: NBP.

per cent. Loans to private enterprises account for 51 per cent of the overall portfolio, whereas loans to SOEs account for 40 per cent. This shows that there has been a substantial shift since 1990 in redirecting credits from state to private enterprises. New commercial banks lent mainly to private enterprises (72 per cent of their loan portfolio). In contrast, the regional commercial banks lent 60 per cent to state-owned enterprises and 30 per cent to private enterprises. This confirms what many would expect. The regional banks, only one of which had been privatized by the end of 1994, continued to be the major creditors of the state-enterprise sector. It may seem surprising that the specialized banks which were also essentially state-owned a substantially higher fraction of their lending to private enterprises (52 per cent). This is probably accounted for by the portfolio of BGŻ whose lending is directed largely towards agriculture which is substantially private. This also accounts for the fact that 82 per cent of the credits granted by cooperative banks were destined for the private sector.

Table 5.11 gives an indication of how the credit channels have evolved since 1990. We note that in 1990 most of the credits granted were directed towards the SOEs. However, given the small size of the private sector at that time, the 34 per cent of new credits destined to private firms meant that early on in the transition process there was already a

TABLE 5.11   Distribution of credit creation (%)

	1991	1992	1993	1994
1. State-owned enterprises	60.55	−48.55	29.89	29.86
2. Private enterprises	34.30	137.96	55.96	58.17
3. Bills of exchange	0.00	6.69	1.50	−1.00
4. Households	5.15	3.91	12.66	12.97
Total household and enterprise credit creation (billion zlotys)	73,387	57,097	83,047	83,697

Source: NBP.

clear redirection of credits underway. This became dramatic in 1992 when credits to SOEs shrunk in nominal terms. This reflected the combined effects of banks choosing to reduce exposure to SOEs as well as the restructuring of these enterprises as some were liquidated or privatized. While the credits granted to private firms grew substantially in 1992, this was insufficient to offset the contraction in lending to the SOEs. The net result was that the net creation of credits in 1992 was 57 billion zlotys in 1992 compared to 73 billion zlotys in 1991. Subsequently, the squeeze on the state sector subsided partially with about 30 per cent of new credits destined for SOEs, but still the real value of credits outstanding to SOEs declined in 1993 and 1994.[13]

Table 5.12 shows that the maturity structure of credits differs significantly for different categories of lender. The loan portfolios of the banks spun off from the monobank (the regional commercial banks and the specialized banks) contain a high proportion of long-term credits. In contrast, the new commercial banks lend very heavily on the short or medium term. In light of the distribution of credits to types of borrowers, this means that SOEs have continued to have relatively preferred access to long-term credits, whereas the new start-up companies have borrowed principally at shorter-term maturities. Another important distinction is that the new commercial banks have a higher proportion of interest arrears in their portfolio. This suggests that in lending heavily to the private sector, the new commercial banks have incurred relatively high levels of problem loans. We will return to the issue in the discussion of the bad-loan problem below.

This review of Polish monetary markets has been somewhat involved, but some relatively clear and simple facts have emerged from it. The development of the market for treasury bills and bonds has effectively

[13] The growth in credits outstanding for SOEs was 21% and 17% in 1993 and 1994 respectively, in both years below the inflation rate.

TABLE 5.12 Distribution of Polish credits by original maturity, 31 December 1994 (%)

	Regional commercial banks	Specialized banks	Cooperative banks	New commercial banks	Total
Up to 1 year	42	32	52	45	39
1 to 5 years	16	16	24	24	18
Over 5 years	37	42	8	10	33
Interest past due	5	10	16	21	11
	100	100	100	100	100

Source: NBP.

securitized the Polish public debt and has paved the way for the use of the tools of modern monetary policy, namely the discount mechanism and open-market operations. However, the NBP has not withdrawn totally from the use of directed lines of credit, as it has channelled subsidized funds to politically favoured segments of the state-enterprise sector. Monetary policy from 1989 was characterized by initially high real rates which have subsequently fallen. This enabled Poland to avoid slipping into hyperinflation and to follow a path of high real growth and high, but relatively stable, inflation. Access to credits has not been uniform as distinctive segments of the banking sector have emerged. The traditional credit channel of state-owned banks lending to state-owned enterprises has tended to perpetuate itself. This segment it large but is being scaled back. The new private banks have directed their lending to new private enterprises. This segment started small but is growing fast. This pattern is not surprising, and, even though some would have wished for a more radical reorientation of credit, it is consistent with a transition path towards an economy where the financial sector fully supports private sector development. More troubling has been the route taken by the state-owned specialized banks and the cooperative banks. The share of credits they account for is large and declining only slowly. These banks lent heavily to housing and agriculture, a practice which has produced significant numbers of bad loans.

5.4. *Deposit Guarantees*

When the nine regional commercial banks and the specialized commercial banks were separated from the NBP in 1989, they were granted comprehensive guarantees of all personal savings deposits. Under article 49 of the Banking Act the treasury is liable for claims in respect of savings deposits held at banks established prior to February 1989 (the NBP, nine regional commercial banks, five specialized commercial banks, and 1,664 local cooperative banks). There is no specific fund backing these guarantees, and they represent a general state treasury contingent liability. New private banks were not covered by the same guarantee. During 1993, as a number of private banks encountered significant problems of non-performing loans, there were reportedly runs in certain provinces. The response of the president of the NBP was to declare that, in advance of deposit insurance legislation, savings deposits not otherwise covered would be insured 100 per cent for amounts up to 1,000 ecu per person and 90 per cent for amounts between 1,000 and 3,000 ecu. In addition to deposit guarantees the NBP has intervened in a number of ways to prevent bank failures. Several potential private bank failures have been averted when the NBP extended refinance credits or arranged for a takeover by a larger bank. This has been done without loss to depositors.

In February 1995 a deposit insurance law came into effect formalizing the coverage as had been assured by the NBP previously. The upshot of these developments is that all depositors in Poland are protected by underfunded, state guarantees. Formally, the State's commitment is limited to no more than 3,000 ecu per person; however, the actions of the NBP may have established the precedent of protecting large deposits as well.

5.5. *Enterprise Restructuring and Financial Distress*

In this section we review the main developments in Polish enterprise-restructuring emphasizing the way that financial institutions have influenced this. The central feature of the transition from socialism to capitalism is the replacement of a diffuse system of economic authority by a better definition of property and control rights (see Hinds 1990). There are three general ways that this can be accomplished: (i) the State may privatize its assets; (ii) state enterprises may fail and their assets may be purchased by private enterprises; or (iii) higher growth rates in the private sector than in the public enterprise sector may diminish state control of productive resources. The financial sector plays a role in all three. Privatization involves the creation of claims on the firms' cash flows; if these claims are made tradable, securities markets are created. Enterprises generally close only under duress; consequently, banks and other financial creditors can play a major role in enterprise reorganization through bankruptcy. Finally, if state enterprises are less efficient than private ones, their rate of return on capital will be lower. Nevertheless, they can continue to flourish and grow relatively if their cost of capital is less. Thus growth rates of private and public enterprises are very dependent upon the way that banks and capital markets determine the costs of funds.

While the development of the private economy is widely viewed as crucial to improving the management of economic resources in the ex-socialist economies, there is less agreement on how the rights to control resources should be allocated. Here, in contrast to the development of monetary policy where something like a standard model is shared by most OECD countries, the West presents a bewildering variety of institutional forms of ownership and control. All these forms are alternative means of dealing with the basic dilemma of providing financial means to insiders who best know the firm and will inevitably make most operational decisions. Given their privileged position these insiders may attempt to run the firm for their own personal advantage and fail to provide the outsiders with the best return on their investment. From this point of view the various financial institutions of the West can be viewed as either favouring effective control of insiders or favouring arm's-length finance. It has been argued that in Eastern and Central Europe the erosion of authority of the Communist Party and its ultimate collapse has effectively left them a system where insiders have most of the power over resources (see Berglöf 1995). In Poland, to a great extent this power was concentrated in the hands of labour (see Frydman and Rapaczyński 1991b). If this is the case, one important consideration in evaluating the trends of private sector development in Poland is the issue of whether outsiders are given sufficient means of control to make them willing to finance the needed investments.

Public and private sector trends

We start with a review of some rough indicators of the allocation of economic resources between public and private enterprises. Table 5.13 records the numbers of state-owned enterprises and private companies annually since 1991. We see there has been a steady and strong reduction in the numbers of state-owned enterprises and a comparably steady growth in the numbers of registered companies and sole proprietorships. This may tend to exaggerate somewhat the importance of the private sector in Poland in part because the state-owned enterprises tend to be very large and private enterprises relatively small. Furthermore, a number of joint-stock companies are wholly or partially

TABLE 5.13   No. of enterprises in Poland at year-end, agricultural sector
excluded

	1991	1992	1993	1994
State-owned enterprises	8,228	7,344	5,924	4,955
Private enterprises[a]	n.a.	69,907	83,283	95,017
Proprietorships (millions)	1,420	1,630	1,784	n.a.

[a] Joint-stock companies and limited liability companies.
Sources: GUS *Statistical Bulletin* and OECD.

TABLE 5.14   Private sector development (% shares)

	1989	1990	1991	1992	1993
GDP	28.4	35.0	45.3	49.7	50+
Employment	43.9	45.1	50.2	53.7	57.5
Employment excluding private agriculture	29.6	30.9	36.6	40.4	45.2

Source: OECD *Economic Survey, Poland* (1994).

owned by the State either because they are in an intermediate stage of
the privatization process or because the State has decided to retain a
long-term strategic share.

Table 5.14 presents some alternative measures of the relative importance of the public and private sectors in Poland. The private share of
GDP is estimated to have grown steadily from 28 per cent in 1989 to
over 50 per cent by 1993. Similarly, by 1993 over 50 per cent of employment was in the private sector. While some of this high fraction is the
result of the large number of private farms in Poland, the trend towards
strong growth of the private sector is clear. We now examine in more
detail the institutional changes that are behind these trends in order to
see in what ways the Polish financial sector has facilitated or impeded
the reallocation of economic resources.

Privatization

Much of the early literature on the transition of Eastern and Central
Europe emphasized privatization. The shared assumption explicit or
implicit in this is that privatization would be the fast route to shrinking
state control of productive resources. In Poland, despite the early and

nearly universal recognition of the importance of privatization, its implementation has been slow. There have been several shifts in policy direction. Furthermore, the process of privatization in Poland emphasizes collective decisions by affected parties, a practice which has undoubtedly slowed the speed of privatization.

Polish privatization law envisages two alternative routes: (i) 'corporatization' or the transformation from a state-owned enterprise to a state-owned corporation (either joint-stock or limited liabilities company) whereby the minister of privatization executes the function of the owner and appoints a supervisory board of which two-thirds are representatives of the State and one-third of the company and (ii) the 'liquidation' route with the dissolution of an enterprise and the privatization of its assets.

The law states that following corporatization a company should be privatized within two years. There are two broad alternative for accomplishing this: individual privatization and mass privatization. The basic procedure for privatization that was employed through 1994 was based on initiative taken by the founding organ of the enterprise with the consultation of labour unions and workers' councils. Since the latter are effectively disenfranchised through the process, there was naturally a reluctance to accept privatization. Poland has experimented with a number of methods.[14] The first to be tried was capital privatization. This consists of transforming the firm into either a joint-stock company or a limited liability company which is then sold. Under Polish privatization law employees may purchase 20 per cent of the shares of the company at a discounted price. The amount of the discount is 50 per cent of the price for the general public or an amount equal to the total wages paid employees in the previous year whichever is less. Alternative privatization methods include employee buyouts and liquidations.

Discussing privatization results as of March 1992, Frydman *et al.* (1993) report that approximately 1,000 SOEs had undergone transformation under Polish privatization law. Half of these were closed down. Of the remaining 500 firms, the most common form of privatization was an employee buyout. This suggests that employee power to block privatizations effectively allowed them to concentrate property rights in their own hands. The process was further facilitated by a feature under Polish privatization law which allows the State to maintain ownership of productive assets and to lease them to employee-owned privatized company. This form of privatization was accompanied by preferential

---

[14] A detailed discussion of Polish privatization can be found in Frydman *et al.* (1993).

conditions: interest was tax-deductible, capped at either 30 per cent or 75 per cent of the refinancing rate, and only 30 per cent of interest due must be paid in the first two years and arrears must be cleared in the third year. In at least twenty-one cases, the new organization was a joint venture between employees and the original firm's founding organization, i.e. the ministry or government unit most directly concerned. In these cases (employee buyout plus lease or employee–state joint venture) the firm has been privatized in a formal sense. However, the State remains as owner of the means of production either solely (when it leases to employees) or jointly (when it is a shareholder). In neither case is it clear that the controlling interest in the organization is in the hands of an agent seeking to maximize profits.

It is perhaps not surprising that piecemeal privatization has been relatively slow and that the process has not removed all fuzziness in firm objectives. Indeed, it was the anticipation of just such an outcome which led many analysts to call for a mass privatization process where traditional power blocs would be neutralized. In Poland, mass privatization has been the subject of constant debate since 1989, but, early in 1995, there were no results under this method. Formally, the method involves SOEs so privatized to become private companies. The shares of the companies included are distributed initially to mutual funds, managed with the help of possibly foreign advisers. Shares in mutual funds are to be placed in the hands of Polish investors through an original issue. Subsequently, shares in firms and mutual funds may be traded. In early 1995 investment managers of the mutual funds had been selected; however, it was still unclear how quickly this process would be implemented and which firms would be privatized in this way.

In awaiting the implementation of Polish mass privatization, a large number of Polish state enterprises have been allowed to operate for six years into transition without any major restructuring. In most cases this probably has meant little effective control by outsiders. Furthermore the form of mass privatization makes it doubtful whether privatization *per se* will do much to create more effective control by outside investors. Shares are to be allocated to the various investment funds on a fairly equal basis. They do not compete (at least explicitly) for these shares. From this starting in principle the funds will need to compete to keep their shareholders. However, if all the funds continue to keep broadly diversified portfolios, they will all have the same performance and private investors will have little reason to shift from one fund to another. In this way, managers can continue to collect their fees without making the effort to exert control in firms where they hold shares. It is true that investment advisers will benefit from superior profit performance. However, it is unclear that the potential benefits from playing the active role of a dominant shareholder would repay the considerable effort this would require.

Financial distress

An alternative route to reallocating the productive assets of SOEs to new owners is through bankruptcy. If the firm is placed on a commercial basis (e.g. as in the case of joint-stock companies wholly owned by the Polish treasury) and if creditors apply the financial discipline of maximizing profits, the firm's budget constraint is effectively hardened. In principle, if the firm is making losses it either changes its operations to become profitable or the creditors use legal means to force it to do so. However, there are a number of factors that may prevent creditors from exerting effective control in this way. First, creditors may not have access to the information necessary to tell whether the firm is distressed. Second, creditors may be dispersed so that gains to the active enforcement of debt contract by any one creditor may be small. For both these reasons, it is generally thought that among possible creditors banks will be best suited to play the role of active monitors of borrowers (see Diamond 1984). Furthermore, if the bankruptcy process in a country is overly complicated or gives most power to the borrower, the cost involved will impede the control of distressed firms by creditors. In ex-socialist countries, the lack of bank experience in enforcing credit contracts and the underdevelopment of bankruptcy procedures suggest that obstacles to creditor activism will be greater than in mature capitalist economies (see Mitchell 1993). Nevertheless, overcoming these difficulties potentially could have a big payoff, since otherwise the informational and other asymmetries between firm insiders and outside could severely undermine investment and growth. We now review the steps taken in Poland to promote creditor activism towards distressed borrowers.[15]

In Poland, the legal means for dealing with financial distress include liquidation, bankruptcy, and judicial reconciliation. Liquidation has proved relatively more widely practised than the other two procedures. The term 'liquidation' is usually taken to mean that the firm's productive assets are broken up and sold off to the highest bidder in order to pay creditors according to absolute priority of claims. In fact, in Poland legal liquidation has been used as part of a more informal process of negotiation among interested parties in distressed firms the outcome of

---

[15] This is also treated at length by Dittus (1994) and Baer and Gray (1994).

which may maintain the assets in place. Once it is clear what form the restructured firm is to take the firm is formally liquidated with its assets acquired by the new firm or by the creditors who then lease to the new firm. The fact that this route is frequently used in Poland suggests that the judiciary is not playing a strong role in making an independent determination of how to best maximize the value of firm assets.

In contrast, formal bankruptcy has been less widely used for resolving financial distress in Poland. One possible reason for this is that under bankruptcy law tax liabilities are given higher priority than financial liabilities. Furthermore, the government has an automatic lien over all property of any party in arrears. Since 1990 a great many enterprises have accumulated very substantial tax arrears.[16] If tax liabilities are large relative to the value of the firm, banks may believe that as junior claimants they have no incentive to provoke bankruptcy proceedings. This is especially the case as bank debt may have been serviced at least partially while taxes went unpaid, implicitly a deviation from normal creditor priority. Of course, for this to work the State must remain passive. As senior claimant one might expect that the State would have had an interest in provoking bankruptcy before asset values are eroded to a level less than the tax liabilities.[17] In fact, this was not the policy adopted by the Polish State during the first four years of transition. In so doing it allowed budget constraints to remain relatively soft. Moreover, all bank loans, whether or not secured, have priority over other creditors even if the latter are secured.

One further means of resolving financial distress that has been available from the outset of Polish transition is court reconciliation (see Belka 1994). Under this procedure a firm may restructure its financial claims, but not its tax liabilities, upon reaching agreement with creditors. For plans which call for 40 per cent or greater write-downs of liabilities, approval is required of creditors representing at least 80 per cent by value of the outstanding claims. Again, since tax liabilities are senior claims and represent a large fraction of the assets in place, financial creditors may have little incentive to agree to plans under court conciliation. However, some features of the conciliation procedure were borrowed in the Financial Restructuring Act of 1993. We shall see below that the modified procedure, called bank conciliation, has emerged as an important means of financial restructuring in Poland.

---

[16] In Poland the tax liability of a firm is not eliminated as its operating net revenues fall to zero. The reason is the *popywek* whereby taxes are assessed on salary increases in excess of an official index. Thus firms can be profitable before tax but loss-making after tax.

[17] In the US banks are frequently senior, and often secured, creditors. In cases of financial distress they are frequently the party to provoke a bankruptcy. See Asquith *et al.* (1994).

Alternatives to privatization or financial distress

Looking for productivity gains principally through privatization and bankruptcy supposes that state-owned enterprises will not willingly be reallocated resources unless their ownership is restructured. Some have questioned this assumption, arguing that exposing these enterprises to competition will force them to restructure. In particular, the resources channelled through the public sector may shrink, at least relatively to the private sector, if SOEs are cut off from subsidies, thus inducing them to abandon uneconomic activities and shed labour.

In Poland several studies have looked at firm-level data to shed light on this issue. Pinto *et al.* (1993) surveyed seventy-five large SOEs covering the period from June 1989 through June 1992. They find that, even though their formal ownership and organizational structure had not been changed, these SOEs as a group had been surprisingly aggressive in adapting to the new conditions of the transition economy. It was estimated that between mid-1989 and mid-1992, employment in these firms fell by 27.2 per cent. Labour was shed both by profitable firms and loss-making firms. The survey suggests that during the course of the three years covered, firms' decision-making was placed increasingly on a commercial basis. For example, initially in the transition period, the use of interenterprise credit rose very strongly but was later reduced substantially. One possible reason for this was that firms gained a clearer idea of the risks associated with this type of credit. The authors of the study thus argue that it is not private ownership *per se* which is the key to making enterprises efficient. They emphasize the importance of hard budget constraints and the expectations of future privatization of the enterprise can be an effective means of inducing change. It should be noted, however, that while the firms may have been cut off from direct subsidies, tax arrears rose substantially for the firms covered so that budget constraints were indirectly allowed to remain soft.

Pinto and Van Wijnbergen (1994) reconsider the same data to carry out some simple tests to see whether there had been a significant shift in firm behaviour. They note that the main changes in behaviour came after they had faced more severe credit constraints. They interpret this as evidence that Polish banks became more aggressive monitors of state enterprises and that tightening of the financial budget constraints could do much to promote the efficiency of state enterprises in advance of privatization. In fact, the credit constraints in Poland became binding when in 1992 the finance ministry forbade banks to advance loans to state enterprises which were not servicing their outstanding loans satisfactorily. Thus the initiative came from the authority of the State and was not the result of the decentralized decisions of profit-minded bankers.

These results are important in that they cast doubt on the overly simplified view that state-owned enterprises are inevitably the source of great waste. However, the limitations of the data mean that the results are open to doubt. In particular, the sample covers only a small fraction of the more than 5,000 SOEs in Poland, and it specifically excludes some of the largest and most politically sensitive of these on the grounds that they would not be representative. However, this is precisely where the inefficiencies are likely to be greatest. Second, the period covers the earliest stage of transition when the widely shared expectation was that early privatization was very likely for most state enterprises. Given the slowness of the privatization process in Poland and the political back-lash to rapid liberalization, the prospect of privatization for the remaining state enterprises is less clear. This change of expectations could have had an important impact on the behaviour of firm managers who no longer needed to be as concerned about pleasing their future private owners nor proving management ability so that they could do well on the job market. Third, the only action of the firms which unambiguously indicated restructuring was their willingness to shed labour. This is very crude and reflects only one aspect of improving efficiency. The ability to perceive and undertake good investment projects is another which is totally absent from the analysis.

The discussion of this section presents something of a paradox. Privatization was meant to be the fastest means of shifting productive resources from public to private control, but in Poland it has proved to be the slowest. Piecemeal privatization has often given rise to employee-owned companies operating state-owned plant and equipment under long-term leases. This is the securitized markets' equivalent of old-style state-owned enterprise. Mass privatization has been delayed because of lack of political will-power. The alternative route to enterprise restructuring through financial distress has been slow primarily because of inefficiencies in the bankruptcy procedure tend to make banks passive and because the State as senior creditor has been shy of provoking bankruptcies. Despite these institutional failures, the private sector is growing and the public enterprise sector is shrinking. And overall industrial growth has been strong since 1993 even though many of the micro-conditions meant to be favourable to gains in efficiency were not yet in place.

How can one account for this set of apparently contradictory circumstances? In part, survey evidence suggests that the restructuring of state-owned enterprises in 1990–1 has been much greater than had been expected. More generally, however, it seems likely that dynamic private firms are simply bidding away resources from the public sector. Where have they obtained the financial means to do this? Inevitably, some of the growth has been self-financed as small start-up firms in most countries grow from retained earnings. However, the credit flows presented in Tables 5.10 and 5.11 showed that the banking sector, with the exception of the large regional commercial banks, has strongly expanded lending to the private sector.

5.6. Bank Recapitalization and the Bad-Debt Problem

One of the central objectives of financial transition is to develop banks and other financial institutions capable of accurately assessing enterprise prospects and monitoring project execution. An important precondition for banks to be efficient monitors is they be adequately capitalized. In an insolvent bank the owners' stake becomes valueless; they have little incentive to see that management performs well. Any marginal improvement of the bank's value will accrue to other stakeholders (such as depositors, deposit insurance funds, or the government). Thus a bank that has been weakened, whether from poor lending practices or from a systemic shock that was outside its control, is unlikely to take the actions necessary to restore itself to financial health. If this occurs in a single small bank, its liquidation may resolve the problem relatively quickly. However, when a system-wide shock has weakened many banks or when the bank is a dominant institution for the financial system, there may be a need for public intervention for bank recapitalization.

In the context of transition the loan portfolio inherited from the communist past consisted essentially of credits granted to SOEs, many of which were assumed to be inefficient and expected to become money-losers after price and trade liberalization. It was to be expected then that commercial banks created out of the monobank may well have negative net worth. Thus in order to create an adequately capitalized banking system had loans need to be eliminated and/or additional capital needs to be placed on bank balance sheets. Since this is a system-wide problem there are evidently some possible gains to dealing with the problem in a comprehensive way. Furthermore, the web of bad debts was pervasive. Consequently, a general forgiveness of the stock of old debts would render the system solvent. According to this line of reasoning, in removing the stock of old, bad loans from the system, the flow of new loans would be assessed on a profit-maximizing basis (see Begg and Portes 1993).

In fact, Poland did not treat bad debts and bank recapitalization in a centralized fashion as a simple matter of accounting. In part this was so for the same reasons that made central planning difficult: a lack of complete information and the organizational distortion of incentives. However, several years into transition, Poland did adopt and ambitious, if partial, programme to deal with bad debts and bank capitalization. Furthermore, according to some analyses this programme contributed directly to the development of efficient bank monitoring and of accelerating the pace of enterprise restructuring (Pinto and van Wijnbergen 1994).

The February 1993 Law on Financial Restructuring was designed for two purposes. First, it introduced on a temporary basis a simplified procedure for financial restructuring of enterprises. Second, it recapitalized selected banks on condition that they restructured their portfolio of designated bad loans. This simplified restructuring procedure, called bank conciliation, is a modified version of court reconciliation described above. A detailed discussion is given by Belka (1994). The main innovations were that (i) an agreement to restructure the liabilities required the approval of at least 50 per cent of the creditors by value (as opposed to 80 per cent under court conciliation), (ii) tax liabilities were included which meant for debtors with large tax arrears a restructuring plan was readily accepted once it has government approval, and (iii) if a secured debtor refused to participate in conciliation his claim was limited to his security. It is clear that these modifications overcame some of the important hold-out reconciliation problems in conventional bankruptcy and court reconciliation (Gertner and Scharfstein 1991). It should be mentioned that bank conciliation permits creditors to accept either new debt or equity or both in exchange for writing off old loans. Furthermore, bank conciliation was available for three years (ending February 1996) to all banks and for all credits whether or not they had been selected for recapitalization.

The recapitalization programme was aimed at state-owned banks, specifically the regional commercial banks and the two largest specialized banks—PKO-BP and BGŻ. It involved giving the banks fifteen-year treasury bonds for which the interest rate is adjusted in line with changes in the discount rate. The amount of the capitalization was chosen so as to raise the capital/assets ratio of banks to 12 per cent. In order to qualify for recapitalization the banks were required to restructure the subset of their loans to state-owned enterprises outstanding at the end of 1991 that had been identified by independent audit as being

TABLE 5.15   Results of Polish 1993 Financial
Restructuring Act for seven commercial banks

Total loans qualified	792
Value (million zlotys)	15,748,795
Credit classification (%)	
1. non-performing	14
2. substandard	8
3. doubtful	8
4. loss	62
unclassified	8
Value of loans processed	15,687,809
Distribution by method (%)	
Bank conciliation	48
Loan sales	6
Liquidation	3
Bankruptcy	10
Paid in full	11
Renewed servicing	22

Source: Polish Ministry of Finance.

bad. The participating banks were required to create a specialized workout department. The restructuring had to be accomplished within one year and could be accomplished by bank conciliation or by methods available in the past including liquidation, bankruptcy, or having the loans returned to performing status. Furthermore, the designated bad loans could be sold on the secondary market. Since the outcome of the restructuring has no effect on the value of assets received under recapitalization, the banks were given the incentive to restructure assets in the most efficient manner possible. This decentralized procedure contrasts with centralized procedures whereby the bad loans are taken over by the state treasury, central bank, or specialized 'bad-loan' bank. One possible outcome of the procedure would be that many bad loans are swapped for equity. This potentially could be an important step towards the emergence of effective universal banking in Poland.

By the end of 1994 the results of the application of the 1993 Financial Restructuring Law to the regional commercial banks had been completed. It was estimated that 1,200 bad loans amounting to 28 trillion zlotys would need to be written off. Seven of the original banks were involved since two others had been recapitalized separately as part of their privatization. These seven banks received 11 trillion zlotys of treasury bonds. Ultimately the total portfolio of loans to be restructured was reduced to 792 loans with a nominal principal and interest outstanding at the end of 1991 of 15.7 trillion zlotys (see Table 5.15). The majority of these loans had been classified as losses. By mid-1994 almost all of these debts had been restructured in one manner or another. Given the slowness of most previous liquidation and bankruptcy procedures, it is clear that the law had the desired effect of accelerating restructuring. Almost half the loans were restructured through bank conciliation. The details of the restructured credits are not reported so that it is not clear what ultimately was the magnitude of the loss realized by the banks. However, one-third of the loans were either paid in full or resumed regular servicing. Given the very low estimated quality of the loan portfolio, this outcome was surprisingly good for the banks. The banks were very reluctant to accept equity as part of the debt restructuring; debt equity-swaps were involved in only 2 per cent of the loans restructured (Dittus 1996).

The specialized state-owned banks were not included in the 1993 Financial Restructuring Act. However, it became apparent in the course of 1993 and 1994 that PKO-BP and BGŻ were facing a very large-scale problem of bad loans, and the Polish authorities attempted to use the same tools to deal with these banks. About 80 per cent of PKO-BP's loan portfolio was for housing. Most loans were extended to building cooperatives with a provision that total loan servicing would not exceed 20 per cent of cooperative members' incomes (see OECD 1994: 113). Many of these cooperatives are now insolvent, with the result that in 1994 some 20 per cent of PKO-BP's loans were bad. During the period 1990–2, the operating losses of PKO-BP were covered by the budget, formally through the purchase of some 29 trillion zlotys of accrued interest. In 1994 the banks was recapitalized with 6 trillion zlotys of treasury bonds. Still the problem loans to the savings cooperative have not been restructured. Despite the apparently bad financial condition of PKO-BP its deposit base grew sharply in 1994 and 1995. This seems to reflect the increased wariness of Polish small savers as a number of new private banks have failed and the government has taken steps to place limits on the extent of deposit insurance coverage. In contrast, the State is seen as totally committed to PKO-BP which therefore is viewed as a relatively safe haven.

The bad loan problem of BGŻ is even more severe than that of PKO-BP. An estimated 45 per cent of its loan portfolio is considered bad (OECD 1995). In part, its problem resulted from having lent heavily to the large state farms which are predominant in the western part of the country and for which privatization or other forms of restructuring have proved very difficult to achieve. In addition, as we have already noted, the banks' owners were the rural cooperative banks which in turn are prime recipients of BGŻ credits. These cooperative banks lent heavily or granted loan guarantees to private agriculture. Many of these borrowers have defaulted, but the cooperative banks and BGŻ have proved incapable of enforcing their contracts or of gaining any value from loan collateral. BGŻ was founded on the principle of servicing agricultural development, and the idea of pursuing profit-maximization through tough credit policies is inimical to its managers. Agriculture in Poland has learned how to use the political process to pursue its interests. Consequently, authorities have been reluctant to introduce radical reforms which would make financial discipline in agriculture felt rapidly.

The first steps to address the problems of agricultural finance were taken in 1994. BGŻ was recapitalized with an infusion of 12 trillion Zlotys of treasury bonds. At the same time, banking in agriculture was to be reformed through the introduction of a three-tier system consisting of BGŻ, nine newly founded agricultural banks, and the cooperatives. The law of 1994 calls for BGŻ to be incorporated with the State initially owning 54 per cent. With this majority position, the State will have a freer hand in restructuring the bank. In the twelve months following these measures some fifty cooperative banks were closed. This left several hundred others which were thought to be insolvent. In light of this, it was widely thought that the 1994 recapitalization was inadequate. It was estimated that an addition 13 trillion zlotys would be required to bring BGŻ to the 8 per cent capital standard sought for the rest of the banking sector.

The Polish approach to resolving the bad loan problem is widely viewed as one of the more successful of the measures taken for institutional development in transition. Indeed, the Financial Restructuring Act of 1993 seems to have stimulated the seven participating regional banks to adopt an active credit policy. The managerial experience these banks have gained in dealing with problem loans will probably contribute to their future performance once they are privatized. This would not have occurred had a centralized solution been adopted, for example, by consolidating bad debts in a single specialized bank as was done in the Czech Republic. Furthermore, the law gave the banks the incentive to minimize losses from bad loans, and the banks appear to have responded by managing to get many of their borrowers to return to scheduled servicing. The question that remains is whether these steps have been sufficient to place the banking sector on a sound footing so that no general state intervention will be required in the future. Unfortunately, the reforms have dealt mainly with the regional commercial

TABLE 5.16   Bad loans in Polish commercial banks (trillion zlotys and % of total loan portfolio)

	1991	1992	1993	1994 (May)
Total loan portfolio	n.a.	n.a.	336	363
Non-performing loans (%)	16.5	26.8	27.4	29
Loss loans (%)	n.a.	n.a.	10	16

Source: NBP.

banks which account for about 30 per cent of banking sector assets (Table 5.2). The specialized state-owned banks account for 50 per cent of the total assets, and in that regard it seems clear that the action taken to date is partial. Future bailouts seem almost inevitable. Furthermore, at least some of the bad loans that burden these banks have been extended since 1991 and have been made to the private sector. So it is difficult to pretend that the State will recapitalize only to deal with a stock of old loans to state-owned enterprises. This raises the issue of whether other banks can hope for future bailouts.

Table 5.16 presents the estimates of the NBP of loan losses for the entire Polish banking system. Non-performing loans are those categorized substandard, doubtful, and losses. Based on estimated losses of 33 trillion zlotys at the end of 1993, it could be hoped that most of the bad loan problem could have been covered by the 1993 Restructuring Act. However, the subsequent revision of total losses to 61 trillion zlotys raises the prospect that the scope of bad loans in the banking system is far greater than can be covered by this Act. This failure of several private sector banks during 1993 and 1994 drew attention to the fact that new banks also have a serious bad loan problem as well. It is estimated that bad loans constituted about 30 per cent of these banks' total loans (see OECD: 115).

As the portfolio of bad debts grows it is becoming increasingly doubtful whether the bank bailout of 1993 will be the only one. The reason the principle of a 'once-for-all' bailout seems incredible is that, while banks may become good at evaluating small risks, the banking sector as a whole is rarely good at accounting for large, system-wide shocks. At this stage of transition in Poland the probability of such large shocks remains high. For example, developments in trade relations with the European Union and Russia could cause important terms-of-trade shocks in the future. Given this, the chances are high that enterprise loans may become non-performing in the future. If the commercial banks become distressed, sooner or later the State must intervene. If it does nothing, reduced capitalization of these banks will induce them to excessive risk-taking, merely increasing the chances of eventual failure. If the State does not recapitalize the banks and they fail, the State, as the deposit guarantor, will inherit the portfolio of bad debts, in effect, a *de facto* renationalization of the banking system. It seems likely that the political process will try to avoid such a prospect and therefore will bail out those banks that become distressed in the future.

5.7. *Financial Market Development*

By some accounts, one of the top priorities for a transition economy is the development of a stock market. Perhaps more than any other single action, this marks the intention of a society to reject the model of socialist planning and to embark on the construction of a market economy. The Warsaw stock market was founded in 1817 and was active until the Second World War. It was closed in 1939 and remained so for the next fifty-two years.

The Warsaw Stock Exchange, refounded in accordance with the March 1991 Act on Public Trading in Securities and Trust Funds, began trading in April 1991. The new market is organized along the lines of the French stock market which itself was extensively reformed in the early 1980s and which has served as a model for reforms in several other countries. For each security there is a daily price-fixing in which an equilibrium price is calculated by crossing the demand curve implied by buy orders with the supply curve implied by sell orders. All transactions take place at the fixing. Securities are computer-registered and are registered at the Polish National Securities Depository. Clearing takes place three days after the transaction is negotiated, which meets the international norm that has been adopted by a large number of countries and is shorter than the clearing period that has been used in a number of active stock markets such as that of London. This is an example of how a transition economy can sometimes leapfrog the West by adopting a new technology.

Trading takes place through brokers licensed by the Stock Exchange Supervisory Board. Membership requirements include the requirement that a broker have a capital of at least 400,000 ecu. Brokers contribute to a guarantee fund maintained by the Depository which is called on in the case of a default by a member. As of March 1995 thirty-two firms were members of the stock exchanges. More than half of these were the brokerage arms of banks. The largest brokers in terms of equity market turnover were PKO-SA and Bank Handlowy. The largest in numbers of investment accounts were PKO-SA and Bank Śląski. Brokers' commissions are negotiable. The Stock Exchange indicates that an average level for small orders is about 1.2 per cent per buy or sell transaction. In January 1995 a stamp duty (turnover tax) of 0.2 per cent was introduced. Dividend income is taxed at a flat rate of 20 per cent. As of 1995 there was no tax on personal income from capital gains. The market is open: foreign investors may purchase Polish securities and may repatriate their profits.

When trading began in April 1991 the shares of five companies were listed on the Warsaw Stock Exchange. This number had grown to forty-one by May 1995. In addition, nine firms were traded in a parallel market which has lighter requirements than does full listing. Most of the listed shares are former state-owned enterprises which have privatized. However, a few new private companies have become publicly listed. Total listed market capitalization grew phenomenally from 70 million zlotys at the end of 1991 to 9.19 billion zlotys in May 1995. However, when compared to the size of the economy as a whole the size of the market remains extremely small. For example, the market capitalization at the end of 1994 represented only 0.002 per cent of the total bank credits outstanding (see Table 5.10) and 0.0006 per cent of 1993 GDP. In contrast, the stock market capitalization exceeds 10 per cent of GDP in a number of OECD countries.

After dull trading for two years, the Warsaw Stock Exchange gained international attention in 1993 by registering an average return of 1,100 per cent. In terms of US dollars the return was 875 per cent, an advance that was far greater than any stock market in the world over a comparable period. Evidently, this advance was based on a deep reassessment of the future prospects of the listed firms: at the beginning of the year prices were 3.7 times earnings, whereas at me year-end the multiple had risen to 32. During that same period, trading activity as indicated by the turnover ratio rose dramatically. Subsequently, trading has tended to slow down.

Prices on the Warsaw stock market have been extremely volatile. After rising to more than 20,000 in March 1994 the Warsaw index fell to about 6,700 in November of the same year. During this time the earnings of the listed companies tended to improve, so that the market's price/earnings ratio fluctuated even more wildly. In equilibrium, competitive stock markets are expected to be efficient aggregators of information concerning the future prospects of the quoted companies. Tests for the most basis form of stock market efficiency applied to the Warsaw market over its first three years of trading fail miserably (Tamborski

TABLE 5.17   The Warsaw Stock Exchange, statistics at year-end

	1991	1992	1993	1994	1995 (May)
No. of listed companies	9	16	21	36	41
Market capitalization (billion old zlotys)	0.07	0.31	1.96	8.92	9.19
Yearly turnover ratio (number of shares trade/number of share outstanding)	18.5	49.1	194	128	59.2[a]
Warsaw stock exchange index	919	1,040	12,439	7,473	7,936
Average price/Earnings ratio	4.0	3.7	32.3	8.9	9.0

[a] 1995 first quarter, annualized.

Source: NBP and Warsaw Stock Exchange.

1995). These are clear sign that the Polish stock market is still relatively immature.

The development of the stock market in Poland is an example of how a private sector initiative intended to produce the conditions for a free market can fail to have much impact if the macro-conditions do not support it. The steps taken to re-establish the Warsaw Stock Exchange in many ways have been commendable. Nevertheless, as of mid-1995 the impact of Polish stock market has been marginal. The cause of this can be found in the course taken by the privatization of Polish state-owned enterprises. Privatization through public sale has proved extremely difficult to bring about. Most of the firms which have been privatized have been sold to employees and other insiders. In principle, if a privatized company is not operated efficiently, investors have an incentive to build up a controlling interest in the firm and then impose a change of direction. With most of the privatized firms being closely held, the stock market cannot be used as a means of taking control. Furthermore, since these firms are not listed, gaining information about their operations is difficult, so that even identifying the interesting takeover targets is very difficult. There is a chance that this pattern may change when the programme of mass privatization is completed. Then a large number of firms will have significant outside ownership. However, this is not likely to have the immediate effect of producing bringing about on the Warsaw stock market. The major interests in these firms will be held by a handful of large mutual funds. It is not clear that these funds will seek to trade their holding, and to the extent that they do, the transactions are likely to be for large blocks exchanged among the mutual funds themselves. In time the funds may turn to the stock market to sell shares to a broader public, either to liquidate a fund's holding or to raise new capital. However, this is likely to be a relatively slow process so that finance by public equity issue is probably going to account for a small fraction of Polish investment for years to come.

5.8.   Assessment

When it initially set out on its path of transition to a market-based economy, Poland made its mark as a rapid reformer by adopting in 1990 a radical liberalization of prices, an extreme opening of its commercial borders, and a severe monetary discipline to cut off incipient hyperinflation. At that time many expected that the approach taken to building the institutional foundation of the market economy would be equally aggressive. In fact, the pace of change in Poland slowed considerably after the initial implementation of the Balcerowicz plan. Opponents to a rapid building of the market economy became increasingly well organized and able to exert a politically effective counterforce. This pattern seemed to fit with the theoretical predictions of some political-economy models of transition (see Dewatripont and Roland 1992b). Rapid initial liberalization failed to build constituencies needed to support change at the same rapid pace.

Given the initially low level of financial development a key part of needed institution building involved the banking sector and to a lesser extent securities markets. Specifically, two-tier banking was needed to clearly separate the activities of making credit decisions from those of monetary control. Banks needed to become active monitors of borrowers and enforcers of financial contracts. The balance sheets of the commercial banks needed to be cleansed of bad debts, and the banks needed to be recapitalized in order to make the financial system secure and to create proper incentives. Finally, market discipline was needed for the commercial banks themselves. This was to involve the removal of subsidies and ultimately bank privatization.

The Polish record on this agenda of financial institution building has been mixed. On the positive side, from the old monobank the National Bank of Poland has emerged as a proper central bank with sufficient independence to maintain consistent policies since 1989 despite successive changes of government. Its policies have been reasonably transparent: high real interest rates have been used to gradually lower the rates of inflation. The development of markets for short-term treasury securities has made it possible for the NBP to make open-market operations a significant tool of monetary policy. In addition it has permitted emergence of a money market in which banks compete for short-term funds.

In the sphere of commercial banking there have been important structural developments that are conducive to competition. A large number of new banks have been created reflecting an absence of significant entry barriers. Thus, while the large commercial banks which were spun off from the old monobank remain dominant, they may face increasing competition as the position of the new banks strengthens. In addition, a well-conceived bank recapitalization programme has done much to improve incentives for risk-taking within banks that had inherited large holdings of non-performing enterprise loans. The innovative feature of that programme was that it did not attempt to deal with the bad-loan problem simply by shifting loans onto the books of a specialized state-owned receiver. Instead, the individual banks keep the loans and are given the incentive to resolve them in a way that maximizes their value.

Still there are many problems that remain. In many ways the shift away from the old monobank is more formal than real. The State is still dominant in banking: first, as owner of the largest commercial banks, formerly attached to the NBP and second, as a significant owner (directly or indirectly through SOEs) of most of the new banks created since 1989. Furthermore, the practice of state-directed credit allocation continues. Admittedly this is no longer directed by the rigid application of a state investment plan. Instead, it seems to be guided mainly by political expediency. Thus, refinance credits have been used to subsidize agriculture, mining, and other politically sensitive sectors. In some respects, these practices are not declining but are even increasing, as in the case of the use of current account refinance credits in order to aid some troubled banks.

One of the greatest difficulties that has been encountered in the transition of the Polish economy has been in attempting to place control over capital in the hands of agents with clear incentives to maximize returns. Privatization has been slow because the process in Poland has bestowed considerable powers on those with vested interest in perpetuating the *status quo*. To date, the most frequent result has been either no privatization or a employee-leveraged buyout with the State as a prominent partner either as shareholder or as owner of the assets that are leased back to the new firm. In terms of clarity of control rights, this is little better than a traditional state-owned enterprise. The corollary of slow privatization is that only a small fraction of firms are listed on the Stock Exchange. Consequently, for most firms it is not possible to link managerial compensation to the share price. This pattern was set to change in 1995 as mass privatization was finally getting off the ground. In this way a large number of state-owned enterprises were becoming privately owned for the first time. However, its design involved creating a small number of similarly composed mutual funds. Given this starting point, there was considerable doubt as to how long it would take these funds to emerge as active investors exercising effective control over management in the firms they own.

Given the disappointing performance in privatization, it was doubly important that banks emerge as active monitors. Here the available evidence is mixed. Enterprise lending by commercial banks shrank from 40 per cent of their balance sheets at the beginning of 1992 to 32 per cent three years later. Banks have preferred to build up their holdings of non-monitored assets, in particular short-term treasury bills. However, the composition of bank loans has changed dramatically as credits have been redirected towards the private sector. By the end of 1994 a majority of bank credits outstanding were extended to private enterprises. So, increasingly, banks have been put into the position to monitor private firms. This has not always resulted in superior enterprise performance; a disturbingly large number of loans to the private sector are non-performing.

The complement of *ex ante* bank monitoring is financial contract-enforcement. Here progress was hampered by important deficiencies in the mechanism for resolving financial distress. Banks often had little incentive to bring about restructuring, and the State, a major creditor which did have the financial incentive to do so, remained largely passive. The bank conciliation procedure introduced in the 1993 Financial Restructuring Act seems to have removed some of the major obstacles for banks to become active agents in resolving financial distress and restructuring enterprises. However, this procedure was introduced on a temporary basis only. Furthermore, it is also unclear how actively banks use this procedure when they do not have added inducements in the form of recapitalization benefits.

We have already stated that Poland has taken a sensible approach to dealing with bad loans. Nevertheless important difficulties remain in dealing with this very thorny problem. In particular, it was naïve to pretend that bad loans were those inherited from the communist past. The 1993 Financial Restructuring Act was intended to deal with bad loans identified in a 1992 audit. This amount has not been outstripped by loans that have subsequently become non-performing. In principle, recapitalization was to be a one-time only cleansing of old bad loans. However, the authorities have already violated this principle by extending the bailout to include BGŻ and PKO-BP whose bad-loan problems have emerged since 1992. As the amounts of bad loans grow it becomes increasingly doubtful that the State will be able to resist pressures for new bailouts. If so, the incentive for banks to maintain credit discipline are undermined severely.

For banks to play the role of financial disciplinarians, they need to submit to financial discipline themselves. One form of discipline can come through privatization, for shareholders have the incentive to see that the bank be an effective monitor and contract enforcer. Of the fourteen large banks created from the old state system, only four had been privatized by mid-1995. A second financial discipline is the removal of subsidies. In trying to eliminate subsidies to commercial banking the State is up against the conflicting goal of maintaining public confidence in the banking system by providing deposit guarantees. Poland introduced deposit guarantees explicitly on deposits in the fourteen main state banks. Subsequently, coverage has been extended to all savings deposits below a ceiling amount. This system does not assess banks' premiums on the basis of riskiness. As a result, even if the premia set so that the system is solvent, it gives a subsidy to those banks with relatively risky asset portfolios. And to the extent that the system is underfunded, it constitutes a state subsidy of the banking system as a whole.

Potentially securities markets can complement and to some extent substitute for banks both in providing funds for investment and in monitoring firm insiders. After a slow start the Warsaw stock market has become very dynamic and appears to be well run. Initially stock prices were extremely volatile, perhaps betraying a lack of investor sophistication, but subsequently this apparent inefficiency has disappeared. Thus, the Polish equity market looks as if it could provide a framework for handling a substantial share of capital market transactions in Poland. For the time being however the course that has been taken in enterprise privatization means that the stock market has been restricted to playing a marginal role.

In transition, building the foundations of the market economy is meant to provide the basis for investment and growth. Despite its mixed success in financial institution-building, Poland was the first transition country to pull out of recession, and, subsequently, it has recorded high rates of aggregate growth. How can we account for this? Undoubtedly the origins of this are complex; however, it appears that the financial sector has contributed to this outcome. First, after the initial efforts to head-off hyperinflation, monetary policy was relaxed considerably. Second, the strong private sector growth has been aided by a dramatic shift of credit flows in favour of the private enterprises. Some of this reflects the growth of new banks which lend largely to private enterprises. However, some of the specialized state-owned banks have also begun lending heavily to the private sector. Third, Poland's state enterprises have done much better than many would have expected. Early on in transition, many survived thanks to interenterprise credits and tax arrears. Some have also benefited from subsidized refinance credits. However, there is also evidence that prior to privatization, many state enterprises had succeeded restructuring sufficiently as to become profitable. This has helped to maintain their size and in some cases to grow.

If the financial sector in Poland has expanded credit to support growth, this has been only partially intentional. Despite the elimination of direct subsidies, the financial sector has allowed enterprise budget constraints to remain soft. Some of the large state enterprises have had their subsidized refinance credits rolled over routinely. Surprisingly, however, the private sector has also benefited from some softness in lending practices. The large specialized banks and the banking cooperatives were aggressive in extending loans and loan guarantees to the private sector. It seems clear that a good deal of this lending was imprudent from the point of view of the individual banks, and the result has been the emergence of a large bad-loan problem involving private borrowers. These losses will be covered by deposit insurance funds, by recapitalizations of the banks, or by credit subsidies or other indirect means of permitting a workout.

Intentional or not, it appears that fairly generous credit has helped get Poland on to a comparatively high growth trajectory. Growth in itself is helping to cure some financial woes as firms are able to pull themselves out of debt. However, the fact that Poland has managed to achieve this without completing a coherent set of market-oriented financial reforms leaves its economy vulnerable on a variety of fronts. First, inflation has persisted and could easily take off again. Second, it is uncertain that the state budget will remain under control; if it does not, the public debt would become increasingly onerous. At the microeconomic level, the emerging financial sector is still far from presenting firms and individuals with a level competitive playing field. The state banks have inherited considerable competitive advantages, and there are signs that the State may move to reinforce them through state-engineered consolidations. Furthermore, credit subsidies and bailouts have become linked to political clout. These represent important distortions which may undermine the flow of funds toward the investments which promise the highest overall returns. Should they persist or become even more widespread, they would undermine Poland's chances for continued strong growth.

6

The Czech Republic

6.1. Introduction

The starting point for the economic transition of the Czech Republic
was the so-called 'Velvet Revolution' of 1989 which brought a Government led by Civic Forum to power in Czechoslovakia and which paved
the way for democratic elections in 1990. In contrast with Hungary and
Poland where a variety of significant market-oriented economic reforms
preceded the political shift towards democracy, in 1989 Czechoslovak
economy still conformed closely to the mould of Soviet-style central
planning. In this chapter we trace the main steps that have been made in
the transition of the financial sector in the Czechoslovak federation and,
since 1 January 1993, in the Czech Republic. To understand these developments it is important to bear in mind that in the heady times of 1989–
90, a sort of consensus among economic thinkers in Czechoslovakia
emerged around ideas put forward by, among others, Václav Klaus who
had been working as a central bank researcher. From early on this
thinking emphasized the importance of privatization as the central task
of economic transition. In his subsequent role as finance minister and,
later, as prime minister, Klaus has been constant in placing privatization
at the centre of the programme. With priority placed on privatization,
other elements of the programme, such as development of banking and
capital markets, have been viewed as necessary companion actions.

At the start of its transition, Czechoslovakia possessed an important
asset—the lack of any substantial foreign debt. This was in distinct
contrast with other liberalizing Central and Eastern European countries, notably Poland and Hungary. As a consequence, there were fewer
constraints imposed on the macroeconomic policy pursued. A further
consequence was that the government of Czechoslovakia was relatively
free to formulate its policy in light of domestic political realities.
Whether for this reason or not, one distinctive characteristic of the
first six years of the Czech transition was the relative political stability.
Of course, the split of the Czechoslovak Federation into Slovakia
and the Czech Republic was a major change in the political scene

with important economic consequences. Nevertheless, there has been considerable continuity in the team that developed economic policy for the federation and later for the Czech Republic. In particular, Klaus has been prime minister of the federal and later Czech governments since 1992 (he was first minister of finance from 1990), and in that capacity has exercised considerable influence over the direction of economic policy.

Did this relative political tranquillity translate into a coherent and effective policy? By some measures the answer is surely yes. Pre-transition Czechoslovakia was one of the countries where central planning had remained little modified during the 1970s and 1980s. In 1989 only about 1.2 per cent of the labour force worked in the private sector. It is estimated that by the end of the second wave of privatization in the first quarter of 1995, almost 90 per cent of productive capacity was in the private sector.[1] On the face of it, this looks like a great success for a regime that has staked much on privatization. In contrast, in Poland the private sector which accounted for some 28 per cent of GDP in 1989 had grown to something more than 50 per cent in 1994. The comparable figures for Hungary were 13 per cent and about 50 per cent. Even more impressive appears to be that this transfer of resources from the public sector to the private has not produced a sharp increase in unemployment. Furthermore, inflation has been successfully controlled.

These are a few macro-indicators which tend to show the Czech transition in a favourable light. Some other indicators are less kind. Table 6.1 shows that the decline in GDP associated with transition has been greater and the return to positive growth has been slower for the Czech Republic than it has for Poland. Furthermore, there have been relatively few bankruptcies in the Czech transition. This raises the possibility that the change in ownership of resources in the Czech Republic has not translated into genuine restructuring of firms into faster-growing activities. Perhaps privatization in the Czech Republic with its emphasis on voucher privatization has failed to create the discipline needed for efficient enterprise management.

These are some of the issues that we will attempt to explore in our review of Czech financial sector development. More generally the main themes that we cover are: (i) the development of commercial banking and the elimination of state-directed credit allocation, (ii) the structure of the commercial banking sector, (iii) the role of banks and financial markets in enterprise restructuring, (iv) the methods for dealing with bad debts and the associated issue of bank recapitalization, (v) the

---

[1] As reported in Filer and Hanousek (1994).

TABLE 6.1   Macro-indicators of transition economies (%)

Year	Inflation rate, December to December			GDP growth rate		
	Hungary	Czech R.	Poland	Czech R.	Hungary	Poland
1991	32	52	60	−14	−12	−7
1992	22	13	44	−6	−3	3
1993	21	18	38	−1	−1	4
1994	21	10	30	3	2	5
1995	28	10	23	4	3	6

Sources: OECD (1995), EBRD (1995), and NBH (1995).

ownership and control of banks, and (vi) the relationship of financial institutional reform for macroeconomic policy and performance. In approaching these issues for the Czech Republic we inevitably describe some developments that occurred in the Czechoslovak Federation. However, unless otherwise indicated, the data we report pertain primarily to Czech institutions.

6.2.   The Structure of the Banking Sector

Until the end of 1989 banking activity, both taking deposits and granting credits, in Czechoslovakia was organized in four well-defined segments based on a simple principle: domestic separate from foreign and institutional separate from individual. Each segment had its single bank (CNB 1994). Domestic banking involving institutions was concentrated in the state bank of Czechoslovakia (SBČS). This was the largest banking institution and corresponds to the so-call 'monobank' that is sometimes thought to characterize socialist banking. The Czechoslovak State Savings Bank (Česká Státní Spořitelna) handled domestic banking for individuals. Foreign banking involving institutions was concentrated in the ČSOB (Československá Obchodní Banka), and that involving individuals was concentrated in the Živnostenská Banka.

The first big step away from socialist banking took effect at the beginning of 1990 with the introduction of two-tier banking. This involved splitting up the SBČS. The Czechoslovak state bank took on the responsibilities of central banking. The commercial banking activities of the SBČS were placed in the Komerční Banka, the Investiční Banka, and the Všeobecná Úvěrová Banka located in Slovakia. The three other state banking institutions became commercial banks and, as such, fell under the supervision of the state bank. In addition, the commercial sector was opened to new entry as the state bank began to grant licences to new banks. The break-up of the Czechoslovak Federation on 31 December 1992 did not affect the basic structure—the Czech National Bank (Česká Národní Banka, ČNB) became the legal successor to the Czechoslovak state bank in the Czech Republic and the 1991 Act on banks was adopted by the new State's legal system.

Since the splitting of the monobank system, the Czech banking sector has grown steadily. This is illustrated by the numbers of licensed banks reported in Table 6.2. Since the start of transition the number of banks operating have grown by a factor of 10. By September 1993 only one commercial bank was wholly owned by the State. This was the Konsolidační Banka (KOB) which was given the specialized role as the receiver for the other banks bad debts. The remaining fifty-six banks constituted the private commercial banking sector, although as we shall see below the separation of public and private sector has not been as neat as this table would suggest. Czech banking has been relatively open to foreigners. At the end of September 1993, only twenty-four commercial banks were wholly Czech-owned. The others had some form of foreign involvement including twelve commercial banks with partial foreign ownership, ten wholly foreign-owned commercial banks, and ten foreign bank branch offices. In addition, a total of forth-one foreign bank representatives' offices performed activities in the Czech Republic. The rate of new bank creation has now slowed down. The number of banks or branches of foreign banks declined to fifty-five due to the merger of the Investiční Banka and the Postal Bank (Poštovní Banka). At the same time, two small banks were under state conservatorship. Now that the privatization process has been largely completed both for industrial companies and for banks, it may be that the structure of banking could undergo considerable changes in the years to come.

Despite the opening of the banking system to new entry and the limited shareholding of the State, the banking system is still dominated by the five original banks created from the monobank system and the consolidation bank. In four of these the State remains the largest shareholder. However, this indirect state dominance is being eroded by the fast growth of new private sector banks. Table 6.3 gives a breakdown of the total balance sheet of the Czech banking system. Although in 1992 more than 80 per cent of the total assets were in the hands of the five original banks, these banks held less than 70 per cent of these assets at the end of 1993. Some of their holdings had been taken over by the

TABLE 6.2   No. of licensed commercial banks the Czech Republic

	1990		1991	1992	1993	1994	1995
	1/01	31/12					
State financial institutions	4	4	5	1	1	1	1
Banks with foreign particip. >50%	0	3	3	4	4	4	4
Banks entirely foreign owned	0	1	8	9	10	10	11
Branches of foreign banks in the ČR	0	0	0	4	10	10	10
TOTAL	5	21	33	45	57	58	55

Sources: ČNB (1993, 1994, 1996).

TABLE 6.3   Distribution of bank assets
in the Czech Republic

	1992	1993
1. Total assets	1,078.990	1,275.800
2. Total 5 ex-state banks[a]	892.158	856.307
3. KOB	n.a.	103.126
2/1	82.68%	67.12%
(2 + 3)/1	n.a.	75.20%

[a] Komerční Banka, ČSOB, Česká Spořitelna, Investiční a Poštovní Banka, Živnostenská Banka.

Sources: Data from ČNB, *Central European Economic Review*, and own calculation.

consolidation bank and therefore remained in the hands of the State. However, the share of the KOB and the five ex-state banks combined stood at 75 per cent in 1993 which was less than the five's share in 1992. Thus growth of new banks appeared to be reducing the role of the State as a major creditor.

Table 6.4 shows that five ex-state banks and the KOB continue to dominate the banking sector from the point of view of capital and primary (i.e. non-interbank) deposits as well. The high fraction of primary deposits is accounted for mainly by the savings bank (Česká Spořitelna) and the postal bank (Investiční a Poštovní Banka). The implication of this is that the smaller banks depend heavily on the interbank money market for funds.

TABLE 6.4   Capital and deposit base in Czech
banks, December 1993

25 largest banks	5 ex-state banks[a]	5 ex-state banks and KOB
Capital	65.7	73.0
Primary deposits	83.3	88.4

[a] Komerční Banka, ČSOB, Česká Spořitelna, Investiční
a Poštovní Banka, Živnostenská Banka.
Source: *Central European Economic Review.*

TABLE 6.5   Czech Republic, distribution of shares in privatized banks (%)

	Komerční Banka	Živnostenká Banka	Investiční Banka	Česká Spořitelna
Vouchers-small individual shareholders	16	11.58	15	8.5
Vouchers-investment funds	37	29.82	37	28.2
Share of NPF	44	5.16	45	40
Restitution	3	1.44	3	3
Foreign capital	0	52	0	0
Free of charge remittance	0	0	0	20

Source: Czech National Bank (1994).

While the involvement of the State in the large banking institutions
has remained, the nature of that involvement has changed considerably
since 1990. The banks and savings bank created from the monobank
were initially given the status of state financial institutions. Subsequently, they were denationalized and transformed into joint-stock
companies in preparation for privatization. As will be discussed below,
a variety of privatization methods have been applied in the Czech
Republic. For the large banks, voucher privatization has been used
extensively. The distribution of share ownership of the four ex-state
banks immediately after the first wave of mass privatization is given in
Table 6.5. In three of these (Komerční Banka, Investiční Banka, Česká
Spořitelna) the State (through its National Property Fund) has maintained a share of 40–47.5 per cent. In contrast, the stake of the state in
Živnostenská Banka is relatively slight with over half its capital being

held by foreigners. The ČSOB was not included in mass privatization but remained the state bank in charge of the promotion of export for the two republics. Instead, the State has retained a majority of shares (51 per cent) with the remaining shares distributed among enterprises specializing in foreign trade.[2] Finally, the State continues to hold 100 per cent of the shares of Konsolidační Banka.

6.3. Patterns of Credit

Clearly, the structure of Czech commercial banking institutions has undergone a radical transformation since 1990. The important issue is whether the change in the practice of banking has been equally great. Has the flow of credit been directed away from the state sector and towards the private? What form do bank assets take—loans or securities? Is there a competitive market for loans? Is there competition for deposits?

In approaching these questions it would be useful to trace the evolution of bank balance sheets since 1990. Unfortunately, the Czech National Bank has compiled a consolidated balance sheet for the commercial banking sector only since 30 June 1994. This is reported in Table 6.6. It should be noted that this includes the balance sheet of the KOB which is a state institution with a specialized function of receiver for the banking sector.

The most important fact that can be observed from this table is that banks lend little to the State. The share of the bank credits to the State, including holdings of treasury securities, is only about 5 per cent of total bank assets. This is a reflection of the fact that the State has avoided running major budgetary deficits. As a consequence, the most important use of funds by banks is in granting credits to non-financial enterprises and to households. Thus in contrast to some liberalizing countries (e.g. Poland and Hungary) state budgetary deficits have not crowded out other borrowers.

In approximately 50 per cent of assets in the form of bank loans, some 39 per cent have been classified as non-performing loans. As in other post-socialist countries, the poor quality of the loan portfolio remains one of the main problems of the banking sector in the Czech Republic. As we shall see, this problem has motivated some of the country's most significant financial institutional developments.

[2] In December 1993, as a consequence of the ČSOB capital increase, the share of the State further increased to reach 90%. The State is represented by the ministries of finance and the NPF of the Czech and Slovak Republics.

The Czech Republic

TABLE 6.6   Consolidated balance sheet of commercial banks,
June 1994 (CZK billion and %)

	6/94	12/94	9/95
Total credit	53.6	53.7	51.3
of which classified	n.a.	38.2	39.0
Treasury issue	4.4	4.9	5.4
Securities	6.6	7.3	9.8
Others	35.4	34.1	33.5
of which: ČNB reserves and cash	6.0	n.a.	n.a.
Credits to financial institutions	20.9	n.a.	n.a.
TOTAL ASSETS	1,385.1	1,538.5	1,733.5
Deposit from non-financial sector	53.4	50.3	47.7
Deposit from financial institutions	18.4	19.9	20.5
Credit from ČNB	5.6	5.1	4.4
of which redistribution	4.8	n.a.	n.a.
Bonds issued	2.3	1.8	2.6
Reserves	7.1	8.7	8.6
Equity	5.1	4.0	3.8
TOTAL LIABILITIES	1,385.1	1,538.5	1,733.5

Sources: ČNB (1994a, 1995a) and own calculation.

Credits granted to and deposits received from other financial institutions stand at about 21 per cent of total assets. This is a relatively high level. This implies a fairly active interbank market for domestic funds. Much of this reflects a structural relationship whereby the major savings banks channel funds towards other banks. Two major banks, Česká Spořitelna and Komerční Banka, together accounted for 67 per cent of total deposits at the end of September 1993. The large banks also receive the main part (90 per cent) of foreign direct investment channelled through the banking system, increasing the asymmetry of the interbank market.

Another important thing to note from the table is the increasing share of the assets invested in securities, other than treasury bills. In September 1995, Czech banks held about 10 per cent of their assets in some form of securities, which is a reasonably high figure given the youth of most Czech securities markets. The Czech banking law theoretically allows for German-style universal banking and the direct shareholdings by banks have increased relatively rapidly. This increase in banks' holding of shares is not without risk. The ČNB has recently underlined the fact that the problematic quality of securities portfolios in many banks affects their liquidity position because many of these shares are currently unsaleable or saleable only with great loss.

Banks may also influence enterprises indirectly by creating investment property funds which receive vouchers distributed to Czech individuals through mass privatization. We will consider below the extent to which this has tended to create effective universal banking in the Czech Republic.

Around 5 per cent of total assets are in the form of treasury securities and about the same amount is in the form of intervention credits which are bills issued by the CNB for the specific purpose of facilitating open-market operations.

Turning to the other side of the ledger, we see that over 5 per cent of total liabilities are in the form of credits granted by the ČNB. These include rediscount and Lombard credits which are means for the central bank to provide short-term liquidity to the system. However, most ČNB credits to banks are longer term, and, of these, most are 'redistributional' credits which were created as part of the initial efforts to cleanse the commercial banks of bad loans. These credits are held in large part by the Consolidation Bank. As a result the rest of the commercial banking sector holds relatively little credit received directly from the central bank. This seemingly innocuous fact has relatively deep implications. It means that the means of direct credit allocation by the State have been dramatically circumscribed in the Czech Republic, though not eliminated. As we shall see below the KOB and the National Property Fund are new institutions that have far-reaching powers to affect the investment funds available to enterprises. However, apart from these institutions, commercial bank lending takes place without the direct involvement of the ČNB.

Because it considers only one date and because it does not distinguish between loans to state and private enterprises, the balance sheet above does not tell us much about how quickly the private sector has gained access to credit. The ČNB has compiled data on total banking sector credits by type of borrower since the end of 1990. These are reported in Tables 6.7 and 6.8.

The first thing to note from these data is that total credit growth in 1991 was clearly lower than inflation. This suggests that credit conditions were generally tight at the beginning of the transition, a fact that may explain in part the decline in inflation from over 50 per cent in 1991 to less than 10 per cent in 1994. The next thing to note is the dramatic shift of credit away from public sector enterprises towards private enterprises. This shift could have occurred in two ways. In part, banks have

TABLE 6.7 Distribution of credits by type of Czech borrowers (%)

	12/1990	12/1991	12/1992	12/1993	12/1994
Public sector	79.40	69.10	47.3	31.9	25.8
Individuals	7.60	7.30	8.0	6.6	5.6
Private enterprises	12.30	22.40	39.30	53.2	59.9
Unclassified	0.70	1.20	5.9	8.3	8.6
TOTAL (ČNB bn.)	417.5	495.40	584.7	701.5	822.2

Sources: ČNB (1994, 1995).

TABLE 6.8 Twelve-month growth rates of Czech
credits and inflation (%)

	1991	1992	1993	1994
Public sector	3.3	−19.3	−19.0	−5.1
Individuals	14.1	28.5	0.0	−0.2
Private enterprises	116.2	104.9	64.1	32.0
Inflation	52.0	12.7	18.2	10.2
TOTAL CREDITS	18.7	18.0	20.0	17.2

Sources: ČNB (1994, 1995).

been extending credit to newly created private enterprises. In part, credits granted to state enterprises have been reclassified as private when those undergo privatization. The aggregate data reported in these tables do not allow us to separate the two sources of change.

All these data concern the *quantity* of credit flows in the Czech banking system. The impact of banking practice on the real economy is also a matter of *price*. Table 6.9 presents average interest rates on loans and deposits in Czech banks at the beginning of the year. These data are for contractual rates rather than rates of actual earned interest by banks. Thus these rates are forward-looking. We also report the annual inflation rates (first quarter to first quarter).

Note in this table that the nominal interest rates were relatively stable. For example, the average rate on all deposits declined slightly from 12.26 per cent at the start of 1991 to 10.43 per cent at the start of 1994. Loan rates fluctuated somewhat more than deposit rates; however, they were smooth compared to wholesale price inflation which went from 70 per cent to about 6 per cent over this period. Czechoslovakia liberalized most prices in 1990, and this gave rise to a rapid inflation. In early 1991 the bank interest rates may have seemed generous to borrowers and punitive for lenders given the then observed inflation rate. However, subsequent inflation was moderate so the *ex post* real interest rates (e.g. interest rate at the start of the year less the annual inflation rate during the course of the year) have been consistently positive since 1991. Indeed, rates on short-term loans were very high in 1993 compared to realized inflation and did not decline much by the start of 1994.

The most striking aspect of this table is that the yield curve (i.e. the rate as a function of the term of the contract) for bank loans has been inverted since 1992. In Western economies this is a relatively unusual condition brought about by near-term monetary tightness pushing up short-term rates. Longer-term rates do not rise as much because the tight monetary policy is likely to slow inflation and result in lower short-rates in the future. In the Czech case, this explanation does not seem to apply because the inversion has persisted for several years and the yield curve of bank deposit rates has been upward-sloping. Indeed, since 1992 the rates on long-term (greater than 4-year) deposits have been substantially above the rates on long-term credits. This anomalous situation of negative interest spread at long-term maturities is difficult to reconcile with competitive interest-rate determination. One possible explanation is that it could be a manifestation of market segmentation and credit rationing. In particular, one possibility is that most of the credits granted on a long-term basis have been extended to selected borrowers but have not been generally available to others. Therefore most borrowers without access to subsidized credits would be forced to borrow short term. This is consistent with the fact that the average intermediation margin reported in Table 6.9 has been consistently positive. Such an explanation still supposes that there is some banking institution that was willing to extend long-term credits at below market-clearing rates. This might reflect persistent government credit subsidies channelled through the banking sector. Alternatively, this could be poor bank management. The aggregate data do not allow us to get at these issues; so the existence and causes of credit rationing in the Czech financial sector will be an issue that we will keep in mind as we explore other available data.

6.4. *Monetary Policy and the Money Market*

The Czech National Bank Act (1993, no. 6) states that the principal aim of the central bank is to assure the relative stability of the purchasing power of the currency. To this end it creates a governance structure of the ČNB which is designed to guarantee its independence. The only constraint on the central bank is the requirement of approval of its annual report by parliament. Moreover, the independence of the central bank is also guaranteed by limiting the direct monetization of the budget deficit to no more than 5 per cent of the previous year's total budget. The members of the ČNB council and its governor are appointed by the President of the Czech Republic. According to the law, the governor of the central bank can only be removed if he commits a criminal offence or suffers from a terminal illness.

The central bank is also charged with assuring the functioning of the monetary payments system and with the supervision of commercial banking. In this last function the ČNB has implemented the Bank Act through the development of a system of prudential regulation.

With the start of two-tier banking in 1990, the central bank had only rudimentary means of monetary control. Since then it has developed a full range of direct and indirect monetary instruments. In the process it has brought into being a money market something like those of the countries of the OECD.

The direct means of monetary control include quantitative credit ceilings and mandatory reserves. Credit ceilings for major commercial banks were cancelled in October 1992. The minimum obligatory reserves apply to primary deposits with banks from non-banking clients, including foreign currency deposits. The level of these reserves has been unified since August 1995 and reached 8.5 per cent for demand deposits as well as for term deposits. Reserves shortages are penalized at a three times the discount rate. These have been raised sharply at times, notably between February and July of 1993, when a strong inflow of funds from the Slovak Republic was experienced following the break-up of the Federation.

The indirect monetary instruments fall into two groups: refinancing credits and open-market operations. In the Czech case refinance can take a variety of forms, the most important being refinance of long-term investment credits, short-term liquidity provision, and auction credits. Long-term refinance is essentially a prolongation of socialist banking practice whereby credits are directed by the State for purposes developed in a central investment plan. Under two-tier banking much the same is accomplished when commercial banks accord credits to selected borrowers (e.g. certain state-owned enterprises) and on this basis receive the required funds as rediscount credits from the central bank. Short-term liquidity provision, on the other hand, is motivated not by some designated investment goal but by the desire to aid the operation

TABLE 6.9   Czech interest and inflation rates (%)

		1991	1992	1993	1994
Nominal interest rates					
Credits	s.t.	13.89	16.28	15.69	13.87
	l.t.	15.10	11.18	9.24	10.43
Deposits	all	12.26	12.88	11.22	10.93
	s.t.	n.a.	10.42	9.45	9.68
	l.t.	n.a.	15.94	14.06	12.83
Inflation					
PPI		70.44	9.90	10.05	6.15
CPI		56.69	11.09	17.09	10.00
Ex-post real interest rates (PPI)					
Credits	s.t.	3.63	5.66	8.99	n.a.
	l.t.	4.73	1.03	2.91	n.a.
Deposits	all	2.15	2.57	4.78	n.a.
	s.t.	n.a.	0.34	3.11	n.a.
	l.t.	n.a.	5.35	7.45	n.a.
Interest margin[a]					
		5.70	7.00	7.10	5.10

[a] Interest margins calculated as the weighted average interest rate on loans minus the weighted average interest rate on deposits.
Sources: ČNB (1994) and own calculations.

of banks experiencing a temporary withdrawal of deposits. The tools used in the Czech Republic—the rediscount and Lombard mechanism—operate in ways similar to those applied in most OECD countries. Finally, the auction refinance is distinctive in that credits are allocated not on the basis of a negotiation between the central and commercial banks but on the basis of a competitive auction in which all commercial banks can take part. In using this form of credit the ČNB sought to create a more competitive market for short-term funds.

In most OECD countries open-market operations, that is, the purchase or sale of securities on the secondary market, is the most important tool for monetary control. The ČNB has moved progressively to such a system so that by mid-1994 it had suspended the use of auction refinance. Open-market operations of the ČNB are sometimes done through the direct purchase and sale of securities in the secondary market but more often through repurchase agreements and swaps. Repos have maturities up to one week. The use of open-market operations by the ČNB was inhibited by the fact that the small state budget deficit implied that the primary market for treasury bills and bonds had been small. To compensate for this, the ČNB issued its own short-term bills as a means of draining liquidity from the banking system.

Since 1993 the ČNB has found monetary control through its conventional instruments made difficult because of a large inflow of capital in the form of portfolio investment and direct borrowing abroad by Czech enterprises. The capital account which showed a surplus of only $US1.9 million at the end of 1992 had reached a surplus of $US2.6 billion one year later and of $US2.4 billion at the end of 1994. In order to sterilize part of this inflow, the ČNB took the unusual step of arranging to drain privatization proceeds from the system. In particular, the National Property Fund (NPF), which had been holding the proceeds of the privatization sales in the form of deposits at commercial banks, transferred a portion of those funds to the ČNB. As we shall see below, the NPF operates as a semi-detached operation of the state budget. The fact that the ČNB enlisted the cooperation of the NPF to execute monetary policy seems to suggest that, despite the formal separation of the authorities of the State and the central bank, there exists a close coordination of monetary and fiscal policy in the Czech Republic. Moreover, the ČNB temporarily froze the deposits of SPT Telecom for an amount of 33.7 billion crowns. This demonstrates the continued willingness of the authorities to intervene in the operations of state-owned enterprises for the purpose of monetary control.

We can trace some of the monetary developments quantitatively through the balance sheet of the ČNB which is reported in Table 6.10. First, note that the total assets of the ČNB grew very sharply at a rate of about 35 per cent annually from the beginning of 1993 through August of 1994. Much of this asset expansion took the form of claims against foreign institutions and was the result of the capital inflow mentioned above. Next, note that credits granted to the State fell sharply over this period whereas treasury bills and bonds grew sharply. In essence this reflected the securitization of much of the domestic public debt.

It is interesting to note that over this period the total claims on domestic banks declined sharply as a share of ČNB assets. These are the various forms of refinance discussed above. Over this period auction refinance was phased out and short-term credits were relatively minor. Most of the refinance credits outstanding in August 1994 were the longer term 'redistribution' credits. The role of these in the clean-up of bad debts will be discussed below.

In our view, one of the main points that emerges from this is that the Czech central bank clearly has moved away from the practice of directing credit allocation. It has relied increasingly on open-market opera-

TABLE 6.10   Balance sheet of the Czech National Bank

	1/1993	12/1993	8/1994
Total assets (ČZK million)	250,945	348,277	405,159
Asset breakdown (%):			
External claims	28.92	39.44	31.84
Claims on domestic fin. inst.	41.40	22.08	19.15
Credit to State	23.78	12.47	8.98
Treasury bills	0.44	0.26	0.49
Bonds	2.58	23.58	35.97
Other assets	2.78	2.16	3.58
Liability breakdown (%):			
Own capital	0.37	0.40	0.35
Currency issue	15.86	19.68	21.54
External liabilities	37.17	34.27	20.25
Liabilities to domestic fin. inst.	17.73	18.89	18.25
Clients deposits	2.09	2.33	2.04
State liabilities	16.56	8.55	12.36
Bonds issues	1.99	10.91	19.75
Other liabilities	8.21	4.98	5.47

Source: Selected indicators of monetary development of the Czech Republic, August 1994, ČNB.

tions and to this end has encouraged the development of a competitive money market. The interbank market for official reserves has developed in step, although it should be mentioned that this has been slowed somewhat by the imperfections of some banks' internal reporting systems and by the fact that penalties for reserve requirement violations are heavy. However, the State has not totally withdrawn from Czech credit market operations. The Konsolidační Banka (KOB) which acts as receiver of other banks' bad debts still relies heavily on ČNB credits. Also, the state National Property Fund (NPF) has emerged as an occasional partner of the ČNB in the execution of monetary policy. We see better how these particular Czech institutions relate to one another when we discuss and privatization and the bad-debt problem below.

6.5.   Bank Regulation and Deposit Insurance

The Czech National Bank has pursued its responsibility to supervise commercial banking by issuing prudential rules and regulations which apply to all banks. The ČNB can enforce these through sanctions including fines, the termination of some activities, limitation of the scope of a banking licence, conservatorship, and lastly the revocation of a licence. The 8 July 1994 amendment of the Banking Act strengthened the supervisory powers of the ČNB and provided a national system of deposit insurance. Starting in 1994, the banking supervision department of the ČNB was substantially reinforced.

The ČNB has issued seven important regulations under the Banking Act. The first five of these are intended to implement the international prudential standards recommended by the Basle committee. The other two are linked to the disclosure of information. According to these provisions, the risk-weighted capital adequacy ratio minima were set at 6.25 per cent by the end of 1993 and 8 per cent by the end of 1996 (ČNB 1993). The regulations set specific credit limits as well. The credit-risk exposure of a bank with respect to any single counterpart is limited to 25 per cent of the bank's capital (80 per cent if the counterpart is a bank). The total of the ten largest credit-risk exposures to single counterparts must not exceed 230 per cent of the bank's capital. ČNB regulations also establish standards for loan-loss reserves. Under these banks classify their loans into five categories: standard, substandard, doubtful, bad and loss. Reserves are required at the rate of 5 per cent for the substandard loans, 20 per cent for the doubtful, 50 per cent for the bad, and 100 per cent for loss loans. Banks are also obliged to publish their annual financial statements which must be audited by internal and external auditors.

With the reorganization of banking in 1990, state guarantees were given to the savings deposits in four banks: Komerční Banka, Investiční Banka, Ceška Spořitelna, and Živnostenská Banka. Konsolidační Banka and the CSOB, as state financial institutions, have received a de facto guarantee.

The 1994 amendment of the Banking Act created a formal deposit insurance system for all banks operating in the Czech Republic. Individuals are insured for 80 per cent of their savings deposits held in a bank up to a maximum of 100,000 crowns per person. The Deposit Insurance Fund is financed by a yearly mandatory fee by each bank amounting to 0.5 per cent of the individual's crown deposits. In cases where the Fund is insufficient to cover obligations, 50 per cent of the necessary additional funds are to be provided by the State in the form of an advance to be reimbursed by the Fund at a later date, and the other 50 per cent are to come from the ČNB in the form of an interest-free credit.

These developments demonstrate that the Czech Republic is reasonably advanced in the creation of a system of banking regulation and deposit insurance formally similar to what can be found in most OECD countries. As the experience of some of these countries has demonstrated, having the formal regulatory structure in place does not necessarily prevent all threats to the stability of the banking system. Furthermore, to the extent that the deposit insurance system does not adequately adjust for risk, such a system can potentially encourage banks to engage in risky lending practices or to take large interest rate exposures. The Czech system is young. We will see below that public policies have kept the levels of business failures low in the initial phase of transition. However, we shall see that events emerged in 1995 and 1996 which have put the new system to a severe test.

6.6. Enterprise Restructuring and the Financial Sector

One view of the objectives in the economic transition of post-socialist systems is to promote efficiency by taking control of most economic resources away from the State and placing it in the hands of economic agents who have the right to use those resources for their own benefit. Stated otherwise, the task is to shrink the public sector and to develop the private. Financial development is crucial to this process because it is through financial contracts (e.g. shares, bonds, etc.) that the rights to control capital are exchanged in market economies (Hinds 1991).

Broadly speaking there are three ways of shrinking the state sector and extending the private. First, resources can be privatized actively by the State. That is, state-owned enterprises (SOEs) can be converted to commercial entities and then sold or otherwise transferred to non-state institutions or individuals. Second, inefficient SOEs can be allowed to fail, and the useful bits recovered by private enterprise through bankruptcy proceedings. Third, the private sector may simply bid resources away from the state sector. In order for the second and third methods to work, direct and indirect subsidies of the SOEs must be removed. As a result some discussions of transition suggest that 'hardening of budget constraints' is a broad alternative to privatization (see e.g. Pinto and VanWijnbergen 1994). However, there are important differences between the second and third methods from the point of view of the financial sector. In particular, an approach based on financial distress relies on creditors taking an active part in restructuring enterprises. This assumes that the creditors themselves have been restructured to effectively seek profits and that bankruptcy laws and courts operate well.

Faced with these options at the start of transition, the Czechoslovak Federation chose to emphasize the early mass privatization of a large part of the economy. What is remarkable is that the political process allowed this approach to be pursued with a single-minded sense of purpose. This has had important consequences for the financial sector. First, it has meant that financial distress has been de-emphasized. In part, this implies that bankruptcy law reform and other related institutional changes were given low priority. Beyond this there may have been an active policy of avoiding bankruptcies for fear they might erode political support and thereby threaten privatization efforts. Second, the privatization process has been applied to the banking sector in the same basic manner it was applied to other industries. In principle, this prepared the way for greater creditor activism. Third, in implementing privatization, new state institutions, notably the National Property Fund, have been created which have been directly involved in the restructuring of the banking sector. Finally, the process of privatization essentially created a primary securities market which will shape both the operations of the secondary securities markets and of future public securities issues. In light of this, it will be useful to understand the basic approach taken to privatization in the Czech Republic before moving on to considering financial distress, bank recapitalization, financial markets, and enterprise monitoring.

6.7. Privatization

Privatization is one of the most studied aspects of the economic transition of ex-socialist systems and this has been particularly true of the Czech Republic.[3] Privatization was started in the Federation in 1990 and was scheduled to be virtually completed in the Czech Republic by the end of 1995. A variety of methods have been used and can be grouped into three broad categories: restitution, small-scale privatization, and large-scale privatization.

Restitution was intended to return to their former owners properties taken over by the State since 1948. This included the return of apartments, offices, industrial buildings, and agricultural or forest land. These were to be returned to private owners. In addition some properties destined for public use were transferred to municipal governments which since 1990 had been reconstituted as independent authorities.

---

[3] General references on privatization in Eastern and Central Europe include Frydman *et al.* (1993) and Bolton and Roland (1992). On Czech privatization see Mejstřík *et al.* (1993), Brom and Orenstein (1993), Mládek (1994), and Filer and Hanoušek (1994).

The thorny issue of restitution properties which were incorporated into larger enterprises was handled by requiring that a fraction of the large enterprise shares be placed at the time of privatization in a restitution fund to be held against future claims.

S*mall-scale privatization* was aimed at transforming small business units into proprietorships. This programme commenced in January 1991 and was completed by the end of 1993. Some 20,000 retail stores, restaurants, and service facilities were sold in this manner (see Mládek 1994).

Large enterprises which made up the largest fraction of value of state property have been processed in the *large-scale privatization* programme which was initiated in 1991. Those enterprises which were not processed by restitution or small-scale privatization were placed in the large-scale programme and were initially divided into four categories: those to be privatized in the first wave of mass privatization, those in the second wave, those left for later privatization, and those that would be liquidated. At the beginning of 1991, the Czechoslovak Government earmarked approximately 6,000 large enterprises for privatization: 4,400 in the Czech Republic and 1,600 in Slovakia (see Svejnar and Singer 1994).

From the earliest stages of the Czechoslovak transition there has been a widespread support for using vouchers as the most equitable means of transferring resources from the state to its citizens. While other methods have been used as well, the use of vouchers has been a distinctive feature of the Czech mass privatization experience. This has meant that share ownership has been within the reach of the entire adult population, thus giving a strong boost to the development of direct channels of finance. However, the privatization programme has involved the creation of some new intermediaries as well.

There are broadly three steps involved in the Czech large-scale privatization process: (i) the development of alternative privatization plans and the selection of one, (ii) the transfer of properties to the National Property Fund, and (iii) the sale of the properties to the private sector by one or more means.

The ministry of privatization has had major responsibility in the organization of privatization plan selection. The legislation framework of mass privatization is based on the Act on Large Scale Privatization and government Rules for Dealing with and Approving of the Privatization Projects. Privatization proposals may be submitted by the management of the enterprise plus any other party including investors interested in acquiring the company. The approval process is complex, involving in addition to the ministry of privatization other ministries concerned plus the enterprise's founding organization. A plan was selected by this group on the basis of criteria that they considered appropriate. They could, for example, select a plan in which the State would retain a significant stake in the privatized enterprise. All privatization projects require the approval of the minister of privatization with the exception of selected enterprises for which the agreement of the whole government is needed.

Table 6.11 summarizes the privatization plans which had been approved under large-scale privatization by August 1994. This encompassed the first two waves of mass privatization. It is clear from the table that a large number of relatively small enterprises were either sold directly or by public auction. A number of somewhat larger enterprises were sold through public tenders. Some 1,800 very large enterprises were converted into joint-stock companies. The privatization plans of these companies specified how shares were to be distributed. In most cases some of the shares were to be distributed for vouchers. Indeed, the treatment of these companies was informally referred to as 'the voucher privatization programme', although it is more exact to recognize that for any given company voucher sales accounted for less than the totality of shares.

The outcome of the first wave of large-scale privatization is set out in Table 6.12. More than 61 per cent of total shares were distributed by vouchers. While this may have fallen short of the early goal of the advocates of vouchers, it is clear proof that the privatization programme through the first wave was following closely the original objective of the government at the outset of the programme. Furthermore, it is seen that the State retained more than a 23 per cent share in the enterprises privatized in the first wave. This means that in many enterprises the

TABLE 6.11   Large-scale privatization in the Czech Republic: properties transferred to the Czech National Property Fund, September 1994

	Total units	Book value (ČZK million)	Book value per unit
Public auction	1,850	9,368	5
Open tender	937	29,095	31
Direct sales	8,770	87,969	10
Joint-stock companies	1,872	746,124	399
Free-of-charge transfer	4,095	45,837	11
TOTAL	17,524	918,393	52

Source: Minister of Privatization (1994).

TABLE 6.12 Large-scale privatization from the start
of the transformation to 9 September 1995

Transformation method	Property value (ČZK million)
Public auctions	6,466
Public competition	17,948
Direct sales	51,812
Conversion of state enterprises into joint-stock companies through voucher privatization	749,657
Free-of-charge transfers to municipalities	36,680
Restitution and restitution with additional purchase	3,873
TOTAL	866,436

State has a controlling interest in the firm if it cares to exercise it. What is remarkable in this table is the very low share that has been distributed to employees. Even though existing management had considerable scope for taking initiative in the formulation of privatization plans, the outcome of the process has not been employee ownership. This is in contrast with the privatization process elsewhere, notably in Poland. It is true that managers may have proposed a privatization plan with a view to maintaining managerial control of the firm. In particular, it may be that a large fraction of voucher sales reflected not only a broadly shared sense of social justice, but also seemed the best way to create a diffuse ownership structure.

The execution of approved privatization plans is the responsibility of the National Property Fund (NPF).[4] Formally, shares to be sold are placed in the account of the NPF. Consequently, in addition to the main task of implementing privatization projects, the NPF also exercises shareholders' rights on behalf of the State. For example, in 1993 the NPF took part in more than 700 shareholders' meetings, in most cases as majority shareholder. The NPF is a legal entity registered in the Companies' Register. Its sole owner is the Czech State. The presidium, the supreme body of the fund, is composed of nine members. The chairman of the presidium is the minister of privatization. The vice-chairman and the seven other members are elected by the house of representatives of the parliament at the proposal made by the government for a five-year term.

[4] Our discussion refers to the Czech National Property Fund. A number of properties have been held in common by the Czech Republic and Slovakia in a Czechoslovak NPF. There is a Slovak National Property Fund as well.

TABLE 6.13   Czech National Property Fund assets
at the end of 1993 (ČZK bn.)

Securities	164.5
Cash	44.2
Subordinated A/C deposit	2.0
Receivable for unsold shares	74.5
Receivable-advances to the clearing	1.3
Other receivable	9.9
Assets not privatized	0.5
TOTAL	297.2

Source: NPF (1993).

As a consequence of the privatization process the NPF has been funded essentially by transfers of capital from the State. In large part its assets take the form of the shares of enterprises whose privatization plans have been approved. As the plans are executed the assets of the fund are transformed into other forms. In the case of monetary sales at market prices, the NPF receives liquid assets which it can employ for other purposes. In the case of voucher sales, it receives virtually nothing as the monetary payment for vouchers goes to cover the operations of the programme. As a consequence its assets shrink by the book value of the assets sold for vouchers, implying a commensurate fall in the net worth of the fund. The assets of the NPF at the end of 1993 are reported in Table 6.13. Of ČZK164.5 billion of shares owned, NPF reported only 28.1 per cent were being held on a permanent basis. The remainder were held because sales were pending or because the plan which was implemented failed to sell out. For some strategic industries such as electricity, gas, mining, and telecommunications, the NPF holds their shares on a permanent basis until a government decision on their best ownership structure. The fund and the government state that the NPF is to be dissolved by the year 2,000, by which time presumably the government will have decided what it wishes to do with the long-term stakes it has taken in industry.

The NPF has generated a huge income from assets sales. Table 6.14 presents a summary income statement of the fund to the end of 1993. This incorporates virtually all of the small-scale privatization and the first wave of large-scale privatization. Despite the heavy reliance on vouchers in the large-scale programme, the total cash proceeds in the first wave of that programme exceeded those of the small-scale privatization programme. Note that the income from share sales was ČZK23.5

TABLE 6.14   Czech National Property Fund: income and expenses (ČZK bn.)

	1991–2	1993	1991–3
Asset sales			
Large scale	26.5	24.4	50.9
Public auction	1.2	1.3	2.5
Public tender	2.3	4.6	6.9
Direct sales	8.4	9.6	18.0
Share sales	14.6	8.9	23.5
Small scale	30.3	1.5	31.8
Other income	1.0	6.6	7.6
Total income	57.8	32.5	90.3
Total expenses	27	19.8	46.8
Balance	30.8	12.7	43.5

Source: NPF (1993).

billion. Referring to Table 6.12 we see that the total book value of shares to be sold in the first wave was ČZK19 billion.[5] This implies an approximate ratio of market value to book value of 123 per cent. This is far larger than the market/book ratio for shares sold through voucher privatization (see below).

The net result of these sales is that the NPF had generated a total cash income of ČZK90.3 billion by the end of 1993 which was equivalent to 9.8 per cent of Czech GDP in that year. This gave the fund enormous power to influence the Czech economy in one way or another. From the outset it was recognized that the income from assets sales should not simply be used to finance current public expenditures. While the idea that proceeds from assets sales should not be consumed immediately may be accepted widely among those conversant with economic principles, it is a demonstration of considerable political maturity to put the idea into effect. The incomes of the NPF may be used only for the purpose stipulated in the law and are not a part of the state budget. The authorized uses of privatizations funds are:

(1)   covering liabilities of enterprises earmarked for privatization,
(2)   compensation of banks for losses realized through bankruptcy proceedings,

[5] This was the sum of sales to foreign investors, domestic investors, employees, and intermediaries.

TABLE 6.15   Bonds issued by the Czech National Property Fund (ČZK bn.)

	Bond title	Value in ČZK bn.	Purpose of issue		Redemption date
			Cash injection	Share acquisition	
1991	Bank recapitalization	7.800		7.8	1.12.96
	Repay enterprise debt	22.200	22.2		1.12.96
1992	Restitution payments	1.000		1.0	30.10.93
	Restitution Fund	2.000		2.0	30.10.93
	Bank recapitalization	23.200	23.2		31.12.97
1993	Fund KOB	3.000		3.0	1.3.98
	Česká Spoř itelna	1.052			31.12.93
	Restitution Fund	10.000	10.0		28.3.94
	Fund KOB	6.000	6.0		25.3.94
	Total issues	76.252			

Source: NPF, *Annual Report* (1993).

(3) covering the operating expenses of enterprises that have been privatized if the NPF has retained a stake and if there are authorized claims outstanding,

(4) for providing security on credits to enterprises in which the fund is holding at least a 50 per cent share,

(5) compensation of environmental damage from a former state-owned enterprises, and

(6) proceeds from the privatization of the Czech Railroad Company to be used in the development of railroad transport lines.

The first four of these uses are various forms of subsidies directed towards what remained essentially the state enterprise sector. Potentially this could have allowed budget constraints of these enterprises to remain very soft for some considerable time after official budgetary subsidies were stopped and these enterprises formally entered privatization. Table 6.14 shows that some ČZK46 billion had been spent by the end of 1993. This can be compared to Table 6.7 where we see the total credit creation in the Czech Republic during 1991–3 was ČZK117 billion. From the same table we see that the total credits to the public sector were reduced by ČZK12 billion over this period. This means that the total expenditures of the NPF would have more than compensated for this reduction in lending. These figures are rough and are only meant to suggest that NPF funds may have alleviated considerably the pressures felt by the state-controlled enterprises. At the same time, this use of privatization income has allowed the budget to be balanced without difficulty.

In anticipation of its revenues from privatization the NPF funded its activities through the issue of bonds. Table 6.15 shows that by the end of December 1993, the NPF had issued bonds amounting to ČZK76 billion. The bonds were for specified purposes so that they tell us indirectly how the NPF has chosen to distribute its expenditures. In 1991 ČZK22 billion was raised to pay off debts of state-owned enterprises. In 1992 ČZK23 billion was raised to recapitalize the banks. In 1993 ČZK10 billion was raised for bank recapitalization and ČZK10 billion was raised for the restitution fund. By the end of 1993 the NPF had paid off ČZK46.6 billion of debt, leaving about ČZK30 billion outstanding. Thus its net proceeds from privatization was used to pay off its debt.

To summarize, the Czech National Property Fund is the agency charged with executing the privatization programme designed by the government. While it has relatively little room to take initiative in the privatization process as such, it still wields great power. In part, this derives from its role in allocating the proceeds from privatization sales. To a large extent these proceeds have been used to recapitalize the banks or to pay the debts of state enterprises prior to their privatization, and of privatized enterprises in which the State retains a significant stake. The NPF is also powerful as the largest single shareholder in Czech industry. It has served as a buffer during the early transition period, preventing the instability of the banking system and excessive disruption of enterprises.

6.8. Resolution of Financial Distress and Bank Recapitalization

We now turn to the description of how the Czech Republic has dealt with its bad-debt problem. The fact that, at the outset of transition, the Czechoslovak economy was heavily concentrated in large state-owned enterprises suggested that the problem was potentially enormous. Many of these enterprises, it was argued, were ill-suited to the coming market economy. They would go bankrupt for sure and in so doing would bring down other enterprises and banks with them.

A decentralized approach to this problem relies on the bankruptcy process. More precisely, the role of the State is to define property rights and contract laws. Private persons and institutions are then left to deal with one another according to the terms of the contracts that bind them together. When a debtor defaults, his creditors use the bankruptcy courts to take over his assets. Since the debtor loses out in the process, he has the incentive to pay when he is able. And the creditors have the incentive to see the underlying assets used efficiently since these are the collateral. Creating correct incentives is a potential advantage of a decentralized approach to financial restructuring. Of course, bankruptcies may be costly in that operations of illiquid but viable firms are disrupted or because they lead firms to invest inefficiently.[6] In transition there is a clear risk that bankruptcies will spread so that a large fraction of enterprises and banks would be involved in legal actions. The argument for a more centralized approach, involving some sort of debt forgiveness, is precisely to avoid the costs involved in generalized bankruptcy.

The Czechs have not left the resolution of their bad-debt problem to the free workings of the market. From relatively early in the transition process it has been actively managed by the government with new institutions specifically created for that purpose. The operating principle was that market forces would work effectively only after property rights had been clearly established through the privatization process. Until that time efforts would be taken to keep most state-owned enterprises from falling into the bankruptcy court. The bankruptcy system itself was not actively developed. In July 1991 the Federal Assembly approved a bankruptcy law containing two procedures. The first was designed for the liquidation of insolvent enterprises. The second was designed to provide temporary protection for solvent enterprises facing liquidity problems mainly because of payments arrears of their customers. In October 1992 parliament delayed enactment of this law. Ultimately the law was amended by the Czech Republic in March 1993 to provide an initial three-month holding period if requested by the debtor with an additional three-month stay being granted if agreed to by the creditors. Under the law if the debtor is a state-owned enterprise undergoing privatization, the ministry of privatization can intervene in the bankruptcy proceedings (for up to six months) until after the privatization.

The law leaves the courts considerable freedom in the operation of the law with the effect that the length of the procedure as well as the likely outcome are all open to considerable doubt. Furthermore, little effort was made to increase the number of trained judges or otherwise reinforce the bankruptcy administration. These factors combined to discourage creditors from filing for bankruptcies. For example, between

---

[6] Underinvestment can occur as in Myers' model of debt overhang (nyers 1977). However, in distress overinvestment can occur as well. See Gertner and Scharfstein (1991).

November 1992 through October 1993, there were 993 bankruptcy filings in the Czech Republic, most of them involving small enterprises. By October 1993 some 400 had been worked out. Thirty companies had been declared bankrupt and were being liquidated. Most of the cases were still in the courts (see Brom and Orenstein 1993).

In developing an active policy to deal with bad debts, the government was aware that since the early 1970s the volume of interenterprise arrears had been increasing. These arrears started to grow very significantly in 1990. As in other transition countries enterprises responded to the removal of budgetary subsidies as well as harsher economic conditions by trying to extend the period of payment of their liabilities. At the end of 1991, arrears amounted to ČZK170 billion, an amount which equalled 25 per cent of total bank credits extended to enterprises. This amount rose to ČZK250 billion in the course of 1992.

By its nature, the problem of interenterprise arrears seems to invite a centralized solution. If one netted the receivables from payables, many enterprises would be restored to sound financial condition. As owner of all of theses enterprises, it would seem a simple accounting matter to clean up most of the bad debts. The Czechs attempted to put this idea into practice through a programme aimed at balancing of claims and debts among enterprises. The ministry of industry and trade founded the Pruômysloý Zápočtový Ústav (PZU) to conduct computerized matching of payables and receivables in industry. The first round was completed on 13 July 1993. In this, 3,482 enterprises participated, registering payables totalling ČZK75 billion and receivables totalling ČZK112.4 billion. Of this only ČZK10.2 billion, or 9.1 per cent of total receivables were cleared. The procedure was attempted during a second round. However, it is recognized that this centralized clearing of interenterprises arrears has done relatively little to relieve the bad-debt problem in the Czech Republic. Overall, this experience was rather disappointing.[7] At the beginning of 1994 interenterprise indebtedness still amounted to 150 billion crowns (see Hanoušek *et al.* 1994).

By far the biggest and most effective governmental efforts to address the bad-debt problem have involved two specialized state institutions: the National Property Fund, which we have discussed already, and the Konsolidační Banka (KOB). This latter institution is the state receiver of bad loans. The KOB was founded by the Federal ministry of finance in February 1991 with the objective of taking over the non-performing assets of commercial banks, to improve their loan portfolio, and at the

---

[7] The government has at times also debt–equity swaps in order to reduce the debt burden and to introduce a more efficient governance structure. However, few creditors have proved eager to hold equity so that these effects have been ineffectual.

same time to help enterprises solve their financial problems during the
period of transformation of the economy. After the break-up of the
Federation, the KOB Praha started its activities in the first quarter of
1993 and is devoted to the management of the bad loans of Czech
enterprises. The KOB has only one shareholder, the State, which is
represented by the minister of finance who is the president of the
supervisory board. In other respects the KOB is formally similar to
commercial banks. The Banking Act applies to it, and it falls under CNB
supervision.

Something of the nature of the Konsolidační Banka can be learned
from its balance sheet at the end of 1993 which is given in Table 6.16. Its
assets totalled more than ČZK100 billion. This was about one-quarter
the size of the ČNB's own balance sheet, so it is clear the KOB was a
large factor on the Czech financial scene. The largest share of the assets
of the KOB consists of credits to its 4,744 clients, mostly formed by
loans taken over from other commercial banks. The ČZK74 billion of
loans outstanding represented more than 10 per cent of total enterprise
credits outstanding at that time (see Table 6.7). The securities in the
assets of the bank consist mainly in bonds of the NPF of ČZK3.0 billion
which was used to capitalize the KOB. The other securities, amounting
to ČZK5.1 billion, come from the securitization of certain loans. It is
notable that the KOB holds very little equity in enterprises, reflecting its
reluctance to agree to debt–equity swaps.

The composition of its liabilities shows that the funding of the KOB is
different from other commercial banks. Very little of its funds come

TABLE 6.16   Konsolidační Banka balance sheet at 31 December, 1993
(ČNB bn.)

Assets		Liabilities	
Deposits with ČNB	16.6	Loans from ČNB	38.8
Deposits with fin. inst.	2.2	Deposits from fin. inst.	29.1
Clients' loans	74.7	Clients' deposits	7.6
Set-up account	0.6	Set-up account	0.7
Securities	8.1	Reserves	1.8
Tangible and intang. property	0.5	Reserve funds	17.1
Other assets	0.4	Capital	5.0
		Other liabilities	2.1
		Profit	1.0
TOTAL	103.1	TOTAL	103.1

Source: KOB (1993).

from client deposits. Instead, it is funded very heavily by the ČNB. We have already seen that the central bank has withdrawn from long-term refinancing of most banks. Lending to the KOB is the exception to this practice. The main part of ČNB funds is in the form of redistributional credits which are the counterpart of the initial loans the KOB took over from the commercial banks. These credits carry a very low interest rate. The repayment of the principal of these loans is scheduled between 1996 and 2002. Given its lack of a branch network the KOB is also active on the interbank market and has received almost ČZK30 billion of loans from other financial institutions. The KOB also holds deposits from non-financial clients but only from legal entities, mainly enterprises and the NPF. These deposits have the same general conditions as deposits in regular commercial banks. In 1993 the capital of the bank amounted to ČZK5 billion and it was increased to almost ČZK6 billion at the end of 1994. The State also decided to increase the reserve funds by resources from the NPF to cover the expected deterioration of the loans.

Most of the loans in the KOB's portfolio were acquired as part of formal clean-ups of selected commercial banks which were identified as holding a major burden of bad enterprise loans. These credits have a uniform maturity initially set at eight-years and an interest rate of 13 per cent. The KOB also intervenes on a voluntary basis in the case of enterprises in bankruptcy proceedings. If an agreement on the restructuring of the enterprise can be reached, the KOB repurchases the enterprise's claims from creditors according to a procedure allowing the restructured enterprise to exit bankruptcy proceedings. The KOB also provides new loans to enterprises. In 1993 these new credits amounted to ČZK2.3 billion. In most cases the KOB, which has only a central headquarters, has participated in a consortium with smaller regional banks. The KOB states that these loans are granted on the same market conditions as would be provided by commercial banks. In 1994 the KOB moved in the direction of development banking with credits for infrastructure in railroads and water purification.

In the same way as other commercial banks, the KOB classifies its credits according to norms of the ČNB. Enterprises which do not repay interest or principal are assessed penalties. When the credits are classified in the loss category, the KOB is allowed to initiate bankruptcy proceedings against the defaulting enterprises. In 1994 the KOB launched more than sixty bankruptcy proceedings. Given that the bank's mission has been to take over bad loans and given that it has over 4,000 borrowers, this suggests that the KOB has not been aggressive in using bankruptcy and has preferred other, more cooperative means of working with its distressed clients.

The make-up of the KOB and indeed of the entire banking sector reflects a series of major clean-up operations orchestrated by the government and involving the ČNB, the NPF, and the KOB. The chronology of these measures is as follows:

(1) In March 1991 a block of credits known as permanent rotating credits issued by the old monobank was transferred from Komerční Banka and Všeobecná Uverová Banka located in Slovakia. These credits had carried a 6 per cent interest rate and uncertain maturity. They were transferred to the KOB. This bank received the associated liabilities in the form of redistribution credits granted by the ČNB for an amount of ČZK38.8 billion. The transferred bank loans now carry the interest rate of 13 per cent with an initial maturity of eight years. At the same time, Investiční Banka kept its permanent rotating credits but received redistribution credits for a total amount of ČZK31.5 billion of which ČZK20.9 billion carried a preferential interest rate (discount rate minus 2 per cent) to cover its loans for housing. In total the ČNB granted redistribution credits for an amount of ČZK70.3 billion.

(2) In October 1991 four large commercial banks—Komerční Banka, Investiční Banka, ČSOB and Česká Spořitelna—were recapitalized. The NPF gave the banks ČZK50 billion in NPF bonds. With this the banks wrote off ČZK38 billion of bad loans. The remaining ČZK12 billion constituted an increase in capital. The bad loans written off were placed in the KOB.

(3) In 1992 the NPF issued bonds worth ČZK23.2 billion which were transferred to Komerční Banka and Investiční Banka to increase their capital.

(4) At the end of 1992 the KOB repurchased from Komerční Banka, Investiční Banka, and ČSOB ČZK15 billion of bad loans for 80 per cent of their face value. The remaining 20 per cent of value was written off by the banks.

(5) In 1993 the NPF provided a capital injection amounting to ČZK3 billion to the KOB.

(6) In January 1994 the NPF provided special funds amounting to ČZK15.8 billion to KOB for income losses due to bankruptcies.

(7) In July 1995 the NPF provided funds to strengthen KOB reserves to ČZK15 billion.

To summarize, there has been no general debt moratorium in the Czech Republic. However, there has been an active public policy to cushion the shock of transition for indebted enterprises. This has been accomplished by subsidizing the operating budgets of selected state enterprises prior to privatization. Furthermore, enterprise loans in certain large state banks scheduled for privatization were transferred to KOB. This may have meant that the borrowers faced a less aggressive creditor than they would have otherwise. It is likely then that the Czech programme has involved a substantial amount of implicit debt forgiveness, although the precise amount is difficult measure. In large part, this programme of debt restructuring has been funded with the proceeds from privatization. Asset sales in the small-scale privatization programme and the cash proceeds from the initial phase of the large-scale programme provided funds to be channelled directly to enterprises still owned by the State and indirectly through the banking system to enterprises more generally. In addition, the programme has been partially funded through interest rate subsidies since the KOB pays below market rates for its long-term redistribution credits. Overall, the recapitalization programme has allowed enterprise budget constraints to remain somewhat soft five years into the transition process.

As a result of these efforts, the financial health of Czech enterprises in the early phase of transition was much better than it would have been otherwise. Table 6.17 reports bad loans in Czech banking system including the KOB. The fast growth of bad loans from 1991 to 1993 reflected primarily the stricter application of classification standards. After stabilizing at about 10 per cent of total assets, bad loans rose precipitously at the end of 1994. As a fraction of the total loan portfolio they represented 38 per cent in September 1995 between those in the KOB and those in the remainder of the banking system (see Table 6.6). The information reported does not break down the total classified loans. However, referring to the figures for December 1993 and to the KOB's balance sheet of that date (the most recent available), we see that at least ČZK80 billion of classified credits remained in the Czech banking

TABLE 6.17   Classified credits the Czech banking system (ČZK bn.)

	12/1991	12/1992	12/1993	6/1994	12/1994	9/95
Classfied credits	13.40	112.00	154.00	180.40	315.4	346.9
in % of total assets	1.16	10.38	10.52	11.29	20.1	20.0
Reserves	12.80	16.50	49.50	60.40	78.5	74.5
Reserve funds	22.30	28.40	48.70	41.50	55.4	74.5
Provisions	0	11.30	20.40	20.90	n.a.	n.a.

Source: *The Transformation of the Czech Banking Sector* ČNB (1994).

system excluding the KOB (under the assumption that all loans in the KOB portfolio are classified credits). Thus despite the major efforts to confine the bad-debt problem in the public sector bank, it remained a very serious problem for the private sector banks. The rapid increase in the classified credits recorded in 1994 and 1995 confirmed the persistence of the problem.

Further information on the health of the Czech banking sector is provided by the risk-weighted capital adequacy ratios (i.e. Cooke ratios) reported in Table 6.18. According to these estimates the capital adequacy of the Czech system as a whole is over 10 per cent, which far exceeds the norm of 8 per cent which was taken as the standard for 1996. As a consequence we see that the government programme of channelling privatization proceeds into bank recaptalization augmented by subsidized credits to the KOB resulted in an apparently healthy banking sector in 1994. However, as illustrated by Table 6.17, the recent increase in recorded classified credits demonstrated that a high level of capital was required.

Czech authorities have called upon a variety of measures to deal with bad loans, and these were successful in keeping the problem under control through the completion of mass privatization. However, beginning in 1994 there were increasing signs that further intervention would be required to maintain the stability of the banking sector. Broadly speaking, it seems clear that the bank recapitalizations and bad-loan clean-ups through early 1995 had probably dealt with the bad loans inherited from the communist system. However, rapid growth of bad loans since 1994 shows that a significant fraction of more recent loans made to new private or privatized entities were also turning out to be bad.

In 1994 and 1995 there were three significant failures of new private banks (Credit and Industrial Bank, AB Bank, and Bohemia Bank). These failures effectively exhausted the newly constituted deposit insur-

TABLE 6.18   Bank resources and capital adequacy
of the Czech banking sector (ČZK bn.)

	12/1992	12/1993	1994
Banks' own capital	54.40	80.10	96.70
Capital	60.70	93.70	107.60
Capital adequacy (%)	6.39	10.21	10.54

Source: The Transformation of the Czech Banking Sector ČNB (1994).

ance fund and left the system vulnerable to further failures. Small banks continued to fail in 1996 and in August 1996 the problem began to take crisis proportions when Kreditní Banka, the country's sixth largest bank, failed. Losses of individuals were covered at a rate of 80 per cent for up to 100,000 crowns by the deposit insurance fund. However, Česká Pojišt'ovna the largest Czech insurance company and largest share-holder in Kreditni promised that it would cover losses on Kreditni depositors in excess of this (up to a maximum of 4 million crowns). This would be financed by a new share issue subscribed by Česká Pojišt'ovna's main owners who included the National Property Fund, the financial company of the Investiční a Pošćovni Banka, Česko-slovenská Obchodní Banka, and Komerční Banka. The first was wholly state-owned and the others were three of the top four Czech banks each of which had the State as the largest shareholder. Thus indirectly this bailout of Kreditní was orchestrated by the State. The hand of the State became even more visible in September 1996 when the country's fifth largest bank, Agrobanka, was placed under the administration of the Czech national bank which announced that it would guarantee *all* the bank's deposits. Agrobanka had begun to suffer major deposit with-drawals soon after Kreditní collapsed. Again it appeared that finance would be provided by the big four Czech banks where the State would exercise its influence as the largest shareholder.

In principle, bank recapitalizations through 1994 were meant to be temporary measures while the major privatization efforts got underway. At some stage the privatized banking sector was to assume full respon-sibility for it own fate within a regulator framework which would deal with isolated cases of bank distress in a routine way. The experience of 1996 demonstrated that this hope has not been realized. Instead, a major banking crisis forced the Czech authorities to continue to play an active role in ensuring bank sector stability. Their response revealed much about the way financial policy operated in the Czech transition: the State used its continuing influence in a number of large, nominally independent organizations in order to find *ad hoc* solutions to the prob-lem at hand.

One of the implications of the Czech banking crisis of 1995–6 was the consolidation of the banking sector as small and medium-sized banks failed and even the country's largest new bank was taken under the umbrella of the State. This seemed to undermine the forces pushing for increased competition in the banking sector. Furthermore, it meant that despite the privatization of the major banks the involvement of the State in the banking sector was persisting and even increasing almost seven years into the transition process.

6.9. *Financial Markets*

Under the communist regime, financial relations among Czechoslovak persons and institutions were conducted within the state bank bureaucracy. Today most financial activities in the Czech Republic still involve banks. While the same could be said of any economy of Western Europe, in a transition economy there is a suspicion that confining financial relations to intermediaries which to a great extent have emerged from the old monobank serves to perpetuate old practices of economic management, not to mention the power of the old *nomenclatura*. The development of financial markets potentially creates methods of finance whereby savers directly provide resources for firms' investment projects thereby bypassing the banks. Even if securities market operations are handled by intermediaries including the banks, their nature differs substantially from traditional banking in that the intermediaries may be serving as a broker between buyer and seller, and in that issuers of securities may disclose information that may be assessed by the investment community generally.

The first important steps towards developing the Czech securities market after the start of transition came in the government bond market which we have already described to some extent. Most of the outstanding government debt has been securitized and takes the form of either bonds with up to four years' maturity of bills with one or three months maturity. Because of the relatively small size of the public debt this market has natural obstacles to becoming a large, deep government bond market of the type that exists elsewhere. The band market has been augmented through issues by the Czech National Property Fund. The Czech National Bank bills which are issued with one or three months to maturity add some depth to the short-term market. This market is essentially an institutional market which is virtually inaccessible to small investors.

The main securities market development in the Czech Republic and the only on e that directly involves individual investment concerns the stock market. This is essentially a by-product of the privatization process. In the space of five years this transformed an economy without a securities market into one in which there are about 1,000 joint companies whose shares are traded on a stock exchange and in which the majority of the adult population own shares. This dramatic achievement has been accomplished through the use of vouchers. We now describe the creation of this market and consider to what extent it has developed into one in which future savings will be channelled into new investment projects.

When Czech state-owned enterprises were transformed into joint-stock companies their shares were initially held by the National Property Fund. These shares became publicly held securities when they were auctioned for vouchers. After the auction, share certificates were issued to the purchasers and shares could then be bought and sold on the secondary market for money. The vouchers themselves could not be legally traded. The shares purchased in this way are common stock, meaning that in addition to receiving a share of the company's profits when dividends are paid, the holder has a voting right at shareholders' meetings. Thus the new Czech stock market has the potential for determining who controls Czech corporations. The development of this market has involved the creation of some new Czech institutions. The main outlines of these were established during the first wave of voucher privatization which started at the end of 1991. However, some modifications were made during the second wave. The main steps in the development of the Czech stock market are shown in Table 6.19.

In the Czech mass privatization programme, vouchers were given to individuals. For slightly over ČZK1,000 crowns an adult received 1,000 voucher points. This represented about one week's wages for the average working person. As a result the cost was more than a symbolic amount but still it was accessible to most Czechs. Ultimately, 75 per cent of those eligible participated in the first wave programme and an even higher percentage participated in the second (see Filer and Hanousek 1994). An individual could either participate directly in the auction or could place some or all of his points in an investment fund. Thus the Czech programme did not impose a system of mutual funds, but allowed them to come into existence. It seems likely that the high participation rate in the programme was the result of the aggressive marketing by some mutual funds, in some cases promising a guaranteed return of 1,000 per cent in one year. In the first round of privatizations more than 70 per cent of all voucher points were invested through mutual funds.

The intermediaries that grew out of voucher privatization were *investment companies* (ICs) and *investment privatization funds* (IPFs). Under a federal decree of September 1991 ICs were companies authorized to found and manage IPFs. IPFs themselves were authorized to receive voucher points and were organized as joint-stock companies similar to closed end mutual funds in the USA and elsewhere. ICs were required to have a capital of ČZK1 million. IPFs were required to be founded by an IC, to have a minimum capital of ČZK100,000, to have a qualified management, and to have a depository bank. These rules applied to the first wave of voucher privatization. They were modified subsequently to allow IPFs to be autonomous (i.e. not related to an IC) and to increase

TABLE 6.19   The chronology of the creation of the Czeth stock market

October 1991	Start of the first wave of voucher privatizations. All adult Czechoslovak citizen-residents were entitled to one look of 1,000 voucher points which could be purchased for ČZK35 ($1.20) plus a mandatory registration fee of ČZK1,000 ($33.30) the equivalent of about one week's average wage.
January 1992	First wave privatization project submissions closed.
February 1992	Registration of newly created Investment Privatization Funds completed.
May 1992	First-wave privatization projects selected. New joint-stock companies registered. First round of voucher bidding begins.
October 1992	Deadline for submitting second wave privatization projects.
December 1992	Fifth and final round of first-wave voucher bidding ends
April 1993	Opening of the Prague Stock Exchange
June 1993	Shares transferred to purchasers. Secondery trading starts.
October 1993	Start of sale of second-wave vouchers to Czech citizen-residents. ČZK50 per book plus ČZK1,000 to register.
November 1993	Registration of Investment and Mutual Funds completed
March 1994	Announcement of companies included in second-wave voucher privatization. First round of bidding started and completed with transfer of share sold.
December 1994	End of sixth- and final-round bidding of the second wave

Sources: Mládek (1994) and Ministry of the Privatization (1994).

the IPF capital requirement to ČZK1 million. The ICs themselves could be owned by another institution. Indeed, many of them are owned by banks (see Brom and Orenstein 1993).

In the first wave of mass privatization, 987 Czech joint-stock companies were included with a total book value of about ČZK331 billion. Of this, some ČZK203 billion was made available for vouchers. Given the participation rate and the nominal price of voucher points, this meant that each voucher point had a book value of about ČZK35. As a consequence, the promise made by some IPFs to return 1,000 per cent within one year appeared attainable.

The operations of the voucher privatization programme were managed by the State. All shares were dematerialized and were registered on a central computer system. Bidding proceeded in rounds. In each round the programme manager announced a price and the number of unsold shares for each firm. In the first round all company shares were given the same price. Each investor could use his remaining voucher points to place orders for the available shares at these prices. If in a round, demand for a company fell short of the total available shares, all demands were filled and the remaining shares were held over to the next round when they would be offered at a lower price. When demand exceeded available supply, the auctioneer attempted to clear the market by satisfying individual orders and rationing IPF orders proportionately. If finding an equilibrium in a stock would require reducing IPF orders by more than 20 per cent, no orders were filled in that round with all available shares offered in the next round at higher price. While the details of price-setting by the voucher programme manager were not public, it seems that it was basically something close to a partial adjustment model with adjustment based on the excess supply or demand. At the start of the auction the total number of rounds was not announced. The first-wave auction lasted five rounds over a seven-month period. About 92 per cent of all shares placed in the auction were sold. Virtually all voucher points were spent (see Filer and Hanousek 1994).

In June 1993, some time after the first-wave voucher auction was completed, share certificates were signed over to their new owners and trading began on the secondary market. The market place is made up of two different stock exchanges and an over-the-counter market (see Brom and Orenstein 1993). The Prague Stock Exchange was opened in April 1993 as a joint venture of twelve banks and five brokerage companies. It is an order-driven system based on the model traditionally used in a number of continental stock markets. There is a periodic (initially twice weekly) price-fixing in which limit and market orders to buy and sell are matched at a price that minimizes the excess supply or demand. Brokers have the option of placing an order for the unfilled supply or demand at the fixing price. All investors must transact through a registered broker. The exchange establishes reporting and other standards for formally listed firms. It also operates the market in unlisted shares. In early 1994 less than ten shares were listed. Approximately 975 companies were traded on the exchange without being listed. The arrival of shares issued through the second wave of large-scale privatization was to bring this to double that number.

Shares trade as well on the computerized RM system which was created originally to handle the voucher auctions. This operates through a computer network available in RM offices located throughout the country. The system is organized on the principle of open access. Thus there are no exchange members. Instead, individuals may place their orders directly for a nominal fee. In order to guarantee their ability to carry out the order, buyers are required to deposit with RM funds equal to the full value of their bid. This has discouraged the use of the system since funds may be tied up for several days before it is known whether the trade has been executed. Prices are set by automatic matching of orders which may be either limit orders or market orders. Volumes in any given share tend to be less on RM than on the Prague Exchange.

Shares trade on an over-the-counter market as well. This is an institutional market made up essentially of IPFs which trade larger-sized blocks of trade. Often it accounts for a much larger total volume of transactions in a given share than do either of the exchanges. Since shares are dematerialized and registered, over-the-counter trade must be cleared through the Centre for Securities. However, only volumes of trade are published so that information about price and the identify of the buyers and sellers is private. This tends to create two distinct market segments: the small investors' market and the institutional market, with the latter being a very non-transparent market. This lack of transparency may facilitate the liquidity of the institutional market as the experience on the London Stock Exchange seems to suggest (see Pagano and Roell 1992). However, it does seem to undermine the usefulness of the Czech stock market for revealing expected returns and other information about economic values.

In the initial trading after the first-wave auction, the value of a diversified portfolio was about ČZK7,000 per voucher book. This represented a 600 per cent return for the investor, but still was short of 35,000 which was approximately the accounting value of the same portfolio. Subsequently, the market rose to reach a peak of about ČZK40,000 per book in February 1994. In the summer of 1994 it was trading at approximately ČZK26,000 per book. At those levels the total market capitalization of the Czech stock market was about ČZK222 billion ($7.6 billion). This represented about 20 per cent of 1994 GDP, which is comparable with what is observable in mature market economies.

Given that it is so new, the Czech stock market might be expected to be very inefficient. By one criterion of efficiency that is often applied to financial markets, the Czech market was surprisingly efficient by the later stages of first-wave voucher privatization (see Filer and Hanousek 1994). Prices appeared to reflect publicly available information. Furthermore, a randomly selected diversified portfolio performed at least as well as the IPFs did. Thus any inside information possessed by the fund managers did not translate into superior performance. But in other respects the market seems to be somewhat inefficient. In particular, IPF shares which themselves are traded carry a price that was on average 57 per cent below the funds' net asset value (i.e. the market value of the shares in the funds' portfolio). While closed-end mutual funds elsewhere are known to trade at significant discounts to the net asset values, the magnitude of the Czech discounts is very large. This might be attributable to the fact that managers of IPFs can receive a large annual fee of up to 3 per cent of assets. However, it might reflect a fear that an investor in a closed-end fund may be hostage to trading by ill-informed traders at a later date.[8] Certainly in the Czech context where a large number of small, inexperienced traders participate, this is a reasonable prospect.

From this description we see that financial market development in the Czech Republic was given a giant push forward through the mass privatization programme. Starting from a economy with no publicly traded firms and no investors, the system has been transformed into one where close to two thousand larger-sized firms are publicly traded joint-stock companies. Furthermore, most of the adult population has gained some first-hand experience of the stock market if in no other way than to choose a mutual fund. The same cannot be said of the USA or the UK, the financial systems widely considered to be most oriented towards securities' trading. It is not clear that this will give rise to a highly securitized method of finance in the future. The test of the maturity of the stock market will be to see if Czechs invest their savings there and if Czech enterprises can succeed in raising funds for new investments by issuing new shares. This in turn will partly depend on whether the Czech stock market reinforces its investor protections and its information disclosure standards which are relatively rudimentary at this stage. Overall, it probably will depend upon whether the return and risk combination achieved by stock market investors will be better than that obtainable through other investment vehicles.

6.10. *Financial Monitoring and Corporate Control*

We have stated earlier that a widely held view of the objective of the transition in an ex-socialist economy is to shift economic resources into the hands of those who have the incentive to maximize the value of those resources. By carrying out successfully a programme of mass privatization, the Czech Republic would seem to have made very significant progress towards that end. However, as the experience in modern market economies elsewhere has shown, having a system based on

---

[8] In the jargon of finance, these traders are called 'noise traders'. For a noise trader theory of discounts in closed-end mutual funds see Lee *et al.* (1991).

private property is no guarantee that efficiency will be achieved. The problem is that in large organizations enterprise owners must delegate decision-making to managers who may seek other goals than maximizing shareholders' wealth. This separation of ownership and management can create important agency costs which can mean that realized returns fall far short of potential returns.[9] In advance capitalist systems a wide variety of institutions are used to deal with such agency problems including managerial incentive contracts, reporting and disclosure rules, takeovers, bankruptcy law, and relationship banking. There is relatively little agreement among scholars or practitioners concerning which are the best such institutions. As a consequence, transition economies find that there is not a single Western model which can be emulated. In addition, in transition the issue of corporate control takes on ethical and possibly political dimensions that are less prominent in most mature capitalist systems. It is widely perceived that under the communist regime power and material rewards were not evenly distributed between most people, the élite holding powerful positions in state enterprises and in the party. There is a fear, then, that members of the old élite will be able to use their initially advantageous positions to ensure that effective control of the resources remains in their control at the end of privatization.

When a firm's managers depend upon outside investors for project finance, the kinds of agency problems that arise will depend upon whether the financial contract involved is debt, equity, or some other contract form. Perhaps the most widespread agency problem associated with debt is the so-called 'asset substitution problem', that is, that in a levered firm shareholders can have an incentive to increase risk-taking since the losses of bad outcomes will fall mainly on creditors. What mechanisms have been put in place in the Czech Republic to deal with this sort of problem? Developments in the area of contract and bankruptcy laws potentially could address this issue. For example, if creditors see that the condition of the firm is deteriorating, possibly as a consequence of past risk-taking, and if a covenant of their loan agreement has been violated, creditors turn to the bankruptcy court so that the firm's assets can be used to cover loan principal before the firm's value erodes further. In the case of the Czech Republic we have seen that much of the thrust of transition policy has aimed at avoiding bankruptcies. The perhaps inadvertent consequence of this policy has been a backlogged bankruptcy process which affords firms' managers protection and which produces unpredictable consequences for creditors. Not surprisingly,

---

[9] For a general statement of the problems of agency and corporate control see Jensen and Meckling (1976).

few creditors have turned to bankruptcy courts to protect their interests. If Czech creditors have been passive, and rationally so, once the loans have been made, it is likely that they are reticent in making loans to any but those borrowers whom they trust most. Thus developments in Czech bankruptcy law to date have done little to alleviate agency costs.

An alternative approach to dealing with agency costs of debt is to try to improve the information flow from borrower firms to creditors. This is one of the main purposes of establishing banking relationships and is the basis of the position of those who have advocated strengthening banking institutions in transition economies.[10] One of the main obstacles to this mechanism in transition economies is that bad debts may produce undercapitalized banks. If the banks themselves are bankrupt, they have little incentive to try to control risk-taking by their borrowers. As we have discussed above, major efforts have been made to recapitalize Czech banks and a major fraction of the proceeds of privatization has been used to that end. The result is a relatively well-capitalized private banking sector which should have the incentives to monitor their borrowers efficiently. However, other aspects of the Czech solution may undermine these incentives. In particular, Czech banks are healthy because they have received bailouts from the NPF and have been able to put their bad loans to the KOB. These two big state institutions still exist and have the means to provide bank rescue operations in the future. The expectation that there will be future bailouts can destroy the incentives for private banks to make monitoring efforts. An important test of the Czech system came in 1995–6 when some privatized banks became distressed because of bad loans. The smaller of these banks were allowed to fail leaving deposits covered only through the new deposit insurance fund up to prescribed limits. However, when the crisis spread to the fifth and sixth largest banks, the State stepped in with additional support. These actions clearly go against the principle of creating proper monitoring incentives and were only justified by the view that the stability of the overall system was in doubt. These actions give a benchmark of how large a bank must be before it is considered to be too big to fail in the Czech political concept. It also leaves policy-makers with the problem of finding how in the future proper credit incentives can be restored. The principle of creating proper monitoring incentives would argue against a new public sector bailout, but what the Czech political climate will actually produce may be another matter. Very similar

[10] For a general theoretical development of financial intermediaries as means of controlling moral-hazard problems see Diamond (1984). For an argument in favour of bank-based finance in transition economies see Carlin and Mayer (1992).

remarks apply to deposit insurance. They system that is being put into place appears to be a measured one with limited guarantees provided to individual depositors. However, experience elsewhere has shown that the public sector through a series of crisis-avoidance measures can create much broader implicit coverage. Should this occur in the Czech Republic, incentives for bank monitoring would again be eroded.

If firms are financed with equity issued to outside investors, a different range of agency problems and means for their solution arise. Since equity holders can vote in company shareholder meetings they participate in appointing top management. This potentially is a much more open-ended and flexible tool for control than those available to creditors. However, because of free-rider problems shareholder control tends to become ineffective when share ownership is dispersed among a large number of investors each with small stakes. These problems can be partially overcome if a large investor emerges holding a large minority stake (see Shleifer and Vishny 1986). However, this is not always a solution, since in very large-scale companies no individual investor may have the wealth necessary to establish a significant stake. If the large shareholder is a big institution itself, this merely pushes back the resolution of the agency problem onto another complex organization. Furthermore, the outside investor may be a competitor or client which may pose problems for industrial competition policy.

In the Czech case, the mechanism of mass privatization would seem to have created severe free-rider problems leaving considerable scope for managerial moral hazard. At the outset all Czechs who participated in voucher privatization were equally wealthy: they each had 1,000 voucher points. Even if they invested all their points in a single firm this would not be a significant stake. Furthermore, most investors chose to diversify their holdings thus exacerbating the problem. Thus Czech mass privatization seems a mechanisms aimed at promoting the entrenchment of the old management remaining after privatization. Indeed, there is evidence that in the first-wave of large-scale privatization, the privatization plans submitted by management were biased towards having a high fraction of shares sold for vouchers (see Mládek 1994). Even though in the immediate aftermath of voucher privatization, share ownership might be very dispersed, this need not be the case forever, If a firm's value can be increased by changing management, then some investors have an incentive to build up their stake to the point where they are able to take control of the firm.

It is too simplistic, however, to say that Czech mass privatization has created exclusively passive equity investors. The Czech case is modified considerably by the presence of the investment companies and the investment privatization funds. During the first round of large-scale privatization a very large number of IPFs were created.[11] However, a small number of funds attracted very large holdings. Furthermore, the same investment company could have more than one fund. Since the same management could control the decision of all these funds, these investment companies could play the role of investors who actively monitor the companies they own. Table 6.20 summarizes the holdings of the fourteen largest Czech and Slovak investment companies which emerged in the first wave of large-scale privatization.

In the Czech Republic and Slovakia combined, the top fourteen investment companies amassed 77 per cent of all voucher points placed in IPFs and 56 per cent of total first-wave points. The top five companies had a 53 per cent share of total IPF resources and 38 per cent of total investment points. The degree of concentration is much the same in terms of numbers of shares purchased. This shows clearly that despite the fact that a very large number of investment funds have been established, a small number of very large investment companies potentially control a large fraction of the shares. They have the potential then to develop a controlling interest in specific firms.

While the form of mutual funds potentially can create controlling blocks of ownership, the Czechoslovak parliament placed certain obstacles in the way of this (Brom and Orenstein 1993). According to the rules of the first-wave voucher privatization, an IPF must hold shares in at least ten different companies. Furthermore, an IPF cannot hold more than 20 per cent of the shares of any single issuer. The funds operated by a single IC cannot account for more than 20 per cent of the shares of a single firm.[12] While these rules were established under the Federation, they have been maintained in the Czech Republic. It is not clear, however, that an effective enforcement mechanism ensures that they have been respected (Mládek 1994). If an investment company violates the 20 per cent rule in an attempt to take control of a company, presumably elements hostile to this could use the violation as part of their defence strategy.

The rules of mass privatization allowed investment companies to be owned by banks. Of the fourteen groups listed in Table 6.20, nine are owned by banks, two are owned by insurance companies and three—Slovenské Investicie Ltd., PPF, and the Harvard Capital group—are non-depository investment houses.

Four on the list are controlled by large ex-state banks in the Czech

---

[11] According to Mládek (1994) a total of 429 funds were registered in the Czech Republic and Slovakia.

[12] The maximum for an IC was initially set at 40% but was reduced to 20% subsequently.

TABLE 6.20   The holdings of the largest Czech and Slovak investment companies at the end of the first wave of large-scale privatization, December 1993

Rank	Name	No. of funds	Voucher points received (billion)	No. of shares purchased (thousand)
1	Česká spořitelna Praha	1	950,432	21,376
2	Investiční Banka group, Prague	12	724,123	13,594
3	Harvard group	8	638,548	15,225
4	Všeobecná Úvěrová Banka, Bratislava	1	500,587	11,985
5	Komerční Banka	1	465,530	11,931
6	Česká Pojišťovna	1	334,040	7,623
7	Slovenské Investície s. r. o.	1	187,917	4,432
8	Slovenská Sprořitelna & VSZ Košice	4	168,864	7,707
9	Creditanstalt	2	116,256	3,610
10	PPF	4	117,624	4,920
11	Slovenská IB	12	145,128	4,432
12	Živnostenská Banka	1	117,541	1,885
13	Slovenská poišťovňa	6	116,682	4,362
14	Agrobanka	17	111,087	3.941
A	Total 1–14	71	4,744,364	119,149
B	Total 1–5	23	3,279,220	74,111
C	Total all IPFs	429	6,134,978	175,979
D	Total all investors		8,541,000	277,800
A/C (%)			0.77	0.68
B/C (%)			0.53	0.42
A/D (%)			0.56	0.43
B/D (%)			0.38	0.27

Source: Czech Ministry of Privatization reported in Mládek (1994).

Republic—Kormerční Banka, Živnostenká Banka, Investiční Banka,
and Česká Spořitelna—which themselves were privatized in the first-
wave voucher privatization. This points to a general fact about ownership patterns resulting from mass privatization.

Since IPFs can invest in banks and other privatized companies which
themselves may have created ICs as subsidiaries, there is a dense web of
institutional ownership and control which binds Czech companies together. It is not possible to gauge the full extent of these interrelations

TABLE 6.21   Cross-holdings of Czech financial institutions, December 1993

Group	Banks in portfolio
Všeobecná Úvěrová Banka IC	Česká spořitelna
	Komerční Banka
	Obchodní Banka
	Všeobecná Úvěrová Banka
	Živnostenská Banka
Harvard Capital and Consulting IC	Česká Spořitelna
	Komerční Banka
	Česká Pojišťovna
Obchodní Banka IC	Česká Spořitelna
	Investiční Banka
	Komerční Banka
	Všeobecná Úvěrová Banka
	Živnostenská Banka
Prvá Slovenská Investicia IC	Česká spořitelna
	Investiční Banka
	Investičná a Rozvojová Banka
	Komerční Banka
	Všeobecná Úvěrová Banka

Source: Brom and Orenstein (1993).

since not all IPFs publish their holdings. Some prominent funds that do are reported in Table 6.21.

This indicates that some bank investment companies have purchased through their IPFs the shares of other banks. In some cases, the bank's IPF has purchased the shares of the mother bank so that the IPFs serve to reinforce the power of the management controlling the bank's IC. However, bank cross-holdings do not translate very simply into the dominance of any single bank or group of banks. For example, all the listed ICs hold shares in Česká Spořitelna, and Kormerční Banka and Všeobecná Úvěrová Banka are held by three of four groups. So that the views of any given group potentially can be contested. Furthermore, one of the groups with significant bank holdings was Harvard Capital and Consulting which was a flamboyant firm which managed to attract a very large number of voucher points by pursuing an aggressive marketing campaign. This group has a very different origin from the ex-state bank groups.

The fact that a small number of very large investment groups hold a significant fraction of total shares does not in itself imply that they exercise effective control in many, or even any, of the firms they hold. In this regard it appears that the big ICs have pursued very different strategies. For example, the Harvard group has attempted to concentrate its holdings, to the extent it can under the rules of mass privatization, with the aim of becoming an active investor that will have an impact on firms' decisions. Others, such as Komerční Banka's IC, have declared their intention of restricting management to that of a portfolio investor which would not generally seek an active role in a firm's decision-making. Finally because of its huge size, the Česká Spořitelna fund took holdings in some 500 Czech companies. It is doubtful whether it has the management resources necessary to play an active role in all of these firms.

The question of whether shareholders will be able effectively to monitor firms does not only depend upon the distribution of share ownership. It depends also upon the procedures in force for firms' decision-making. According to the Czech Commercial Code, joint-stock companies must have two boards: an executive board responsible for firm management and a supervisory board which reviews financial statements prepared by management and the executive board. In large companies (more than fifty employees) a third of the supervisory board are employees elected by an assembly of all the employees. Shareholders elect the remaining members of the supervisory board (i.e. two-thirds for large firms and all members for small firms). Thus an element of employee representation serves to limit shareholder power. Under the law the executive board may either be appointed by the supervisory board or may be elected from by the shareholders' assembly. The law does not specify whether shareholders may or should sit on either the executive or supervisory boards. The question has been openly debated within some firms with management insisting that shareholders should not be present on the executive board (Brom and Orenstein 1993). Because of the size of the IPFs, shareholder representatives in the Czech context tend to be employees of the ICs. In the initial stages after the first wave of voucher privatization, there were indications that in some firms a coalition of ICs was able to gain control of a firm's executive board (Brom and Orenstein 1993).

Some observers of Czech financial development have suggested that Czech finance is being cast in the German mould in that large banks play a dominant role (see Mládek 1994; Grosfeld 1994). There are certainly elements in the picture we have presented that support such a view. It is true that the voting rights of many individual shareholders have been signed over to investment groups many of which are controlled by banks. This is similar to German finance where banks gain much of their influence by controlling the proxy rights of the shares for which they are custodians (Franks and Mayer 1994). Furthermore, some of the firms with the best prospects are those which have been able to benefit from debt relief that has been channelled through the banking system.[13] However, the pattern of ownership and control at the end of mass privatization is just the initial starting position for a future evolution of industrial and financial restructuring that will be played out within the new Czech financial market place. There are aspects of the new rules of the game which will make a banks' or investor groups' position contestable. First, Czechs have now acquired some experience of shareholding. This may mean that future financing may be channelled through the stock market thereby circumventing the banks. Second, many of the investment funds for the second wave of voucher privatization have adopted the open-ended or variable capital form. This means that a fund that underperforms is likely to shrink in size. This in turn means that even if a bank's funds may initially have the resources that allow it to influence companies, it will keep these only if its performance warrants it.

A factor that could determine the course of future industry restructuring is the degree to which takeovers and mergers will be facilitated or obstructed on the Czech stock market. Currently there is little experience or formalized structure to this aspect of the market. While investment and IPF share ownership are limited to a maximum of 20 per cent in a given company, the same is not true of other institutional owners. In principle, this means that large holdings could be amassed through the growth of a single company. The fact that large blocks of shares can be traded off exchanges with no reporting of price or of the identity of the transacting parties would facilitate this process. If an investor sought to buy out other firms, one of his principal obstacles would be finding the necessary finance. Debt might be the most accessible means. If that is the case, it would seem that building up larger industrial groups would require the cooperation of banks. It is difficult to predict with any confidence the particular path likely to be taken in the future, for experience of mature capitalist economies suggests that financial restructuring through takeovers and leverage buyouts can take many forms and can lead to unforeseen results.

Finally, one dimension of the Czech case is very different from that of the German or indeed most mature capitalist economies. This is, that despite the large advances that have been made in mass privatization, the Czech State remains the largest owner of productive assets. This is

[13] An example is the machinery company Škoda. See 'Money and Markets', *Central European Economic Review* (February 1995: 34).

reflected in the shares retained by the NPF in the companies that have been privatized. In particular, we have seen that the State has retained a dominant share of some of the largest commercial banks. Furthermore, some enterprises have not yet been sold to the private sector and are being held by the NPF. How the State chooses to exercise the control rights it holds will have a big impact on certain areas of Czech industry. Furthermore, if and when it decides to dispose of these holdings, the way in which in does so could alter prevailing patterns of ownership and control. For example, as a shareholder the State may be able to block the acquisition of one firm by another. If it sells out to dispersed shareholders, the takeover might then go through. Consequently, the political objectives of the Czech government in the future can have an important influence on the development of Czech industry and finance.

6.11.   Evaluation

In transition the Czech financial sector has been the handmaiden to large-scale privatization of industry. Since all other aspects of the transition were subordinated to this task, they must be judged in this light. At the outset of the transition, the Czech Republic had comparative advantages over neighbouring countries: the absence of major macroeconomic imbalances and, in particular, the absence of large external debts. These advantages have been helpful in implementing mass privatization, and, at the same time, have provided a window of opportunity for the State to intervene in structural problems such as bad loans and banks undercapitalization.

As in Poland and Hungary, the installation of two-tier banking was a clearly defined carly goal. By 1994 this reform was successfully completed. In its normal activities the ČNB has withdrawn from directing credit allocation and relies mostly upon tools employed in any OECD country. It cannot be said that the State withdrew rapidly from the banking sector, in that commercial banking was concentrated in institutions created directly by the State or by state-owned enterprises. This ambiguous position was changed to a certain extent when most banks were privatized. However, the State (through the NPF) holds a blocking minority in the large banks, suggesting that banking is still viewed as being of strategic importance; however, this is not unknown even within OECD countries. Moreover, the presence of the State in the banking system has not hampered the massive reallocation of savings in favour of the private sector.

The particular vision of privatization adopted in the Czech Republic spawned two unique state institutions that were intended to play a decisive role in the privatization process and in the creation of sound marked-based finance. Both were vested with monopoly powers within their initially circumscribed sphere. As a consequence of its founding principles, the NPF was destined to be a major player on the Czech scene, long after the privatization process was completed. The corollary is that the NPF controls a very significant portion of total Czech wealth in the name of the Czech people, but from all appearances, with considerable autonomy. This has allowed it to channel its funds into low-interest loans, bail out commercial banks, and be a partner in a macro-stabilization policy.

The Konsolidační Banka is similarly a large state monopoly introduced in the name of creating a functioning capitalist economy. It has taken over unwanted loans from the commercial banks at terms that in part reflected legislative intent and also some loosely structured commercial bargaining. Its has been funded by a variety of *ad hoc* means including low-interest long-term loans, asset gifts from the NPF, special credits from the ČNB, as well as the occasional above-the-table transfer from the national budget. Under the dubious principle of 'sharing the costs of bankruptcy', it was vested with an open-ended responsibility to buy out commercial banks' bad loans issued to bankrupt firms at a legislated 60 per cent floor price or better. Despite its original temporary and privileged status, there is now an open debate as to whether the KOB should become a permanent feature of Czech commercial banking. Moreover, the principle of back-door-bank-bailout is yet to be tested as the bankruptcy process in the Czech Republic is still not widely used. Therefore, the credibility of the once-for-all banks' recapitalization plan has not yet been proved.

Another by-product of the mass privatization programme implemented in the Czech Republic is the rapid development of the stock exchange market. Even if Czech enterprises cannot really use shares issues as a substitute for banking financing, the development of the stock market launched by voucher privatization allows an improvement-in enterprise governance. In this environment, control can shift quickly since investors can accumulate a large, even a majority stake in firms by buying shares on the open market.

Whatever the future may hold, the NPF and the Konsolidační Banka have joined with the government and the ČNB in devising ingenious, *ad hoc* solutions to the emerging problems on the Czech path to capitalism. Needless to say this ingenuity has been made possible by the rather thick veil that has shielded most of the crucial deal-making from the public eye. Generally, the Czech establishment seems aware of this lack of transparency but is not particularly troubled by it. It can be plausibly argued that a flexible, non-transparent system has been useful in keeping the momentum in developing the Czech market and as such has contributed to the political stability experienced to date. But it seems equally justifiable to argue that the persistence of significant state monopolies in the financial sphere operating without a clear legislative basis or defined purpose could prove very useful for very different ends should the Czech political scene ever come to be dominated by reactionary forces intent on 'humanizing', not to say dismantling, the market.

7

Comparing Financial Transition in the Czech Republic, Hungary, and Poland

7.1. Introduction

In the preceding three chapters we have examined in some detail the development of the financial sectors of the economies which are widely viewed as leaders in Eastern Europe in the transformation of the socialist economy into a thoroughly market-based one. Hungary, Poland, and the Czech Republic are often grouped together as sharing a common heritage of Soviet dominance which was thrown off at roughly the same time and in similar circumstances. However, at the outset of their transition to the market these economies faced very different sets of conditions. Both Hungary and Poland had very large foreign debts whereas Czechoslovakia's foreign debt was relatively small. Poland's foreign debt was to a large degree owed to official creditors whereas Hungary's was largely owed to large banks and other private creditors. Hungary had for many years introduced important elements of the market system into the operation of its economy. Poland had also experimented with market socialism but less extensively than had Hungary. However, throughout the post-war period much of Poland's large agricultural sector had operated with private farms and relatively free markets. In contrast, Czechoslovakia had made few enduring efforts to introduce markets, so that at the outset of its transition the economy conformed relatively closely to the classical socialist system introduced by the Soviet Union. Finally, these countries differed in the degree to which labour movements had emerged under socialism. In particular, to a greater extent than its counterparts elsewhere in Eastern Europe, Polish labour had acquired significant powers both in the management of enterprises and in national politics.

Our discussion has also shown many important differences in the paths that subsequently have been taken in these countries. To some extent this reflected the ideas of those in power just after the collapse of Soviet control. It was also the consequence of trying to adapt different sets of institutions to the needs of the market. It is important, however, to not overstate the differences in the conditions of the three countries. The countries had economies whose overall design came from the same socialist inspiration. Furthermore, most political groups within these countries agreed that their economies should move towards something like the market systems that can be found in mature capitalist economies. Thus it is natural to try to compare these countries. In making comparisons it is useful to try to look past relatively superficial differences to see how far they have come towards achieving the fundamental objectives that are implied by the broad choice of moving the economy towards a market-based system. Our approach in this chapter is to pose a series of basic questions about financial transition and then to try to provide answers for each of the economies that we have studied in depth.

7.2.   Has the State Retreated from Controlling the Allocation of Savings?

One of the most fundamental functions of the financial sector of an economy is the allocation of savings to alternative possible investments. It is a precept of traditional socialism that the State should play a central and active role in determining this allocation. Under capitalism it is the decentralized interactions of private savers and investors which do so. Thus if the countries of Eastern Europe are to make the transition to a market-based economy, the State must retreat considerably in order to give the private sector the scope to develop and to increasing decide how capital will be deployed. Put in these terms, the need for state withdrawal in transition economies is so obvious as to hardly be a matter of dispute. However, state control has been exerted through formidable institutions which were hardly abstractions. The withdrawal of the State implies reducing the powers of these institutions or transforming them to operate within the context of a market. The inertia associated with large institutions opposes such changes. Thus it is interesting to see to what extent the policies that have been adopted in our target countries have been effective in overcoming the persistence of state dominance in finance.

The retreat of the State is problematic also because a market economy requires a legal and commercial framework which in most capitalist countries is provided to some degree by the State. Thus, in transition the State is to withdraw from certain kinds of activities while at the same time taking on new ones. Furthermore, the act of creating the institutions of the market economy requires a significant degree of collective action which inevitably will be the responsibility of the State. As a consequence, policies and events which serve merely to weaken the State can have the perverse effect of retarding private sector development. An example of this would be a rapid liberalization which left the banking system unstable. If public confidence were lost, the banks would cease serving their basic payments function, and economic activity would be disrupted.

In most mature capitalist economies, financial intermediaries play a key role in channelling savings towards investment projects. Thus one important issue in transition economies is the relation of the State to the banking sector. Under socialism the structure of banking was very similar in our three target countries. There was no clear separation of monetary control and credit allocation. All banking activities passed through a large state banking bureaucracy consisting of the national bank and a few specialized intermediaries. In all three countries, one of the first steps in financial transition was the implementation of two-tier banking where the national bank spun off its commercial banking activities into separate institutions. This created a commercial banking sector that was still essentially state-owned and controlled. Reducing the role of the State in making detailed decisions of credit allocation was to be accomplished by privatization of state-owned banks on the one hand and the emergence of new private banks on the other.

Table 7.1 provides some summary indicators of the relative importance of the banks where the State has a controlling interest. According to these indicators, the State continues to dominate commercial banking in each of the three countries. This emerges despite the fact that the three countries have had very different experiences in privatizing state-owned banks. The Czech Republic has moved aggressively to privatize its banks by including most state-owned banks in mass privatization. Nevertheless, the State has retained large, minority interests in the privatized banks. At the same time, the rules of privatization have tended to result in relatively dispersed private shareholding thus leaving the State as the largest single shareholder. Furthermore, KOB, the bank specializing in bad loans, is very large and remains entirely state-owned.

In Poland, case-by-case privatization resulted in the sale of five state-owned banks of mid-1995. After these sales, state-owned banks still accounted for about two-thirds of total bank assets. Furthermore, the State remained an important minority shareholder in the privatized banks. Thus the State had the potential to exert strong control over

TABLE 7.1 State dominance in commercial banking

	Hungary[a]	Poland[b]	Czech Republic[c]
Asset share of state-controlled banks (%)	70.2	66	75

[a] Includes six largest banks in which state directly or indirectly owned at least 44%. Figures are for end of 1993 (see Ch. 4).
[b] Assets as of end 1993. Based on the ten non-privatized banks listed in Table 5.3.
[c] Figures at the end of 1993. Includes privatized banks because in all but one case the state retained a large minority stake of at least 40%.

much of the commercial banking activities of the country. In Hungary efforts sell off some of the large state-owned banks was repeatedly thwarted by difficulties in reaching terms with potential buyers and because of lack of political consensus on the direction of the privatization programme. This stand-off left most commercial banking in state hands.[1]

Thus in the three transition leaders, the State has been relatively slow to withdraw from controlling the banking sector. Bank privatization has been slower than privatization of industry. And in most cases where bank privatization has occurred, the State remains a large minority shareholder. What explains this continued dominance of the State in banking ownership? One reason may be a general concern for the stability of the financial sector. There are indications that some of the new banks in the region have had difficulty in calculating and managing risks. Had these countries moved too aggressively towards placing banking in the private sector, perhaps there would have been increased risk of collapse of the financial system. A second reason is that the banking units that were spun off from the national banks inherited considerable competitive advantages. If these banks had been privatized very rapidly, it might have created a private sector oligopoly that would have been essentially unregulated. It is true that these same banks had some inherited disadvantages as well, in particular a portfolio of bad loans. However, this was largely corrected by state efforts to deal with the bad-loan problem which were directed towards these banks exclusively. Finally, in the case of Poland and Hungary, the slowness of bank privatization seems to be partially the consequence of the strategy of seeking strategic foreign partners as part of the privatization plan.

[1] This pattern was perhaps set to change at the end of 1995 when it was finally announced that a privatization plan had been agreed upon for Budapest Bank.

Foreign banks have been reluctant to make very large investments in the region. This reluctance has translated into their demanding very favourable terms before they were willing to take long-term stakes in a privatized bank. In most cases the governments of Poland and Hungary have been unwilling to meet these terms.

Some would argue that the speed of privatization of state banks is determined by the pace of reforms elsewhere in the economy. In particular, it may have been thought that it was preferable to find a general solution to the bad-loans problem before bank assets would be privatized. Thus the fact that Poland did not recapitalize the banks until 1994 meant that until recently there was an important obstacle to their privatization. Even though Hungary moved early to address the bad-loan problem, each policy measure that has been taken has almost immediately been seen to be inadequate. The state-owned banks always seemed to operate under a crushing burden of non-performing credits thus making it difficult to sell them off at an attractive price. In the Czech Republic the resources devoted to resolving the bad-debt problem have been considerable. In particular, KOB, the specialized receiver bank, accounts for about 8 per cent of the banking sector assets, and the proceeds from privatization have been regularly used to recapitalize state-owned banks. This was sufficient to allow the large state-owned banks to be included in the mass privatization along with industrial enterprises.

It is not clear that all these reasons are sufficient to account for the continued prominence of the State in the banking sectors of these countries. In particular, they do not really seem to explain why the State has retained strategic stakes in those banks that have been privatized. Our view is that at least as important as the considerations we have just mentioned is a basic perception that the banking sector exerts considerable leverage on the rest of the economy. In particular, bank monitoring of large enterprises means that whoever controls the banks can have an indirect influence over a large number of organizations. This has given rise to a reluctance to fully cede this power to the private sector.

Furthermore, there has not emerged a clear consensus as to the definitive shape of the financial sector. In particular, there has been a conflict between those who would favour an open competitive banking sector and those who see the sector being built around a very small number of dominant banks. To the extent that the State retains significant control of the privatized banks, it will be in position to directly influence which vision prevails in the future. This is related to the issue of whether the State should bring about bank mergers in order to achieve a more concentrated banking sector. A hint of what might emerge as a more general tendency was given in late 1995 when the Polish parliament voted to transfer the 42 per cent stake that it had retained in Bank Przemysłowo-Handlowy to the larger Bank Handlowy of Warsaw which was still state-owned. The intention was that in this way the merger of these two banks would be brought about. More generally this reflected growing support for the idea that the State should be active in bringing about the consolidation of the banking sector. In the Czech Republic the call for consolidation of banks has been less strong. Nevertheless, even after mass privatization the State has the potential to use its power as an owner of bank assets to bring about changes of direction in the banking sector. In particular, the KOB is a major player whose fate remains a subject of open debate. Conceivably, it could be called upon to take over future bad debts from large privatized banks in which the State has retained a large interest. In this way, it would contribute to the emergence of these banks as the dominant competitors in Czech banking for years to come.

Even if the State were to withdraw entirely from the ownership of commercial banks it would be possible for it to maintain effective control of the allocation of credit if the policies employed by the central bank were sufficiently intrusive. Thus one aspect of the issue of the withdrawal of the State from the financial sector is the degree to which monetary control is exercised through the use of indirect policy tools that leave most of the details of credit allocation to be determined by the market. In this regard all three transition countries we have targeted have clearly moved to put monetary policy on the same footing as in mature capitalist economies. By 1992 all three had eliminated interest rate controls and quantitative limits on credits allowed in banks. Furthermore, short-term monetary policy adjustments are accomplished through central bank operations on the money market which itself has become reasonably liquid.

While the main direction of monetary policy has been achieved by relatively indirect, non-intrusive tools, not all directed credits have been removed. In Poland, while overall refinance credits account for a shrinking portion of central bank assets, certain categories of refinance remain important and are used to channel certain targeted sections of industry a regular subsidy in the form of credits at below-market interest rates. Similarly, in Hungary refinance credits have been severely restricted. Nevertheless, long-term refinance credits have been maintained as a subsidy to favoured sectors. These constitute more than 10 per cent of the long-term credits outstanding to the private sector. The pattern is substantially the same in the Czech Republic. Subsidized long-term credits have been sufficiently important for average interest rates received by banks on long-term credit to be less than the rate they were paying on long-term deposits. A large component of these credits were those granted to KOB and Investiční Banka in order to finance the bad loan consolidation programme. These credits represented 17 per cent of the CNB's balance sheet in 1994.

The fact that the State may decide to support investment in certain sectors by giving them subsidies is hardly unique to the countries of Eastern Europe. What is more significant about these subsidies is that they have occurred at a time when the State was publicly pursuing a policy of removing direct budgetary subsidies. These indirect subsides were probably chosen because they are somewhat disguised as their cost is not directly observable. Furthermore, in a number of cases the subsidies were clearly destined for declining industries where the main motivation was to avoid the social costs and political fall-out that would be associated with the immediate restructuring of the enterprises. Thus for some lucky or politically well-connected enterprises, financial budget constraints have stayed soft well after the time when direct subsidies have been removed.

Finally, it is possible for the State to dominate the financial sector and to distort the allocation of savings to investment even if does not own banks and even if monetary policy is conducted entirely through the open market. In particular, if the State has a heavily imbalanced budget it may finance itself by borrowing heavily. Thus even though the financial sector is completely private and based on competitive markets, if the public sector absorbs the entire private savings of the country it could not be considered that the State has withdrawn from dominating the financial sector. Table 7.2 gives some indication of the degree to which the government sector has crowded out private and state-owned enterprise sector investment. Here we see the situation differs dramatically among the three countries we have considered. In Hungary the worsening imbalance of the state budget and the high level of foreign indebtedness has led it to borrow very heavily on the domestic market. In 1994 the Hungarian Government accounted for nearly 60 per cent of domestic credit creation. This was significantly more that the comparable figure for Poland which in turn had significantly more crowding out than in the Czech Republic.

To summarize, Hungary, Poland, and the Czech Republic have had broadly similar experiences in the degree to which the State remains active in the workings of the financial sector. The Czech Republic has gone further in bank privatization than the other two; however, the State retains large shareholdings and the dispersion of private shareholders means that the State can act as a dominant shareholder if it

TABLE 7.2   Crowding out, 1994

	Hungary	Poland	Czech Republic
Government share of domestic credit creation (%)	59.0	45	29.2
Credit to government/total central bank assets (%)	20.8	22	5.3

[a] Public sector in Hungary does not include state-owned enterprises.

Sources: NBH (2/1995), NBP, and ČNB (9/1994).

wishes to do so. These three countries are also similar in that they have clearly moved to exercise monetary control through indirect tools which interfere little with the market determination of interest rates. Each of the three has nevertheless employed subsidized credits as a means of channelling resources to privileged sectors. The one area where the experience of state withdrawal has clearly differed for the three is in the degree of crowding out of private investment. In Hungary the government's commitment to expanded social programmes and the continuing service burden of the foreign debt has meant that the government's borrowing requirement has been the major drain on domestic savings. Inevitably this makes it considerably more difficult for private sector investments to obtain the needed finance than their counterparts in Poland and the Czech Republic. The lesson of this is that even though reforms might introduce greater efficiency in the financial sector this does not translate into an increased flow of resources into private investment if the government's own finances are severely imbalanced.

7.3.   Is the Banking Sector Competitive?

In banking as in other sectors the socialist economies of Eastern Europe were organized around state monopolies. A key to gaining the efficiency benefits of a market system is to introduce an adequate degree of competition into banking. Hungary, Poland, and the Czech Republic made it possible to create new, privately owned banks more or less at the same time that two-tiered banking was introduced. Licensing requirements were not very stringent, with minimum capital requirements varying from about $10 million in the Czech Republic to about $15 million in Poland to $18 million in Hungary. This allowed entry of private commercial banks at about the same time that the State broke

TABLE 7.3   Numbers of commercial banks

	1988	1989	1990	1991	1992	1993	1994	1995
Hungary	24	24	31	37	35	42	42	42
Poland	6	14	75	86	87	95	85	75
Czech Republic	n.a.	5	21	33	45	57	58	55

off state-owned commercial banks from the national banks. The result has been a significant growth in the number of commercial banks throughout the region.

Table 7.3 summarizes these developments for the three countries we have studied. As we noted in Chapter 4, Hungary began to allow entry of new banks in the 1980s. In the 1990s the number of new banks introduced in Hungary has been significant, but still moderate compared to the very rapid introduction of new banks in Poland and the Czech Republic. The latter was the last to introduce two-tier banking. Nevertheless, within three years of its introduction the total number of commercial banks operating in the Czech Republic stood at fifty-seven which is greater than the number in Hungary, a country of comparable size.

Initially, licensing requirements were extremely loose in Poland, to the point where some new banks relied on borrowed funds for their initial capital. The result was that the number of commercial banks grew more than tenfold in the two years ending in 1990. Subsequently the numbers of new entrants fell as one might expect; however, this also reflected a change of policy on the part of the National Bank of Poland which became very reluctant to grant new licences. There were two motives for this policy shift. On the one hand, the NBP became aware that inexperience and low capitalization threatened the stability of some of the new banks. It central bank was understandably reluctant to encourage the entry of still more small banks which it might need to bail out later. In addition, the NBP refused licences to foreign banks as part of a policy to encourage the foreign banks to purchase stakes in state-owned banks being readied for privatization or to buy out financially weak private commercial banks. In effect, the NBP was using licensing as a tool for bank consolidation and restructuring. The process was beginning to show its effects as a number of bank failures and distressed mergers began to reduce the number of active banks by 1994.

The strong growth of new banks in Eastern Europe potentially creates competitive pressures that will improve the level of bank services

TABLE 7.4   Asset concentration, December 1993 (as % of commercial bank assets)

	National bank offshoots	Five largest banks
Hungary	75.5	69.5
Poland	85.1	56.3
Czech Republic	75.6	82.7

Source: *Wall Street Journal Europe* (1994).

and will force the restructuring of the commercial banks emerging from the national banks. Initially, however, there are clear signs that some banks benefit from considerable market power. Table 7.4 presents two measures of industrial concentration in banking. First we see that at the end of 1993 the commercial banks that had been spun off from the national bank or otherwise emerged directly from the socialist bank bureaucracy still accounted for at least 75 per cent of total bank assets in all three countries. This shows that despite the tremendous growth in the numbers of private banks, there was considerable inertia which favoured the continued dominance of the old banks established by the State. We also report five-bank asset concentration ratios. Here the concentration is high but less so than for the ex-monobank offshoots. Furthermore, there is significant variation across the countries. In particular, in Poland the relatively low five-bank share is the result of breaking the national bank commercial activities into nine regional banks.

Concentration ratios are not always good indicators of market power: However, in the context of transition countries we feel that they do suggest some clear reasons for being concerned about the strength of competition. It is clear that at the end of 1993 the main competitive threat for a bank that had emerged from the monobank were other banks similar to itself. Managers in these banks tended to know one another. Furthermore, most of these banks had not yet been privatized. Consequently, we feel that it is probable that competitive pressure was not as fierce for these banks as it would have been if their main competitors had been large, secure privately owned banks.

It is also not clear that the relevant bank market-place was the country as a whole. As a consequence some banks have greater market shares in their effective markets. In particular, the fact that Polish state-owned commercial banks were set up on a regional basis meant that with the exception of the Warsaw region each bank had at most one or two serious rivals. Since some industries in Poland are regionally specialized, this also meant that some banks and some large state-owned enterprises were mutually dependent on one another. Furthermore, in all three countries, the state savings banks inherited dense agency networks which gave them a clear competitive advantage in retail banking (see Abel and Székely 1995).

It is widely believed that potentially the strongest competitive pressure in banking in Eastern Europe could come from foreign banks. In fact, given the established branch networks of the large domestic banks, it is likely that foreign banks would face higher funding costs than their domestic competitors. Also domestic banks already have established relations with borrowers; however, given that many of these may be unprofitable state-owned enterprises, this may be more of a competitive disadvantage. In Table 7.5 we report the number of licensed banks with foreignownership operating in the three target countries. These totals exclude portfolio investments of foreign individuals but include wholly foreign-owned new banks, new banks with mixed ownership, and privatized banks where foreign companies have taken an identifiable stake. The basic message that comes from this table is that Hungary and the Czech Republic have been quite open to foreign banks whereas Poland has not.

Hungary has had a reputation for openness to foreign banking since its national bank began a joint venture with Citibank in 1986. In the eyes of many the arrival of foreign banks with a significant presence in the early 1990s created considerable competitive pressures on Hungarian banks despite the fact that most of the latter remained state-owned. These pressures may have aggravated the problems of domestic banks in dealing with their portfolios of non-performing loans because good quality borrowers switched to the foreign competitors. However, foreign competition apparently has not squeezed margins which as we

TABLE 7.5 Banks with foreign ownership

	1990	1991	1992	1993	1994	1995
Hungary	n.a.	n.a.	15	19	23	23
Poland	n.a.	n.a.	n.a.	8	11	15
Czech Republic	6	13	20	25	25	25

Sources: NBH. *The Banking System in Poland* (1993), *Poland International Economic Report* (1994–5), Hrnčíř (1993), and Wachtel (1995).

noted in Chapter 4 have remained high for the banking sector as a whole.

One possible benefit of openness in banking is that it may help to promote foreign direct investment. The foreign investor may be faster to move into a new market if aided by a banker whose methods he understands and trusts and who has a knowledge of the new market. Cumulative foreign direct investment from 1989 to 1994 has been $6.9 billion for Hungary, $3.5 billion for the Czech Republic, and $3.8 billion for Poland (EBRD 1995). Thus, in the case of the three countries we consider there is a correlation between the openness to banking (indicated by the number of foreign banks present and the length of time they have been established) and the amount of foreign direct investment that has occurred to date.

The presence of foreign banks may be as much a reflection of the openness of the economy to foreign trade. Since it is a less open economy than are Hungary and the Czech Republic, this may partially explain the relatively small number of foreign banks in Poland. However, it seems that a more important reason is that the Polish authorities have actively used licensing policy to limït entry of new foreign banks. With a limit on licences for foreign banks the only way to enter the Polish market was to buy out an existing Polish private bank or to take a stake in a bank undergoing privatization. Both of these have indeed occurred in Poland, so the authorities may feel that the strategy has worked. However, the uncalculated cost of the policy has been other foreign banks have been kept out when they would have entered had a licence been forthcoming. As a result, the large state-owned banks have been partially shielded from competitive pressure during six years of transition.

Given the socialist heritage of numerous and elaborate intrusions of the State in the functioning of the economy, one important question regarding the competitive environment in a transition economy is whether the policies of the state favour one group of competitors over another group. In particular, one might ask whether state-owned banks are treated differently from private banks. One area where state intervention has been manifestly unequal in all three of the target countries is in the handling of bad loans and bank recapitalization. Despite important differences in the approach taken in these areas, all three countries have developed programmes essentially aimed at the state-owned banks which have inherited a portfolio of loans extended to state-owned enterprises. The original intention was to deal with the stock of old bad loans. And even if, as we have argued in Chapters 4–6, the bailouts were expanded to include some recently issued loans, the programmes followed maintained the original logic in restricting the programmes to the state-owned banks. In the early stages of transition this approach made very good sense. Clearly, the offshoots of the monobank were severely undercapitalized, and some case-by-case measures were required to make them healthy enough to compete. It would have been foolish to delay this or to distort the process by applying anti-monopoly policy too early to these institutions. At some stage, however, these banks will he expected to compete on their own and further access to bailout could severely distort the competitive environment. With the exception of the treatment of BGZ and PKO-BP in Poland, the public stance in three countries is that the bailouts are over. However, that was the stance in Hungary at the time of the first of its several recapitalization plans. Our view is that future bank bailouts remain fairly likely given the uncertainties of a transition economy. If they do in fact occur, continuing to link them to whether the bank is or was state-owned or to whether the bank's clients are state-owned would be clearly anti-competitive.

To summarize, for a variety of good and bad reasons competition was very imperfect in the banking sectors of Hungary, Poland, and the Czech Republic up to 1995. As time goes on and important aspects of building the institutions of the market economy are brought to completion, maintaining this uncompetitive environment will be harder to justify. It would seem then that competition policy should increasingly become a high priority in banking in these economies. Despite this, it appears that in some quarters there is growing support for state-directed consolidation in the banking sectors. Thus there is a risk that the banking sectors may become less rather than more competitive.

7.4.   *Do Investors Direct the Use of Capital?*

In Chapter 1 we argued that one of the widely recognized failings of socialism in Eastern Europe was that it left a void in the monitoring and control of capital. Capital was owned collectively or by the workers of the enterprises. In either case, a lack of clear incentives as well as a large free-rider problem meant that too often no one acted to ensure that capital was used efficiently. Thus a central motivation for adopting capitalist forms of economic organization was to fill this void.

One aspect of this question is the extent of private sector development in the transition economies. This in turn depends upon the pace of privatization and the growth of new private companies. A rough indicator of the status of the private sector is the share of GDP produced by the private sector. The European Bank for Reconstruction and

Development estimates that in 1995 these shares stood at 70 per cent for the Czech Republic and 60 per cent for both Hungary and Poland (EBRD 1995). These should be taken as rough estimates. So in our view what is important in these figures is not whether the Czech Republic has a greater or smaller private sector share than the other two, but rather that it has achieved about the same level as the other two in such a short time and starting from an extremely low level of private sector development in 1989. Our reviews of the privatization processes in the three countries gives a clear explanation of this. In the Czech Republic the group directing the transition process has pursued privatization with single-minded determination. Indeed, in response to the argument that other reforms were being neglected in order to further privatization, the Czech prime minister Klaus repeatedly argued that the key was to privatize after which time private agents working through the market place would bring about the restructuring of the economy. The consequence has been that the Czechs had successfully completed two waves of mass privatization by 1995, leaving most of the former state-owned enterprises with private owners. In contrast, Hungary and Poland had not seriously used mass privatization in the first stage of transition. Privatization was approached with great energy, but the case-by-case approach ended by slowing the privatization process as clearly defined groups battled with one another in order to move privatization in the direction that favoured their interests.

Even though privatization has proved difficult to accomplish quickly in Poland and Hungary, it may be that some progress was achieved early in transition by the State itself operating its own enterprises on a commercial basis. In this regard, by 1995 both Poland and Hungary had succeeded in changing most state enterprises into legal entities which were subject to company laws. Furthermore, there were a number of concrete steps that were taken by the authorities to enforce harder budget constraints and to bring about restructuring in enterprises in advance of privatization.[2] However, the commitment of the government to running their enterprise for profit competes with other priorities. Thus, in the long-run increasing the efficiency of most of the enterprises still owned by the State will require that sooner or later they are privatized.

Finally, private ownership does not necessarily mean that efficiency is achieved. Agency problems can cause private firms to fall far short of the best results that are technically possible. In the face of this, mature

---

[2] e.g. the survey evidence of Pinto *et al.* (1993) suggested that the Polish ministry of finance's decision to prevent its state-owned enterprises which had become delinquent from receiving further credits seems to have induced labour-shedding.

capitalist economies have developed laws and other means of helping shareholders and other outside investors to maintain effective authority within an organization. What have been the developments in this regard in transition economies?

Much of the dynamism in the private sectors in Eastern Europe has been in small enterprise, often in services. Much of this activity takes place with sole proprietorships or partnerships where the owners are also managers. For such small organizations agency problems should be slight. The concern is mainly with those economic activities which must take place in larger-scale enterprises which are managed by complex management organizations. Most existing large firms in Eastern Europe were state-owned in the past even if they are privately owned now. To what extent are these firms emerging from privatization with owners that are willing and able to restructure the firms as required to achieve efficiency?

This question amounts to asking whether post-privatization large shareholders have emerged to exert control and to bring about management changes. In Hungary a number of the large enterprises, especially those which were privatized early on, were sold to foreign buyers who took large stakes. In these cases, we would say that privatization has resulted in a clearer concentration of decision-making power in the hands of the owners. Later Hungarian privatization began to favour sales to domestic buyers. The result was a large number of sales to managers and other employees. In many cases shares are held widely by employees which weakens the incentives of top management to maximize returns.[3]

In Poland the privatization process resulted frequently in sales to employees, often with the plant and equipment leased from the State. In our view, this was probably about the worst outcome that could have occurred in privatization. It changed the formal legal status of the enterprise, but left the effective control of the enterprise more or less as it was before the firm was privatized. In fact, it might have been worse than no privatization at all in that when the State remains the nominal owner of the enterprise it is able to intervene directly and may do so when the need for it is sufficiently clear. The mass privatization programme that was finally underway in 1995 was designed so as to give one investment fund a large stake in the firm. Theoretically this should favour active monitoring. However, the investment funds themselves will have large diversified portfolios as their assets and extremely

---

[3] A 1993 World Bank Survey of 200 Hungarian enterprises included some 24 firms privatized that are classified as having insider ownership. Of these employees held 46% of shares and managers held 35% See EBRD (1995: 130).

dispersed shareholdings. It is not clear to what extent their managers will seek to run the funds as very active shareholders as opposed to passive portfolio investors.

In the Czech Republic most large firms have gone through mass privatization. This has left them with a dispersed ownership structure. However, most of the shareholdings have been channelled through investment funds. Among the many investment funds, some have emerged as giants. And some of these have pursued a strategy of trying to accumulate large holdings in selected firms. In such cases effective control of the enterprises lies in the hands of the investment companies which manage the funds. Even though there is a legal limit on the size of the share that a single fund or single investment company can own, the fact that there is no organized system of proxy voting means that a fund with 20 per cent of the shares could easily have a majority of the votes of those shareholders who attend a shareholders' meeting. Furthermore, there is no legal obstacle to investors accumulating a large, even majority, stake in the firm by buying shares on the open market. There are signs that this has been occurring during 1995.[4] A small group of investors began to accumulate large holdings of companies whose prices had been severely depressed in the stock market failure that followed the initial privatization stock market boom. In doing so they created empty-shell companies for the purpose of asset diversion and otherwise used the looseness of Czech securities laws in order to disguise their hand. Once in control they changed management with the result that the share price improved. Building on these gains they repeated the process on progressively larger and larger firms until eventually they gained control of the fifth largest Czech bank. Thus in the environment created by voucher privatization control can shift quickly in Czech enterprises. Ultimately this may induce a deeper restructuring in Czech industry than was observed while the privatization process was being developed and brought to completion.

Large shareholders are not the only investors who may effectively decide the direction for an enterprise. Potentially, large debtholders, in particular the banks, may actively monitor the firm and may use the tools available to intervene. In transition one of the problems that received the earliest attention was that the banks appeared to be very passive in dealing with non-performing borrowers (see Mitchell 1993). In part this seemed to be due to defects in the laws and procedures for dealing with financially distressed firms. Thus one approach to developing debtor control over enterprises is to improve bankruptcy procedures. In this regard the three countries we have studied have taken

---

[4] See 'Investment Coup Rattles Prague', *International Herald Tribune*, 21 Dec. 1995.

strikingly different paths. Hungary pursued the bankruptcy route most aggressively by passing a law which made bankruptcy mandatory for firms that fell behind in debt service more than a moderate amount. The result was an explosion of bankruptcies in 1992 which overwhelmed the courts and provoked a banking crisis which forced the government to intervene with further recapitalization at a time when it had considered it had completed its bank recapitalization efforts. It was soon clear to virtually everyone that this law had gone too far, and steps were taken to moderate its effect. Some have argued that the Hungarian bankruptcy reform produced important benefits in the form of forcing the banks to deal with problem credits actively and that the programmes' defects could have been corrected with modifications of detail (Mizsei 1995*a*).

The Czech Republic has taken the opposite approach to bankruptcy from that of the Hungarians. In effect, they have reformed their law but they have done little to encourage the use of bankruptcy as a means of bringing about the restructuring of enterprises. This was consistent with a strategy of delaying the restructuring of large enterprises until privatization had been completed. This approach is open to the possible criticism that the delay was costly in terms of lost growth during the period when industry was allowed to continue much as in the past. It is hard to say for sure that such a view is correct since privatization itself might have taken a very different course had firm restructuring increased unemployment or other social costs early on in the transition process. What is clearer in our view is that in opting to invest little in improving bankruptcy proceedings in the Czech Republic, the authorities made bankruptcies unnecessarily costly. Now that privatization is largely complete, financial discipline can be expected to become increasingly severe. This will naturally create more distressed firms. In this environment, a costly bankruptcy process may mean that restructuring of distressed firms will not occur when it should, and that lenders may be unwilling to provide the necessary finance for new projects which would allow the firms to grow.

Poland's basic bankruptcy law left creditors little incentive to pursue their delinquent borrowers through the courts. It appears that the most effective use of these laws occurred when creditors and managers would strike a deal on the form of a reorganized firm, in which case formal liquidation was simply a step used to bring the intended reorganization about. The main step taken towards creditor restructuring of firms was the Financial Restructuring Act of 1993. This introduced bank conciliation procedures which simplified the restructuring process and gave large creditors, in particular banks, clear incentives to succeed in putting through a reorganization plan. The results in Poland show that it was widely used and that it effectively removed the bankruptcy roadblock. This procedure has been often praised and has been suggested as a model of what might be used in other transition economies. However, not everyone is pleased with the law. Indeed, the law streamlines the process by reducing the powers of small creditors and creates the possibility of reorganization plans that may be harmful to these groups of creditors. Therefore there has been a challenge to the constitutionality of the Financial Restructuring Act. Because of this the use of bank conciliation was not continued beyond 1996 when the original coverage of the Act lapsed.

Finally, banks become active in firm management when they become large shareholders or if they control blocks of shareholder votes. In this area also each of the three countries we have studied has taken its distinctive approach. In Hungary there are important legal distinctions between commercial banks and investment banks which make it difficult for the commercial banks to be active shareholders in firms. In the Czech Republic commercial banks have considerable freedom to become shareholders in firms. Furthermore, through the mass privatization process several banks have created investment companies which control large numbers of the shares that had been sold for vouchers. Thus indirectly the banks potentially can gain access to the board of directors of companies to which they lend. Some banks say that they are passive investors who do not seek to intervene in management decisions; however, the possibility clearly exists for Czech banks to develop very close ties with firms in much the same way that occurs in German universal banks (see Franks and Mayer 1994).

Polish law allows for universal banking. Nevertheless, no Polish banks have emerged as actively using share ownership as a means of intervening in the restructuring of firms who borrow from them. In particular, it appears that debt equity swaps were not very widely used in the reorganizations accepted by the seven regional commercial banks covered by the Financial Restructuring Act. This is consistent with a general reluctance of bankers in transition countries to take equity stakes in their clients (as Dittus (1996) has argued). In part, this seems to reflect their desire to keep senior claims. However, his interview evidence suggests that at least as important is the belief that the banks themselves do not possess sufficient management personnel of the appropriate type to use shareholder voting power to an effective end. There is a third possible explanation. If banks believe that there is some chance that partial bailouts of the banking system will occur in the future, they probably realize that bailouts would usually occur in response to a decline in the quality of a loan portfolio rather than a decline in stock prices. If so, they would be even more reluctant to swap debt for equity. This would be consistent with the prediction of the model of Berglöf and Roland (1995).

7.5.   Are Securities Markets Developing?

Through a series of money market reforms taking place during the 1980s and 1990s, liquid government bond markets have become a regular feature of mature capitalist economies. In a few years following the introduction of two-tier banking, Hungary, Poland, and the Czech Republic have made impressive progress in imitating this example and have now developed reasonably liquid markets for treasury bills. In some cases, notably Poland, this has spawned the growth of trading in other short-term instruments. As elsewhere, efficiency in the government's efforts to develop this market was forced by the very practical need to finance its deficit. In this regard, the budgetary discipline of the Czech State had the perverse result of slowing the development of the monetary market in relative terms. In other ways, developments on the Czech fixed-income market have been relatively advanced. For example, early on in transition, some Czech firms were able to raise funds by selling bonds on the domestic market.

   The establishment of a stock market is an important step in giving privately owned firms access to finance by means of securities issues. From almost the outset of transition, steps were taken in Hungary, Poland, and the Czech Republic to open stock exchanges for the first time since the old exchanges were closed during the Second World War. The development of these markets has been strongly shaped by the courses taken by privatization in these countries, as can be seen from the summary statistics listed in Table 7.6. Hungary and Poland have adopted a case-by-case approach to privatization with only a small minority of firms going through the process of a public sale (IPO). The result is a small number of large firms are traded on the stock exchange. The total value of stock outstanding represents about 4 per cent of GDP in each country.[5] In many mature capitalist economies stock market capitalization represents 20 per cent or more of GDP. So by this criterion equity markets in Poland and Hungary remain quite underdeveloped. In contrast, mass privatization in the Czech Republic has resulted in more than 1,000 Czech firms having publicly traded shares

---

[5] This ignores treasury and other bonds traded on the exchanges. In the case of the Budapest exchange these are very substantial.

TABLE 7.6　Stock market development

	No. of publicly traded firms	Stock market capitaliztion (% of GDP)
Hungary (1994)	40	4
Poland (1995)	41	4
Czech Republic (1994)	1,000+	20

outstanding, representing a total market capitalization that puts the Czech Republic in the company of mature capitalist economies. Furthermore, the majority of the adult population has now had the experience of owning shares, a situation that does not exist even in the USA which is generally thought of as the economy most strongly oriented towards securities market finance.

If stock market development is the yardstick of progress in a transition economy, the Czech approach must be considered very successful. However, there are reasons to believe that this comparison of the number and value of traded firms overstates the degree of equity market development in the Czech Republic. While a large number of firms can be traded on the Czech exchanges, in fact liquid markets exist only for a relatively small number of them. A still smaller subset of these firms have met the requirements for full listing on the Prague Stock Exchange. Furthermore, Czech citizens bought their shares with vouchers, not money.[6] Thus the Czech equity market has not proved its ability to attract financial capital. In this regard, the exchanges of Warsaw and Budapest have a longer and stronger track record than does the Prague market. In our view one should not make too much of this point. In all mature capitalist economies, new equity finance funds only a small share of investment (Mayer 1990). And the volume of secondary trading in a year vastly outstrips the value of new issues. Thus the importance of stock markets is first in providing liquidity for investors and a means of exchanging corporate control. As we mentioned in section 7.4, there are already signs that the Czech equity market is playing this role. There are even suggestions that through mergers and leveraged buyouts the number and value of publicly traded firms in the Czech Republic may decline in the future (Mejstrick *et al.* 1996). Thus it is distinctly possible that the net contribution of the Czech equity market to funding of new investment may turn *negative* for a time as was the case on the American

---

[6] More exactly, they bought shares with vouchers which were purchased with money at prices which were only a small fraction of the book value of the shares being auctioned.

equity market at times during the 1980s. In our view such a development would demonstrate the importance of Czech stock trading as a market for corporate control.

In turning to other securities-markets developments in the region, it is clear that the growth of mutual funds has also been strongly affected by the course taken by privatization. In the Czech Republic mass privatization allowed the free creation of investment funds, with the result that more than 400 mutual funds were traded after the first wave of voucher privatization in 1993. These ranged in size from the very small to some huge funds run indirectly by the major banks. In contrast, the development of mutual funds was slow in Hungary and Poland. This may change in 1997 when the fifteen funds created as part of Poland's mass privatization start trading on stock exchanges. Otherwise, there have been some attempts to introduce the trading of derivative instruments in the region, the main example being the reopening of the Budapest Commodity Exchange (see Anderson and Powell 1993). Prior to the Second World War, this commodity exchange was very active, reflecting the importance of Budapest in the agricultural trade in Central Europe. When it reopened in 1990, the exchange introduced the trading of futures contracts for agricultural goods, primarily wheat and maize, which have historically been important export crops for Hungary. As far as possible the exchange tried to imitate the Chicago Board of Trade which has the largest market for grain futures in the world. Again following the example of Chicago the intention is to follow the trading of agricultural futures with the trading of futures on financial instruments, notably treasury bonds. Given the significance of the Hungarian government bond market, it would seem that the potential for growth in this area is considerable.

The main lesson that emerges from this review is that for a transition economy, the choice between bank-based or market-based finance is made essentially at the time the path of privatization is chosen. If a country uses mass privatization and designs the programme so that shares become securities in the sense that they can be freely traded on exchanges or over-the-counter markets, then the country can make a giant step towards the development of securities-market finance for the private sector. Otherwise, it appears that equity markets are likely to be restricted to a relatively small section of the private economy. In stating this conclusion, we do not underestimate the importance of banks in the Czech Republic. Indeed, Czech law and the structure of Czech banking gives the large banks considerable power to influence the course of finance in the economy. At the same time we do not underestimate the considerable efforts that have been extended to build the institutions

of securities markets in Hungary and Poland. However, these microeconomic developments are overwhelmed by influence of the privatization programme. Stated otherwise, the potential of using securities
markets to finance growth, to restructure firms, or to force banks to pay
a competitive return on deposits is much greater in an economy where
the existing stock market capitalization represents 20 per cent of GDP
than in one where it represents only 4 per cent of GDP.

7.6.   Is Outside Finance Supporting Economic Growth?

Stated in the most general way, the objective of the transition is to
change the organization of ex-socialist economies in order to promote
rapid economic growth. Despite the fact that they were complex, indus-
trialized economies, the levels of income achieved were far less than
those of advanced capitalist economies of the West. For example, in
1992 the GDPs per capita in the Czech Republic, Hungary, and Poland
were respectively $7,160, $5,740, and $4,880.[7] This compared to an aver-
age of $19,600 in G-7 countries in 1992. The shared hope of all those
committed to the transition is that these gaps can be closed very considerably in a period of ten or fifteen years.

The development of the financial sectors of these economies contributes to this end in a variety of ways. It can help to stimulate the savings
rate that will provide the funds needed for investment. More importantly it can guide the allocation among alternative investment opportunities so as to favour those promising the highest return and thus making
the greatest contribution to growth. It can help to establish proper
incentives for managers of firms to maximize returns rather than pursuing their own personal goals. By overcoming these 'agency' problems
the financial sector can make those agents with funds to invest willing to
give them to those agents with access to the most promising investment
projects.

Central to all of these activities is the idea that the savings of one
agent will probably be most productive if they are used to finance
another agent's project. In fact, there is a strong tendency for enterprises to be self-financed, and this tendency is true for advanced
capitalist economies as well as developing economies. Nevertheless
there appears to a positive correlation between economic growth and
financial depth (see King and Levine 1993). One aspect of financial

---

[7] These figures are based on purchasing power exchange rates. See EBRD (1994).

TABLE 7.7 Financial depth

	1990	1991	1992	1993	1994
A. Total bank assets (% of GDP):					
Hungary	77.0	79.8	72.5	76.1	72.2
Poland	22.2	32.5	32.1	28.0	32.8
Czech Republic	n.a.	n.a.	n.a.	89.0	94.8
B. Growth of commercial bank assets (% of GDP):					
Hungary	n.a.	n.a.	n.a.	16	10
Poland	n.a.	n.a.	16	17	18

Sources: A. EBRD (1995); B. OECD, NBH, NBP, and own calculations.

depth is the degree of development of financial intermediaries which by their nature play the role of directing savings to investment. Table 7.7 reports some crude indicators of the banking sector coverage in the three countries we have considered. In panel A we report total bank assets in relation to GDP. There are very large differences in this measure across the three countries considered. By this measure the Czech Republic has a bank coverage approaching that of many mature capitalist economies. In contrast, Hungary and, especially, Poland have a considerably lower bank coverage. One factor that may explain these low levels of coverage is the relative importance of the rural population in Poland. For example, the cooperative banks which service largely rural areas are not taken into account in the consolidated balance sheet of the commercial banking sector. A second factor that distinguishes Poland and Hungary from the Czech Republic is their considerably higher rates of inflation. This tends to discourage savers from holding bank deposits. The fact that high and variable rates of inflation tend to discourage intermediation is one way in which inflation can hurt economic growth.

The current levels of bank coverage strongly reflect the heritage of the past. It is important to see whether these patterns are being altered by the course of transition. In this regard the growth of bank coverage in Poland from 22 per cent to 32 per cent of GDP in the course of four years of transition appears encouraging. In contrast, during the same period in Hungary the trend was for bank coverage to shrink. These divergent trends are seen also in panel B where we report the growth of bank assets from the consolidated balance sheets reported in Chapters

TABLE 7.8   Private sector credit (% of domestic credit creation)

	1989	1990	1991	1992	1993	1994
Poland[a]	n.a.	n.a.	n.a.	80.0	29.9	29.53
Czech Republic[b]	n.a.	12.3	22.4	39.3	55.4	59.9
Hungary (small enterprises)	1.2	2.6	3.3	3.7	3.6	3.2

[a] This is obtained by combining information from Table 5.11 with share of non-financial credits in total domestic credit creation (including non-financial credits, public sector credits, treasury bills, and bonds).
[b] Based on Table 6.7.
Sources: NPB, ČNB, and NBH.

4 and 5. We see that in 1994 in particular there was a relatively weak expansion of the Hungarian banking sector.

Aggregate measures of financial depth give us a crude indication of the degree to which outside finance is available for investment projects of all types. At least as important is the question of whether outside finance in transition economies is being made available to the emerging private sector. Given the newness and small size of many private enterprises, there is reason to fear that the banking sector may prefer lending to large established enterprises in preference to new private enterprises.

Table 7.8 reports some data relevant to this question. For Poland and the Czech Republic we are able to see the fraction of domestic credit creation which takes the form of loans to private enterprises. It is extremely striking that in 1992 the private sector received 80 per cent of new credits in Poland. This was at a time when still relatively little of the state enterprise sector had been privatized; as a consequence much of this credit was received by new enterprises in industry and services or private enterprises in the agricultural sector. The fact that the Polish system was able to channel significant amounts of credits to the private sector early in the transition process may well have contributed positively to pulling the economy out of the recession in 1992. In the Czech Republic the share of credit destined for the private sector grew steadily over the period 1990–4. This trend paralleled the pace of privatization of the economy. Much of the increase in private credit appears to be explained by the passage of established enterprises from the state sector to the private sector. This is consistent with the fact that a large proportion of outstanding long-term credits originated before 1990 (see EBRD 1995: 162).

Hungarian credit statistics do not report credit growth by ownership category of borrower. As a result we do not have data which can be compared directly with those we report for Poland and the Czech Republic. However, we can try to piece together the available information in order to infer something about overall bank lending to the private sector. First, we have already documented the fact that the State's heavy borrowing requirements to cover the budget deficit severely restricted lending to enterprises as a whole (Tables 4.11 and 4.12). Therefore, increasing private sector lending could only have come as the result of a very large shift in the composition of enterprise lending away from state-owned enterprises to private enterprises. Hungarian data do distinguish large and small enterprises, the latter being privately owned. As can be seen from Table 7.8, the share of small enterprise loans in total domestic credit creation rose from 1989 to 1991 but has been about level since then. It is unlikely that the treatment of large private enterprises has been dramatically very different than that of small enterprises. Therefore, we can safely infer than there has been no dramatic shift in lending to private enterprises in Hungary. This is confirmed by the relatively high proportion of financing by Hungarian firms provided by foreign creditors.

Finally, foreign direct investment provides an alternative to domestic credit as a means of financing project investment. Gross foreign direct investment is not reported on a systematic basis by the statistical authorities of the three countries we have considered so these must be estimated on the basis of data from diverse sources. Table 7.9 reports one set of estimates over the period 1989–94. These data show that Hungary was relatively more successful than the Czech Republic or Poland in attracting foreign investment in 1991–3. The performance appears even more impressive in relation to the size of the economy: FDI in 1993 stood at 3.6 per cent of GDP in Hungary whereas it was 1.4 per cent and 0.6 per cent for the Czech Republic and Poland respectively.[8] This ability to attract foreign investment relatively early in the transition process may have been a beneficial by-product of Hungary's relative openness to foreign banks (Wachtel 1995). However, it also was the consequence of a privatization path which initially involved selling many state assets to foreigners. This view is consistent with the decline in FDI in 1994 after that privatization policy was essentially reoriented to favour domestic investors. As a result Hungarian FDI changed the ownership of existing real assets but may not have financed much real investment. In this sense, its contribution to growth would have been limited to the indirect effect of improving management.

---

[8] Calculated using purchasing power exchange rates. See EBRD (1995).

TABLE 7.9 Gross foreign direct investment ($US million)

	1989	1990	1991	1992	1993	1994
Czech Republic	10	166	200	1,210	1,100	800
Hungary	120	311	1,538	1,471	2,339	1,100
Poland	60	88	470	830	1,100	1,300

Source: Koping-Datorg (1995).

What emerges from this review is that in mobilizing finance in order to support economic growth led by the private sector, the three countries under review have had very different experiences in the first years of transition. Poland stands out first by the low level of financial depth at the outset of transition, and second by the dramatic shift of credit favouring the expansion of the private sector. It would be astonishing if this change had been brought about solely by the uncoordinated changes in lending practices of individual banks. The detailed discussion of Chapter 5 suggests that the aggressive approach adopted by the Polish finance ministry in preventing state-owned banks from increasing credits to delinquent state enterprises contributed directly to the shift. Furthermore, the specialized state banks, rural cooperatives, and new private banks were all aggressive in lending to the private sector. Since the priorities of governments can change rapidly and since some of the aggressive lending practices helped spawn Poland's bad-debt problem, one might question whether these factors provide a solid basis for healthy credit allocation in the future. Nevertheless, we fell that it should be recognized that these factors did converge to produce a climate favourable for growth at a time when this was badly needed.

7.7. Is the Financial System Stable?

If the financial system is to be able to support microeconomic tasks of credit allocation and monitoring, it must also fulfil the fundamental requirement that it be adequately stable. Under normal conditions when agents engage in financial contracting their counterparties should be able to fulfil their side of the bargain, and the chances that they will not do so can be ascertained on the basis of information that can be obtained with a reasonable amount of effort. When the financial system as a whole is unstable, all efforts involved in contracting can be swept aside by waves of defaults which are difficult for the individuals to foresee and against which there is little protection save that of not entering into the financial contract to begin with. Furthermore, deep instability of the financial sector can leave the banking system unable to fulfil its basic payments function thereby having an immediate negative impact on trade in goods and services as well. Thus the last question we ask in this section is in some sense the most fundamental: have the transition economies that we have studied assured the stability of the financial systems as a whole?

At the outset of transition the stability of the emerging commercial banking sectors was clearly threatened by the burden of outstanding loans made to state-owned enterprises that were unprofitable or were soon to become so as a result of price and trade reforms. All three countries we have studied have made major efforts to clean up bad debts and to recapitalize their banks. Have these efforts eliminated the bad-debt problem? Table 7.9 reports the evolution of non-performing loans in commercial banks of Hungary, Poland, and the Czech Republic through 1994. We have relied on statistics collected by the countries' central banks. The methodologies employed to construct these data and the timing of the efforts to conduct audits of outstanding loans differed across these countries. As a result precise comparisons across countries or even across years are somewhat difficult. Nevertheless, these data are suggestive of a number of important conclusions. First, the proportion of bad loans within the bank's portfolios of enterprise and individual loans remained high in 1994 several years into transition and after the countries programmes to clean up had had time to work. This points out what we have emphasized in our discussions of the individual countries, namely that the bad-loan problem in these countries originates as much from the risks of lending in transition as from the mistakes of the past. For this reason the bad-loan problem has not gone away and is likely to remain a major preoccupation of policy-makers for years to come.

Second, the data suggest important differences in the status of the bad-loan problem in the three countries. In Hungary in 1994 the reported level of bad loans was almost 30 per cent of all loans but only 11 per cent of all bank assets. This reflected the relatively small and declining share of bank loans in total bank assets as the banks held large amounts of treasury securities, central bank reserves, and liquid assets. In contrast, Czech had loans in 1994 represented 38.8 per cent of the loan portfolio and 20.1 per cent of all bank assets, reflecting the relatively large share of bank loans in the assets of Czech commercial banks. One possible consequence of the State crowding out enterprise loans in Hungary might have been the more severe screening of borrowers so that only relatively safe borrowers could obtain credits. Instead, the

TABLE 7.10   Non-performing loans

	1991	1992	1993	1994
As per cent of bank loans to enterprises and individuals:				
Hungary	9.4	20.7	42.6	30.2
Poland	16.5	26.8	27.4	29.0
Czech Republic	2.7	19.3	22.1	38.8
As per cent of total assets:				
Hungary	4.1	7.5	15.7[a]	11.0
Poland	6.9	10.2	9.7	9.8
Czech Republic	1.2	10.4	10.5	20.1
As per cent of GDP:				
Hungary	3.5	5.4	11.9	7.9
Poland	2.2	3.3	2.7	3.2
Czech Republic	1.9	14.2	9.3	30.4

[a] Starting in 1993 this includes savings cooperatives.

Sources: National Banks of Hungary, Poland, and the Czech Republic.

data suggest that borrowers were screened only by high interest rates leaving banks with high-risk borrowers, as predicted by models of credit rationing.

Third, one's impressions of the relative significance of bad loans for the countries might be influenced by whether data are reported as a percentage of total loans, total assets, or GDP. For example, Czech bad loans reported in 1994 were in line with those of Poland and Hungary when stated as a percentage of total loans. But when expressed as a percentage of GDP, Czech bad loans exceeded those of Poland and Hungary. The reason is that in the Czech Republic loans figure large in the balance sheets of banks and bank coverage is greater than in either Poland or Hungary. This points to what might be the dark side of the transition strategy adopted by the Czech Republic. In giving priority to bank recapitalization and privatization, the Czech authorities may have prevented latent problems from surfacing as enterprises were subsidized in a variety of ways and bankruptcy proceedings were systematically avoided. Now that privatization is largely completed, enterprise restructuring is likely to increase. Thus, the number of loan defaults may begin to rise considerable. Were it to do so this would quickly become a problem of alarming proportions given the scale of enterprise loans for the economy as a whole.

As the scale of the bad-loan problem in these transition countries

TABLE 7.11   Deposit insurance coverage

Hungary	1 million forint ($9,000)
Poland	3,000 ecu ($3,500)
Czech Republic	80% of deposits, up to 100,000 korunas ($3,500)

became known, there would have been an immediate banking crisis if depositors had not been given adequate assurance of the safety of their bank funds. The treatment of this problem has been similar in the three countries we have reviewed. In the first instance the State guaranteed the deposits in the state-owned banks and in this way covered the vast majority of bank deposits. The new banks did not automatically receive the same guarantee. Subsequently, the three countries took steps to set up formal systems of deposit insurance. This effort was motivated by the desire to extend coverage to deposits in private banks and to establish limits to the coverage of individual depositors. The scale of coverage is roughly comparable in the three countries with Hungary being the most generous of the three (see Table 7.11). The systems are funded through premiums. In Hungary there is some attempt to adjust the premiums for risk, which is not the case in Poland and the Czech Republic. As in other countries, explicit deposit guarantees are probably supplemented by implied guarantees of uncertain dimension. In all three countries, the authorities have intervened in banks that had collapsed. The interventions took a variety of forms including arranging mergers with healthy banks and extending cheap refinance credits. The upshot is that all major losses to depositors have been avoided. This appears to establish a precedent for generous coverage through deposit insurance. However, many of these steps pre-date the introduction of explicit guarantees which arguably provide the authorities with a basis for allowing some depositors to lose in future bank failures.

The second line of protection against banking system instability is to establish minimum capital standards for deposit-taking institutions. In the case of traditional state-owned banks, the issue of capital adequacy did not arise in any direct way since the depositors were fully guaranteed by the State implying that it would make infusions of funds should they be needed. In contrast, capital levels become crucial once a bank takes the form of a private company (e.g. joint-stock or limited liability company). In setting capital standards for these banks the three countries followed the BIS approach that has had widespread acceptance internationally. Poland and Hungary were relatively aggressive in setting a capital standard of 8 per cent of risk-adjusted assets by 1994. The

Czech Republic adopted an intermediate target of 6.25 per cent which was set to rise to 8 per cent by the end of 1996. While these targets have been publicly declared, only fragmentary information has emerged from the central banks about the standards that have been achieved to date. As a result it is difficult to form an assessment of either the number of banks meeting the standards or about the distribution of actual capital ratios throughout the banking system.

Hungary, Poland, and the Czech Republic adopted the BIS standards in part because they sought to conform to the internationally accepted norm and in part because their systems initially fell far short of those standards so that such targets meant making a serious step towards assuring banking system safety. It is unclear how much of the banking system meets the standards chosen. Furthermore, one can question whether such standards really provide sufficient safety given the risks associated with lending in transition economies. For these reasons, we think that the safety of the banking systems is probably not assured on the basis of the deposit insurance systems that have been put in place and the levels of capital and reserves in the banks. That is, there is a real chance that systematic losses in loan portfolios could exceed bank capital by an amount which would exhaust deposit insurance funds. Should this occur, the safety of the banking system would hinge on the response of the government on the one hand and the central banks on the other. The former could intervene with capital infusions for distressed banks. The latter could intervene by lending to the distressed banks or by loosening credit more generally. As a result we are led to conclude that assuring the safety of the banking system is likely to remain an important concern as the transition process continues and that it is likely to exert significant pressure either for future bank bailouts or for relaxing monetary discipline.

7.8. Conclusion

We have tried to provide a comprehensive review of the approaches taken to financial development in Hungary, Poland, and the Czech Republic in the first six years after the collapse of communism. In the process we have seen many similarities and many differences in the paths taken. It is perhaps worth asking what are the broad lines which most distinguish each country from the others. Each reader is free to distil from the details of each country's story an answer to this question. Our own is as follows.

Hungary is frequently labelled the gradualist in its approach to reform. We have seen, however, that some of the measures taking towards liberalizing its financial sector have been more aggressive than those of either Poland or the Czech Republic. In particular, it adopted a radical approach to financial restructuring through the use of bankruptcy proceedings. This forced both distressed firms and their creditors to acknowledge loan delinquencies and in so doing prodded them to take concrete action to address the problems. Hungary has also been a leader in opening its financial sector. It has allowed foreign banks to enter the Hungarian market, and at the same time Hungarian firms have had access to foreign capital either as direct investment or through loans from foreign banks. In these ways Hungary has taken strong steps aimed at creating the microeconomic conditions needed for the financial sector to become market-based and competitive. Until now the benefits of these measures for the Hungarian economy have been hindered by an approach to bad-loan clean-up in which one insufficient bank recapitalization was succeeded by another. This has left the impression that the State stands ready to help out the banks when they make mistakes. This undermines the financial discipline that was being sought through strong bankruptcy laws, and at the same time it tends to nullify the effect of bank competition since the experience has shown that the large banks that emerged from the monobank are those most likely to be helped out when in trouble. Beyond all this, Hungary stands out as the country where the painful efforts to get the financial sector on good microeconomic foundations have been severely compromised by bad macroeconomics. The heavy budgetary deficit, which is due in part but not entirely to the huge foreign debt which Hungary has continued to service through the transition, has crowded out both state-owned and privately owned enterprises. The consequence probably has been a lower rate of investment and growth than might have been the case otherwise.

Financial reform in Poland took a very liberal course in the initial months of transition. The banking sector was completely restructured by splitting up the monobank into smaller units and by allowing the creation of many new banks. At the same time a very restrictive monetary policy was used to cut off an incipient hyperinflation. Subsequently, in the face of a ballooning bad-loan problem and a severe recession which threatened he stability of the banking sector, both policy directions were reversed. Monetary policy was relaxed noticeably, and new entries to banking were stopped. In addition, the government took strong steps towards redirecting credit from state enterprises towards private ones. The tools used were crude, but starting from 1992 they had a noticeable effect. The credits which flowed to private enterprises probably helped to feed the rapid private sector expansion. This was aided by the fact that public sector borrowing was somewhat restrained. In this regard Poland was undoubtedly helped by the having found relief from some of the burden of its external debt. Shifting credit away from public towards private enterprises occurred largely without the benefit of the institutions of a capitalist financial sector which in Poland have had a slow and somewhat painful gestation. The stock market is dynamic but still plays a relatively marginal role in Polish finance. The banking sector remains dominated by state-owned banks as bank privatization proceeded even more slowly than did the privatization of industrial enterprises. This deliberate pace in bank privatization may have avoided the creation of large but very weak banks that would soon have required the support of the State for their survival. Similarly the Poles did not rush to recapitalize their banks; however, the programme that was completed in 1994 for the seven large regional commercial banks appears to have had the virtue of discouraging them form believing that in the future the State would be quick to rescue them if they were in difficulties.

Czech transition has been marked by political stability and continuity of leadership. This has given rise to policies that are the coherent reflection of a particular vision of how to proceed with transition. Privatization has been the priority, with voucher privatization being the favoured method. The logic of this is that enterprises should be restructured by private owners. Voucher privatization was the means of assuring that enterprise control was retained by the nation. This strategy implied a clear sequence of reforms. For example, it was decided to avoid having firms restructured by creditors prior to privatization. As a result, bankruptcy procedures remained inefficient and little used. On the other hand, bank recapitalization was treated as a high priority, with a centralized receiver-bank cleaning the state banks' balance sheets in time for them to be privatized along with industrial firms. Enterprise privatization is far more advanced in the Czech Republic than in the Poland or Hungary so, by its own standards, the Czech strategy appears to be succeeding. However, it has left a number of important problems to be resolved in future. Voucher privatization created almost overnight a stock market with a market capitalization level comparable to that of mature capitalist economies. However, much of the market it illiquid. And the lack of investor protection or market transparency has created a gulf between insiders (including banks and managers) who control the enterprises and Czech small shareholders. Furthermore, the by-product of mass privatization has been the creation of powerful state institutions, notably the consolidation bank and the state property agency, which have the power to perpetuate the practice of state intervention in the allocation of savings and investment. Finally, as the privatized firms advance in the process of restructuring their activities to cut costs and develop new markets, the burden of bad debts may grow considerably. If so, the underdeveloped tools of the private economy for dealing with the problem—notably the bankruptcy courts and deposit insurance—could easily be overwhelmed. Thus, the Czech approach to financial transition involves a considerable commitment to a single long-term strategy. Like other large, long-term bets, this represents a big gamble.

There is one additional question which we have so far refrained from addressing. Has the financial transition been completed in Hungary, Poland, or the Czech Republic? In Chapter 1 we sussgested that the economic transition of the ex-socialist countries had three distinct aspects: stabilization, liberalization, and building the institutions of the market economy. At this stage, the first two steps have been largely accomplished in the financial sectors of the economies we have studied. While much has been done to establish the framework for the market economy, it seems clear to us that much remains to be done before we see that aspect of transition to be at an end. In particular, it strikes us that patterns of ownership and control are still in extreme flux in these economies. As a consequence, agents who acquire a financial asset are still basically uncertain about the rules of the game that will determine how the underlying real assets will be managed or how cashflows will be paid out to various competing stakeholders. Until this becomes more settled, we cannot say that the structure of the market economy has been established and shown to function. And, as such, financial transition has not been completed in any of the three countries.

8

Financial Policy for Transition Countries

8.1. Introduction

After devoting seven chapters to the description and analysis of the financial development in transition economies as represented by the Czech Republic, Hungary, and Poland, we now adopt for the first time the point of view of the economic policy-maker. This is in contrast with much of the early literature on transition which was motivated by the need to provide guidance in making pressing choices of policy. As was inevitable at the time, polemics preceded analysis. Now, several years into the transition process in Eastern and Central Europe, we and others have had the time to analyse the facts and to observe some of the consequences of the policy choices that have been taken so far. It is hoped that the result will contribute to making more informed policy choices in the future. We feel obliged to go one step further and state explicitly what we believe are some of the lessons suggested by our analysis.

In order to be convincing, recommendations for policy should be linked to objectives. What are the goals that should guide financial sector policies in transition economies?[1] In a broad sense, financial policy in a transition country in Central and Eastern Europes is successful if it helps to put the country onto a path of sustained growth leading to the ultimate convergence with the mature capitalist economies of Western Europe. The financial sector contributes to this end through the supply, allocation, and monitoring of funds for investment. These functions of finance apply to any economy, but in the context of a transition economy they take particular forms. Socialist institutions biased the flow of investments in certain directions favoured by the State which did not necessarily have the promise of a high return. In

---

[1] Our thinking on these issues has been aided greatly by our discussions with Lóránd Ambros-Lakatos, Erik Berglöf, Kálmán Mizsei, and Mark Schaffer within the context of a forum on banking policy organized by the CEPR and the Institute of East-West Studies. See Anderson *et al.* (1996).

transition, policies for the financial sector are required to put into place institutions which will select investments on the basis of their productivity. Beyond this, the need for monitoring investments takes on special meaning in a transition context where in the past collective ownership of capital endowed managers and other insiders with great discretionary power in directing enterprises. Finally, even if under socialism the aggregate level of savings was adequate, there is no assurance that this will continue to be so in transition. In particular, if the macroeconomic context is not sufficiently stable, savings may be diverted away from the economy in pursuit of relatively safer investment vehicles.

In light of these considerations we see four general goals for financial policy-making in transition economies:

- assuring a stable financial environment,
- enhancing the quality of enterprise governance,
- promoting the liquidity of real and financial asset markets, and
- facilitating the retreat of the State.

These objectives underlay much of the discussion in Chapters 1–7 and do not require much further elaboration. Without financial stability savers will not have confidence in securities or bank deposits. As a result savings will be discouraged or will find their way to leave the domestic financial circuit. In either case, domestic growth is undermined. Corporate governance has been a major preoccupation in transition economies where the diffuse authority within state-owned enterprises has been blamed for much of the economic underachievement of the past. We have seen that privatization has not been easy to implement and that, even where it has occurred, effective control may remain with managers and other insiders whose ownership stake may be very small relative to the power they wield. Liquidity enhances the value of financial assets and therefore enables borrowers to obtain more funds for the same level of commitment of future repayment. If real asset markets are liquid, productive resources can be directed into the hands of those who are best able to manage them effectively. When this is the case there can emerge a genuine market for corporate control.

Making the retreat of the State an explicit objective of financial transition may require further comment. We have repeatedly argued that, given the starting point of state planning and a banking bureaucracy which actively managed the flow of funds for investment, this is at the core of the transition process. On balance, investments should be directed towards profitable projects, where profits are calculated on the basis of market prices. This does not mean that the State does not have a role to play in the workings of the private financial sector. As in

mature capitalist economies, the State may be required to set and enforce rules of conduct within the market system. However, given the
history of massive state interference in the detailed workings of the
economy, the risk is that ex-socialist states may have difficulty limiting
themselves to being even-handed regulators who implement policies in
non-intrusive ways and who leave private agents to compete on a level
playing-field. Given this likely bias towards excessive state intervention,
it is important to scrutinize each policy choice to see whether the end
served is economic efficiency or bureaucratic prerogative.

We now consider the major financial policy choices facing the countries of Eastern and Central Europe after several years of effort aimed
at developing market-based economies. Our discussion is structured
along the lines of operational areas of policy-making. Typically, any
particular policy tool will affect each of the four general policy goals that
we have identified. In light of our detailed analyses in previous chapters,
we will concentrate on Hungary, Poland, and the Czech Republic. However, many of the same policy choices confront other countries of the
region, in particular those which have entered into association agreements with the European Union.[2] Consequently, our comments will
also apply to other transition countries in the region. However, we
assume that there is a minimum of institutional structure in place
and that there is some stability in the macro-environment. Consequently, the discussion may not yet be relevant to some parts of former
Yugoslavia or the former Soviet Union.

8.2.   Assuring Financial Safety

Mature capitalist economies rely on a battery of policy instruments
which are intended to maintain the continuous functioning of the
financial system. These include:

- self-regulation and credit assessment,
- capital and solvency standards for banks,
- restrictions on asset holding by banks,
- deposit guarantees, and
- existence of a lender of last resort.

The market itself provides the tools needed to assure contracts are
respected or to alert financial partners of the danger of breakdown.

[2] These are Bulgaria, the Czech Republic, Estonia, Hungary, Latvia, Lithuania, Poland,
Romania, Slovakia, and Slovenia.

Credit-rating firms are an example of this. In the banking sector this is supplemented by public regulations aimed at assuring that banks are managed prudently. Finally, the confidence of the general public in the banking system is supported through the provision of deposit guarantees. In normal circumstances these protections will suffice to assure financial stability. Occasionally, a large shock to the system will require the authorities to intervene more actively in order to prevent a banking failure or to prevent the failure in one institution from spreading to the rest of the system. This is done by the central bank extending credits to distressed banks or, in extreme cases, by the State intervening to restore bank solvency. In a mature capitalist economy, the use of these forms of state bailout represent a failure of the normal system of protection. In contrast, in a socialist banking system direct state involvement was the primary means of assuring the overall solvency of the system. Thus one of the major policy concerns for the financial sectors of transition economies is to develop the institutions that will assure the stability and smooth functioning of the banking sector without the regular intervention of the State.

In fact, our detailed analysis has shown that in the six years of transition most of the financial policy effort has been directed to solving the bad-loan problem and recapitalizing the state-owned banks. The same is true of the other transition countries of the region which we have not discussed in detail. To varying degrees these efforts have been successful in lessening the burden on the banking sector of non-performing loans extended to unrestructured state-owned enterprises. However, they remain essentially *ad hoc* measures which have done little to guarantee that in the future financial safety will be achieved by market-based institutions and routine regulations without active state intervention. Indeed, the governments in the region suffer from a credibility problem when they state that there will be no bailouts in the future. In attempting to deal with the stock of old bad loans they have not prevented a flow of new bad loans. In our view, the only way out of this problem is to reinforce the other safety tools listed above and to allow them to carry the burden of dealing with bank failures in the future.

Increasingly, in Western financial systems, explicit deposit insurance has emerged as the policy tool to deal with severely distressed banks. Indeed, since 1994 European Union rules require member States to maintain a deposit guarantee scheme that meets certain standards, including setting an upper limit on the degree of coverage. The advantage of making deposit guarantees explicit is that it removes the incentive for bank runs. By placing limits on deposit insurance coverage, it leaves large depositors with some exposure, thus giving them an incentive to monitor the bank and thereby serving to check abuses of the scheme by bank managers.

We have seen that Hungary, Poland, and the Czech Republic have all created explicit deposit insurance systems with maximum coverage limits. In this sense they are leading the way in the region. However, important issues remain to be addressed before these schemes will function as they should. First, the funding of these schemes remains a problem. Nominally, the schemes are to be funded by premiums levied on deposits. However, the schemes may well be underfunded which leaves open the question of who pays if the funds are exhausted. Indeed, this issue quickly arose in the Czech Republic where two bank failures exhausted the available funds. When in 1995 a third bank failed, the State responded by bailing out depositors from budgetary funds. Thus despite having a modern deposit insurance law on the books, in reality a bank failure forced the State to intervene with an *ad hoc* bailout. Once again it looks as if the workings of the soft budget constraint have taken new institutional forms.

A related problem is that in Central and Eastern Europe implicit deposit guarantees are probably much greater than are explicit ones. Of course, this is hard to determine with certainty because what matters is what depositors and bank managers expect the central bank and government to do in the event that the bank becomes severely distressed. This problem probably exists for all of the commercial banks that have emerged from the old monobanks, for with few exceptions these banks are either state-owned or the State has retained a significant stake after privatization. It is particularly acute in the case of the savings banks where the expectation of unlimited state backing is taken for granted.

In our view, policy should be aimed at making explicit deposit insurance schemes credible by increasing their level of funding through insurance premiums. In addition, there should be a clear message that in the case of bank failures the consequences will be felt by managers through loss of jobs and prosecution for fraud if this occurred, by shareholders through loss of all their equity in the bank, and by large depositors through loss of interest and some of their principal. These policies will begin to have effect only if severely distressed banks are allowed to fail. In Hungary, the Czech Republic, and Poland banks that had failed up to the end of 1995 were all relatively small banks. Now that some large banks have been privatized in these countries, it will be important to make it clear that the State is prepared to see these banks disappear. The Baltic countries stand out in the region for the hard line taken on distressed banks. Large banks have been allowed to fail, including in Latvia the largest commercial bank. However, these are very small countries which had a very low level of bank penetration at the time the bank failures occurred. It is unlikely that they serve as a model for the other countries of the region. We think a much more viable approach is to allow the State to intervene in a failed large bank by restructuring its balance sheet and its management including the possibility of selling it to a large foreign investor.

In developed capitalist countries regulation of minimum capital in banks is the second main tool for assuring the stability of the banking system. As we have seen the goal in the leading transition countries has been to achieve the Basle 8 per cent, risk-adjusted norm. In our view, however, it is an open question whether this norm is appropriate for transition countries. First, this norm was selected on the basis of the experience of mature capitalist economies with relatively stable institutional frameworks and macroeconomic contexts. We have seen that the onset of transition brought several large shocks to these economies. There is no assurance that there may not be significant 'after-shocks' during the years to come. For example, these could come in the form of major shifts in domestic politics, major changes in Russia, or a failure to accede to the European Union. If the risks in transition economies are greater than in mature capitalist economies, then seemingly capital requirements should be greater. However, it is not a simple matter to state what is the appropriate standard for these countries. In particular, we have documented that raising capital standards in the region has had important costs in the form of discouraging bank lending to enterprises and biasing the flow of savings towards financing the state deficit.[3] Thus our analysis does not justify us in recommending a particular capital standard to be applied in all transition countries. Instead, we would view the Basle standard as a probable lower bound for the target for capital standards.

There is much more to banking regulation than just setting capital and liquidity norms. Poland, Hungary, and the Czech Republic have adopted rules for bank supervision which are comparable to those *in effect* in Western Europe, and in this regard they set the example for other transition countries. However, having a set of rules is one thing, but enforcing them is another. Here, the initial efforts in Eastern and Central Europe were inadequate. In our view, reinforcing banking supervision should be a high priority for policy-makers. In part, this is matter of having more staff and improving their qualifications for the

---

[3] More generally it has been argued that the risk-based, Basle capital standards tend to aggravate problems of credit rationing. See Thakor (1996).

job expected of them. However, it is also a matter of having adequate means of forcing banks to remedy rule violations. In our view, in transition economies it is best if the main responsibility for banking supervision be given to the central bank. Generally in the region, central banks are better able to attract qualified staff and have available a variety of 'carrots' and 'sticks' in order to spur banks into acting.

However, it cannot be assumed that central banks in the region will be independent of the government. This opens the door for using political influence to shield a well-connected bank from costly or disagreeable safety standards. As a check on this it is desirable that deposit insurance funds develop their own competence in bank supervision. This requires establishing the funds as independent authorities. Furthermore, in order for them to be effective, the funds must have the means of penalizing imprudent banks. Probably the most effective means of doing this is for deposit insurance authorities to withdraw the coverage of such banks. Thus in light of this we oppose giving blanket coverage to all depository institutions.

A totally different approach to assuring bank safety is to increase the security of the loans that the banks grant. This can be done by having the banks require higher levels of collateral. Indeed, we have seen that this was a clear tendency of some better-managed banks in the early stages of transition. However, setting very high collateral levels is costly economically and can discourage growth. Thus, a more attractive alternative is to enhance the value to banks of any given collateral. In transition countries, this has been hampered by the poor definition of property rights and by other institutional failures that reduce the liquidity of collateral. For example, small and underdeveloped securities markets mean that borrowers do not have available securities which in many circumstances provide attractive bank guarantees. Inefficient bankruptcy procedures have been an additional problem. Hungary has relied heavily on bankruptcy reform, and, after having corrected some clear mistakes in the system, probably has the most developed means of dealing with defaults and distress. The Czech Republic has left its bankruptcy regime in a relatively undeveloped state. If this is not remedied, inefficient bankruptcy may emerge as a serious liability which could obstruct the restructuring of Czech enterprises now that they have largely been privatized.

The thrust of these policy prescriptions is to reinforce the decentralized and institutionalized means of assuring a stable banking system so that the State's intervention is only occasional and circumscribed. Thus the objective is to avoid continuing the massive debt clean-ups and bank recapitalizations that characterized the first five years of transition. A failure to accomplish this would strike a major blow against financial discipline and would undermine the efforts to put the allocation of savings on a market basis. Thus stopping regular bank bailouts should be a priority of financial sector policy-making. However, in our view it is counter-productive to pretend that there could never be a widespread bailout in the future. Given the continuing large and uninsurable risks in transition countries, policy-makers must be prepared for the possibility that the central bank or the State more generally will be called upon to intervene in the capacity of the lender of last resort. Pretending that this is not the case is simply not credible. Thus policy-makers must look to other means to counteract the possible incentive for excessive risk-taking or other forms of managerial moral hazard. To our mind the most effective means of doing this is to demonstrate through action the fact that a bailout is disagreeable for both managers and shareholders. Managers must lose their jobs. Furthermore, their non-salary compensation should be linked to the value of company shares. In the case of bailouts, equity values for old shareholders, including managers, must be reduced or wiped out entirely.

It might be thought that an alternative means of limiting the amount of bailouts would be to fix a predetermined amount of resources that could be available for recapitalizing banks. For example, in the Czech Republic recapitalization has come from the proceeds of privatization. Thus, the government could say that recapitalizations could not exceed the resources of the National Property Fund. In our view, this would be a mistake for several reasons. First, it is arbitrary. Second, this creates an incentive to come relatively early with a claimed loss. And, finally, it does not really address the issue of credibility since it is clear that once a given fund is exhausted the State will still be confronted with its responsibility as the lender of last resort.

Another alternative general approach to assuring financial safety might be through the granting of monopoly power to the banking sector, e.g. through restricting entry (Stiglitz 1994: ch. 12). Indeed, it might be argued that in the aftermath of the Second World War, financial stability in Western Europe was assured largely because of the dominance of large banks which benefited from considerable market power. The major problem with such an approach is that the costs of assuring bank solvency come in the form of monopoly rents which are difficult to trace and even more difficult to remove. Furthermore, it has come to be recognized that specific public policies can assure safety within a competitive banking sector. We now assess the policy measures which might influence the degree of banking competition in transition countries.

8.3.　Banking Competition Policy

In Chapter 7 we concluded that after some initial efforts to introduce an element of competition into banking, there has been much less emphasis on competition policy. This has been particularly true in Poland where the government has actively taken some steps to consolidate some existing banks into larger units. In our view, this is a reaction to the initial pro-competitive policy which gave rise to a large number of new private banks many of which were undercapitalized and quickly succumbed to loan losses resulting from sloppy, and in some cases fraudulent, lending practices. In retrospect, some of the initial efforts towards 'demonopolization' in transition economies, in banking and in other sectors, were clearly misguided. In many cases, a monopolistic state enterprise was broken up into smaller units along lines borrowed from the old, administrative hierarchy which made little sense from an economic point of view. The extreme example of this was the break-up of the old monobank in Bulgaria by making virtually every branch office an independent bank (Wachtel 1995). The result was that the number of banks went from ten in 1990 to seventy-eight in 1991, the majority of which had bank capital of less than $1 million. These proved unmanageable for bank regulators. In the face of a huge bad-debt problem, the government was forced to consolidate banks (Dobrinsky 1994). The result was that eleven relatively large, state-owned banks emerged from the consolidation so that by 1995 the number of banks in Bulgaria had dropped to 42.

It is not only in transition countries that there are signs that severe competition can undermine bank safety. The Savings and Loan Association crisis in the USA can be interpreted as evidence of this. Indeed, some of the savings banks that expanded most rapidly by offering the most attractive terms on deposits were precisely those that failed.[4] Thus we must acknowledge that there is some justification for thinking that the benefits competitive policy in banking must be balanced against costs which may be more significant than in other sectors such as retail sales. However, in the transition economies, some of those arguing that safe banking requires large banks shielded from 'excessive' competition are clearly motivated by self-interest. The prime examples of this are the commercial banks that emerged from the monobank. In most cases these have not yet been privatized and until now they have been supported through bad-loan clean-ups and bank recapitalizations. As a

---

[4] However, increasing deposit insurance coverage at the same time as reducing resources for bank supervision appears to be at least as important a cause. See White (1991) for a discussion.

result, their restructuring has been slower and less deep than it might have been otherwise. These organizations would be likely to be put under pressure once they were privatized if the banking sector becomes increasingly competitive.

In our view the fact that there have been numerous bank failures in the region is the consequence of the risks inherent in the transition process and not a sign that competitive pressure in banking has been excessive. In fact, the large banks that have emerged from the monobank have inherited large deposit bases and extensive branch networks which tend to give them a competitive advantage. Admittedly, they inherited portfolios laden with non-performing loans; however, with time and after numerous bailouts, this burden has been lightened considerably. Thus, on balance public policy should be aimed at increasing competitive pressures in banking. This does not mean that large banks should be broken up. Indeed, the trend in mature capitalist economies is towards larger, more fully integrated banking firms. This suggests that there are significant economies of scale and scope in banking. Banks in transition economies should be free to pursue these as well, even if it means that some of the existing banks will join together to form still larger units. Bank mergers may be a response to an increasingly competitive climate but they contribute to such a climate as well. Thus the persistence of large banks and a significant degree of concentration in banking in transition economies is not a public policy concern so long as barriers to entry have been removed.

This does not mean, however, that the governments of transition countries should actively promote increasing concentration within the banking industry. The risk of such a policy is that the State itself may erect barriers to new entry in the banking sector. This is particularly a matter of concern when the State has retained a strategic share in privatized banks. Thus we regard the efforts towards government-led bank consolidation in the Czech Republic and, especially, Poland to be very negative developments. They are likely to perpetuate the close relationship between the State and banking, resulting in banks that are too big to fail and overly protected from competitive threats.

Generally, bank entry is regulated in transition economies, as in other economies, through granting or denying banking licences. In the first period of transition, licensing requirements tended to be extremely liberal. The result was an enormous growth in the total number of licensed banks, some of which subsequently became distressed. In this environment, it is natural that the number of new bank entries has slowed considerably. However, in the case of Poland the authorities refused to grant new banking licences to some willing applicants. In our view, it is a mistake to use licensing as a tool of industrial policy aimed at reducing the total number of banks in operation. Instead, the authorities should concentrate on whether a bank to be newly licensed would be sound. The most important test of this is the capital adequacy of the bank. Poland, Hungary, and the Czech Republic have all adopted minima which are in line with international norms.[5] However, these minima have not always been strictly enforced. For example, some banks have opened with 'capital' that had been obtained from borrowed funds. Therefore, if there is a public policy problem, it is one of rule-enforcement rather than rule-setting.

Beyond capital requirements, the newly adopted banking regulations in countries leaving the transition attempt to make sure that top bank managers are qualified for their jobs. The fact is that many of the institutions in the financial sector of a transition economy are new and that imperfect regulatory controls may attract dishonest people. As a consequence, we view it as entirely appropriate that bank regulators check top management for criminal records or for significant rule infractions in previous employment. These controls should be limited to questions of character leaving the main responsibility for choosing management to shareholders. However, the screening should be a serious one. Fraud is a real and potentially very important problem in these economies. The experience with the Latvian banking crisis, to pick just one example, has amply shown this. It is easier to exert a control at the licensing stage than it is to remove management on the basis of suspicious practices.

Probably the most controversial question of market access is whether foreign bank entry should be restricted or eliminated altogether. Policy in this regard has varied considerably in the region. Hungarian banking has been quite open to foreign banks. In contrast, in Poland after an initial period when foreign entry was encouraged, the stance has been to restrict foreign entry and to try to channel it into taking strategic stakes in banks undergoing privatization and where the State is to retain a large share. In our view, foreign banks in Hungary have played a positive role in competing for the business of major borrowers by applying modern credit evaluation practices and by offer attractive terms. They have also provided depositors with a range of new products. It is likely as well that the presence of foreign banks in Hungary has helped to raise the inflow of foreign direct investment. While foreign banks in Poland have played somewhat the same role, undoubtedly their influence has

---

[5] These three countries' standards exceed that of the Second European Banking Directive (1989) which sets the minimum initial capital at 5 million ecu.

been less than if foreign banks had been given access to bank licences on the same terms as domestic investors. In short, opening the banking sector to foreign entry is the single most pro-competitive action available to the authorities in a transition economy.

What is the risk that foreign entrants will overwhelm the local incumbents so that banking will become the exclusive preserve of foreigners? The experience of the European Union in the fifteen years since the liberalization of capital controls can give some indication of this. In recent years there have been important international mergers of commercial banks with investment banks. It is important to realize, however, that this tendency reflects the desire of large money-centre banks to achieve the scale necessary to be competitive in such areas as international merchant banking or derivatives market-making. At the same time efforts to consolidate retail banking have often proceeded relatively slowly. For example, the penetration of commercial banks into the retail markets of other countries of the European Union has been very slow, and banks, such as Crédit Lyonnais, which have been aggressive are apt to have suffered from pursuing this strategy. The reason that large foreign banks have been slow to push aside smaller local rivals is that the latter possess an important asset in the form of an existing branch network and existing clientele.

What are the implications of these trends for the transition countries of Central and Eastern Europe? Much of the task of channelling domestic savings to domestic investment is likely to be left to intermediated finance. In this activity, domestic banks have very significant assets which should allow them, provided they are reasonably well-managed, to maintain a large share of banking business. Of course, if local banks waste their opportunities and bank entry is reasonably free, foreign banks will try to seize opportunities and establish a toehold in Central and Eastern Europe. However, experience elsewhere suggests that building from the toehold to penetrate deep and wide in a region is a risky and slow process. Consequently, there does not seem to be an overwhelming need to protect domestic banks from foreign competition.

The countries of Central and Eastern Europe have committed themselves to some degree of openness to foreign banks through their association agreements with the EU. However, these agreements will begin to have real effect only in 1999 at the earliest, and once they do the transition countries will probably retain some leeway in applying the agreement. It is important that transition countries see opening their banking sectors as bringing with it important benefits and therefore a desirable objective in itself.

Even if there is open access to bank licensing, the State may create other, indirect barriers to entry and thereby undermine the effects of competition. We have seen in the three countries we have studied in depth that despite efforts to remove budgetary subsidies to industry, a number of indirect subsidies persist within the banking sector. One form of these is the refinance credits accorded to industry at subsidized rates. The primary recipients of these are the industrial borrowers who are supported in this way. However, these loans typically pass through state-owned or recently privatized commercial banks which receive a substantial processing margin despite the fact that the loans are state-guaranteed. New banks typically do not have access to this business.

A more important form of subsidy to banking is the aid for dealing with bad debts which has been directed at the commercial banks that emerged from the monobanks. These include the remedies for non-performing loans such as bond–loan swaps which value the loans at levels that are actuarially unjustified. In effect, this allows certain banks to lend to high-risk high-return projects and have the risks borne by taxpayers. These also include explicit or implicit deposit guarantees that may be more generous for deposits in state-owned banks or former state-owned banks which have been privatized. The coverage may be more generous for large banks generally because they are viewed as crucial to the stability of the banking system. If certain banks have greater insurance coverage for which they do not pay the full economic value, they clearly have an advantage in attracting funds away from their competitors.

The policy stance that would most favour banking competition would be the removal of all forms of indirect subsidies. However, this is not necessarily easy to do. As we discussed above, even in the transition leaders it is not clear that the bad-loan problem is past. If future bailouts remain possible, it will be difficult to avoid the expectation that the state-owned banks and those in which the State retains stake will be the first to receive assistance. Whether or not this turns out to be the case, the *expectation* of this alone gives these banks a competitive advantage. The same applies to implied deposit guarantees. Here the principle of 'too large to fail' can be invidious for banking competition. Bank mergers and consolidation may be motivated not by scale economies, but as one of the pillars of the banking system the bank will feel assured of government or central bank assistance in times of need. In our view, the measure we advocated in section 8.2 for the reasons of instauring financial discipline also favour competition. Explicit deposit insurance should be reinforced and fairly priced so that the role of implicit guarantees will be reduced. Once state-owned banks have had their debts cleaned up they should be privatized. In the future, any intervention to aid a failing bank, whether privatized or *de novo*, should result in the cost of economic losses being borne first by shareholders and next by large uninsured depositors.

Even if these steps are taken, it is likely that some banks very closely related to the State will continue to enjoy significant insurance benefits. The savings banks are probably the primary ones. Even if the available deposit insurance funds were be insufficient, it is inconceivable that a government would allow a failure of the large savings banks to result in major losses for small depositors. If this is the case, public policy should be clear-sighted about this fact. In particular, it means that the State will remain an important stakeholder in the savings banks whether or not they have been privatized. It should also be recognized that given their competitive advantage in attracting deposits these saving banks should be profitable. If they are not, then their economic rents are being dissipated away in the form of overly generous conditions on loans, on deposits, or from managerial waste. Furthermore, if their deposit insurance coverage is greater than other banks, then the level of banking surveillance should be higher. It should be verified that the asset-management practices of the saving banks are consistent with the low-risk nature of their deposits. This may mean restricting the forms of asset holding to treasury securities and diversified holdings in other financial intermediaries. In effect, we believe that the course taken by Hungary sets a poor example for policy towards savings banks. In the first instance the quasi-privatization of OTP has given it an ownership structure composed of about 20 per cent public social security funds, 25 per cent privatization funds, and the remaining 55 per cent dispersed small holdings. This tends to obscure the continuing stake of the State in the operations of the savings bank and makes it more difficult for the State to intervene when necessary. Second, by granting the privatized bank a general banking licence, it is able to have a relatively unrestricted hand in choosing its assets with the consequence that it is more difficult to ensure that the bank maintains a low-risk profile appropriate with the high level of guarantees enjoyed by its depositors.

A number of specialized banks in the region also benefit from having a privileged treatment by the State. This has been especially the case with agricultural banks. Perhaps the largest and most difficult example of this type is the Polish Bank for the Food Economy (BGŻ). We have seen that the BGŻ received very significant assistance in dealing with its bad-load problem and that the clean-up is still far from complete. The question is whether real reform will ever come. There are clearly some groups that view BGŻ as providing part of a set of permanent subsidies directed to the agricultural sector. Solving the problems of BGŻ are far from simple; they will require coordination with efforts to reform agriculture. However, in our view it is clear that BGŻ should cease trying to play the role of caretaker for agriculture and start acting like a bank, albeit one with an intimate knowledge of the agriculture sector. If subsidies are to be given to agriculture, they should be made explicit. The legal status of BGŻ has been changed to give the State more direct control over its activities. This should be used to put into place strict accounting and modern credit practices. These should be made preconditions for any further recapitalization.

8.4.   Bank Ownership Structure

Given a banking system which was entirely state-owned and controlled, one of the most important questions of financial sector policy in transition economies is how to put most banking matters in the hands of the private sector. In part, this is determined by the pace of creation and growth of new private banks. These are affected by licensing policies, capital standards, and other prudential regulations. However, inertia favours the position of the offshoots of the ex-monobank. Consequently, bank privatization policy is the most important instrument for the development of a private sector banking.

The countries of Central and Eastern Europe have taken a variety of approaches to bank privatization, and their experiences allow us to say something about the desirable time to privatize a state-owned bank. Hungary and Poland started by privatizing stronger banks for which it was relatively easy to find investors. However, the pace of privatization has been slow, and the result is that after more than five years of transition state-owned banks still have a large fraction of the market. Thus the pace of bank privatization has been slower than the privatization of industrial enterprises. In contrast, in the Czech Republic, the large state-owned banks were included in mass privatization along with most large industrial enterprises. The approach taken in the Baltic countries, notably Latvia, was to privatize banking quickly.

On the basis of these experiences we would propose the following rule for the timing of bank privatization. Banks in transition countries should be privatized as soon as they are financially sound and an enabling environment for a stable banking sector is in place. In part, this says that prior to privatization existing bad debts should have been dealt with and the bank recapitalized on an adequate basis. This does not necessarily mean that non-performing loans have been taken off the books. However, if they remain, they should be covered by loss provisions. Our proposed rule of thumb also requires that a minimal capacity for prudential regulation also be in place before banks be privatized. We have seen consistently that one of the challenges of transition is for the State to take on the role of providing a stable institutional framework within which private agents and enterprises can interact efficiently. For depositors to trust banks, they need to know that bank regulators have access to information on how bank assets are managed and will take corrective action if fraudulent or excessively risky practices are revealed. However, this is not just a matter of bank regulation. It also requires that the basic legal framework for commercial banking exists. The legal system should enforce financial contracts. There should be a framework for taking collateral. Bankruptcy law should function to some degree. Of course, all these aspects of institution building take time themselves. There must be some judgement of what is 'adequate' in the circumstances. However, if banks are privatized or private banks are allowed to grow very quickly without this environment, experience suggests that this will be likely to result in a full-scale banking crisis. Indeed, there are signs that the underdevelopment of contract and bankruptcy law in Bulgaria directly contributed to its banking crisis (see Dobrinsky 1994).

In our view bank privatization should be treated somewhat differently from that of other enterprises because we feel it should await the creation of at least a rudimentary bank regulatory framework. For most industrial enterprises specific regulation is probably not required before privatization nor possibly after. Depending upon the pace of the privatization initiative generally, this might imply privatizing banks after industrial enterprises. However, in the transition countries we have studied in detail, it proved possible for the central banks to improve their competence in bank supervision very considerably in the space of one or two years. Consequently, the lag in privatizing banks need not be very long.

It should be noted that our criterion for deciding the timing of bank privatization does not make bank restructuring or building managerial competence prerequisites. This reflects the view that deep restructuring is best left to private sector owners. Also we have seen that the experience of Poland and Hungary suggests that state-owned enterprises took significant steps towards restructuring when it appeared that privatization would not be delayed. This tendency is likely to operate for state-owned banks as well. Delaying bank privatization in the hopes that installling superior management will improve the reception of the privatization issue is likely to be counter-productive. The same remark applies to the idea of holding up bank privatization in order to find a foreign bank willing to take a long-term strategic stake in the privatized bank. In Poland this is one of the reasons why it proved impossible to meet the objective of privatizing all the State's regional commercial banks by 1996.

There are even more reasons for stating that bank privatization should not delayed in order to consolidate the banking sector into a small number of large, powerful banks. There is every reason to doubt that the State has the competence needed to form a modern bank that fully realizes the potential for economies of scale and scope. Rather, starting a process of state-led mergers is likely to favour incumbent management in its desire to create a banking empire which will entrench their positions. Furthermore, this policy risks falling into the trap of granting enterprises monopoly power in the name of maximizing the proceeds from privatization.

The upshot of this discussion is that in our view the policy towards bank privatization in Poland is misguided. The recapitalization of the regional banks was accomplished by early 1995, by which time the banking regulation was operating at a reasonable level. All the remaining regional banks should have been privatized in the course of that year. Instead, time was lost in pursuing the strategy of finding foreign banks to take long-term strategic stakes in the baks at the time they were privatized. Then in the end of 1995, with six of the nine regional commercial banks still awaiting privatization, the government embarked on a policy of consolidating the banking sector into larger units. This is likely to add considerably to the delay in privatizing them and raises the prospect of the State retaining its controlling interest in these banks indefinitely. The policy pursued in Hungary can also be criticized as being too slow; the tentative nature of its bad-debt clean-up has made it difficult to declare the state-owned banks as financially solid at any particular time. However, at the time of writing it appears that bank privatization is going forward.

The Czech policy on bank privatization involved completing the major bad-debt clean-up in time to include most of the large state-owned banks in mass privatization. As such, this policy appears to comply with our criterion of the timing of bank privatization. Our only reservation is that it is probably too early to tell whether the regulatory environment was ready to deal with privatizing virtually all the major banks at the same time. So far, none of the very largest banks has been hit with losses that threaten its solvency. However, the failures within the second tier of banks have already tested the regulatory framework severely in that the deposit insurance fund has been exhausted. The State has continued to invent *ad hoc* solutions to prevent the banking crisis from spreading.

The challenge is to move from crisis management to a stage when the deposit insurance fund will suffice to assure stability.

Timing is not the only important consideration involved in bank privatization policy. The approach taken to privatization can have important implications for who retain control of the banks and for the liquidity of the market for bank shares. The countries we have studied have used three distinct approaches: initial public offerings in Poland, directly negotiated sales to a consortium of investors in Hungary, and voucher privatization in the Czech republic. In Poland and Hungary, the result was that post-privatization there were identifiable institutional investors with large minority stakes in the banks. Potentially they could attempt to exert control in these banks and put in place management of their own choosing. The difficulty in Poland was that in several cases the State retained the largest single holding, so that major changes in bank direction might be difficult without its agreement. The same was true of the 1995 MKB privatization in Hungary which transferred 42 per cent of shares to investors. In the Czech Republic the technique of mass privatization did not automatically create large shareholders who would actively participate in corporate governance. The emergence of some very large investment funds most of which are associated with the large banks has meant that bank management indirectly controls a significant fraction of bank shares. However, the position of bank management does not appear unassailable. There are already groups of active investors who have build up the size of their positions by taking control of underperforming companies. These have already attempted to take control of a major bank and may do so in the future. Since the National Property Fund has retained large minority stakes in the major banks, the State will be able to have an important influence on any such control contests.

In our view, it is difficult to say this experience demonstrates that any one method is particularly well suited to bank privatization. The Polish and Hungarian methods resulted in large holdings by institutional investors; however, these investors may have been picked by the State for favouring a particular management policy in preference to other investors who would have put the bank on an alternative, perhaps more profitable, course. The Czech approach ran the risk of dispersed ownership leaving management with great power. However, the new Czech securities markets creates the potential for a market with corporate control.

Independently of the method of privatization used, these experiences point to the great difficulty in getting the State to withdraw from controlling the banking sector. This manifests itself by the slowness of privatizations. It also shows itself in the large minority stakes retained by the State in the large Czech banks. In our view, the main task for bank privatization in the coming years of transition is to reduce the holdings of the State to zero in almost all commercial banks. The sole justifiable exception to this policy concerns the large savings banks. If the lack of competition in deposit-taking results in these banks having a large fraction of small-saver deposits and therefore being critical for the overall stability of the banking sector, then it is appropriate for the State to remain a large shareholder. The objective of the State in managing its holdings in these banks should be to ensure the prudent management of assets under the control of the bank at the same time as it offers deposit rates that make it profitable. It may be expected that as a result of this policy the banks' share of deposits will diminish over time and that in the not too distant future the size of the banks will be such that the State can sell its stake.

8.5. *The Organization of Securities Markets*

In our study of Hungary, Poland, and the Czech Republic we noted that in the immediate aftermath of the collapse of communism there was a strong interest in reconstructing stock markets. The symbolism involved in this was clear. However, it was generally recognized that in the development of the financial sectors the main effort should be aimed at creating strong, well-functioning banks (Corbett and Mayer 1991). Indeed, this is where most of the effort to build financial institutions has been channelled in the first years of transition. While the stock markets of Budapest and Warsaw are dynamic, the overall levels of stock market capitalization are still relatively low. In the Czech Republic mass privatization has led to large amounts of traded shares; however, policy efforts were concentrated on running a successful auction procedure so that the stock market itself remains relatively underdeveloped relative to its size.

Much work remains to develop the banking sectors in transition economies, and we have emphasized some of the important policy choices that will influence the course of that development. However, in our view, as the banking sector begins to function without the crisis-driven intervention of the State, and as large numbers of the industrial enterprises have now been successfully privatized, securities market development should become an increasingly high priority for policy-makers. This is not to say that market-based finance is more important than bank-based finance. Indeed, we think that the recurring debate on the virtues of these two modes of organizing financial sectors places undue emphasis on the trade-offs between the two. In the leading transition economies, the reinforcement of the stock markets will complement efforts in building the banking sectors.

If stock markets are able to attract savings, they will provide an important financing alternative for companies seeking to grow. Even if stock market issues are relatively infrequent, the potential to finance investment in this way serves as a market discipline for banks. We have seen that the State has continued to dominate the banking sectors of the transition economies and that much banking business is concentrated in a relatively small number of banks. While we have emphasized that reducing the involvement of the State and improving banking competition should be priorities for the next phase of financial development, we cannot be very confident that this will occur. Consequently, it seems that private industry will have a strong incentive to see stock market finance develop as a viable alternative to bank finance.

However, the main contribution of the stock market is likely to be felt through means other than new securities issues. Data on the flow funds in developed capitalist economies show that the proportion of investment financed by stock issues is typically small compared with that financed by banks or by retained earnings (Mayer 1989; Corbett and Jenkinson 1994). The same is likely to be true in the transition economies. However, this does not mean that the stock market plays no role in directing investments. Financing investment from retained earnings is a form of equity finance. If management works in the interest of shareholders, these investments would be pursued only if the firm has investment opportunities that are at least as attractive as those available to shareholders on the market generally. The question is whether management will maximize share values or will pursue its own personal objectives. Having shares traded on a stock market can help to ensure that managers pursue shareholders' interests (Roell 1996). For example, management compensation can be linked to share performance by supplementing salaries with payments in stock or stock options. Furthermore, the stock market can help to discipline managers who do not perform. This happens when investors buy up cheap shares of underperforming companies in order to take control and make management changes. Alternatively, stockholders may fire managements when they are seen as responsible for bad decisions as reflected in depressed share prices.[6]

Thus, a developed stock market can contribute to improving corpo-

---

[6] For a fuller discussion of the use of publicly traded shares in order to overcome agency problems see Roell (1996) and Holmström and Tirole (1993).

rate governance and to disseminating information about company prospects. We have seen that in transition economies managers and other
insiders inherited considerable power in state-owned enterprises and
that in many cases privatization has not directly changed this. Thus
developing means of overcoming agency problems is at least as high
a priority for transition economies as it is in a developed capitalist
economy. Banks may play a monitoring and control role. However, the
banks' interests will not generally be the same as the shareholders'.
Furthermore, given the continuing dominance of the offshoots of the
monobank, there is a clear risk that bankers will align themselves with
management. Improving the functioning of the stock market will give
shareholders some carrots and sticks that will help in making management more sensitive to shareholder interests. And when banks and
management pursue some end other than profits, the fall in the share
price on the stock market can at least document this fact.

Developing a stock market that will perform these functions well is
not an easy thing. In some of the region, the stock markets are very
rudimentary. The efforts to build stock markets in Warsaw, Budapest,
and Prague have been relatively significant; however, even in these
markets much needs to be done. These experiences suggest that import-
ing up-to-date trading technologies is quite feasible in transition economies. However, having a trading system that can process orders well
does not necessarily guarantee the emergence of a liquid market. Indeed, trading in many shares in Eastern and Central Europe is often
very illiquid. This means that prices often move substantially in
response to order to sell or to buy. Frequently there is simply no
counterparty willing to carry out transactions in given shares. For example, some investors find they must advertise in the popular press in order
to attract sellers for the shares they are seeking. This illiquidity discour-
ages investors from buying shares in transition economies and tends to
depress the average stock prices.

It is difficult to assure liquidity in shares if there are only a small
number of potential buyers or sellers of the shares. Thus if the company
is small, the probability that investors will wish to trade in any given
period of time tends to be small. This reduces liquidity. Even for a
relatively large company, if most of the shares are held by long-term
investors, the natural rate of turnover will tend to be low. For these
reasons, very small firms are not usually listed on stock exchanges. Nor
are larger firms that are closely held by a small group of investors. In this
regard, the relative illiquidity of shares of many Czech companies is not
surprising. It is likely that over time some of these shares will be taken
private. That is, some investors will buy up a controlling interest in these

companies and then will delist the company. However, we believe that coupon privatization presents a major opportunity to develop a stock market that will emerge into a relatively liquid, smoothly functioning market place. Therefore, it would be unfortunate if the Czech market is allowed to become moribund.

Illiquidity and depressed stock prices (as indicated by relatively low price/earnings ratios) can sometimes be the consequence of deficiencies in securities laws. For example, experience in capitalist economies has shown that laws are needed to protect the interests of small shareholders. When they do not, most small investors are wise to stay away from the market. There are a variety of ways that a controlling group of shareholders can divert earnings to themselves without paying the rest of the shareholders. For example, they can vote to increase the number of shares and they arrange to sell these new shares to themselves at low prices. Or they can open a company that will become a supplier to the firm and direct the firm to buy exclusively from the supplier at inflated prices. Securities laws are needed to protect shareholders from these types of abuse. However, the laws in place in Eastern Europe are often deficient and the capacity of the judicial system to enforce the laws is in doubt. Further development in this area would contribute considerably to the development of securities markets in the region.

Poland has adopted severe American-style securities regulation and is probably the leader in the region. Indeed, the standards are so severe that some investors question whether there may a degree of regulatory overkill. In contrast, the Czech stock market is relatively underregulated. In addition to the Prague Stock Exchange and the computerized stock market, there is an active over-the-counter market where the big transactions and probably most of the volume are directed. Prices on the latter market are unreported. As a result there may be several prices for the same stock at the same time and imperfect information prevents arbitrage from eliminating these discrepancies. An additional problem is the limited protection offered to investors in the Czech market. These deficiencies are being brought to light with the consolidation of ownership of privatized firms. For example, investors could buy a majority stake in the company, put its chosen directors in place, and then delist the company all without consulting the minority shareholders. In effects, the rules of the game in the Czech market strongly favour insiders.

A separate but related matter concerns laws and accounting rules affecting information disclosure requirments. If corporate insiders are be able to trade on information before it is made available to the investing public at large, then portfolio investment in the stock market is discouraged. This type of insider dealing was long unchecked on a number of continental European stock markets and contributed to restricting the use of equity finance. Over time, these market places have moved towards introducing insider trading laws similar to those initially introduced in the USA and Britain. Such laws are underdeveloped in transition economies. At this stage their development should be made a priority by policy-makers.

To some extent the market itself can develop responses to problems of insider dealing and protecting the interests of minority shareholders. If the law provides for basic protection, there is still a problem that very small investors may not find it worth the time and effort necessary to use the law to protect themselves. This problem can be overcome or reduced by mutual funds since the manager of the funds would spread the costs of monitoring efforts over many investors. However, this poses another set of agency problems. In particular, what guarantees that the managers of the mutual funds will pursue the interests of their own shareholders? For example, the Czech privatization funds managed by investment companies attached to large banks potentially face a significant conflict of interest. They may tend to protect the bank's interests in preference to those of the investment fund. Securities laws in transition countries need to reinforce the fiduciary responsibilities of mutual fund managers so that investor interests are served above all others.

8.6.   Central Banking and the Money Market

We have seen that the first major step towards reforming the financial sectors of the socialist economies of Central and Eastern Europe was the introduction of two-tiered banking which stripped the monobank of it commercial banking departments leaving what remained to concentrate on the activities of central banking. In the case of Hungary this reform preceded by two years the decisive political events of 1989 which initiated the transition process more generally. In Poland and Czechoslovakia and elsewhere in the region this reform coincided roughly with the start of transition.[7] Given this early start, we would expect that the practice of central banking would be relatively well developed in the region. Generally, our detailed review of Hungary, Poland, and the Czech Republic shows that this is the case. Nevertheless, further work needs to be done. And some other transition countries are not so advanced.

[7] The dates of banking laws instituting two-tier banking are: Bulgaria, 1989; Romania, 1990; Slovenia, 1991; Estonia, 1992; Latvia, 1992; and Lituania, 1993. *Source*: EBRD (1995).

It is often said that one of the objectives of financial reform should be to ensure the existence of an independent central bank. In fact, central bank independence is a complex phenomenon that is not easy to operationalize. Most of economics literature supposes that an independent central bank will tend to favour price stability (see Curkierman 1992). In fact, this is contradicted by the experience of Russia during 1992 and 1993 when the central bank governor went against the desire of the government and pursued a highly inflationary policy aimed at keeping enterprises afloat. Furthermore, it cannot be said that in the mature capitalist economies there is an agreed view that an independent central bank is necessary to secure price stability. In the case of Britain, key tools of monetary policy are under the explicit control of the government. At the opposite extreme is the Bundesbank which is probably the prime example of central bank independence. Still, the consensus seems to support something like the Bundesbank model. For example, this is essentially what has been accepted by the European Union as the design for the new European Monetary Institute. Beyond this, in the immature democracies of the CEE countries, our view is that insulating monetary policy from political pressures is important if these economies are to have reasonably stable prices. Furthermore, it is important as well to establish in these economies an organization that is competent in matters of financial policy which will assure continuity in policy-making even if the governments go through frequent changes.

Transition countries have employed a number of legal means to ensure formal central bank independence. For example, in Poland, Slovakia, and the Czech Republic the president or prime minister appoints the bank chairman for a term which exceeds their own elected term. In the Czech Republic the sole macroeconomic responsibility of the central bank is to guarantee price stability. The central banks of Hungary and Poland are legally obliged to support the government's economic policy as well as attain price stability. There are statutory limits on the amount of a government expenditures that can be financed by monetary creation. In the Czech Republic this is placed at 5 per cent of previous revenues, whereas in Poland and Hungary the limits are apparently more restrictive, being placed at 2 per cent of budget expenditures and 3 per cent of planned revenues respectively. Using a variety of indicators borrowed from political economy, Siklós (1994) constructs indices of central bank independence and finds the following ordering (starting with the most independent): Czech Republic, Poland, Hungary, and Slovakia.

Formal independence of the central bank is no assurance that it will be effectively independent. We have seen that despite the strict limits on deficit monetization allowed for in Hungary's central bank Act, other means have been found to force the central bank to help finance the government's deficit. The Czech Republic has a number of legal measures insulating the central bank from the government. Furthermore, it has been the model of fiscal discipline in the region and has gained the reputation for being the transition country with the greatest commitment to monetary stability. Nevertheless, there are ample signs that Czech monetary policy has been developed through close collaboration of the government with the central bank. An illustration of this arose in 1994 when an influx of foreign direct-investment tended increase the money supply beyond levels the central bank deemed desirable. Given the limited numbers of treasury securities on the bank's balance sheet, it was difficult to limit this increase through open-market operations. In order to deal with the problem the central bank called upon the co-operation of the National Property Fund which agreed to withdraw a large amount of liquid bank deposits from the commercial banks and to write them down as a loss of capital. Such an operation was an *ad hoc* measure with no real legal basis.

More generally, statutory limitations or other formal measures can do little when fiscal pressures become intense. Regarding the creation and distribution of seigniorage in the Czech, Hungary, and Romania, a study by Hochreiter *et al.* (1996) finds that in Hungary seigniorage was four times the benchmark of Germany and Austria and in Romania it was thirty times the benchmark. In Hungary seigniorage was roughly the magnitude of the government deficit so that 100 per cent of the deficit was financed by money creation. In contrast, in the Czech Republic seigniorage was about the same as in Germany. These differences in outcomes cannot be explained by the relatively minor formal differences in the status of the central banks.

The lesson of this is that there is no easy legal way to ensure that monetary policy will give high priority to pursuing price stability. A sufficiently determined government can usually find the means of forcing the central bank to pursue the government's agenda to the detriment of monetary stability. Probably the best protection against this is to make the actions of the government as transparent as possible. One way to do this is to promote the liquidity of the monetary markets. Such markets will respond to an inflationary monetary development moving up rates sharply on government bills. These higher rates will be felt by enterprises in the form of higher financing costs. In this way, some agents in the economy will be activated to bring political pressure to bear on the government which will tend to counteract the forces tending towards monetary prodigality.

The liquidity of the money market is favoured by increasing its size. For this reason, it is important to require government borrowing to take the form of issuing standardized bills and bonds. This is the purpose of central bank laws that place statutory limits on the degree of direct monetization of the government deficit. Even though these laws can be circumvented, by forcing the government to introduce the legislation that overrides the central bank law, the government will be called upon to justify its willingness to undermine the monetary stability of the country.

A related issue is the use of directed lines of credit by the central bank. If these credits are given at rates that are below those that commercial banks would offer otherwise or are destined to borrowers who would not otherwise be deemed creditworthy, there is a distortion of credit from what would prevail under a free market. Typically the sectors benefiting from this favourable treatment are those with political influence. In this way directed lines of credit can sometimes substitute for budgetary expenditures and therefore reduce the government's financing needs. For example, low-interest loans can be used to keep a sick enterprise alive. This maintains employment in the sector, thereby reducing the government's expenditures on unemployment benefits. The negative consequence of this is that at the margin an investment opportunity with a better risk–reward profile will be crowded out. Furthermore, if increases in directed credits are not compensated by a relative tightening of monetary policy, the effect will be to contribute monetary pressure.

We have seen that overall there has been a reduction of the use of short-term redistribution credits in the three economies we have studied in detail. However, in Poland and Hungary, long-term redistribution credits have been persistent. It is perhaps not a just a coincidence that these two countries have found it difficult to reduce the inflation rate below 20 per cent per year. In our view, the continued use of credit subsidies is a means of avoiding fiscal discipline and as such contributes to the pro-inflation bias of policy. It is an invidious practice because it is so hard to eradicate. Measuring the extent of subsidies requires comparatively subtle reasoning so that it tends to not become the focus of political debate. In our view, it would be useful to modify central bank laws to constrain or eliminate the use of long-term redistribution credits. This would help to eliminate credit subsidies and to force governments to make subsidies for favoured sectors explicit and therefore more readily scrutinized by the political process.

Finally, we feel that one aspect of the relation of monetary policy and banking competition requires some attention in transition economies.

Specifically, these countries have a variety of methods for issuing government securities, typically under the control of the central bank. Participating banks bid for government paper either to keep on their own account or, what is more likely, as dealers who then sell to other investors. In high-debt countries, especially Hungary, this market is large relative to the size of the financial sector as a whole. Therefore, competitive conditions on this market can have a significant influence on bank profitability. Since the central bank may have an influence on the outcome of these auctions, it is important to recognize that this could potentially be a means of perpetuating the dominant position of the banks which emerged from the monobank. Policy should be aimed at ensuring a level playing-field in which banks would have equal access to this market.

8.7.   *Financial Reform and the Negotiation of Entry into the European Union*

The transition countries of Central and Eastern Europe as a whole have signalled their desire to turn towards the West by entering into association agreements with the European Union (EU).[8] Among other things these agreements established a framework for discussions that could ultimately end in these countries joining the European Union as full members. In 1993 the Copenhagen European Council specifically declared the intention that the associated countries of Central and Eastern Europe should ultimately be allowed to join the Union. As with previous enlargements, the countries seeking to accede are expected to adapt their institutional structure to be compatible with those found within the Union. Depending on how strictly these countries are expected to conform to the various European directives, they could find themselves constrained to developing policy along definite lines. Within the political context of Central and Eastern Europe, a broad consensus in favour of entering the Union is a factor tending to give a coherence to policy choices despite the multiplicity of political parties or the rapid shifts in the political balance. Overall, this probably tends to give a pro-market bias to policy. However, Brussels is not a single-minded protector of the free market. In this section we consider to what extent seeking to join

---

[8] The countries signing association agreements are: Czechoslovakia 1991; Hungary, 1991; Poland 1991; Bulgaria 1992; Romania, 1993; Estonia 1995; Latvia, 1995; Lithuania, 1995; and Slovenia, 1995.

the European Union really binds financial policy-making and in what directions.

The association agreements were negotiated on a bilateral basis between the European Union and each of the associated countries. Consequently, the details of the agreements differ from one country to another. However, they all call for a ten-year period of adjustment in order to prepare the country for membership in the Union. Initially, the agreements place relatively few constraints on the countries, but as the agreements approach their term they are expected to achieve a progressively higher degree of harmonization with the institutions of the Union.

In 1995 a White Paper of the European Commission set out the steps involved in the preparation of the associated countries for integration into the European Union (COM(95) 163 FINAL, 3/5/95). In particular, a number of concrete steps are required to bring legislation into alignment with the policies of the internal market. In addition, the White Paper establishes the principle that integration of the associated countries will require that they get onto a path of sound macroeconomic policy. It is notable, however, that the White Paper does not say that this would necessarily involve adherence to the Maastricht criteria.[9] The White Paper also advances the principle that reforms in the associated countries must have proceeded to the point where their economies are able to stand up to the rigours of competition within the single internal market.

The obligations of member States concerning the organization of their financial sectors are set out in a series of EU Directives on Banking and Securities Markets. The Commission White Paper identifies those parts of the Directives that are to be treated by associated States as high priority and to be attained relatively early on in the agreements. These include the basic laws on licensing of credit institutions (First Banking Directive), the definition of own funds to be used in determining solvency (Own Funds Directive), setting the minimum solvency standard at 8 per cent (Solvency Directive), and creation of deposit insurance schemes (Deposit Guarantee Directive). In regard to securities markets the only measure identified by the Commission as a priority to be treated in the first stage of the agreements is the conformity to ecu norms on laws on creation of mutual funds. The White Paper also identifies Second Stage measures which are to be implemented after the

---

[9] The Treaty of Maastricht (1992) criteria for entry into the European monetary union include a limit on government deficits of no more than 3% of GDP, a limit on public debt of no more than 60% of GDP, as well as exchange rate and inflation criteria.

higher-priority measures. For credit institutions, these are the Second Banking Directive which establishes a minimum initial capital of 5 million ecu and the principle that banks licensed in one member State can conduct business in other member States, the Capital Adequacy Directive which sets out how a bank's trading book is to be treated for the purposes of calculating capital adequacy, and the Large Exposures Directive which limits the exposure of a bank to a single client to be no more than 25 per cent of the bank's own funds. Second stage measures also include the Investment Services Directive which specifies that a country must create a regulatory framework for licensing investment companies and calls for the Capital Adequacy Directive to be applied to investment firms.

While it is clear that the association agreements condemn these countries to learn the ins and outs of EU law as well as the sometimes stilted language that is employed in Brussels, it is less clear that these measures will have a large impact on the functioning of their financial sectors. Ultimately, whether or not these countries enter the EU will probably depend on a broad judgement of whether they are sufficiently similar to existing members. Given the increased diversity created by the enlargement of the Union in recent years, it is clear that the countries of Central and Eastern Europe will not be required to conform rigidly to any specific model. In our view, the most important consideration touching on the financial sector will be judgement of whether the banking sector is stable. Clear failure to enforce prudential standards, collapse of the deposit insurance schemes, or an inability to deal with insolvent banks all would weigh against a country seeking entry. The principle of single-country licensing means that after gaining membership a country's newly created banks would be able conduct business throughout the EU. A country that is incapable of ensuring that these banks are adequately supervised is less likely to be seen as ready for entry.

The countries hoping to gain accession to the EU will also be under pressure to open their banking sectors to entry by EU banks since this is the basic principle underlying banking regulation among existing members. However, some of the association agreements (e.g. Poland's) specifically allows for the country to restrict entry of foreign banks during the association period. If this is interpreted to mean that the countries have until about 2004 before they must open their banking sectors, there will be ample time to create banks with entrenched market power that will be difficult for potential entrants to overcome. The consequence could well be a persistent oligopoly in banking. This is not necessarily the case. If this is made a negotiating priority, the EU probably could pressure the associated countries into opening their

banking sectors to foreign banks in the Second Stage of the Associatı
agreements. We have identified the move towards non-competitiv
banking as one of the more worrying trends of the financial sectors of
transition countries. Consequently, in our view pressuring the associated countries to address this issue would be one of the most positive
possible contributions of the EU to development of the economies of
Central and Eastern Europe.

Epilogue

We have studied an exciting and unique historical episode. The collapse of the Soviet Bloc left its members free to structure their economies as they saw fit. With varying degrees of resolve they have set off on their particular paths toward a market system. In so doing they have provided economic researchers with the closest we can hope to come to a laboratory experiment in system-wide institutional change. Our aim has been to study the data generated by this experiment, focusing on finance in the countries which are immediate eastern neighbours of the European Union and which are in many respects the leaders in the transition to the market. In these countries many of the fundamental reforms now have been implemented, and, for better or worse, future developments will be shaped by these. In the Czech Republic, Hungary, and Poland, the countries we have treated in detail, we have seen that market institutions are functioning increasingly smoothly. This might give the impression that after some fairly minor adjustments to their institutional frameworks these countries will be fully integrated into the mainstream of the capitalist West. However, our own view is that the work that remains to build a solid and efficient financial sector should not be underestimated.

Six years after the initial major shocks to their systems, the level of risk in transition countries remains significantly higher than in Western Europe or North America. As a consequence the new institutions in these countries probably will be subjected to severe tests for years to come. As we write, there are clear signs of this in the Czech Republic where, by design, the major task of restructuring enterprises was delayed until after privatization so that the market could decide their fate. In 1996 major enterprise restructuring took place at least at the financial level with the result that many firms have not fully serviced their debts. This has shaken the Czech banking system to its foundations and has induced the government to reinforce its links to the largest banking institutions. In Poland the course of events has been different. However, that country's early commitment to demonopolization in banking is giving way to a clear current favouring cartelization centred around large banks formed by the state. At the same time the essentially unreformed state savings bank continues to use its protected st. attract a large fraction of savings, leaving new banks to struggle to r depositors. In Bulgaria the continuing inability of the commercial ba. created by the State to exercise basic credit discipline allowed bad loan to balloon in 1995 and 1996. Perhaps in the hope of growing out of this problem, the central bank exacerbated it by providing easy refinance credits, with the result that inflation was running out of control by mid-1996. Under pressure from the IMF Bulgaria's president is seeking to replace the central bank by a monetary board; however, this move is resisted by parliament.

In bringing up these issues, we do not wish to predict constant banking crises in the region for years to come nor to suggest that there will necessarily be a renationalization and centralization of banking. Rather, our message is that the institutional changes of recent years are not irreversible steps toward building the market economy. If there were a major change in political orientation or even a slackening of the will to carry market-oriented reforms further, it is perfectly conceivable that private sector growth could dry up and that state direction of economic activity could increase. In such a shift of direction, finance could play a pivotal role. For in transition countries at this stage the banking sector remains closely linked to the state through direct state ownership, and even where this is absent, banking regulation, deposit insurance and the conduct of monetary policy all present continuing opportunities for indirect state intervention in the economy generally. Our hope is that our analysis has helped to make these linkages more transparent and in this way aid the understanding of the full implications of policy choices in the future.

We have devoted much of our attention to the new financial institutions that provide the microeconomic foundations of the market economy. However, one of the general lessons to emerge from our study is that, in transition, good microeconomics cannot make up for bad macroeconomics. This was particularly true in the early days of transition. It is clear in Poland that a basic change in microeconomic conditions, namely price liberalization in 1990, set the stage for dynamic growth of the private sector which pulled the economy out of recession in 1992, two years before Hungary or the Czech Republic. Nevertheless, in our view monetary policy also played a big role in this. In particular, the decision to relax credit restrictiveness in 1991 and the finance ministry's prohibition of lending by state-owned banks to state enterprises with non-performing loans combined to push credit toward the private sector thus helping to relieve one of the most severe bottlenecks found in transition. Other macroeconomic conditions also favoured this, in

...lar the fact that the government had managed to obtain some ... on the external debt and that it maintained a degree of budgetary ...cipline. The ensuing growth has encouraged the microeconomic ...stitutional reforms which were politically difficult to put through, including bank recapitalization, bank-led financial restructuring of enterprises, and privatization.

In contrast, Hungary early on took important actions to build the microeconomic foundations of the market economy. It was the first transition country to attempt to recapitalize the banks. It reformed laws to make bankruptcy a vehicle for enterprise restructuring. It was quick to open a stock market. Nevertheless growth did not come very quickly because the private sector and industrial enterprises were starved as the state budget deficit absorbed a growing share of credit as a consequence of fiscal indiscipline and the heavy burden of its external debt.

As time goes on the investments in microeconomic foundation building will start to pay off, and this will hopefully allow growth to be sustained for a long period and to allow the economies of the region to join the economies of Western Europe on an equal footing. However, even as the transition progresses macroeconomics will continue to be very important. Fiscal discipline is needed to assure that private sector growth will not be choked off. Monetary discipline is needed to assure that inflation remains moderate and reasonably predictable. These last remarks apply as well to mature capitalist economies. However, they are worth repeating here because they relate to the potential for a change in the direction of economic development in Central and Eastern Europe. If there is strong shift in political direction its effects will probably be felt first at the macroeconomic level since it is there that changes of policy tools would have the widest impact.

References

Abel, I., and Székely, I. (1993), 'The Conditions for Competition and Innovation in the Hungarian Banking System', paper presented at the Eighth Annual Congress of European Economic Association, Helsinki.

—————(1995), 'Retail Banking in Central and Eastern Europe', Institute of East-West Studies, New York.

Anderson, R. W., and Powell, A. (1993), 'The Hungarian Agricultural Commodity Exchange and Liberalization in Hungarian Agriculture', in S. Claessens and R. Duncan (eds.), *Managing Commodity Price Risk in Developing Countries*, Johns Hopkins U. Press, Baltimore.

——and Tangermann, S., (1991), 'Agricultural Price and Trade Policy in Poland', Working Paper 1, *Agricultural Price and Trade Policy and Agricultural Budget*, World Bank, Washington, DC.

——Berglöf, E., Mizsei, K., *et al.* (1996), *Banking Sector Development in Central and Eastern Europe*, CEPR, London.

Arrow, K. J., and Lind, R. C. (1970), 'Uncertainty and the Evaluation of Public Investment Decision', *American Economic Review*, 60(3):364–78.

Asquith, P., Gertner, R., and Scharfstein, D. (1994), 'Anatomy of Financial Distress: An Examination of Junk Bond Issuers', *Quarterly Journal of Economics*, 109(3):625–58.

Baer, H. L., and Gray, C. W. (1994), 'Debt as a Control Device in Transitional Economies: the Experiences of Hungary and Poland', Working Paper, World Bank.

Balcerowicz, L. (1988), 'Polish Economic Reform, 1981–1988: An overview', in *Economic Reforms in the European Centrally Planned Economies*, UN Commission for Europe, New York.

——(1993), 'Common Fallacies in the Debate on the Economic Transition in Central and Eastern Europe,' EBRD Working Paper, 11.

——and Gelb, A. (1994), 'Macropolicies in Transition to a Market Economy: A Three-Year Perspective', Paper presented at the Annual World Bank Conference on Development Economics.

Begg, D., and Portes, R. (1993), 'Enterprise Debt and Financial Restructuring in Central and Eastern Europe', *European Economic Review*, 37(2–3):396–407.

Belka, M. (1994), 'Financial Restructuring of Banks and Enterprises: The Polish Solution', Paper presented at the International Conference on Bad Enterprise Debts in Central and Eastern Europe, CEPR, London.

Berg, A. (1993), 'Measurement and Mismeasurement of Economic Activity during Transition to the Market', in Eastern Europe in Transition: From Recession to Growth?, IMF and World Bank, Washington, DC.

——and Sachs, J. (1992), 'Structural Adjustment and International Trade in Eastern Europe: The Case of Poland', *Economic Policy*, 14:117–56, 161–73.

Berglöf, E. (1995), 'Corporate Governance in Transition Economies: The Theory and Its Policy Implications', in M. Aoki and H-K. Kim (eds.), *Corporate Governance in Transitional Economies*, World Bank, 9:354–75.

References

-and Roland, G. (1995), 'Bank Restructuring and Soft Budget Constraints in Financial Transition', *Journal of Japanese and International Economics*.

-olton, P., and Roland, G. (1992), 'The Economics of Mass Privatization: Czechoslovakia, Germany, Hungary, Poland', *Economic Policy*, (15):275–303.

Bonin, J. P., and Schaffer, M. E. (1995), 'Banks, Firms, Bad Debts and Bankruptcy in Hungary 1991–94', Paper presented at the meetings of the American Economics Association, Washington, DC, January 1995.

Boote, A., and Somogyi, J. (1991), 'Economic Reform in Hungary Since 1968', IMF Occasional Paper, 83.

Boycko, M., Shleifer, A., and Vishny, R. W. (1994), 'Voucher Privatization', *Journal of Financial Economics*, 35(2):249–66.

Brom, K., and Orenstein, M. (1993), 'The "Privatized Sector" in the Czech Republic: Government and Bank Control in a Transition Economy', Institute for East-West Studies, Prague.

Bruno, M. (1993), 'Stabilization and Reform in Eastern Europe: Preliminary Evaluation', in *Eastern Europe in Transition: From Recession to Growth?*, IMF and World Bank, Washington, DC.

Calvo, G., and Coricelli, F. (1993), 'Output Collapse in Eastern Europe: The Role of Credit', in *Eastern Europe in Transition: From Recession to Growth*, World Bank Washington, DC.

——and Kumar, M. S. (1994), 'Economic Performance in Former Socialist Economies', *IMF Staff Papers*, 41(2):314–49.

Carlin, W., and Mayer, C. (1992), 'Restructuring Enterprises in Eastern Europe', *Economic Policy*, (15):311–46.

——Van Reenen, and Wolfe, T. (1994), 'Enterprise Restructuring in the Transition: An Analytical Survey of the Case Study Evidence from Central and Eastern Europe', EBRD Working Paper, 14.

Chadha, B., Coricelli, F., and Krajnyak, K. (1993), 'Economic Restructuring, Unemployment, and Growth in a Transition Economy', *IMF Staff Papers*, 40(4).

CNB, (1993), *Provision on Capital Adequacy of Banks*.

——(1994), *Monetary Policy Implementation: 1990–1994*.

Coase, R. (1960), 'The Problem of Social Costs', *Journal of Law and Economics*, 3:1–44.

Colin, J. (1995), 'Too Much of a Good Thing', *The Banker*.

Conseil central de l'économie (1995), 'Europe Centrale et Orientale, la Transition des économie', *Letter mensuelle socio-économique*, Brussels.

Commander, S., and Coricelli, F. (1993), 'Output Decline in Hungary and Poland in 1990/1991: Structural Change and Aggregate Shocks', in *Eastern Europe in Transition: From Recession to Growth?*, IMF and World Bank.

Corbett, J., and Mayer, C. (1991), 'Financial Reform in Eastern Europe: Progress with the Wrong Model', *Oxford Review of Economic Policy*, 7(4):57–75.

Coricelli, F., and Milesi-Ferretti, G. M. (1993), 'On the Credibility of "Big Bang" Programs', *European Economic Review*, 37(2–3):387–95.

Curkierman, A. (1992), *Central Bank Strategy, Credibility and Independence: Theory and Evidence*, MIT Press, Cambridge, Mass.

Czech National Bank (1994), *Annual Report*.

——(1995), 'Report on Monetary Development in the Czech Republic'.

Dabrowski, M. (1995), 'The Role of the International Agencies and the West in the

References

Post-Communist Transition: Some Selected Aspects', Paper prepared f. American Economic Association Convention 1995, Washington, DC.

Dewatripont, M., and Maskin, E. (1990), 'Credit and Efficiency in Centralized a Decentralized Economies', mimeo.

——and Roland, G. (1992a), 'Economic Reform and Dynamic Political Constraints', *Review of Economic Studies*, 59(4):703–30.

————(1992b), 'The Virtues of Gradualism and Legitimacy in the Transition to a Market Economy', *Economic Journal*, 102(411):291–300.

————(1997), 'Transition as a Process of Large Scale Institutional Change', in D. Kreps and K. Wallis (eds.), *Advances in Economic Theory*, Cambridge University Press, Cambridge.

——Tirole, J. (1994), *The Prudential Regulation of Banks*, MIT Press, Cambridge, Mass.

Diamond, D. W. (1984), 'Financial Intermediation and Delegated Monitoring', *Review of Economic Studies*, 51(3):393–414.

Dittus, P. (1994), 'Corporate Governance in Central Europe: The Role of Banks', Basel Bank for International Settlements, Working Paper, 42:72.

——(1996), 'Why East European Banks Don't Want Equity', *European Economic Review*, 40:455–62.

Dobrinsky, R. (1994), 'The Problem of Bad Loans and Enterprise Indebtedness in Bulgaria', Paper presented at the International Conference on Bad Enterprise Debt in Central and Eastern Europe, Budapest.

Espa, E. (1992), 'Western Aid and the Transitional Economies', Paper presented at the AIECE meeting, Brussels.

Estrin, S., Hare, P., and Surányi, M. (1992), 'Banking in Transition: Development and Current Problems in Hungary', Centre for Economic Performance Discussion, Paper, 68.

——Schaffer, M., and Singh, I. (1993), 'Enterprise Adjustment in Transition Economies: Czechoslovakia, Hungary, and Poland', in *Eastern Europe in Transition: From Recession to Growth?* World Bank, Washington, DC.

European Bank for Reconstruction and Development (EBRD) (1994a), 'Selected Economic Indicators', *Economics of Transition*, 2(2–4).

——(1995), *Transition Report*, London.

——(1994b), *Annual Report*.

Fan, Q., and Schaffer, M. (1994), 'Government Financial Transfers and Enterprise Adjustments in Russia, with comparisons to Central and Eastern Europe', *Economics of Transition*, 2(2):151–87.

Filer, R. K., and Hanousek, J. (1994), 'Efficiency in Newly Emerging Capital Markets: The Case of Czech Voucher Privatization', Working Paper, CERGE, Prague.

Franks, J., and Mayer, C. (1994), 'The Role of Banks in Corporate Governance in German Finance', Paper presented at the JFI Symposium, Amsterdam, May.

Frydman, R., and Rapaczyński, A. (1991a), 'Markets and Institutions in Large-Scale Privatization: An Approach to Economic and Social Transformation in Eastern Europe', in V. Corbo, F. Coricelli, and J. Bossak (eds.), *Reforming Central and Eastern European Economies: Initial Results and Challenges*, World Bank Symposium, World Bank, Washington, DC, 253–74.

————(1991b), 'Privatization and Corporate Governance in Eastern Europe:

References

a Market Economy be Designed?', Working Paper, New York University onomic Research Reports, 91–52:48.

――and Earle, J. S. *et al.* (1993), *The Privatization Process in Central Europe: Central Economic Environment, Legal and Ownership Structure, Institutions for State Regulation, Overview of Privatization Programs and Initial Transformation of Enterprises*, CEU Privatization Reports, i, Budapest, London and New York, Central European University Press, 262.

Gertner, R., and Scharfstein, D. (1991), 'A Theory of Workouts and the Effects of Reorganization Law', *Journal of Finane*, 46:1189–222.

Gomułka, S. (1994), 'Lessons from Economic Transformation and the Road Forward', Centre for Economic Performance, Occasional Paper 5(12), London School of Economics, London.

Government of Poland, European Community and World Bank (1990), *An Agricultural Strategy for Poland*, Washington, DC.

Greene, J., and Isard, P. (1991), 'Currency Convertibility and the Transformation of Centrally Planned Economies', *Journal of Multinational Financial Management*, 1(4):87–126.

Grosfeld, I. (1994), 'Financial Systems in Transition: Is There a Case for a Bank-based System?' CEPR Working Paper, 1062.

GUS (1994), *Statistical Bulletin*, May.

Hanousek, J., Izák, V., and Klokočník, O. (1994), 'Monetary Policy During Transformation', CERGE Working Paper, 47.

Harada, Y. (1994), 'Lessons from Japanese Policy-based Finance', in *Transition: Private Sector Development and the Role of Financial Institutions*, EBRD Working Paper, 13.

Hinds, M. (1991), 'Issues in the Introduction of Market Forces in Eastern European Socialist Economies', Managing inflation in Socialist Economies in Transition, Economic Development Institute Seminar Series, World Bank, Washington, DC, 121–53.

Hochreiter, E., Rovelli, R., and Winckler, G. (1996), 'Central Banks and Seignorage: A Study of Three Economies in Transition', *European Economic Review*, forthcoming.

Holmström, B., and Tirole, J. (1993), 'Market Liquidity and Performance Monitoring', *Journal of Political Economics*, 101(4):678–709.

Hrnčíř, M. (1993), 'Reform of the Banking Sector in the Czech Republic', Working Paper, Czech National Bank.

Hungarian State Holding Company (1993), *Annual Report 1992/1993*.

International Monetary Fund (1992), *International Financial Statistics*, Washington DC.

――(1994), *International Financial Statistics*, Washington DC.

Jensen, M. C., and Meckling, W. H. (1976), 'Theory of the Firm, Managerial Behavior, Agency Costs, and Ownership Structure', *Journal of Financial Economics*, 3(4):305–60.

Jerschina, J. (1995), 'Consolidation and Privatization of Polish Banks in the Light of Sociological and Market Research', Paper presented at conference on the Competitive Position of the Banking Systems in East European Countries, Jagiellonian University, Kraków.

References

Kane, E. J. (1993), *The S&L Crisis: How Did It Happen?* The Urban Institu. Washington DC.

King, R., and Levine, R. (1993), 'Finance, Entrepreneurship, and Growth: Theory and Evidence' *Journal of Monetary Economics*, 32(3):513–42.

Kopint-Datorg (1994), *Eastern Europe*, 3(2).

——(1995), *Eastern Europe*, 4(1).

Kornai, J. (1992), *The Socialist System: The Political Economy of Communism*, Princeton University Press, Princeton, NJ.

——(1995), 'Eliminating the Shortage Economy: A General Analysis and Examination of the Development in Hungary', *Economics of Transition*, 3(1):13–37.

Lane, T., and Dinopoulos, E. (1991), 'Fiscal Constraints on Market-oriented Reform in a Socialist Economy', IMF Working Paper 75.

Layard, R., and Richter, A. (1995), 'How Much Unemployment is Needed for Restructuring: The Russian Experience,' *Economics of Transition*, 3(1):39–58.

Lee, C. M.-C., Shleifer, A., and Thaler, R. H. (1991), 'Investor Sentiment and the Closed-End Mutual Fund Puzzle', *Journal of Finane*, 46(1):75–109.

Maskin, E. (1994), 'Theories of the Soft-budget Constraint', Paper presented at *Institutional Dimensions of Transition*, conference held at ECARE, Brussels, 7 May.

Mayer, C. (1990), 'Financial Systems, Corporate Finance, and Economic Development', in R. G. Hubbard (ed.), *Asymmetric Information, Corporate Finance, and Investment*, a National Bureau of Economic Research Project Report, University of Chicago Press, Chicago, 307–32.

Mejstěík, M., Laštovička, R., Marcincin, A., and Semetillo, D. (1993), 'Privatization and Opening the Capital Market in the Czech and Slovak Republics', CERGE, DP 21.

——Marcincin, A., and Laštovička, R. (1996), 'Voucher Privatization, Ownership Structures and Emerging Capital Markets in the Czech Republic', Paper presented at the Congress of the European Economics Association, Prague, August 1995.

Mitchell, J. (1993), 'Creditor Passivity and Bankruptcy: Implications for Economic Reform', in C. Mayer and X. Vives (eds.), *Capital Markets and Financial Intermediation*, Cambridge University Press, Cambridge.

Mizsei, K. (1995a), 'Lessons from Bad Loan Management in the East Central European Economic Transition for the Second Wave Reform Countries', in J. Rostowski (ed.), *Banking Reform in Central Europe and the Former Soviet Union*, Central European University Press, London.

——(1995b), 'Regulation of Bank Failures in Economies in Transition', Institute of East-West Studies, New York.

Mládek, J. (1994), 'Mass Privatization in the Czech Republic', Czech Institute of Applied Economics, Prague.

Myers, S. C. (1977), 'The Determinants of Corporate Borrowing', *Journal of Financial Economics*, 5(2):147–75.

National Bank of Hungary (NBH) (1991), *Annual Report 1990*.

——(1992), *Annual Report 1991*.

——(1993), *Annual Report 1992*.

——(1994a), *Annual Report 1993*.

References

——(1994*b*), *Monthly Report*, various issues.

——(1995*a*), *Accounts for the Year 1994*.

——(1995*b*), *Annual Report 1994*.

——(1995*c*), *Monthly Report*, various issues.

——(1996), *Monthly Report*, various issues.

Newbery, D. M. (1991), 'Reform in Hungary: Sequencing and Privatization', *European Economic Review*, 35(2–3):571–80.

Nuti, D. M. (1992*a*), 'Impediments to the Transition: The East European Countries and the Policies of the European Community', Working Paper, European University Institute, Florence.

——(1992*b*), 'The Role of the Banking Sector in the Process of Privatization', Commission of the European Communities, Economic Papers, 98.

——(1992*c*), 'Socialist Banking', in P. Newman *et al.* (eds.), *New Palgrave Dictionary of Money and Finance*, Macmillan, London.

Obláth, G. (1992), 'Hungary's External Debt: Past Trends, Constraints, and Policy Options', Paper presented at the conference 'Impediments to the Transition', European University Institute, Florence, Feb. 1992.

OECD (1993), *Hungary*, Economic Studies, Paris.

——(1994), *Czech and Slovak Republics*, Economic Studies, Paris.

——(1995*a*), *National Accounts Central and Eastern Europe'*, Paris.

——(1995*b*), *Mass Privatisation: An Initial Assessment*, Paris.

Pagano, M., and Roell, A. (1992), 'Auction and Dealership Markets: What Is the Difference?', *European Economic Review*, 36(2–3):613–23.

Perotti, E. C. (1993), 'Bank Lending in Transition Economies', *Journal of Banking and Finance*. 17:1021–32.

Pinto, B., Belka, M., and Krajewski, S. (1993), 'Transforming State Enterprises in Poland: Evidence on Adjustment by Manufacturing Firms', *Bookings Papers on Economic Activity*, (1):213–61.

——and Van Wijnbergen, S. (1994), 'Ownership and Corporate Control in Poland: Why State Firms Defied the Odds', Working Paper, University of Amsterdam.

Portes, R. (1993), 'Integrating the Central and East European Countries into the International Monetary Systems', CEPR Occasional Paper, 14.

Rask, K. J., and Rask, K. N. (1994), 'The Pivotal Role of Services in Transitional Economies: Lessons from the West', *Economics of Transition*, 2(4):467–86.

Rodrik, D. (1992), 'Making Sense of the Soviet Trade Shock in Eastern Europe: A Framework and Some Estimates', CEPR Working Paper, 705.

Roell, A. (1996), 'The Decision to Go Public: An Overview', *European Economic Review*, 40:1071–81.

Rosati, D. K. (1992), 'Problems of Post-CMEA Trade and Payments', CEPR Working Paper, 650.

——(1994), 'Output Decline during Transition from Plan to Market', *Economics of Transition* 2(4):419–41.

Shleifer, A., and Vishny, R. (1986), 'Large Shareholders and Corporate Control', *Journal of Political Economy*, 94:461–88.

Siklós, P. (1994), 'Central Bank Independence in the Transitional Economies: A Preliminary Investigation of Hungary, Poland, and the Czech and Slovak Republics', in J. P. Bonin and I. P. Székely (eds.), *The Development and Reform of Financial Systems in Central and Eastern Europe*, Edward Elgar, Cheltennam.

Sinn, H.-W. (1991), 'Macroeconomic Aspects of German Unification', NBER Working Paper, 3596.

Slay, B. (1994), *The Polish Economy: Crisis, Reform and Transformation*, Princeton University Press, xvi and 229.

Stiglitz, J. E. (1994), *Whither Socialism?* Wicksell lecture, MIT Press Cambridge, Mass., xii and 338.

Svejnar, J., and Singer, M. (1994), 'Using Vouchers to Privatize an Economy: The Czech and Slovak Case', The Economics of Transition, 2(1):43–69.

Swain, N. (1992), *Hungary: The Rise and Fall of Feasible Socialism*, New Left Book, Verso (eds.), London, vii and 264.

Tamborski, M. (1995), 'Efficiency of New Financial Markets: The Case of the Warsaw Stock Exchange', Working Paper, IRES, Catholic University of Louvain, Discussion Paper 9504.

Tanzi, V. (1992), 'Financial Markets and Public Finance in the Transformation Process', IMF Working Paper, 29(26).

Thakor, A. V. (1996), 'Capital Requirements, Monetary Policy, and Aggregate Bank Lending: Theory and Empirical Evidence', *Journal of Finance*, 51(1):279–324.

Várhegyi, E. (1993), 'Key Elements of the Reform of the Hungarian Banking System: Privatization and Portfolio Cleaning', CEPR, Discussion Paper, 826.

Wachtel, P. (1995), 'Foreign Banking in Central European Economies in Transition', Institute of East-West Studies, New York.

Wall Street Journal (European Edition) (1994), 'Central European Economic Review', 2(4), Autumn.

Warsaw School of Economics (1994), 'Poland: International Economic Report 1993/1994', Warsaw.

Weitzman, M. (1993), 'Economic Transition: Can Theory Help?'. *European Economic Review*, 37:549–55.

White, L. (1991), *The S&L Debacle, Public Policy for Bank and Thrift Regulation*, Oxford University Press.

Winiecki, J. (1993), 'Heterodox Stabilisation in Eastern Europe', EBRD Working Paper, 8.

World Bank (1994), *World Debt Tables*, Washington, DC.

Zemplińska, T. (1995), 'Privatisation of the Polish Banking Sector', Paper presented at conference on the Competitive Position of the Banking Systems in East European Countries, Jagiellonian University, Kraków, July.

Index